LOFT JAZZ

LOFT JAZZ

Improvising New York in the 1970s

Michael C. Heller

UNIVERSITY OF CALIFORNIA PRESS

University of California Press, one of the most distinguished university presses in the United States, enriches lives around the world by advancing scholarship in the humanities, social sciences, and natural sciences. Its activities are supported by the UC Press Foundation and by philanthropic contributions from individuals and institutions. For more information, visit www.ucpress.edu.

University of California Press
Oakland, California

© 2017 by The Regents of the University of California

Publication of this book was supported by a grant from the H. Earle Johnson Fund of the Society for American Music.

Library of Congress Cataloging-in-Publication Data

Names: Heller, Michael C., author.
Title: Loft jazz : improvising New York in the 1970s / Michael C. Heller.
Description: Oakland, California : University of California Press, [2017] | Includes bibliographical references and index.
Identifiers: LCCN 2016040707 (print) | ISBN 9780520285408 (book/cloth : alk. paper) | ISBN 9780520285415 (book/pbk. : alk. paper) | ISBN 9780520960893 (ebook)
Subjects: LCSH: Jazz—New York (State)—New York—1971–1980—History and criticism. | Jazz—Social aspects—New York (State)—New York—History—20th century.
Classification: LCC ML3508.8.N5 H45 2017 | DDC 781.6509747—dc23
LC record available at https://lccn.loc.gov/2016040707

Manufactured in the United States of America

26 25 24 23 22 21 20 19 18 17
10 9 8 7 6 5 4 3 2 1

To two inspirations:
Richard Heller and Juma Sultan

CONTENTS

List of Illustrations and Table .... *ix*

1. Fragmented Memories and Activist Archives *1*

PART ONE: HISTORIES

2. Influences, Antecedents, Early Engagements *19*
3. The Jazz Loft Era *34*

PART TWO: TRAJECTORIES

4. Freedom *65*
5. Community *94*
6. Space *127*
7. Archive *145*

8. Aftermaths and Legacies *179*

Acknowledgments *191*
Notes *195*
Bibliography *229*
Index *245*

ILLUSTRATIONS AND TABLE

FIGURES

1. Juma Sultan outside of Studio We 9
2. Group of musicians in front of Studio We: Ted Daniel, Milford Graves, Frank Lowe, Juma Sultan, Noah Howard, James DuBoise, unknown (possibly Bobby Few), Sam Rivers, and Ali Abuwi. June 1973 37
3. We Music House rehearsal at Studio We: Jimmy Vass, James DuBoise, Sonelius Smith, and Eugene Jackson 38
4. Flyer for Studio We's festival "Three Days of Peace between the Ears" 39
5. List of demands sent by NYMJF organizers to George Wein, Newport Jazz Festival 43
6. Central Park jam session at the conclusion of the New York Musicians' Jazz Festival, July 10, 1972 46
7. Studio Rivbea brochure and schedule, April 1973 51
8. Leon Thomas performing at Studio Rivbea, circa 1972–73 52
9. Menu from Studio 77 / Ali's Alley 53
10. Pharoah Sanders performing at Marcus Garvey Park, July 7, 1972 106
11. Letter of support for Studio We park concerts, from the office of Staten Island Borough President Robert T. Connor 108
12. Poster template for trumpeter Eddie Gale 110
13. Flyer for Andrew Cyrille and Maono 111
14. Flyer for African Street Carnival at The East 112
15. Flyer for William Parker's Aumic Orchestra 113
16. Map from flyer for the Jazz Forum 114

ix

17. Map created for liner booklet for Muntu box set *115*
18. T-shirt image featuring map of jazz lofts, created for WKCR Lofts Festival, 1993 *116*
19. Japanese map poster of the New York loft scene *117*
20. Performance at Studio We: Hakim Jami, Mark Whitecage, James DuBoise, and Shelly Rusten *131*
21. Page from packet of materials sent by Nation Time Productions, circa 1971 *167*

TABLE

1. Jazz Works with Titles Including the Word "Freedom," 1917–1965 *66*

1

FRAGMENTED MEMORIES AND ACTIVIST ARCHIVES

Archives do not simply reconnect us with what we have lost. Instead, they remind us ... of what we have never possessed in the first place. If that is a paradox, it is perhaps the paradox of modernism itself.
—SVEN SPIEKER

The date was November 19, 1975. We know this because the document is dated. It is the first page of a letter addressed to the Volunteer Lawyers for the Arts, a nonprofit group providing free legal services to artists and organizations. The remainder of the letter has not been found. Though the signature is absent, it appears to be written by bassist and percussionist Juma Sultan, director of the New York Musicians Organization (NYMO) and concert organizer at a small, lower Manhattan loft called Studio We. The page provides a general introduction to the goals and current activities of NYMO. We can speculate that subsequent pages outlined the reasons why Sultan was contacting the Volunteer Lawyers—reasons that, in 2009, Sultan could not recall.[1] It begins with a basic mission statement:

> The New York Musicians Organization (N.Y.M.O.) is a non-profit corporation established in 1972, to provide New York and elsewhere in the United States:
>
> (1) A jazz complex housing auditoriums, concert halls, seminar rooms, archives and other facilities enabling the fullest communication of the jazz medium to the public.
> (2) Employment for the jazz musicians for whom there are insufficient professional engagements, because of the restrictions in the commercial market.
> (3) To improve the quality of jazz and the public knowledge thereof.
> (4) To preserve the cultural heritage of all forms of jazz music, which will disappear unless the traditions of the music are passed along from one generation to another through sheet music, recording and other mechanical devices, training and listening.[2]

It is a mission that is striking in both ambition and range, combining aspects of commercial production, cultural promotion, job creation, historic preservation, and artistic training. Jazz fans will recognize, however, that NYMO was hardly the first musician-run organization to pursue such goals amid the heightened social and political consciousness of the 1960s–70s. Collectives like Chicago's Association for the Advancement of Creative Musicians (AACM),[3] St. Louis's Black Artists Group (BAG),[4] and Los Angeles's Union of God's Musicians and Artists Ascension (UGMAA)[5] all used similar language to advance their own grassroots efforts. Closer to home in New York, NYMO emerged within a crucible of small-scale organizing activity that spread throughout lower Manhattan beginning in the 1960s. In warehouses and tenements, in parks and on street corners, in churches and community centers, New York artists were developing a broad array of alternative spaces and strategies to promote their work. But their activities eventually became most closely associated with the abandoned factory spaces that littered the neighborhood and provided frequent settings for concerts. In time, the movement would be known throughout the world as the "loft scene."

If NYMO's primary mission centered upon empowerment, it is striking how the creation of a historical archive figures prominently in items (1) and (4) of these early goals. Alongside plans to produce, promote, and educate, the impetus to preserve a yet unwritten legacy and to facilitate the writing of history is much more than an afterthought. The archive is not merely a thin residue of the past to be combed over by future historians—it is positioned as a central, active agent within the group's vision of musical and social change. If this seems like overstatement, it is worth noting that, forty years later, the archive is the last remnant of the NYMO enterprise, and it is still maintained by its original organizer. Through the physical materials of the archive, the goal of re/constructing a new musical history, marked by particular ideals of beauty, progress, and development, becomes possible. In fact, it is only through the archive that this early document—fragile, fragmented, and forgotten—reaches us in the first place.

But perhaps I'm getting ahead of the story. After all, many readers have never even heard of the New York loft scene, much less NYMO's short-lived role within it. A more conventional approach would start by relating the background of the organization itself, using strategically positioned documents to sketch out a noble musical legacy. But the key to an archival project like NYMO's goes beyond merely corroborating dates and details—it provides more than just documentary proof that "we were here." Rather, to place the archive at the center of a broader campaign for musical and social empowerment is to recognize its *generative* force in the construction of narratives. It constitutes a vital facet of the artists' efforts to reclaim control over their work, their finances, their legacy. It appears not as a scrap from the past that falls to us in the present, but the vision of a possible future conceived at/as the group's inception.

LOFTS, JAZZ, LOFT JAZZ, JAZZ LOFTS

The goal of this book is to examine histories and discourses surrounding New York's so-called "loft jazz era," one of the least-understood periods in jazz history. Spanning from the mid-1960s until about 1980, the jazz lofts were a dense network of musician-run performance venues established (mostly) in and around the former industrial buildings of lower Manhattan.[6] The majority of these spaces were also musicians' homes, a factor that allowed them to operate with minimal overhead costs (though also with some sacrifice of privacy). In various contexts, lofts acted as rehearsal halls, classrooms, art galleries, living quarters, and meeting spaces. Their most visible role, however, was as public performance venues, especially for younger members of the jazz avant garde. At a time when few commercial nightclubs were interested in experimental styles, the lofts became a bustling base of operations for a growing community of young improvisers. When musicians couldn't find gigs in the city's shrinking club scene, they could often arrange a performance at a loft—though performance conditions were sometimes less than ideal.

The loft years were nothing if not divisive. To those who remember them fondly, the scene was vibrant and fertile, effervescing with musical and social activity. For players and listeners alike, lofts provided no shortage of sounds to hear, places to play, people to meet, and things to do. The settings were generally casual—sometimes literally inside of living rooms—and young musicians had endless opportunities to interact with veteran players. The proceedings overflowed from day into night, from night into day: jam sessions, rehearsals, performances, workshops, conversations, gatherings. With few commercial restrictions, artists were free to explore their most adventurous visions. Free-blowing affairs could last for hours, as players grappled with extended techniques, extreme volumes, group interaction, and long-form improvisation. And when one marathon session finally ended, the close proximity of the spaces meant that another was always waiting a few blocks away.

But the period was not without its detractors. By the end of the 1970s many musicians voiced pointed critiques of the lofts. The spaces were often small, had shoddy acoustics, and were sometimes poorly managed. Most gigs only paid musicians from the meager ticket sales earned at the door, rather than offering a guaranteed fee. Since loft spaces generally had little to no budget for advertising and promotion, audiences were often scanty, further limiting the potential to earn a livable wage. Loft performances could be sloppily planned and sloppily executed. In an atmosphere of complete freedom, some players lacked discipline, leading to endless blowing with little evident musical direction. Perhaps the most infuriating development came when some writers began to use the term "loft jazz" to denote a particular musical style, one that seemed to pejoratively imply that experimental improvisation was best suited to meager circumstances.[7] In short, critics argued that on every level (economics, acoustics, respectability) the lofts failed to do justice to the seriousness of the music.

There is, of course, truth in both perspectives. At various points the loft scene could be both vibrant and messy. Unfettered and undisciplined. Filled with promise and devoid of direction. It soared toward unexplored heights and crashed headlong into glass ceilings of its own creation. To understand such an environment requires grappling with a range of complex and conflicting stories, memories, and perspectives on a deeply fragmented musical moment. It is such an effort that this book attempts to undertake.

RE/CONSTRUCTING JAZZ NARRATIVES OF THE 1970S

Since the mid-1990s, scholars of the "new jazz studies" have increasingly worked to problematize canonical narratives of jazz history. Instead of presenting the music as a linear progression of influence from one legendary figure to the next, musical practices have been reimagined in terms of the elaborate interactions among aesthetic, social, and historical discourses. This perspective has reconceived the function of music as a living entity that emerges not merely at historic moments or through "great works," but as a tradition residing in the everyday lives of artists, listeners, and the culture at large. It has been especially productive for considering the music through a variety of interpretive lenses, including critical race and gender theory, twentieth-century political history, and postmodernism.[8]

A particularly fruitful approach is the crafting of studies that focus on jazz communities rather than on individual artists or recordings. Community-based approaches allow scholars to examine a broad swath of musical meanings that spill over into other spheres. They challenge us to traverse paths of musical circulation other than solely commercial recordings, which tended to dominate much earlier scholarship in the field. As Jed Rasula has argued, jazz records—though a seductive starting point—fail to account for the more ephemeral movements, exchanges and social networks that generate music's changing meanings over time.[9] By shifting attention away from the musical product (records) and toward the musicking practices that emerge among social groups, it becomes possible to construct histories that use the essential information found on recordings without overstating their role within the broader context of musical culture.[10]

Perhaps no period has benefited more from this methodological shift than the 1970s, an era of jazz that has never fit easily into linear narratives. Where earlier decades are commonly—though reductively—linked to the rise of particular subgenres (swing in the '30s, bebop in the '40s, hard bop and cool jazz in the '50s, free jazz in the '60s), the surfeit of styles in circulation by the 1970s makes any such characterization insufficient and problematic.[11] At the same time that fusion artists experimented with rock rhythms and electric instruments, bebop and mainstream styles underwent a revival that rejuvenated the careers of many older musicians.[12] The nascent jazz repertory movement also gained steam through groups like the New York Jazz Repertory Company and the adoption of jazz curricula at several universities. Meanwhile, avant gardists continued to develop the language of free jazz in new directions, often supporting their work through European touring and collective organizing.

This diversity—some might call it fractioning—of the jazz scene makes it difficult to fit the decade into the types of evolutionary frameworks that remain common in survey texts. Authors have attempted innumerable ways of getting around this, each of which is fraught with issues. Some concentrate exclusively on just one subgenre in order to preserve the narrative structure, the most common candidate being fusion.[13] Others depict a battle pitched between advocates of old and new styles, a discursive echo of the 1940s conflicts between modernists and "moldy figs."[14] Still others gloss over the new stylistic developments completely, focusing instead on the ongoing careers of earlier legends as they navigated a rapidly changing musical landscape.[15]

More nuanced approaches avoid lumping the decade into a particular category, instead choosing to acknowledge the decade's deep fragmentation. A refreshingly confessional example can be seen in a chapter introduction written by Joachim-Ernst Berendt and Günther Huesmann:

> Up to this point, we have been able to match each decade with a particular style—certainly at the cost of some fine distinctions, but with greater clarity as a result. With the beginning of the seventies, we have to drop this principle. This decade showed at least seven distinct tendencies:
>
> 1. Fusion or jazz-rock . . .
> 2. A trend toward European romanticist chamber music . . .
> 3. The music of the new free jazz generation . . .
> 4. An astonishing comeback for swing . . .
> 5. An even more amazing and widespread comeback for bebop . . .
> 6. European jazz found itself . . .
> 7. The gradual development of a new kind of musician who moved between jazz and world music.[16]

As the authors imply, fragmentation did not originate in the 1970s and can be noted in earlier periods as well.[17] Still, the decade's explosion of stylistic diversity creates narrative complications that historians are forced to confront.

The movement toward community-based approaches has been a powerful tool in addressing this challenge, and has led to some of the most nuanced work on the period. Especially impressive are several excellent studies of musician-run collectives that sprang up in cities throughout the United States, including George Lewis's seminal research on Chicago's AACM, Benjamin Looker's examination of St. Louis's BAG, and Steven Isoardi's chronicling of Los Angeles's UGMAA.[18] In all three examples, a transition away from individual biography and toward a communal and/or organizational emphasis has allowed these authors to articulate more precise questions, and to employ a wider variety of source materials. Furthermore, by concentrating on particular cities, these studies are capable of addressing national discourses of music and politics while retaining a sharp focus on the way musicians work within and/or confront their own unique local environments.[19]

If a standard tendency among survey texts is to portray the 1970s as a time of dissent and contentiousness, community-based studies act as a corrective by foregrounding solidarity, organization-building, self-sufficiency, collaboration, and friendship. This is no small point, as it implicitly argues for the musical/cultural relevance of the decade by acknowledging that it was more than a series of petty squabbles. Such studies are far more effective than discographical or magazine-centric accounts at conveying the perspectives of musicians who worked in these communities and found meaning within them. I argue that such work therefore constitutes a *reconstructive* project aimed at unearthing layers of musical significance as remembered and cherished by musicians, despite being overlooked in other secondary sources. The approach does not dispute the role of fragmentation—indeed, it relies on it—but adds clarity by demonstrating how the music continued developing within various types of (often hidden) sociomusical networks.

While the lofts shared a great deal with these previously mentioned jazz collectives, they differed starkly in that they were not governed by any centralized organization. Instead, a downturn in the lower Manhattan real estate market (discussed in chapter 2) allowed hundreds of artists to obtain and develop their own spaces, mutually independent from one another. Such independence led to a more diffuse set of activities than manifested elsewhere—further fragmentation in an already fragmented time.[20] Loft organizers pursued a diverse range of artistic and social priorities that were not always evident to the listening public. Some spaces featured mostly straight-ahead styles, others spotlighted free jazz, and still others interfaced with contemporary European music. Some participants envisioned themselves as champions of black solidarity, while others employed language emphasizing racial universality and multiculturalism. Some attempted to position themselves within national and global discourses, while others saw their work as primarily connected to neighborhood concerns. Contradictory impulses could even manifest within a single venue, with attitudes and strategies shifting set-by-set and night-by-night. Although these varied activities were, and often still are, referred to as a cohesive "loft movement," "loft era," or "loft scene," their disjointed nature presents endless complications for scholars and enthusiasts approaching the period as a whole.

Despite such challenges, despite the fragmentation and self-contradictions and shortcomings of the lofts, I nevertheless conceive of reconstruction as a central motivation for this book. It operates on several levels. First, I claim reconstruction as a historiographic approach to problematizing and revising narratives that would frame the lofts as governed only by dissent and stagnation. Following the work of the scholars above, my emphasis is instead on generative ideals of institution-building that informed musical practices, even when those institutions were unsuccessful in achieving their goals. Second, reconstruction provides a framework for reflecting upon the ways that musician-organizers aspired to re/build communities and foster self-empowerment as a strategy for confronting hardship. In this sense, the term carries echoes of the Reconstruction Era in the postbellum United States, especially through musicians' efforts to reformulate issues of race in terms of economics and cultural ownership. Third, the text will attempt to reconstruct not only historical details, but also look at central, unsettled discursive debates that animated the loft movement. In this sense the term calls attention to the historian's delicate task of re/constructing nuanced narratives out of a web of archival fragments and personal recollections. Fourth, later chapters (especially chapter 7) will engage deeply with musician-curated archives that document loft activities. Such projects have served as meaningful rendezvous points for former loft artists, some of whom had not corresponded in decades. In this way, historical projects not only generate accounts for posterity, but work to rebuild personal relationships among living figures, reconstructing bonds that were dispersed across time and space.

In all of these ways, I employ reconstruction not in opposition to deconstructive approaches to historical writing, but as a corollary to them.[21] This is intended to reflect the goals of musician-organized movements more broadly. Though such groups always tacitly imply a deconstructive analysis of the jazz industry, I have found that musicians are rarely content to merely revel in a landscape of unmoored postmodern pastiche. Instead, deconstruction is comprehended as a prelude to new forms of growth and institution-building, to re/construct a position of strength through self-ownership. This book makes no attempt to rebuild grand narratives, nor do I seek to insert an alternative group of "major figures" into an extant canonical model. Rather, by excavating specific threads of musical and social significance, I hope to provide the groundwork for considering the lofts as an attempt, however flawed, at generating a productive, empowered, and independent sphere for musical exploration.

JUMA SULTAN AND THE ACTIVIST ARCHIVE

If the fragmentation of the loft scene creates one type of challenge, a second arises from a noticeable gap in source material. This lack is especially apparent in regard to commercial recordings. Due to an economic recession and a downturn in the jazz industry during the 1970s, musicians in the lofts made significantly fewer records than earlier artists, leaving a dearth of widely accessible material. Echoing Rasula, it is clear that a history based only on commercial records would drastically underrepresent the overall richness of the period. It becomes imperative to look elsewhere for source material.

Luckily, what is missing from the public sphere is more than adequately compensated in the substantial private collections of musicians. Throughout the 1960s and '70s, the increasing affordability of amateur tape equipment allowed many artists to record their own work. Several such collections have come to light in recent years, though these materials vary widely in scope and audio fidelity. Ephemera such as flyers, programs, photos, and business documents also abound, scattered in the files, drawers, and closets of dozens of individuals. Our challenge, therefore, is not that research materials don't exist, but that they survive as singular, unpublished, hidden artifacts that remain in private hands. Since these sources are not generally accessible in record stores, and have not yet been catalogued in libraries or posted online, a deep engagement with private archives is necessary in order to reconstruct the loft period.

Much of the source material for this study comes from one such archive, compiled by the aforementioned Juma Sultan of the New York Musicians Organization (NYMO). Sultan is one of those fascinating figures of the 1960s and '70s who seemed to float effortlessly through a string of groundbreaking movements. Originally from Monrovia, California, he spent much of the early 1960s in San Francisco, enjoying the height of counterculture activity near Haight-Ashbury and playing drums at events staged by the Black Panthers. He moved east in 1966, splitting time between New York's Lower East Side and communal living spaces in the vicinity of Woodstock. It was at the latter that he met rock legend Jimi Hendrix, and Sultan soon became a staple in the guitarist's final bands (he even played in Hendrix's legendary set at the 1969 Woodstock festival).[22] After moving to New York full-time in the early 1970s, Sultan became active in the lower Manhattan free jazz scene, playing bass and hand percussion at jam sessions, coffee shops, and clubs. In 1972, he was instrumental in organizing the New York Musicians' Jazz Festival, an episode that proved to be a germinal moment for the loft scene. Through the remainder of the decade, Sultan continued organizing concerts, festivals, and workshops, working primarily out of an Eldridge Street loft called Studio We (Fig. 1).

Sultan was an avid recordist, and often brought reel-to-reel equipment to rehearsals, performances, and events that he attended. With help from multi-instrumentalist Ali Abuwi, he built a recording studio in Studio We that musicians could rent to record rehearsals, demos, or even commercial records.[23] Over the course of about ten years, Sultan accumulated over 400 tapes. Many of these

FIGURE 1. Juma Sultan outside of Studio We. Photo mounted on painted wood with design by Ori Oba. Image courtesy of the Juma Sultan Archive (Print 001).

included artists who are scarcely documented in commercial sources. In addition, he saved over 10,000 pages of documents related to his work, including contracts, budgets, photos, flyers, and other materials relating to his business operations. After leaving the city in the early 1980s, Sultan transferred this collection to his new home in upstate New York, where it remained largely untouched for almost twenty-five years. In 2005, he launched the Juma's Archive Project, which seeks to preserve these materials and make them available to scholars and listeners. To date, the project has received support from the National Endowment for the Arts, Clarkson University, and Columbia University. Since 2011, the project has begun issuing selected items on CD and LP, including a three-disc boxed set titled *Father of Origin* and the compilation *Whispers from the Archive*.[24]

Sultan's collection is hardly unique among musicians who performed in the lofts, though it is currently among the largest to be made available to researchers. Smaller collections were compiled by dozens of individuals, most of which remain with their original owners. By chronicling individual experiences within a larger social-economic-aesthetic context, such archives put pressure on the assumed boundaries between public history and private lives, a topic that will emerge repeatedly throughout this book. In many ways, this destabilization of conventional historiographic channels seems somehow fitting in relation to the lofts, a movement which saw factories transforming into homes, homes into studios, and studios into stages.

The Juma Sultan Archive rests firmly within this conceptual break, blurring the boundaries between personal collection, corporate archive, and historical repository. It is far from a representative sample of the total swath of loft activities and vastly overrepresents Sultan's own career as an organizer and performer. Rather than conceding this as a shortcoming, this book will attempt to use the private nature of the Sultan collection as an entry point for a decidedly nonhagiographic history. Instead of identifying dominant narratives, I aim to expand outward from the private sphere, examining the movement from the most local level. My guiding questions are less about pinning down "What happened during the loft era?" and more about asking, "How did a series of shifting discursive landscapes affect the lives of musicians on an everyday level and how, in turn, did these individuals react and feed back into these broader discourses?"

BLUEPRINT FOR RE/CONSTRUCTION

The primary research for this book took place during a five-month period of fieldwork at the Sultan archive in the fall of 2009. My work was not limited to studying the collection, but also entailed assisting Sultan in various administrative tasks. Over the course of my time there, I helped create a full catalog of his holdings, and oversaw the digitization of 143 tapes, 203 photos, and several thousand documents. I assisted in drafting grant applications for further preservation efforts, and facilitated requests from musicians who wished to obtain copies of materials. I also conducted a series of interviews with Sultan, both to provide annotations for particular items and to record his memories, perspectives, and present goals. By living, working, and studying alongside Sultan, I sought to intertwine the research modalities of written documentation, recorded sound, and living memory. Sultan's ongoing contributions as collaborator, fact-checker, archivist, guide, primary source, generous host, and friend have contributed immensely to the interpretation and analysis presented in these pages.

I supplemented my work at the Sultan archive by conducting interviews with other musicians, organizers, and listeners who were active in the lofts. My interview choices were guided in part by the archive itself; I purposely sought out figures who appeared frequently in the collection. Certain names may be unfamiliar—even to dedicated fans and discographers—but their footprint in the archive speaks to the ways that music circulates outside of the most familiar channels. Their contributions were essential in grappling with the everyday significance of the period. These archival and interview sources are juxtaposed against a wealth of periodical and secondary accounts to provide further historical context.

Though the chapters that follow draw from a variety of inspirations, I am especially indebted to two scholarly models. The first is Ingrid Monson's 2008 study *Freedom Sounds*, which analyzes the role of jazz in the civil rights era by considering three analytical levels: discourse, structure, and practice. Monson uses these levels to break down the complex interconnections between musical and social movements, arguing that simpler models[25] fail to account for the myriad forms of tension that arise between rhetoric (discourse), context (structure), and action (practice).[26] Applying this framework to the lofts creates enormous potential for reading diverse sources against one another in fruitful ways. Even the term "loft jazz" itself seems to rest precariously between these three modalities, as it refers to the discursive moniker coined to name the movement, the various structures (physical, economic, social) that underlay it, and the artistic practices developed by artists to navigate a complex urban ecology.

Beyond Monson's approach, I am additionally concerned with issues relating to memory, artifact, and contested technologies of historicization. Following the example of Gabriel Solis, I conceive of history as an ongoing process of negotiation, subject to influence by musicians, writers, and material objects.[27] Through the interplay of personal memories with physical and/or sonic materials, musicians act as decisive—though under-acknowledged—agents in developing a historical discourse. Examining the fluid processes of histori(ographi)cal *trans*cription across modalities (performances, memories, interviews, texts, artifacts, narratives), rather than simply a process of historical *in*scription (from event to account), is a key critical goal. Musicians' present-day memories are placed in dialogue with archival materials, exploring how past and present can speak to one another in manifold ways. This effort is not made to favor one modality over another, but rather to demonstrate how, to quote David Scott, "Memory and tradition are inextricably intertwined."[28]

. . .

With these objectives in mind, this book is not organized as a purely historical chronicle, but as a mosaic of overlapping themes that arose repeatedly throughout my research. By weaving through a range of (sometimes conflicting) accounts,

I intend for the text to reflect the messy vibrancy of the scene itself. It is not a tale with a single message or protagonist, but a dense web of meanings, memories, and experiences.

Chapters 2 and 3 are the most straightforwardly historical, and together provide a detailed sketch of the period. The story begins with an overview of the lofts' primary influences and contextual backgrounds in chapter 2. Details about its organizational forebears (including earlier jazz collectives) and descriptions of the unusual urban ecology of early 1970s New York serve to situate the movement's beginnings. An account of the scene's emergence follows in chapter 3, starting with an in-depth look at the 1972 New York Musicians' Jazz Festival. The movement is traced through its peak around mid-decade, and into its subsequent decline amidst a string of new financial and structural challenges. These final years also saw a growing number of critiques leveled by musicians who disputed the efficacy of the lofts. Whereas the movement had begun as a campaign against industry exploitation, its failure to develop viable alternatives ultimately made it vulnerable to the criticism that lofts merely repackaged the inadequate conditions of nightclub performance.

The remaining chapters each follow a single discursive trajectory, each of which offers a different perspective on the loft period. Drawing from Robin Kelley's scholarship examining the "freedom dreams" of African American activist movements, in chapter 4 I consider the multifaceted ways that loft artists envisioned freedom as an inspiration for their work. Rather than hewing to a single definition, however, artists employed the term to connote a wide variety of different meanings. The chapter examines several in succession, including definitions that foreground: (1) collectivist or communalist practices, rooted in civil rights and 1960s counterculture movements; (2) self-creation and identity politics; (3) off-the-grid living strategies; (4) transgression and transcendence, and (5) "energy music" aesthetics that feature minimal pre-composed elements. In the end, the term "freedom" emerges as powerfully overdetermined, as it is used to reference a number of interrelated goals and values.

Chapter 5 examines discourses of community (as well as contradictory discourses of isolation) that arose within the lofts. While references to community involvement were quite common, the symbolic boundaries that defined and demarcated loft community/ies were often described in highly divergent ways. I begin with a survey of several scholarly models for conceptualizing collectivity before proceeding to outline four boundary discourses that were referenced most frequently by loft artists (discourses of pay, play, place, and race). Although conceiving of the lofts as a community provides certain benefits, the discussion concludes by attempting to reframe the period in terms of network- and scene-based theoretical approaches, arguing that each model offers potential insights.

The physical spaces of the lofts are considered in chapter 6, which asks how the surrounding environment afforded certain types of performer and listener experience. In contrast to architectural accounts of loft conversions for high-end housing—which often romanticize the industrial history of old factories—musicians' accounts tended to be largely devoid of nostalgia for a bygone era. Instead, descriptions of loft jazz venues generally focused on the creative possibilities enabled by the presence of large, raw spaces. By emphasizing the liberatory potential of blank space, rather than the nostalgic echoes of industrial place, organizers stressed underlying values of reclamation and community-building. The second half of the chapter goes on to discuss descriptions that referenced markers of domesticity in loft venues, a factor that carried additional resonances in regard to gender politics. All of these factors worked to differentiate lofts from other types of music venues (especially nightclubs) by constructing new types of relationships between artists and audiences.

The topic of private archives returns in chapter 7, which looks at the various challenges (both conceptual and methodological) that such collections pose to historical research. This observation is no mere esoteric exercise; many musician-archivists explicitly situate their work as an intervention into historiographical processes—an intervention that mirrors the musician-run ethos of the lofts themselves. These topics are explored through an ethnographic account of my own involvement in the Juma Sultan Archive. I divide the discussion into three sections that correspond to different storage media in the collection: audio tape, paper, and human memory. Each of these media carries particular affordances and limitations, and they converse with each other in interesting ways. Drawing from literature of the recent "archival turn" in the humanities, I argue that engaging with these affordances is essential to understanding the role of the archive as a generative force (and not merely a passive repository) in the writing of history. By including this reflexive account at the end of the study, I also aim to situate my work within a larger histori(ographi)cal process of inscription in which my role as a scholar necessarily makes me implicit.

A final chapter concludes the study by considering multiple musical legacies that emerged in the aftermath of the loft era. By tracing the most prominent narratives and historical initiatives to emerge since the 1980s, the conclusion grapples with the ongoing resonance of the loft era, which continues to influence musician-organized activities in New York to the present day.

. . .

Several caveats should be noted from the outset. First, this work makes no attempt at providing a comprehensive treatment of the loft era. Considering the deeply multivalent nature of the loft scene and its countless participants, such a goal would lie well beyond the scope of a single monograph. Instead, I have sought to collect, consolidate, and analyze the materials and recollections provided to me by a subset of several dozen consultants, situating them within the context provided by secondary source material. Due to its size, the Sultan Archive is my primary point of entry, though even it—as noted above—is starkly incomplete. Following the example of Antoinette Burton, it is my goal to take this incompleteness not as a weakness, but as a strength.[29] The archive provides an opportunity to explore the private, lived experiences of a handful of individuals as they navigated an intricate network of discourses and structures. There are scores of other artists who I might have chosen to interview, and whose stories remain to be told. My choice of trajectories is also necessarily selective. Substantial issues like the politics of gender, the development of specific musical techniques, the commercial discographies of loft artists, and the scene's connections with other experimentalist communities in lower Manhattan (from minimalism to punk rock) are only touched on briefly. Conversely, certain topics reappear in several places in connection with different threads. It is my hope that this book will provide a productive starting point, and that future work will push further in many additional directions.

Second, although I present much of my analysis as a historiographic intervention away from hagiography, it is less certain whether the musicians I spoke with would share this goal. Some would likely be more content to carve out their own place within extant canonical discourses. In some of my interviews, it seemed more like my correspondents would have preferred me to simply write them into the canon as the next "great figure." Though I do hope that my work brings recognition to these individuals, my broader aim is to look at the lofts through the lens of rapidly changing contexts and discourses, rather than appealing to notions of artistic genius and/or timelessness. Following the work of Monson, Solis, and others, I find this to be a more productive way to convey the full scope of an era's musical and social significance.

Third, although I often frame the discussions that follow in terms of artist agency, it is clear that I, as the author of this book, am complicit in the ongoing historicization of the period. Unlike a scholar like George Lewis, I can make no claim for this work as an insider account or "autobiography of a collective,"[30] despite my close collaborative relationships with many of the musicians cited herein. Instead, I conceive of this study through the practice of ethnography, especially through its emphasis on living alongside a community in order to study its patterns and values. My status as a participant-observer at the Sultan archive offered a unique perspective on musicians' goals in dictating their own histories. This text acts as an extension of that collaboration. I gladly acknowledge my role in advancing the history presented here (including my role in building the Sultan Archive), while also maintaining that it is Sultan's initiative as musician-archivist that constitutes the more radical move. Were it not for the discursive complex of sounds, words, objects, and memories that he and others have created, researchers like myself would lack the most basic groundwork for engagement.

Lastly, although I strive to present a multiplicity of viewpoints, undoubtedly some participants will disagree with certain parts of my account. To an extent, such disagreement is unavoidable when constructing an account of a phenomenon that included so many diverse goals and activities. Even the choice of what to call the period remains a constant struggle. Some musicians like Ahmed Abdullah insisted on referring to it as the "loft movement," a phrasing that highlights the progressive politics of self-determination.[31] Others, like Cooper-Moore, expressly disputed the idea of the lofts constituting a movement, arguing that the absence of coordination among organizers would seem to contradict the term's association with unified struggle.[32] "Community" is another possibility, but as I discuss in chapter 5, the word came to mean different things for different individuals. While the phrase came up often, it was rarely used in the construction "loft community."

Perhaps no moniker is more contentious than the very term "loft jazz," which I ultimately chose (not without certain reservations) to use as the title for this book. Some musicians have protested that the phrase misleadingly suggests itself as a discrete musical genre, like swing or hard bop. The period's wide range of musical styles would support this objection; there may have been "jazz lofts," but there was certainly never a thing called "loft jazz." Even more pointedly, others contend that such phrasing might imply that progressive black art is best confined to meager, low-budget venues. Some musicians even object to the very mention of the lofts in the first place, arguing that talking about a type of building may detract from the importance of the actual music being produced. And on top of all of this, some of the artists involved didn't consider their work jazz at all, and many performances did not take place in literal lofts (at least defined by architectural standards).

I have no intention of ignoring or sidestepping these criticisms. In the context of a culture that has long marginalized African American artistic work, it remains imperative to respond to reductive commentaries when and where they appear. In using the title "Loft Jazz," then, I make no attempt to defend it as a discrete category. To the contrary, I hope to engage with the layers of discourse evoked by both terms—loft and jazz—as well as with their juxtaposition at a particular moment in time. These include issues related to race, class, land use, gentrification, urban repurposing, musician-organized initiatives, industrial romance, and inequities surrounding the reception of African American art music of the late twentieth century. I even briefly considered titling the book "Loft / Jazz" to reinforce the tenuousness of the connections between them. Though the designation is not without its problems, the fact that such a diverse set of associations came to be perceived as linked suggests a revealing moment in New York's musical history. It remains worthy of study, even as we subject it to ongoing critical pressure.

But loft performance wasn't exclusively seen as a straitjacket, either. Despite occasional claims that the spaces were universally deplored,[33] my discussions with numerous musicians told a very different story. For many, the lofts represented a fertile opportunity to come together and create new visions of artistic practice and social mobility. Lofts were not a prison meant to confine the music, but a gathering place to come together in a spirit of exploration and joy. As the late violinist Billy Bang told me when I asked for his reaction to the phrase "loft jazz":

> I just know [loft jazz] defines a period and it defines a happening. It's not just a coincidence because everybody used their lofts . . . to have music. I love the fact that they all agreed—individually and collectively—let's have some music! So they called it loft jazz, but I don't think of it as a sound of jazz. I think of it as some different guys coming together. But the guys that came together under this umbrella are the guys that I like a lot . . . If it means that, then great![34]

Rather than focusing purely on restrictive definitions ascribed from the outside, it is the lofts' empowering, revolutionary potentials—for community, for creativity, for resistance—that this book seeks to explore.

PART ONE

HISTORIES

2

INFLUENCES, ANTECEDENTS, EARLY ENGAGEMENTS

In extant music literature, jazz lofts exist mostly as a fleeting detail, an offhand mention, an aside. Though it's quite common in interviews, for example, to find musicians referencing loft events in which they participated, their accounts generally frame loft performance as commonplace and self-explanatory: the spaces were there, so musicians used them. They rarely consider the larger musical and social surroundings that gave rise to the lofts, nor do they interrogate the shifting rhetoric that circulated around loft practices at various times.[1] The spaces are considered incidental, superfluous backdrops to more important musical matters.

Yet taking a step back to consider the movement as a whole gives rise to a series of questions. Why did jazz performance in old factory spaces become so common in the 1970s? Why didn't it happen earlier? Why did they fade away by the 1980s? How did the loft environment affect the experience of musicians or audiences? What function did they serve? What meanings did they imply? In short: why were all of these musicians playing in lofts, anyway!?

The following two chapters will begin to answer these questions by presenting a basic historical account of the period. I begin below by providing background on early motivations for the lofts, arguing that the movement emerged at a unique intersection between national discourses on musician empowerment and local urban ecologies specific to late 1960s New York. This chapter will trace these influences through the arrival of the earliest, private loft events that began cropping up in the 1960s. This is followed in chapter 3 with an outline of the loft scene itself, focusing on the more formally administered venues that characterized the height of the movement in the mid-1970s. Special attention is given to the 1972 New York Musicians Jazz Festival, an event cited by many musicians as a germinal moment for the scene. I close with a description of the lofts' decline in the late 1970s, focusing on an increasing degree of criticism leveled by musicians.

GUILDS, GROUPS, AND ASCENSIONS: MODELS FOR MUSICIAN EMPOWERMENT

The lofts are best considered within a tradition of artist-run initiatives in African American music dating to the early twentieth century. George Lewis has traced the genesis of such activities to New York's Clef Club, founded in 1910 by James Reese Europe and Will Marion Cook. The club operated as both a labor union and a booking agency for black performers in genres ranging from classical to popular to protojazz styles. Europe and Cook emphasized the importance of securing economic and creative control for artists, a goal that was envisioned as both a strategy for professional advancement and a means to advocate for racial uplift during the era of Jim Crow. This combination of practical concerns (securing work) and broader campaigns for social recognition would become a hallmark of many future initiatives. Among other accomplishments, the group produced one of the first appearances by African American musicians at Carnegie Hall, a concert led by Europe himself in 1912.[2]

Jazz saw a noticeable uptick in musician-organized activities in the 1950s. Most took the form of commercial business ventures, including Dizzy Gillespie's Dee Gee record label (1951), Charles Mingus and Max Roach's Debut label (1952), and the Melotone and Totem Music publishing companies founded by Gigi Gryce and Benny Golson (1955). It was not only black artists who employed such strategies; other labels were founded by Dave Brubeck, Lennie Tristano, and Woody Herman. Brian Priestley has attributed this sudden upswing to a lack of major label interest in jazz following the second American Federation of Musicians (AFM) recording ban in 1948.[3] Whatever the impetus, this increased focus on business ownership was geared toward claiming greater economic benefits from the publication and sale of one's work. As Lewis points out, the nature of these 1950s efforts as business ventures *within* the music industry was quite different from the collectives that would follow in later decades. Rather than attempting reform within industry structures, these later groups strived for a broader goal of "reconceptualizing the discursive, physical, and economic infrastructures in which their music took place."[4]

In New York, several initiatives during the 1960s began striving toward broader collectivist ideals. Arguably the first was the short-lived Jazz Artists' Guild (JAG), once again spearheaded by Mingus and Roach. The group was formed during the summer of 1960 in the aftermath of an artist-run counterfestival in Newport, Rhode Island. This so-called "rump festival" was staged to protest the hiring policies of the better-known Newport Jazz Festival. By extension, it functioned as an overt critique of economic inequities that permeated the jazz industry.[5] As reported by Nat Hentoff, the counterfestival fostered a distinctly emancipatory atmosphere by distancing itself from standard power brokers of the music industry: "It was exhilarating for the musicians involved to realize for once in their careers, they were capable of formulating and sustaining their own ground rules without booking agents, impresarios, and other middlemen."[6]

On the final day, Mingus and Roach announced the formation of JAG, a collective designed to continue advancing the festival's goals.[7] The group would support musicians by facilitating negotiations with record producers and club owners while simultaneously producing their own independent concerts. They even outlined plans to establish an artist-run school in upstate New York. Unfortunately, most of these goals would not come to fruition. Although they produced a series of concerts in Manhattan that August, they failed to recapture the excitement of the counterfestival and drew disappointingly small crowds. The series was cancelled in its second week and the organization folded soon thereafter.[8] Despite JAG's short lifespan, it is notable how their proposed agenda would resurface as the basic blueprint for several later collectives: self-presentation in suitable venues, collective bargaining in the music industry, artist-run educational programs, and an egalitarian organizational structure.

Four years later, another successful festival would spark a second attempt at collectivism in New York, this time galvanized by trumpeter Bill Dixon. After organizing the "October Revolution in Jazz" in 1964, Dixon convened a group of avant garde players to form the Jazz Composers' Guild (JCG). Despite the similarity in name, Dixon cited little influence from the earlier JAG, instead claiming inspiration from an extended study of the medieval guild system. Like its predecessor, the organization proposed using collective bargaining strategies to advocate on behalf of member musicians. Strict bylaws dictated that no member could accept a performance opportunity unless the offer was also extended to, and agreed upon by, the entire membership. Anticipating that this would initially impede external opportunities, the guild began producing their own independent events, hoping to build upon the success of the October Revolution. By remaining visible (and audible) to the public while removing themselves from the commercial market, they hoped to generate a grassroots demand for their work. In theory, this would create the dual benefit of generating income for members while also strengthening the group's bargaining position within industry contexts. But despite a more regimented organizational structure, the JCG was also unable to maintain the buzz that surrounded their original festival. Internal dissension over various topics soon began dividing the membership, and by mid-1965 the group would dissolve altogether.[9]

The seed of a third New York collective also began taking shape in 1965, as John Coltrane, Babatunde Olatunji, and Yusef Lateef discussed plans to form their own cooperative venture. The written goals of this "Triumvirate" once again highlight concerns for egalitarian structure, collective bargaining, and educational initiatives:

1. To regard each other as equal partners in all categories.
2. Not to allow any booking agent or promoter to present one group without the other two members of the Triumvirate.
3. To explore the possibility of teaching the music of our people in conservatories, colleges and universities where only European musical experience dominates and is being perpetuated.[10]

It is likely that these goals were influenced by those of the Jazz Composers' Guild. Coltrane would have been aware of the earlier group, as Dixon had previously approached him about assisting in a JAG-organized strike against nightclubs.[11] The goals of the Triumvirate seem to echo the guild approach on a smaller scale, especially in refusing to work for presenters who would not hire all three members. Plans for the group were tragically cut short by Coltrane's death in 1967.[12]

It is striking how these examples of 1960s New York collectivism were all rooted in guild and / or trade union strategies. In all three cases, artists envisioned temporarily removing themselves from the commercial market in order to enhance their negotiating leverage as members of a larger movement. Through collective bargaining, the musicians hoped to transcend internal squabbles and stand as a united front against industry exploitation. Unfortunately, the relatively small size of the organizations made such an approach untenable. In a city saturated with musicians, financially motivated club owners could always find other artists to hire, even if a handful had removed themselves from the market. Despite their success in generating attention for particular events (especially the festivals of 1960 and 1964), none of these groups managed to build an alliance large enough or long-lived enough to realize their principal goals.

But New York musicians were not the only artists to explore collectivist strategies. The latter half of the 1960s saw the rise of a different brand of collectivism out of the Midwest. The primary model was Chicago's Association for the Advancement of Creative Musicians (AACM), founded in 1965. Unlike the short-lived New York guilds, the AACM succeeded in building a sturdy coalition of African American artists to pursue a series of goals, including concert production, promotional initiatives, and educational programs. The group was remarkable in establishing a high degree of discipline and professionalization among its membership. Their organizational mission, best exemplified by the motto "Great Black Music—Ancient to the Future," articulated a vision of black creativity that embraced flexibility and experimentalism rather than a static model of predetermined racialized constraints. The AACM's unprecedented success helped launch the careers of several generations of Chicago improvisers while laying down a template for future initiatives. It remains the world's best-known jazz collective and is the only group from the period that remains active today.[13]

In 1968, a second instance of Midwest collectivism surfaced in St. Louis with the founding of the Black Artists' Group (BAG). A close descendant of the AACM, BAG introduced a strong focus on community activism, which they pursued through offering free workshops and public performances. Interdisciplinary collaboration—though somewhat present in the AACM—was an even greater emphasis for BAG, which included musicians, writers, actors, poets, and visual artists. With funding support from urban renewal grants, the group established a headquarters and community center on Washington Boulevard that thrived for several years. During that time, the group's cooperative atmosphere and strong sense of civic engagement helped cultivate a vibrant local arts scene. When grant money began drying up in the early 1970s the group largely dissolved, though many members went on to prominent careers in Europe and New York.[14]

Looking even further west, a different approach can be seen in Los Angeles's Union of God's Musicians and Artists Ascension (UGMAA), founded in 1961 by pianist Horace Tapscott. In terms of organizational structure, the group was less collectively conceived than those above; Tapscott was unquestionably its chief architect and leading voice. Nevertheless, the group mirrored their Midwest counterparts by building an atmosphere that championed black experimentalism while stressing a deep devotion to community engagement. Based primarily around Tapscott's big band The Pan Afrikan Peoples Arkestra, UGMAA members performed regularly in community-oriented contexts, including coffee houses, "churches and mosques, schools and social centers, with nationalist and socialist revolutionary organizations, as well as with Democratic Party politicians."[15] The group's local visibility became especially meaningful in the turbulent aftermath of the Watts riots in 1965. By organizing workshops and performances, the UGMAA offered alternatives to violence while still presenting a strong image of black identity and racial empowerment. Like other collectives, the group also provided a vital forum for avant garde performers at a time when few clubs were supporting the more radical developments in jazz.

How might one account for the relative success of these Mid/Western collectives in contrast to the more rapid dissolution of the New York guilds? While a number of explanations could be advanced, I would suggest that one factor lies in subtle but pivotal differences in the groups' organizational philosophies.[16] In focusing primarily on trade union strategies, the New York guilds tended to orient their pursuits toward establishing negotiating leverage with commercial presenters. In this context, self-production is framed less as an end in itself, and more as a bargaining chip to achieve more equitable status. The Mid/Western organizations inverted this relationship by making self-presentation a central tenet, seeking to build their own institutions from the ground up. This subtle adjustment had notable repercussions, especially regarding the ability to accept outside work. Unlike their New York counterparts, AACM, BAG, and UGMAA members were generally not precluded from accepting outside offers, nor from working with musicians unaffiliated with the collective.[17] Rather than viewing such appearances as a subversion of negotiating power, they saw them as a way of raising broader awareness for their efforts as a whole. In this way, the Mid/Western groups succeeded in expanding their public visibility through multiple channels rather than withholding their presence until their terms were met. Such an approach also helped to minimize (though not entirely avoid) the types of internal rifts that continually plagued the New York guilds, often resulting in their dissolution.

A second facet of Mid/Western collectivism was an increased emphasis on racial identity/ies, especially regarding the status and ownership of African American music. Unlike the interracial guilds of Mingus and Dixon, the three Mid/Western groups maintained all-black memberships and articulated diverse constructions of blackness in their goals, projects, and mottos (Great Black Music, Black Artists' Group, Pan Afrikan Peoples Arkestra, etc.).[18] As many others have argued, such shifts are indicative of jazz musicians' long-standing engagement with the fast-changing landscape of twentieth-century racial politics. A few overzealous commentators have gone so far as to suggest that the new collectives were simply dogmatic descendants of black nationalist and/or black power ideologies.[19] Certainly some musicians held such affiliations, but it is a mistake to draw such conclusions too starkly; doing so flattens essential distinctions within each group's membership, all of whom grappled with variegated viewpoints on race and politics. This point can be illustrated through a brief detour examining parallel debates that occurred in all three collectives over the potential role of white collaborators.

In the AACM, controversy erupted over the collective's lone white member, vibraphonist Emanuel Cranshaw (formerly Gordon Emanuel). Cranshaw had been a member of the group since 1967, after being recommended by saxophonist Fred Anderson and AACM president Muhal Richard Abrams. Over a period of two years, his presence slowly became a point of contention, with some members wishing to establish an entirely black membership. The debates culminated with Cranshaw's expulsion from the group in early 1969. In later recollections, members recalled the vote as one that weighed personal relationships against concerns of political efficacy and organizational identity during a period of intense national discourse over race. Lewis describes the episode as follows:

> In the context of the burgeoning influence of a newer kind of African American cultural and political nationalism, one could well imagine the AACM coming under considerable pressure regarding its bona fides as a truly "black" organization as long as Cranshaw remained a member ... [F]or a number of members, ambivalence about the affair persists to this day. "These people did not hate him, but they didn't want that mixed image," noted Abrams. "The image was just as important as a real fact. The image was elevated to reason."[20]

Lewis quotes several members who opposed the ouster either at the time or subsequently, yet no other white members would ever be admitted into the organization. Despite this policy, collaboration between white artists (including Cranshaw) and AACM members was not prohibited by the group, and continued in the ensuing years.

Strikingly similar debates cropped up in St. Louis and Los Angeles during the same period. Following the AACM's lead, BAG also chose to maintain an all-black membership, which they saw as integral to both economic control and the development of a black aesthetic. Once again, however, the decision was not accepted tacitly, but became an ongoing point of discussion and dissension. As Benjamin Looker describes:

> The group's philosophical orientation was by no means monolithic. BAG actress Portia Hunt remembers "a whole range of feelings about blackness in the group. Some of our members felt strongly about a very clear black identity, and a lot of individuals were multi-culturalists." . . . In what [Malinke] Elliott describes as "one of the big, central fights throughout BAG," members sharply debated the degree to which white allies should participate in artistic projects. This issue surfaced in running disputes over whether to close the BAG building to whites, whether to hire white instructors to train the group's actors, and whether to solicit white tech support and audiences. For a time, at least, these kinds of disagreements stoked the intellectual energy of the group rather than fueling an explosion.[21]

In Los Angeles, UGMAA members confronted similar dilemmas. One musician recalled an occasion when he brought a white friend to the group's headquarters in the late 1960s:

> A couple of [members] got pissed off at me because it was all black. "Taumbu, what are you doing bringing this cat over here? You're cool. You're part of the family, but we don't know this guy." It was nationalist time. I said, "Well, if I'm part of the family, you can trust me that I wouldn't bring nobody here unless they were cool." But Leroy [Brooks] didn't like it. So I said, "Okay, man, you gotta leave." And I left, too.[22]

I draw attention to these parallel moments because they speak to the emergent and disputed quality of the linkages connecting politics and art during the late 1960s. These stories run against assertions that jazz collectives were simply transparent extensions of political ideologies.[23] Unlike the earlier Black Arts Movement—which self-consciously presented itself as an aesthetic arm of black nationalism—the late '60s collectives did not arise out of a single, clearly defined political agenda. Instead, artists were actively wrestling with complex questions surrounding aesthetics, politics, race, and the endless discursive connections linking them. Like the black community at large, musicians were highly invested in political issues, but also frequently conflicted about the most efficacious route forward. As Juma Sultan described: "It was an internal struggle. On one hand, you want to go peaceful with Martin [Luther King], and on the other you want to say 'By any means necessary—*because I'm hungry!*' It was a dichotomy, if you can understand that." In the end, the final decisions by the Mid/Western collectives to racially restrict membership may be less illuminating than the nuanced debates and internal dissensions that consistently surrounded such choices.

The success and visibility of the Mid/Western collectives prompted a string of smaller initiatives in other cities, including Detroit, New Haven, and Boston. Though their strategies may have differed slightly, such groups were linked by a set of common concerns including experimentalist aesthetics, political action, economic self-sufficiency, racial consciousness, and community engagement. But when the aftershocks of this Mid/Western revolution reached New York in the late 1960s, musicians would encounter an urban landscape very different from those found elsewhere in the country.

CHANGING LANDSCAPES OF NEW YORK'S LOWER EAST SIDE

The middle decades of the twentieth century found lower Manhattan embroiled in a continual process of social and environmental restructuring. The proposed changes were massive, encompassing both physical landscapes as well as their proposed usage by industrial, residential, and commercial constituencies. With so much at stake, disagreements became rampant between opposing interest groups, resulting in a host of battles that left the area's fate in flux for decades. While this instability proved vexing to those with long-term interests in the neighborhood, it also enabled the rise of unexpected new types of institutions that thrived within this fast-changing urban wilderness.

The bulk of the debates centered on former factory buildings that dotted the area, whose capacious, unpartitioned stories were known as lofts. When they were built in the late nineteenth century, lofts housed a variety of light industries including garment-making, printing, machinery-manufacturing, textiles, storage, and shipping.[24] Their physical characteristics were designed to facilitate assembly-line work and the use of small machinery in an era before large-scale mass production. The most common features of loft buildings are described in detail by sociologist (and longtime loft resident) Sharon Zukin:

> Usually they have five to ten stories, with two thousand to ten thousand square feet of space on each floor. Older loft buildings only have a freight elevator, but newer ones also have passenger elevators. Ceilings are high—twelve to fifteen feet—and are supported by either vaulted arches (in smaller buildings) or columns. Architectural detail is often classical, reflecting late nineteenth-century taste for the Italian Renaissance. Columns in loft buildings are frequently fluted, and the building façades are

generally cast iron, which marks an important innovation of the time in the industrialization of construction technique. In contrast to the construction materials used in modern buildings, those used in loft buildings are more solid (brick and iron) and more valuable (often oak flooring and even copper window sills).[25]

Zukin goes on to note that many of these elements have come to be perceived as progressively chic since the 1970s, despite carrying no such associations in earlier years. Prior to the 1960s, lofts generally evoked images of sweatshop-style labor rather than fashionable urban opulence.[26]

The usage patterns of manufacturing lofts began changing sharply in the decades after World War II, a period characterized by rapid deindustrialization of the city, particularly the island of Manhattan. Between 1950 and 1970, the percentage of New Yorkers employed in manufacturing dropped from 29.5% to 20.5%, a loss of over 300,000 jobs. Two main factors prompted this falloff: first, newer and more efficient machinery decreased the need for human labor, and, second, manufacturing began migrating out of the city toward newer, larger suburban factories in other parts of the country. With this exodus, vacancies soon proliferated inside these increasingly outdated models of urban commerce. Over time, their supply began to drastically outpace demand.[27]

As one would expect, the situation prompted a slew of proposals for urban renewal projects that began in the 1950s. The most ambitious plans were drafted by the Downtown Lower Manhattan Association (DLMA), a consortium of businessmen convened by David Rockefeller.[28] The DLMA proposed an expansive list of potential changes to lower Manhattan, including the construction of an enormous office complex (the World Trade Center), high-rise apartments, a sports stadium, and a massive elevated highway called the Lower Manhattan Expressway (LOMEX). In spirit, the plans echoed the slash-and-burn tactics of infamous New York power broker Robert Moses (who had, in fact, been involved in early proposals for LOMEX in the 1940s).[29] Such construction would have required wide-scale displacement of both industrial tenants and working-class residents, many of whom were members of long-established immigrant communities.[30] Older structures would be razed in favor of high-priced units marketed to Wall Street businessmen, who could now live and work in the same area of the city. Not coincidentally, the Rockefeller family already owned a great deal of property on Wall Street itself. In conjunction with the city Planning Commission, the DLMA outlined many of their intentions in a 1966 document titled *The Lower Manhattan Plan*.[31]

But while Moses had successfully launched similarly sweeping projects during the 1930s–50s, several factors prevented *The Lower Manhattan Plan* from being realized. The proposals were fiercely opposed by numerous constituencies, including advocates for the lower classes (who commanded increased respect after a wave of urban unrest in the early 1960s), labor unions, and—perhaps most crucially—historic preservationists.[32] This last group would prove especially influential in the debates that ensued. Their objectives were bolstered by the city's brand new Landmarks Preservation Commission, which was established in 1965 amid a national wave of support for protecting historic buildings. This preservationist surge was sparked, in part, by uproar over the recent demolition of several nineteenth-century landmarks, including New York's Penn Station. As a result, the commission had far-reaching powers to prevent alterations on buildings or neighborhoods designated as having "Special character or special historical or aesthetic interest or value."[33] Among the first neighborhoods to make use of this new authority was Greenwich Village, an older residential area on the west side of Manhattan. Under the leadership of activist Jane Jacobs, the neighborhood obtained Historic District Status in 1969, protecting it against intrusive redevelopment projects.[34] Soon thereafter, residents in adjacent neighborhoods began seeking similar protections for loft buildings, citing the aesthetic value of their cast-iron façades as grounds to oppose the disruptive plans of the DLMA.

Perhaps the most unwittingly consequential aspect of these debates was their interminable length, stretching from the mid-1950s to the early 1970s. Throughout this time, it was impossible to know which side would triumph, or what the subsequent landscape of the lower Manhattan would look like. This sustained uncertainty led to a protracted stretch of disinvestment from the region. Landlords were reluctant to renovate or even provide basic upkeep on their buildings, as the outcome of the redevelopment plans might suddenly render any expenditure worthless. In the lofts, the withdrawal of industrial tenants left few options for filling vacancies since zoning laws prohibited the buildings from being used for residential or commercial purposes. Many structures fell into disrepair, attracting squatters and drug abusers and exacerbating negative perceptions of the area that had circulated since the nineteenth century. Some landlords simply abandoned their properties outright after realizing that they were losing money by retaining them.[35] In a close echo of the South Bronx's fate after the construction of the Cross-Bronx Expressway (another Moses project), lower Manhattan found itself trapped in a vicious cycle of financial evisceration, abandonment, and urban blight.[36]

But as the area grew more hostile for residents and costly for landlords, it also slowly began to attract a somewhat unexpected new population of residents: artists. Painters and visual artists were the first to flock to lofts, where open floor plans and copious amounts of natural light facilitated the creation of large-scale works. In addition to using them as living and work spaces, some artists also opened their lofts for public gallery showings and sales. Best of all, the glut of available space prompted landlords to lease them at remarkably low rents. Residence was technically illegal due to existing zoning restrictions, but for many artists the allure of large, cheap space offset the risk of possible eviction. Landlords were equally happy to overlook legal issues, since having tenants (even at low rent) would help to offset their financial losses. Because the arrangements were illegal anyway, there was no need to comply with city housing codes, thereby avoiding the additional expenditures of providing basic amenities like heat and hot water, which many lofts lacked. This also meant that the residents could be readily evicted should a more profitable opportunity present itself (such as a sale to redevelopers). In short, while this collusion between artists and landlords constituted a somewhat uneasy alliance, the prolonged uncertainty hanging over the neighborhood made such arrangements mutually beneficial, and led to increasing numbers of artist residents throughout the 1960s.

Although the size and context of this influx was remarkable, it was hardly the first time that downtown New York served as an important artistic center. As Christopher Mele has observed, lower Manhattan has been the nerve center for a string of avant garde cultural movements spanning the twentieth century: bohemian culture in the 1920s, the beatniks in the 1950s, the hippies in the 1960s, punk and queer subcultures in the 1970s and 1980s.[37] Mele notes that each of these groups attempted to romanticize the area's working-class population as an incipient critique of bourgeois culture. Such attempts generally failed, however, when the middle-class background of the movements' participants put them at odds with actual residents. In many ways, the 1960s loft artists also fell into this pattern, yet their arrival amid debates over the fate of the neighborhood prompted quite a different reception. Resident activists began framing the burgeoning artistic activities as indicative of evolving usage patterns of loft buildings, transforming them from sites of industrial manufacturing to sites of cultural / aesthetic production. By providing a new identity for the region *within* existing spaces, the artists' presence implicitly created a compelling new argument against the need for disruptive redevelopment. They were thus embraced as key allies of local residents and historic preservationists, a reception that differed sharply from those of earlier groups described by Mele.

By the early 1970s, artists had become the most vocal constituency lobbying for preservation and tenants' rights in lower Manhattan. The center of the movement was the newly christened area known as SoHo, a twenty-six-block region bounded by Houston, Canal, West Broadway, and Crosby Streets.[38] There, artists formed a series of community organizations to advocate for their right to live in lofts, including the Artists Tenants Association (ATA), the SoHo Artists' Association (SAA), and the Lower Manhattan Loft Tenants (LMLT).[39] In 1971, the SAA successfully lobbied the city's Board of Estimates to pass a zoning resolution legalizing the occupancy of loft residents in SoHo.[40] A few years later, in 1973, they obtained historic landmark status for the region and its distinctive iron façades, precluding any future attempts at demolition.[41] Over time, their efforts overwhelmingly altered common perceptions about loft structures, transforming them from threatening skeletons of outdated industry to visually pleasing and historically significant sites for new cultural production.

Walking through SoHo today, it seems almost unfathomable that the neighborhood was once viewed as a paragon of obsolescence, criminality, and urban decay. The same brawny structures in which artist-squatters once huddled without heat or hot water now number among the most expensive properties in the city. Ironically, the staggering success in reforming the area's image would quickly lead to snowballing gentrification that priced many of these artist residents out of the neighborhood (despite constant attempts to protect their rights through rent control). Today, the streets teem with high-end galleries, boutiques, and multinational corporations. The very phrase "SoHo loft" has come to evoke visions of luxurious urban domesticity that are recognized throughout the world (a phenomenon explored in greater length in chapter 6).

But in the 1960s and 1970s, lofts promised no luxury. They offered only possibility.

"REHEARSALS AT MIDNIGHT": EARLY JAZZ LOFTS IN THE 1950S AND '60S

Jazz history is rife with stories about musicians congregating in informal gathering spaces. In New York alone, several sites have become immortalized in the music's lore. In the 1920s, for example, Harlem's legendary rent parties became critical incubators for the virtuosic "stride" piano style, spurred on by fierce battles between giants like James P. Johnson and Willie "The Lion" Smith.[42] In the 1940s, a small nightclub called Minton's Playhouse became renowned for the blistering after-hours jam sessions that helped foster the creation of bebop.[43] Several musicians' homes were equally important. Both Mary Lou Williams's apartment in Harlem and Gil Evans's on 55th Street maintained something of an open-door policy in which musicians would wander in and out at all times of day and night.[44] Commercial venues that were perceived as being friendly to artists (such as the Café Society in the late '30s, or several clubs during the heyday of 52nd Street) played a similar role, as did certain West Village coffee shops in the early 1960s.[45] The music's long history within these sorts of communal semipublic environments set the stage for the emergence of loft activities.

The first performances of jazz in lofts date at least to the mid-1950s. Early events often consisted of informal gatherings and jam sessions inside the homes of musicians, artists, or supportive fans. The sheer size of lofts was conducive to such activities, comfortably accommodating pianos, drum sets, or large ensembles. Their location in industrial areas was another advantage, since there were fewer neighbors to disturb with excess noise. This lack of sound restrictions—a rarity in the cramped confines of New York—allowed sessions to continue deep into the night.

An especially well-documented early loft was the home of W. Eugene Smith, a successful photographer for *Life* magazine. Smith's loft was not in SoHo, but located at 821 Sixth Avenue, just north of 28th Street in the city's flower district. Other units in the building were also occupied by artists at various points, including composer Hall Overton, pianist Dick Cary, and painter David X. Young. During a period spanning from 1957 to 1965, Smith's loft developed a well-known reputation for hosting jam sessions. A piano and drum set were always available, and Smith himself maintained a hands-off, open-door attitude where musicians could drop in at any time of day or night. The space was visited by hundreds of musicians over this time, including major luminaries like Thelonious Monk and Charles Mingus. Though never open to the public, it became a vital hangout, after-hours spot, and meeting place.[46]

Smith's home represents a poignant early example of jazz in lofts, but his was hardly the only space to put on such events. Twenty-five blocks to the south, record collector Dan Serro fostered a similar environment in his loft at 9 Great Jones Street. His account of moving into the space in 1961 highlights several common themes among early loft presenters: low rent, casual jam sessions, and the conversion of the structure into a mixed-use living and work space:

> I think I was the first artist in residence in the building. I built it into a living space and working space . . . I don't think anything was there before I moved in. The [landlord] was glad to rent it. I think we were playing $125 a month. It was a whole floor, 2,400 square feet . . . We did not have a club, but musicians used to just drop by and we'd have sessions. Just the musicians.[47]

Like Smith, Serro also made attempts to document the events that transpired.

> I had a Scully tape recorder, which was a professional tape recorder at that time. I used to record a lot of the sessions that we had.[48] People like Sam Rivers, Prince Lasha, [and] Roy Brooks. Elvin Jones was there, but he never played . . . I always felt that all the music that was happening was being lost. In those days free jazz musicians didn't write, they just played. It was free music, period . . . Even when I went to clubs I used to record because I felt that all this music was being played and some of the greatest things—music, sounds, whatever you want to call them—was being played and just disappeared! And some of it was just so unbelievably fantastic. So I started recording everything that I [organized].[49]

Serro recorded thirty-five reels of tape on Great Jones Street, along with hundreds more at other locations. Later, he would use his engineering skills to launch two separate record labels, Kharma and Danola.[50]

By 1963, loft events had become common enough to be featured in a *Down Beat* column by Amiri Baraka. The piece, titled "New York Loft and Coffee Shop Jazz," is the first published account of loft jazz activities. It portrays them as a proactive solution undertaken by avant garde musicians who were being ignored by commercial clubs. Although Baraka mentions several coffee shops by name, he refers to the lofts only by their locations: "a large loft on Great Jones Street"[51] and "a loft down on Clinton Street, which is deep on the Lower East Side where nobody lives but poor and new Americans or artists."[52] Despite this anonymity, these concerts were open to the public, a crucial development that clearly set them apart from earlier, private loft affairs.[53]

Baraka's account is glowingly enthusiastic about the musicians he heard at these early events, including relative newcomers like Archie Shepp, John Tchicai, and Henry Grimes. Yet it is notable that his prose displays little romanticism for the value of self-presentation itself. Instead, much of the piece is devoted to chastising club owners for neglecting avant garde artists:

> I have been impressed for a long time now with the fact that the jazz club owner is the only entrepreneur who knows absolutely nothing about the product he is peddling. And I have suggested many times to my friends that some Samaritan ought to put out a jazz club owners' consumer's report to better equip these naïfs in the handling of their own businesses . . . [T]he jazz audience, at least here in New York, is changing, in fact, has changed a great deal already. One of the formal jazz clubs had better take this change into consideration when hiring their talent and get some of the exciting younger musicians into their clubs. There's a lot of them around The Apple now, who could even be used as the second group opposite some *name*. It's bad enough to let so much talent go to waste, but it's worse to let it starve.[54]

At least at this time, Baraka appears to see little potential in the spaces as sites for artist empowerment or industry protest. For this reason, his overall assessment of loft performance seems somewhat conflicted: the music is groundbreaking and the atmosphere welcoming, but ultimately the spaces are bemoaned for their poor acoustics and lack of cultural respectability.

Such attitudes gradually began changing in the years following Bill Dixon's highly successful October Revolution in 1964. The festival furnished a powerful example of the potential advantages of alternative performance space. It had taken place at the Cellar Café, an Upper West Side coffee shop similar to those discussed ambivalently by Baraka. In Dixon's hands, however, the event aimed to transcend and transform the meager surroundings into a suitable venue for serious music. It was billed as a "Festival of Contemporary Music," and one journalist even described the setting as "not really a café, but a small concert hall with sandwiches and coffee."[55] Where Baraka saw misfortune in the need to play in atypical surroundings, Dixon saw an opportunity to build new institutions controlled entirely by musicians. This transformation from a discourse of reactionism to one of institution-building would become a keystone for subsequent organizations. Even Baraka himself would soon embark on several such initiatives, including the Black Arts Repertory Theater and School (founded 1965) and the Spirit House (1966).

As the 1960s progressed, a growing cadre of musicians followed the lead of visual artists and began obtaining their own lofts for use as living and rehearsal spaces. Like Smith and Serro, their activities often began informally as private get-togethers, circulated by word of mouth. Pianist Dave Burrell moved into his first loft in 1965, a space at the corner of Bond Street and the Bowery that he shared with drummer Bobby Kapp and saxophonist Byard Lancaster.[56] Burrell recalls frequent rehearsals and meet-ups at all hours of the day and night. Over time, more and more musicians began showing up, helping the young Burrell plug in to the city's musical network.

> We had rehearsals at midnight . . . we could do it without disturbing anybody . . . We were very outgoing so we actually attracted all of these folks who would hear the music and wonder what's going on in there . . . [We would tell them,] "Well tomorrow at midnight we're gonna do this again." [And they would say], "Oh really? Okay, I'll tell my friends!" We had Valerie Wilmer there. Elvin [Jones] and Gil [Evans] came. Then Marion Brown came and he brought Grachan Moncur III. And then they started giving us gigs![57]

Saxophonist Mark Whitecage has similar recollections of his own arrival in 1967. Whitecage gravitated to the Lower East Side, an area just east of SoHo that became known for low rents and a high concentration of musicians.

> I found a pad for fifty-seven dollars a month. I could work a couple days a month to pay for that. So money was easy in those days because the rents were so low . . . The whole town was full of musicians. You'd walk down the street in the spring and the windows would open up. You'd hear a trombone player up there, a violin over here. All these guys have been shedding all winter and they finally open the windows! You'd hear them all![58]

Like Burrell, Whitecage recalls the ease of meeting other artists within the neighborhood's rich musical ferment. He met bassist Steve Tintweiss, for example, simply because he was walking through Tompkins Square Park with his tenor saxophone. Tintweiss saw the instrument case, flagged him down, and asked if he could attend a rehearsal a few days later. Within a relatively small area of the city, a dense network of like-minded experimentalists was beginning to come together. Before long, this group would begin to seek out spaces to present their creations to the world.

3

THE JAZZ LOFT ERA

Although jazz events in lofts have been documented as far back as the 1950s, the phrases "loft scene" or "loft era" are most often reserved for the activities of the 1970s. This usage points to an important change in how loft performances were produced and perceived at that time. While earlier events were mostly private affairs held for the enjoyment of musicians, the lofts of the 1970s began adopting more methodical business models in order to promote their music to audiences and critics. Social logics gave way to presentational logics as organizers sought to position their spaces as viable alternatives to commercial clubs. By opening their homes as public showcases, musicians developed a new type of performance setting that combined the intimacy of the jam session with the rhetoric of self-empowerment derived from other jazz collectives (as well as civil rights activists). Lofts began adopting memorable venue names, programming ongoing schedules instead of sporadic events, and advertising their activities through flyers and newspaper advertisements. Over time, their visibility increased to the point where the New York lofts acquired an international reputation as a center for avant garde music.

EARLY PROTOTYPES: ARTIST HOUSE AND STUDIO WE

The years between 1968 and 1970 saw the formation of two key prototypes for 1970s jazz lofts. The first was Ornette Coleman's Artist House, established inside his home at 131 Prince Street in SoHo. Coleman acquired the space in April of 1968,[1] initially envisioning it as a location to hold rehearsals: "I didn't have any idea that it was going to be [a public concert space]. I was just trying to find a place where I could go and make music at any time."[2] By 1970, he had begun hosting occasional performances of music and dance, fostering an informal atmosphere that was typical of loft gatherings.[3] Photos of the space are visible on Coleman's album *Friends and Neighbors,* which was recorded in the loft that year.[4] Several other musicians also lived in the building at various times, including AACM veterans Anthony Braxton and Leroy Jenkins.[5]

Artist House acted as a significant transitional entity between the more casual get-togethers of earlier years and the more publicly oriented lofts that followed. Though it foreshadowed later spaces by adopting a memorable name and achieving slightly higher visibility, events at Artist House remained sporadic and were often open to the pubic with no admission charge. In addition to staging his own concerts, Coleman also made the space available to other artists, an opportunity that left a deep impression on drummer Rashied Ali:

> Ornette would give out the space to musicians. It wasn't even about renting the space. He would give it to you for almost nothing. We would produce and perform our own concerts there. We were the producer, the performer, did all the legwork, the P.R. work and everything like that in order to get people to come. That was a hell of an experience. It taught me a lot. It gave me an incentive to open up a space like that.[6]

These lessons would prove useful later on when Ali opened his own nightclub, Ali's Alley. The musicians I interviewed uniformly recalled Coleman offering support to young artists, despite some characterizing him as remaining somewhat distant from the later loft scene.[7] Nevertheless, Artist House was an influential predecessor to subsequent activities, and its importance was bolstered by Coleman's own status as a musical innovator. The space hosted events through 1974, closing its doors just as the lofts began to enter their most celebrated period.[8]

An even more archetypal early loft was Studio We, which began hosting concerts around 1969. The space was located in a vacant factory building at 193 Eldridge St., about seven blocks east of SoHo. In the mid-1960s, it was home to pianist Burton Greene, who obtained it through a somewhat unorthodox arrangement with one of the neighborhood's many absentee landlords:

> I didn't "own" the loft on Eldridge St. I got it from the landlord in Brooklyn who didn't want to go near the building after a while, since the coffee shop downstairs and the neighborhood was infested with junkies. I had free rent in return (supposedly) for "keeping the junkies" out of the upstairs lofts (Lots of Luck!), and for keeping the stairways clean, and to do occasional repairs to the roof (Lots of Luck Again!!)[9]

By the time he moved in, Greene had already been evicted from several other lofts in the area, including one in which a landlord called the fire department to expel several artists who—while technically living there illegally—had been paying rent for months. His arrangement on Eldridge Street was somewhat more stable, and Greene grew comfortable enough to obtain a nine-foot grand piano to use for practicing and group rehearsal.[10]

In 1969, Greene was preparing to embark on his first trip to Europe, an excursion scheduled to last about one month. Prior to departing, he was approached by trumpeter James DuBoise, a Pittsburgh native who had played with Greene on several occasions. DuBoise expressed interest in looking after the loft while the pianist was away, noting that he had been in search of a location to host jam sessions and rehearsals. Despite having previously received another offer of $2,000 for the space, Greene was impressed by DuBoise's vision and decided to grant his request. Though the arrangement was initially planned as temporary, Greene ended up staying in Europe for over a year, eventually relocating there permanently by the mid-1970s. In his absence, DuBoise became the space's permanent steward, inheriting Greene's prior arrangement with the landlord.

DuBoise is a figure who has been almost entirely overlooked in jazz literature, yet his organizing work at Studio We played a pivotal role in launching the loft era. A brief detour into his biography will help lay down the context for his contributions. Born in 1932, DuBoise received his earliest musical education in his native Pittsburgh, where he played in rock-and-roll bands before becoming interested in jazz as a teenager.[11] He developed a deep admiration for a venue called The Musicians' Club, a hall operated by Pittsburgh's black musicians union: Local 471 of the American Federation of Musicians (AFM). The space was administered entirely by union members and operated as a nightclub, rehearsal hall, meeting facility, and business center. In addition to providing work opportunities, the Club was an important community gathering place, as well as an advocacy group that lobbied for the rights of African American artists.[12] It remained in operation until 1965, when Local 471 merged with the city's white Local 60 as part of a nationwide initiative to integrate AFM chapters.[13]

The Musicians' Club's model of self-production by black artists left a major impression on DuBoise. As he stated in a radio interview from the early 1990s, much of his professional activity centered on the premise that, "Musicians should be in control of their own affairs."[14] DuBoise began putting this idea into practice early in his professional life. During a brief period living in Cleveland in the 1950s, he made a first attempt at organizing concerts at a space on Superior Avenue that he named the Cleveland Cultural Center. Back in Pittsburgh in the early 1960s, he acquired another space in an abandoned glass factory on Centre Avenue. Around this same time, he established a nonprofit organization called the Society of Universal Cultural Arts (SOUCA) that focused on producing concerts and providing musicians to play at local events.

DuBoise moved to New York in the mid-1960s to advance his musical career, but was disappointed to find few opportunities available. He moved into an apartment on 6th Street where he lived with drummer J. C. Moses (a fellow Pittsburgh native) and bassist Juney Booth. DuBoise described the area as, "A musician's paradise because the rent was cheap! You could get a place for seventy-five dollars a month!

FIGURE 2. Group of musicians in front of Studio We. L–R: Ted Daniel, Milford Graves, Frank Lowe, Juma Sultan, Noah Howard, James DuBoise, unknown (possibly Bobby Few), Sam Rivers, Ali Abuwi. June 1973. Photo by Thierry Trombert.

A lot of musicians gravitated to the Lower East Side."[15] Throughout this time, DuBoise dreamed of organizing a venue that could re-create the vivacious professional ambiance of the Pittsburgh Musicians' Club. The acquisition of the loft on Eldridge Street presented him with an ideal opportunity. Soon after Greene's departure, DuBoise resurrected SOUCA and began preparing to host public events.

But before they could do so, DuBoise had to address a number of serious structural flaws in the building. An account written by the trumpeter in 1974 describes the initial condition of the building as "an archetype of urban blight," and provides a telling glimpse into the state of many loft structures: "Riddled with fire and building violations, lacking heat, electricity and adequate water facilities, displaying gaping sockets where doors and windows once had been, trash heaped in the hallways and basement—the building stood as a reeking, rotting shell destined for destruction by neglect."[16] With assistance from drummer Harold Smith, DuBoise embarked on a series of major renovations. The two musicians installed a new roof and plumbing fixtures and fixed cracks in the walls and brickwork. They also installed a small stage on the sixth floor and soon began hosting jam sessions. To emphasize his hope for an open, welcoming atmosphere, DuBoise called the space "Studio We: A Community Music Project" (Fig. 2).

FIGURE 3. We Music House rehearsal at Studio We. L–R: Jimmy Vass, James DuBoise, Sonelius Smith, Eugene Jackson. Archival damage visible. Image courtesy of the Juma Sultan Archive (Print 101).

Attendees often recall the early years of the studio as being characterized by lengthy, raucous jam sessions that stretched deep into the night. Saxophonist Daniel Carter, who came to the city in 1970, remembers getting an abrupt introduction to the high-energy New York school of free jazz:

> My first impression of Studio We was as kind of a wild and woolly, no-holds barred [environment with high] numbers of horn players. Sometimes there were drummers, [but they were] shy on having bass players. It was all these horns! I was writing [notated] music before I came to New York, so a lot of times I'd be like, "Okay, when are these horns going to stop and we can do something?" They really initiated me to the value of all-out group playing.[17]

Open blowing sessions comprised just one part of the loft's total activities; at the other end of the spectrum were more straight-ahead groups that performed jazz standards, including DuBoise's own ensemble We Music House, which became something of a house band at the loft (Fig. 3).

The venue began staging public concerts by late 1969. Like other lofts, the performances were initially sporadic, and heavily featured members of DuBoise's inner circle of musical associates. A watershed moment took place in July 1970, when the loft hosted an extended festival titled "Three Days of Peace between the Ears." A promotional flyer shows that the event included several musicians who would later open their own venues, including Sam Rivers and Rashied Ali (Fig. 4).[18]

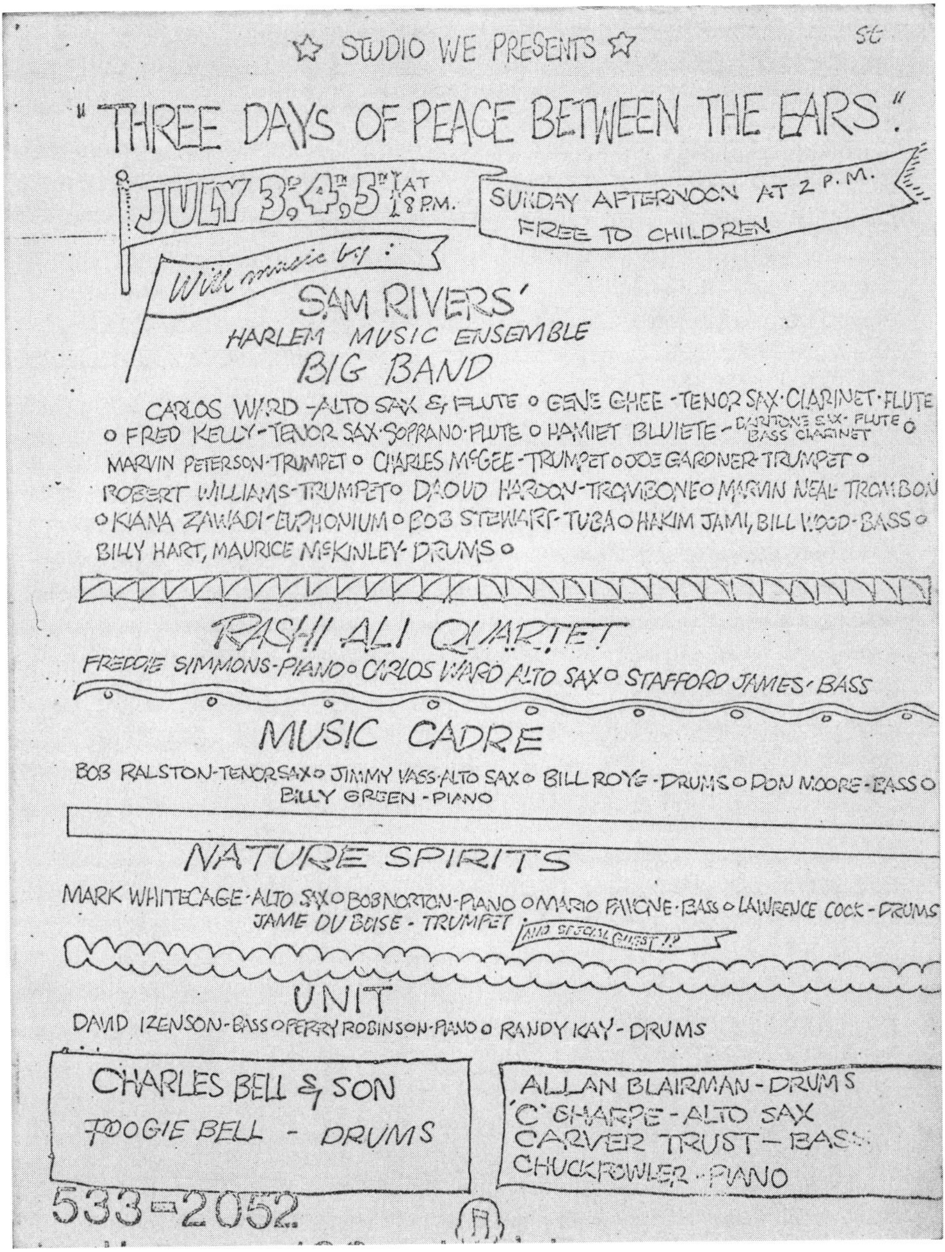

FIGURE 4. Flyer for Studio We's festival "Three Days of Peace between the Ears." July 1970. Image courtesy of the Juma Sultan Archive (F0054.19).

Since DuBoise had access to several of the building's vacant floors, the festival presented simultaneous sets in multiple rooms at once. On top of the advertised groups, a wave of other players showed up with their instruments, leading to additional, impromptu sets. This excess of activity made it difficult when DuBoise tried to halt the proceedings at the end of the night: "So many musicians showed up we had to expand it from the sixth floor to the fourth floor and to the second floor . . . One day the music got started and I couldn't stop the music! . . . I would stop the music on the second floor, and then when I'd go up to stop the music on the fourth floor, the music on the second floor started playing again!"[19] The success of such events prompted a gradual expansion of Studio We's programming. Their funding base expanded as well. Through the auspices of his nonprofit SOUCA, DuBoise obtained his first presenting grant from the New York State Council on the Arts (NYSCA) in 1972, allowing him to stage another ambitious series that spring. The model of courting grant funding for special events, interspersed with a dense schedule of more casual presentations, would become increasingly common at Studio We, and would later be adopted by several other loft spaces.

Despite the successful models provided by Studio We and Artist House, loft performance remained a relatively minor part of New York's jazz landscape at the dawn of the 1970s. The full flowering of the scene would not begin until the summer of 1972, when a string of tumultuous events prompted an extraordinary reassessment of loft practices.

COMPLAINING TIME IS OVER: THE NEW YORK MUSICIANS' JAZZ FESTIVAL

In January of 1972, impresario George Wein announced that the Newport Jazz Festival was moving to New York. The move was not undertaken entirely by choice. The previous summer, the festival had fallen victim to its second riot in just over a decade. It was hardly the first outdoor event to be marred by crowd violence during the period. Several similar outbursts had occurred in the preceding years, including the well-documented murder at the Altamont Free Concert (1969) and crowd disturbances at the Isle of Wight and Atlanta International Pop Festivals (both 1970). Though Newport's identity as a jazz festival might seem to cater to a different clientele, the inclusion of groups like Led Zeppelin, Jethro Tull, and Sly and the Family Stone in 1969, as well as the Allman Brothers Band in 1971, made it a plausible destination for rock fans seeking outdoor music events in the wake of Woodstock. In a deeply ironic (and perhaps apocryphal) twist, at least one newspaper account had the riot peaking when audiences broke down the fences during Dionne Warwick's performance of "What the World Needs Now Is Love."[20] Within days of the riot, the Newport City Council voted to ban the event from the city. The Newport Jazz Festival would not return to its namesake city until the summer of 1981.[21]

Rather than seek another outdoor venue in the mold of Newport, Wein chose to relocate the festival to New York City, a move necessitating substantial changes in format. Instead of operating at a single site, concerts would take place in several venues, including Carnegie Hall, Lincoln Center's Philharmonic Hall, and Radio City Music Hall. The shift from outdoor stages to more tightly organized concert venues had the dual benefit of lessening security risks while also attracting prestige by presenting jazz in spaces normally associated with concert traditions.[22] The schedule moved away from popular music[23] and focused primarily on well-known jazz artists from the swing and bebop eras.[24] The festival was welcomed with open arms by city officials, and both Mayor John Lindsay and former mayor Robert Wagner accepted honorary chairmanships on festival planning committees.[25] An extensive publicity campaign was launched in the spring, featuring a bright red apple as its iconic logo. By both public figures and press alike, the festival was promoted as a way to boost the city's flagging jazz economy, which Wein later referred to as "at a low ebb in 1971."[26]

But as many in the city eagerly anticipated Newport's arrival, the reaction among some musicians was more skeptical, especially from those who had been left out of the schedule. Rather than celebrating the festival as a rebirth, many saw it as an intrusion and an insult to their own efforts to maintain a vibrant and innovative jazz scene. The festival provided gigs for established artists, but it did little to attract attention for lesser-known players, especially younger musicians and those involved in the avant garde. As a result, many were disappointed that Newport was merely presenting, in the words of James DuBoise, "the same musicians that we'd been hearing down through the years."[27]

The racial and economic ramifications of Newport's arrival also became the subject of scrutiny. Musicians accused Wein of neglecting black communities by presenting most of the performances at pricey Midtown concert halls. In an article in the *New York Times*, Juma Sultan states: "We tried to bring to the attention of Newport producers that they weren't doing anything for Harlem and other black communities in the city . . . We tried to point out that George Wein, the producer, wasn't hiring black musicians who are part of and represent this city in jazz today."[28] In a fascinating reversal, what Wein had thought would be seen as an effort to raise the cultural status of black music was instead viewed as an attempt to pull jazz away from the community that created it. Later in the same article, saxophonist Archie Shepp levels the additional criticism that despite Newport's presentation of black artists, the festival included no input from black musicians at the organizational level: "We felt that if [Wein's] festival was going to move from Newport to New York City then it should reflect that change from a rural to an urban setting where blacks want to control where and how their music is performed . . . The entrepreneurs have been able too long to determine what the musicians will play, where they'll play it and when."[29] Inspired by the cultural nationalist tenor of the

Black Arts Movement, such calls for direct control by black musicians would become progressively more frequent in the coming years.

These growing complaints soon manifested in a series of meetings at the University of the Streets, a community center on 7th Street and Avenue A. Several figures took central roles in the organizing process, including DuBoise and Sultan, saxophonists Sam Rivers and Noah Howard, and percussionists Rashied Ali, Milford Graves, Ali Abuwi, and Eddie Heath.[30] This group possessed a wealth of organizing experience among them. In addition to DuBoise's work with SOUCA and Studio We, Sultan and Abuwi had founded a presenting organization and performance group in Woodstock called the Aboriginal Music Society.[31] Rivers had previously sought to establish a teaching studio in Harlem, before relocating to lower Manhattan and opening his own loft called Studio Rivbea.[32] Howard had launched the record label Altsax in 1971,[33] while Graves and Ali had both been involved in Bill Dixon's October Revolution in 1964.[34] Thus, while the musicians were challenged with the task of organizing in a relatively short time, members of the group had already been considering strategies of self-determination through other ventures in the preceding years.

The musicians compiled their complaints in a list of ten demands sent to Wein that spring. These demands can be seen in Figure 5.[35] Taken as a whole, the list points to three main goals: (1) providing musicians with greater control over their performances, including financial aspects, (2) close involvement with local communities (especially in black neighborhoods) through direct outreach and ticket subsidies, and (3) acknowledgment of the centrality of the African American community in jazz's development. Racial critiques are especially palpable in the list, as seven of the ten items make direct reference to black artists and/or outreach efforts in Harlem.

It is fair to question whether Wein was used as something of a scapegoat during the course of these debates. In many ways, the musicians' militancy seems directed less at Wein himself than at the music industry more broadly. A solid majority of Newport's lineup each year consisted of black artists, and Wein himself had long been a vocal supporter of civil rights causes. Even before receiving the list of demands, the producer had pledged to donate half of the festival's profits to the civil rights group the Urban League. And though it is true that the festival did not plan any official concerts in Harlem that year, Wein and his wife Joyce—herself African American—did arrange for singer Eddie Jefferson and saxophonist James Moody to appear as late additions to a Harlem street fair organized by activist Kimako Baraka.[36]

In the heated atmosphere surrounding jazz and race during this period, it was not unusual for lines to be blurred between personal attacks and wider critiques of structural inequality. As Ingrid Monson has noted: "These debates were in some ways public rituals of racial catharsis in which the white representatives were made

NEW YORK MUSICIANS ORGANIZATION

193 Eldridge Street, New York, New York (212) 260-1211

This is a list of demands, served upon the Producers and Planners of the Newport New York Jazz Festival, 1972, held in New York City, July 1, through July 10, 1972.

1. That a minimum salary be guaranteed to the bands.

2. That musicians have determination as to what location they will play.

3. Black Musicians to be consulted regarding total activity coordination of the Jazz Festival. A committee for such purpose to be set up through Black Musicians United.

4. That each day of the Festival, there be a major activity in Harlem.

5. That during the Festival, a day be set aside to honor Marcus Garvey and the formal Community dedication of Marcus Garvey Memorial Park (Now Mt. Morris), with his "Black is Beautiful", theme.

6. From the funds received by the Urban League, renovation of the Marcus Garvey Building, 204 Lenox Avenue, housing the Music Workshops and the Black Indepth Thinking Classes dedicated to rehabilitation of Addicts with a stress on Musicians and providing premises for the Black Musicians to create and teach.

7. Liaison between the Urban League and Community based programs on the wants and needs of the Black Musicians. The pilot project development to be in Harlem.

8. That the Urban League set aside, on a quarterly basis, funds, for a School of Music in Harlem.

9. That free tickets to the Festival locations outside of Harlem, and within Harlem, if tickets are required, be dispersed in needy area.

10. That there be 100% support to the above demands.

FIGURE 5. List of demands sent by NYMJF organizers to George Wein of the Newport Jazz Festival. Circa late 1972. Image courtesy of the Juma Sultan Archive (F0248.03).

to stand symbolically for the whole history of white racism and the African American representatives were made to exemplify the entire history of racial injustice. During heated arguments the distinction between the personal and the sociological, the micro and the macro frequently collapsed as the structural became personal."[37] Wein, like other white producers, had undoubtedly benefited from societal inequalities that facilitated white entrepreneurship,[38] yet the sweeping tenor of the musicians' demands indicate that their critiques struck deeper than the producer alone.

A particularly notable aspect of the list is its multiple references to the funds pledged to the Urban League, a decidedly nonmilitant civil rights organization. Although the league is not criticized directly, the presence of three demands to specifically earmark the donation suggests that the musicians were not fully satisfied with Wein's gesture. Like many discourses emerging in the wave of what Eric Porter has called the period's "Black Arts Imperative,"[39] their demands point to a greater influence from black cultural nationalism rather than the moderate integrationism favored by the league. This stance is especially evident in the overt concern with obtaining direct control over revenue flows as a way to reclaim aesthetic and financial agency.

In a broader sense, the musicians' reaction to Wein's Urban League donation was reflective of the position of the civil rights movement in the period, which sat at a critical crossroads in 1972. In the wake of both the gains made by 1960s civil rights legislation and the tragic assassinations of leaders like Martin Luther King and Malcolm X, activists wrestled with the next steps for social reform. The first National Black Political Convention—which took place that March in Gary, Indiana—gives us a window into this fraught process. The event brought together leaders from many disparate ideologies, including elected officials, moderate reform organizations, cultural and revolutionary nationalists, land-based separatists, and Pan Africanists. Despite an initial goal to work together under the principle of "unity without uniformity,"[40] the event revealed deep rifts between liberal and nationalist factions that ultimately impeded widescale action.[41] The musicians' demands seem to suggest a similar tension. It is notable, for instance, how the musicians are careful not to criticize the Urban League directly, yet there is nevertheless a clear undertone of dissatisfaction. The text echoes several other early documents written by the group in deploying a slightly tentative (or perhaps conflicted) brand of black cultural nationalism. Rhetoric framing jazz as the product of African American communities is frequent but the group never goes so far as to restrict the participation of white artists, who were involved early on in festival activities.

The list was sent to Wein that spring, but the group received no response. After further meetings, the musicians decided to stage a counterfestival in protest, calling it the New York Musicians' Jazz Festival (NYMJF). The event was designed as a corrective to the various shortcomings they saw in Newport. In contrast to the larger festival's use of expensive Midtown concert halls, the NYMJF staged events in all five boroughs of the city, including many that were free to attend. The jazz club Slugs volunteered to host some performances, but in order to keep costs low, most were held at venues obtainable for little or no cost, including city parks, community centers and, significantly, lofts. Studio We, Studio Rivbea, and Artist House all presented nightly events throughout the festival.

Concerts were also staged at the Space for Innovative Development, a converted church on 36th Street that hosted events produced by the collective Free Life Communication. Founded in 1970 by musicians Dave Liebman and Bob Moses, the group had formed with the mission of bringing the music being played in the (then private) lofts into wider public view. Free Life Communication occupied a unique role in the scene as a collective made up of mostly white members, but one that was modeled closely after Chicago's AACM.[42] The organization achieved rapid success; within a year it had registered as a nonprofit, secured a long-term home for hosting events, and received a multiyear grant of $10,000 from NYSCA.[43] Though it is likely that the group's racial makeup provided certain advantages in securing funding (especially in the highly charged atmosphere surrounding black organizations of the early 1970s), their orientation was centered on similar ideals that mobilized black collectives, including self-organization, the use of alternative space, and experimentalist artistic practices. Their inclusion in the NYMJF—in spite of the counterfestival's emphasis on black identity—points to both the group's position within the burgeoning loft movement and the fluidity of racial discourses that surrounded the festival planning.

Contrary to some newspaper stories that portrayed the festival's organization as being somewhat haphazard,[44] an examination of NYMJF documents held in the Juma Sultan Archive reveals the immense level of planning that was involved. Within a matter of months, the group established a basic organizational structure, with a governing board made up of DuBoise, Sultan, Rivers, Ali, Graves, and Howard. Formal contracts were drafted for every participating musician in highly legal language.[45] Permits were obtained to perform in eight different city parks, with the festival culminating in a massive jam session in Central Park (Fig. 6). An initial source of revenue was secured through dues paid by the groups performing, each of which was asked to contribute twenty-five dollars.[46] Later, the musicians were also awarded two grants (one from the Parks Department) in support of their efforts, which allowed them to offer guaranteed payments to each artist (instead of a percentage of ticket sales). Recognizing the event's historical significance, plans were made to record as many concerts as possible, with several also filmed by cinematographer McKinley Karma Stanley. The group even hired staff photographers, drawing up a contract outlining fee scales and intellectual ownership of the negatives. This documentation was ultimately intended to create a feature-length film about the festival, to be titled "The New Music Scene in New York City."[47]

FIGURE 6. Central Park jam session at the conclusion of the New York Musicians' Jazz Festival. Chiitra Neogy and Alan "Juice" Glover (Akinjorin Omolade) in the foreground. Archival damage visible. July 10, 1972. Photographer unknown. Image courtesy of the Juma Sultan Archive (Print 134).

By all accounts, the counterfestival was an enormous success. On the day the curtain rose on Newport's first two concerts at Philharmonic and Carnegie Halls, the NYMJF presented eleven events all over the city. This abundance continued throughout the ensuing eleven days, totaling over two hundred fifty performances at one hundred discrete events in twenty-two venues, dwarfing the earlier protest festivals arranged by Mingus and Dixon. Even the Newport Festival itself staged only twenty-six events at six venues over nine days, with over ninety percent taking place in Manhattan.[48] The counterfestival also received a great deal of positive press coverage. Its biggest champion was *New York Times* columnist Les Ledbetter, one of the few black writers employed by the paper.[49] International publications covered it as well, including Japan's *Swing Journal* and France's *Jazz Hot* (the latter ran a cover story on the NYMJF in their September issue).[50] This recognition from

European writers would yield benefits later on, as European festivals became important presenters of loft artists. In all, the festival's success and the surge of public interest that followed provided a powerful demonstration of the potential of musician-organized events in alternative spaces.

Early NYMJF planning documents show that the organizers envisioned more than simply a one-time event. Rather, they echoed earlier collectives in hoping that the festival could serve as a launching pad for a permanent organization:

> This Festival is being put on by the Jazz Musicians themselves as a first *co-orporate* venture in unison. Musicians are traditionally healers and spiritual transporters and we recognize that if our tradition is to remain pure, it must remain under our own direction as before. The recognition of Black Men in charge of their own creative works is the recognition of unclouded vision into tomorrow. We have come together out of [a] long discussed need to present the vast areas of music previously ignored, that our people in the community need to hear in unison for rebuilding internationally.[51]

The notion of a "co-orporate" endeavor—a neologism combining cooperative strategies and corporate goals—appears in several of the group's documents. A more expansive agenda was laid out in an internal memo circulated around the same time:

> In keeping with forward plans for our organization to be of benefit and long life to our members, a New York Musicians' Fund will be established. The purpose of the fund will be to meet present and long range needs of our membership. The fund will be used to establish our own Legal Department, Managing, Booking and Producing Departments, a library for books and records, schools, workshops, Publishing Department, transcribing service, copy service, Film and Record Production Department, pressing plant, distribution and sales outlet, music stores, communication research center, scholarship foundation, Advertising Department, Real Estate Department, hostels, Theater/Concert Hall, Import/Export Department, health food co-ops, our own Bank, and a Church of African Liberation to keep the force of ourselves spiritually correct. All of these are steps toward self-sufficiency and are within our future with consistent, serious effort. Complaining time is over.[52]

While such plans can be read as vastly overambitious, the document demonstrates aspirations that include wholesale involvement in all aspects of the music industry and, subsequently, the community more broadly. Regardless of feasibility, it is instructive to note the multifaceted ways in which the musicians hoped to interface with larger social, cultural, and political milieus of the early 1970s. This is especially evident in regard to the focus on community-based ownership strategies informed by black cultural nationalism.

In September, two months after the festival's conclusion, the organizers announced the formation of the New York Musicians Organization (NYMO), a collective designed to expand upon the gains made by the NYMJF.[53] Sultan was named its first president. Their purpose would be to "produce, promote and distribute original works of its members through free and paid concerts, festivals and recordings."[54] The organization launched with the Central Park premiere of Sam Rivers's composition *Zodiac*, initially slated to include one hundred fifty musicians and dancers[55] (subsequent reports placed the final number at about thirty).[56] Plans were also made to establish a music school at Studio We. A pilot program ran briefly during the fall but soon collapsed due to lack of funding.[57]

But like their predecessors in the New York guilds, the musicians found that the exhilaration surrounding a defiant underdog counterfestival was much more difficult to sustain on a permanent basis. While the NYMJF had been characterized by cooperation and consensus in the face of a common foe, this unity began to dissolve in the year that followed. The splintering started in early 1973 when an offer arrived from Wein to join forces with Newport the following summer. NYMO members were deeply divided about this possibility. Some, including Sultan, DuBoise, and Rivers, saw it as something of an olive branch. Since a major complaint in 1972 had been a lack of recognition and respect, the proposal to collaborate seemed to acknowledge the value of their work. But for others, especially Rashied Ali, aligning with Newport was akin to giving up the values of self-control upon which the organization was founded. For Ali, to collaborate with the jazz establishment would implicitly promote the very sort of economic structures that they had struggled to combat. When the membership voted to go forward with the collaboration, Ali and several others left the organization. He would later write a scathing essay about the episode titled "Exploitation Among NYC Musicians," though the piece was never published.[58]

Two other members of the board also left between the 1972 and 1973 festivals. On March 19, 1973, Sam Rivers sent a letter asking to resign his position on the NYMO board of directors. The text is reverential in its praise of the group, but Rivers cites other commitments—including the growing operations of Studio Rivbea—as leaving him little time to devote to NYMO work.[59] The board responded on March 26 in equally glowing fashion, granting Rivers his resignation but asking that his name be retained on a list of the group's founders.[60] A second loss occurred when Noah Howard emigrated to Paris in late 1972. Despite never officially resigning, he would remain abroad for the rest of his life and ceased being actively involved in the New York scene.

The departures of Ali, Rivers, and Howard were a tremendous blow. Not only had NYMO lost half of its board members (the remaining three being Sultan, DuBoise, and Milford Graves), but it lost three members with particularly high levels of public recognition. The split also destroyed any pretense that the organization spoke for a consensus of African American musicians or the downtown scene more broadly. This perception, while perhaps overstated at the time, had proved powerful in promoting the 1972 festival. Under Sultan's directorship, NYMO continued to function through much of the decade, with many of its events overlapping with those of Studio We and SOUCA.⁶¹ The group's summer festivals continued into the 1980s under several names, including the Five Boroughs Jazz Festival and the Studio We Park Concert Series. From 1974 to 1976 it obtained major sponsorship from the American Revolutionary Bicentennial Administration, prompting another renaming to the "Bicentennial Jazz Festival."⁶² Far from the aggressive, racially charged tone of the first year, by this point the festival advanced a decidedly more populist image of jazz as a beacon of American culture; DuBoise even applied to receive a ten-foot-tall statue of Uncle Sam to decorate the festival stage.⁶³ But despite their continued success, after 1972 NYMO could make little claim as an all-inclusive city-wide collective. Instead, it was merely one out of dozens of smaller initiatives producing events in the city.

Although NYMO failed to establish the type of long-term, broad-based collectivism that its founders envisioned, the success of the 1972 festival acted as a powerful catalyst for subsequent musician-organized activities. NYMJF organizers and participants would go on to run several of the most successful loft venues, including Studio Rivbea, Ali's Alley, Ladies' Fort, Studio WIS, Firehouse Theater, and Sunrise Studios.⁶⁴ By demonstrating the viability of grassroots strategies, the festival inspired a generation of musician-organizers who soon flowed into the city's lofts, parks, churches, and galleries.

"VENUE[S] FOR MUSICIANS LIKE US": LOFTS IN MID-DECADE

The stature of jazz performance in lofts mushroomed quickly in the years following the NYMJF. The period witnessed both the creation of new venues as well as the expansion of public offerings at those already in operation. Spaces that previously held only sporadic concerts began programming more regular events on a weekly or nightly basis. This burst of activity slowly transformed the lofts into a central destination for performers and listeners of avant garde jazz.

The single most influential jazz loft was the aforementioned Studio Rivbea, run by saxophonist Sam Rivers and his wife, Bea. The couple had lived and worked in the space since 1970, using it primarily for teaching and rehearsals. For the most part, they did not focus on hosting public concerts until after the 1972 festival, which Sam directly cited as his inspiration. In his resignation letter from NYMO, he writes:

> During the Summer Festival which was produced by the NEW YORK MUSICIANS ASSOCIATION [sic], STUDIO RIVBEA . . . was Host to some of the most talented Musicians creating some of the most exciting Music of our Times.
>
> It was from and because of those performances that STUDIO RIVBEA became internationally recognized for the presentation of New York's most talented Musicians of Contemporary Music.⁶⁵

Newspaper advertisements from 1972 confirm that it did not take long to make this leap into regular public presentations. Within three weeks of the festival's conclusion in early July, the space began holding weekly concerts on Friday and Saturday nights.[66] By mid-August, the schedule expanded to include Thursdays and Sundays, and by September the venue was presenting music seven nights a week.[67] Figure 7 shows a Rivbea brochure produced in April of 1973, including a representative schedule.[68]

In addition to concerts, events included workshops by various musicians (often Rivers himself) as well as weekly Sunday afternoon jam sessions. The brochure's mission statement frames the space as a cultural organization and center for musical development, but notably lacks the oppositional tone that had characterized early NYMO documents.[69]

A vital organizing force behind this expansion was Bea Rivers, who managed the loft's business operations. Sam, meanwhile, coordinated the bookings and served as music director.[70] Under Bea, Rivbea quickly established an organizational structure that was considerably more robust than either Studio We or Artist House. The 1973 brochure—produced less than a year into the space's public life—already notes affiliations with several other arts organizations including SOUCA, The Harlem Cultural Council, the Collective Black Artists, the Center for New Music, and the Creative Music Foundation. NYSCA also supported their activities within the first year, awarding a grant in 1973 for the space to host its own Studio Rivbea Summer Music Festival (which ran alongside the second year of both Newport and the NYMJF).[71] By the mid-1970s, the space developed a revenue structure in which grant funding provided guaranteed payments for musicians during the annual festivals while more casual "door gigs" (performances that paid based on ticket sales) kept the space active through the rest of the year.[72]

Rivbea's summer festival soon surpassed the NYMJF as the preeminent annual showcase for loft artists (Fig. 8). A compilation of festival recordings from 1976 was famously released as a five-LP set titled *Wildflowers: The New York Loft Jazz Sessions*.[73] Despite frequently being out-of-print, it remains by far the best-known recorded document of the entire loft era.[74] Both the venue's success and Sam's own prominence as a musical innovator and "unofficial mayor of the lofts"[75] led to Rivbea being consistently recognized as the quintessential musician-run space.

Rashied Ali followed a similar path in the wake of the 1972 festival. Starting in 1973, he began staging concerts in his spacious SoHo loft at 77 Greene Street, initially naming the space Studio 77.[76] After about a year, Ali chose to renovate the space and convert it into a full-fledged nightclub called Ali's Alley. A far cry from the couches and floor seating at other lofts, Ali's club featured tables, a full bar, and a soul food menu (Fig. 9).[77]

Speaking in 2007, Ali recalled that his main inspiration stemmed from the avant garde's exclusion from other jazz venues:

studio rivbea

24 bond st. new york, n.y. 10012

APRIL 1973

473-4378

MAY

FRIDAY 4, SATURDAY 5
SUNNY MURRAY

FRIDAY 11, SATURDAY 12
PAUL BLEY

FRIDAY 18, SATURDAY 19
ROBIN KENYATTA

FRIDAY 25, SATURDAY 26
MELODIC ART-TET

JUNE

FRIDAY 1, SATURDAY 2
FRANK LOWE

FRIDAY 8, SATURDAY 9
DEWEY REDMAN

FRIDAY 15, SATURDAY 16
KEN McINTYRE

FRIDAY 22, SATURDAY 23
TED DANIEL

FRIDAY, JUNE 29, 1973
STUDIO RIVBEA WELCOMES THE NEWPORT JAZZ FESTIVAL NEW YORK

STUDIO RIVBEA IS A CULTURAL ACTIVITY, a non-profit Organization dedicated to the promotion and exposure of talented Artists deserving wider recognition.

At present, STUDIO RIVBEA receives no funds from any sponsoring Organization.

STUDIO RIVBEA exists from the cooperation of the Artists that perform here and the donations of the enthusiastic Audiences.

STUDIO RIVBEA also provides workshop and rehearsal space for the development of New Music.

Through the presentation of these Artists, STUDIO RIVBEA hopes to stimulate a greater public interest in Contemporary American Music.

STUDIO RIVBEA is affiliated with:
THE HARLEM CULTURAL COUNCIL
THE SOCIETY OF UNIVERSAL CULTURAL ARTS
THE COLLECTIVE BLACK ARTISTS
THE CENTER FOR NEW MUSIC
THE CREATIVE MUSIC FOUNDATION

ACTIVITIES COORDINATED BY:
SAM RIVERS
DIRECTOR-STUDIO RIVBEA
DIRECTOR-HARLEM ENSEMBLE
VISITING ARTIST-WESLEYAN UNIVERSITY

CONCERTS: FRI.& SAT.   DON. $3.00
CONCERTS: MON,TUES,WED,THURS $2.00
WORKSHOPS: $1.00

---

studio rivbea
24 bond st. new york, n.y. 10012

APRIL 1973

SUNDAY 1 8 15 22 29
3:00 PM
JAM SESSION

6:00 PM   WORKSHOP
ORCHESTRAL EXPLORATIONS

A CONTEMPORARY APPROACH TO MUSIC COMPOSITION, TECHNIQUES OF ORCHESTRATION AND PERFORMANCE FOR YOUNG MUSICIANS, STUDENTS AND HOBBYISTS.
SAM RIVERS

9:30 PM   CONCERT
ABDULLAH

FRANK LOWE   REEDS
ARTHUR DOYLE   REEDS
AHMED ABDULLAH   TRUMPET
RICHARD DUNBAR   FRENCH HORN
BRO EARLE   BASS VIOLIN
RA-SHID SINAN   DRUMS

CONCERTS: SUNDAY DON. $2.00

MONDAY 2 9 16 23 30
6:30 PM   WORKSHOP
COMPOSITIONS FOR
WOODWIND ENSEMBLE
SAM RIVERS

9:30 PM   CONCERT
MUSART BAND

GEORGE BRAITH   REEDS
CARL CORNWELL   TENOR SAX, FLUTE
JOHN ORE   BASS VIOLIN
DOUG HAWTHORNE   VIBES
STEVE HAAS   DRUMS
BOB STHULER   DRUMS
ANGEL ALLEMDE   PERCUSSION

TUESDAY 3 10 17 24
6:30 PM   WORKSHOP
COMPOSITIONS FOR
JAZZ ENSEMBLE
DANIEL CARTER

9:30 PM   CONCERT
ESSENCE

SHELLY RUSTEN   PERCUSSION
MARK WHITECAGE   REEDS
JAY CLAYTON   PIANO-VOCALS
FRANK CLAYTON   BASS VIOLIN

WEDNESDAY 4 11 18 25
6:30 PM   WORKSHOP
COMPOSITIONS FOR
BRASS ENSEMBLE
SAM RIVERS

9:30 PM   CONCERT
PETER LA BARBERA

PETE YELLIN   ALTO SAX
BUTCH JONES   FLUGELHORN
DAVE SHAFIRO   BASS VIOLIN
GREGG BANDY   DRUMS
CHIP WHITE   DRUMS

THURSDAY 5 12 19 26
6:30 PM   WORKSHOP
COMPOSITIONS FOR
FLUTE ENSEMBLE
BECKY FRIEND

9:30 PM   CONCERT
MONTY WATERS
QUARTET

CONCERTS: FRI. SAT.   DON. $3.00
CONCERTS: MON,TUES,WED,THURS $2.00
WORKSHOPS: $1.00

FRIDAY 6 13 20 27
7:00 PM   WORKSHOP
COMPOSITIONS FOR
JAZZ ORCHESTRA
PAUL JEFFREY

10:00 PM   CONCERT

FRIDAY 6, SATURDAY 7
FREE ENERGY

MIKE MOSS   REEDS
WILDEN KING   VIOLIN
LAUREN BROWN   OBOE
MARK WHITECAGE   REEDS
MARTY COOK   TROMBONE
CHARLES STEPHENS   TROMBONE
JOHN FICHER   PIANO
JOHN SHEA   BASS VIOLIN
FRANK CLAYTON   BASS VIOLIN
DAVID EYGES   CELLO
SHELLY RUSTEN   DRUMS
MIKE MAHAFFEY   PERCUSSION

FRIDAY 13, SATURDAY 14
KARL BERGER
AND FRIENDS

FRIDAY 20, SATURDAY 21
JAZZ OPERA ENSEMBLE

ED TAYLOR- DIRECTOR
JEANNE FAULKNER   BRENDA FELICIANO
ROBERT DONALDSON   BEVERLY MASON
SAM RIVERS   WARREN SMITH
VISHNU WOOD   LINDA TWINE

FRIDAY 27, SATURDAY 28
SAM RIVERS

CECIL McBEE   JEROME COOPER

FIGURE 7. Studio Rivbea brochure and schedule. April 1973. Image courtesy of the Juma Sultan Archive (F0113.24).

FIGURE 8. Leon Thomas performing at Studio Rivbea. Circa 1972–73. Graininess from archival source. Image courtesy of the Juma Sultan Archive (Print 106).

If you look at the records from Ali's Alley, most of the avant garde musicians played there. They had a place where they could play for a week-long gig and do well and make money on their own because all the money that came into the place went to the musicians. I just sold the liquor and the food and the musicians took the money that came in the door. It was about having a place to present your music and having a venue for musicians like us to play because we weren't playing in the Village Vanguard and the Village Gate and Sweet Basil. We weren't doing that because we weren't invited to those places. We couldn't even get gigs in those places. So Ali's Alley was a place for struggling musicians to work.[78]

Good Vibes
come with
neighbors
children
lovers
present ex or future
husbands and
       wives
good vibes

À la carte Menu

Chicken sandwich
  (served with salad) $3.00
Fish sandwich
  (served with salad) $3.00
Avocado sandwich $3.00
Chef's salad $2.75
Potato salad .... $ .85
Candied yams .... $ .85
Collard greens .... $ .85
Black-eyed peas .... $ .85
Brown rice with
  sauteed vegetables $1.50

DESSERTS

Homemade fruit pie .... $ .85
Fruit cobbler .... $ .85
Bread pudding .... $ .85
Fresh fruit dessert ...... $ .85

BEVERAGES

Coffee .... $ .50
Tea .... $ .50
Herb teas with honey ..... $ .75
Apple cider .... $ .75
Carrot juice $1.00

Dinner Menu

Choice of:
  * Gourmet spiced
    chicken or fish
  • Vegetable Platter
  • Fruit dinner

* Choice of two:
    vegetable salad
    potato salad
    candied yams
    collard greens
    black-eyed peas
    brown rice
    sauteed vegetables
    green beans

              PRICE -- $4.00

FIGURE 9. Menu from Studio 77 / Ali's Alley. Image courtesy of the Juma Sultan Archive (F0007.07).

Unlike other lofts that worked to obtain grant funding, Ali's efforts were rooted in the idea that self-presentation could be a profitable business model, while still providing a welcoming setting for musicians. Ali also founded the label Survival Records during the same period, which constituted a second extension of musician-owned business practices. Ali's Alley operated throughout the decade and was later renamed "Alley's Bars" for a brief period in the early 1980s before closing entirely.[79]

A stream of other venues also emerged between 1973 and 1977. Despite the fact that many were not housed in literal lofts (i.e., former factories), loft practices came to be defined by a number of key characteristics, including (1) low admission charges or suggested donations, (2) casual atmospheres that blurred the distinction between performer and audience, (3) ownership/administration by musicians, and (4) mixed-use spaces that combined both private living areas and public presentation space. These criteria demonstrate how the designation of "jazz loft" described much more than physical spaces; it implied a broader complex of presentational strategies that gained resonance throughout the period.[80] Some spaces were called lofts despite being housed in other types of buildings, while others that *were* in loft structures were nevertheless denied the label.[81]

The flood of activity soon began attracting attention from the local press. A 1974 profile in the *SoHo Weekly News* was the first of many to characterize loft jazz as a coherent (if somewhat disjointed) movement. It included profiles of Rivbea, 236 E. 3rd St. (formerly LaMama), 501 Canal Street, Artist House, and the Space for Innovative Development, praising each as offering adventurous music in a warm, welcoming atmosphere.[82] Similar articles—all attempting to sketch a larger movement through short descriptions of multiple spaces—would appear in the *Village Voice* in 1975 and the *New York Times* in 1976 and 1977.[83]

Newspapers also began reviewing loft concerts as part of their regular arts coverage. Such articles were scarce early on, but by about 1976 they were common fare for writers like Gary Giddins, Peter Occhigrosso, Robert Palmer, and J. R. Taylor. A tremendous boost took place in 1975 with the arrival of writer and drummer Stanley Crouch from California. Not long after moving to the city, he began writing reviews for the *SoHo Weekly News* (usually under the title "Concrete Rainforest Safari") and the *Village Voice*. Crouch proselytized for both the value of the new music and the significance of musician-ownership. His most effusive paean appeared in a 1977 *New York Times* feature titled "Jazz Lofts: A Walk through the Wild Sounds."

> The emergence of these jazz lofts, like that of various "little" magazines and SoHo art galleries, was a reaction to the closed doors of the professional marketplace. Though the music they are creating has broken the bounds of familiar jazz, both in form and instrumentation, the burgeoning loft movement is reminiscent of the historic gatherings of jazz musicians that took place in New Orleans and Chicago in the 20's, Kansas City in the 30's, and New York in the 40's.[84]

Crouch's efforts to position the lofts within a noble lineage of jazz history was characteristic of his writing style. Though his predilections would later move sharply away from the avant garde, his impact at the time was unmistakable. Within months, other writers followed suit in stepping up their loft coverage. The assertiveness with which Crouch presented his opinions—both in print and in person—also played a role. Perhaps the most succinct account comes from saxophonist David Murray, a former student and frequent collaborator with Crouch in the 1970s. Speaking about his own rapid rise upon arriving in New York, Murray said, "I've just been lucky with the press. I don't know why. (*Pause*) Well, I guess I do know why. One reason was Stanley . . . He came in and he intimidated all the rest of the writers and told them that I was the greatest saxophone player in the world!"[85]

Crouch and Murray were not the only new arrivals to New York in the mid-1970s. To the contrary, these years saw a massive influx of artists arriving from the Mid/Western jazz collectives.[86] Some quickly began establishing their own venues: Bobo Shaw and Joseph Bowie organized events at the Children's Workshop at the La MaMa Theater on 3rd Street, while Crouch and Murray formed Studio Infinity in a loft on the Bowery. Others became active participants at spaces that were already in operation. John Fischer—the pianist, visual artist, and organizer of the loft Environ—recalled how his space hosted numerous AACM concerts after he was approached by pianist Muhal Richard Abrams:

> Sometime in the late Summer of '75, Richard Abrams shows up at Environ.
> "You John Fischer?"
> "Yeah."
> "I'm Muhal Richard Abrams. I'm one of the directors and creators of the AACM. Do you know what that is?"
> Then he looks around and says, "I see you have a very good piano. Can I try it?"
> "Go right ahead." . . .
> [After we got to know each other] he decided John Fischer can play and he's really a nice guy. So he said, "We would like to introduce some musicians here. Is that okay?" I said, "Go right ahead." So then all of the people who were at that time in the AACM one-by-one called and made a date for a gig.[87]

In a relatively short time, Midwest and West Coast musicians became a forceful presence in the scene. They soon began receiving the lion's share of press attention, often overshadowing earlier loft participants. Crouch led the way in promoting their work, praising their disciplined approach in contrast to the shortcomings he saw in the New York school of "energy music."[88] A Gary Giddins review from 1977 was titled "[Arthur] Blythe and [David] Murray Tower over Loft Underground," asserting the preeminence of the two saxophonists from Los Angeles.[89] This attention helped to spur new professional opportunities for musicians as well. In 1978, Blythe became the first artist from the lofts to be signed to a major recording company, cutting the albums *In the Tradition* and *Lenox Avenue Breakdown* for Columbia Records.[90]

Several of my respondents reported a degree of tension arising due to the level of coverage given to the new arrivals. One musician described the situation as follows:

> [The new arrivals] reaped the benefits by going into the lofts, which is what we had set up. Which is what *NEW YORK* musicians had set up. But the New York musicians didn't get any press at that time. If you go back and look through the papers like the *Village Voice* and the *Times*, you're going to see Chicago. You're not going to see anything about the New York musicians. You're not going to see it! I'm working down at Rashied's every Monday night and sometimes all week, but you don't see nothing! But you will see about [the Midwesterners]. I'm not angry, that's just politics. That's all that is! The guys from Chicago didn't make that happen. They're just trying to come here and play.[91]

Like many who expressed such opinions, the speaker went on to note that he had very positive relationships with many of the Midwest and West Coast musicians, and bore them no ill will for their success in the New York media. Nevertheless, statements like this display a certain degree of factionalism that arose due to the number of musicians and spaces competing for the same audiences.

For all the attention that loft performance received, it never became a particularly lucrative source of income. Most of the artists' fees remained tied to ticket sales, a situation that many musicians decried as demeaning to their work. Audience turnouts to loft events were often small, even at the height of their prominence. If unified organizations like the Jazz Composers' Guild had found it difficult to draw consistently large crowds in the mid-1960s, the challenge was exacerbated by the 1970s profusion of small events competing for the same crowds. Most venues had few funds to devote to promotion and relied on the musicians themselves to post handmade flyers. Unable to survive on New York performances alone, many musicians turned to invitations from European festivals and record labels to supplement their income.[92]

Yet where many venues might have crumbled due to paltry ticket sales, lofts managed to persevere due to the astoundingly low overhead costs of keeping them running. So long as rents remained cheap or landlords remained absent, artists could continue their activities with minimal interference. And since musicians controlled the spaces, music-making could continue day and night. This unprecedented ease of finding space was perhaps the largest structural factor distinguishing the lofts from other musician-run initiatives. Intoxicated by an atmosphere where staging a concert seemed so simple, loft organizers made few efforts to build larger coalitions. Instead, the scene developed as a scattered array of disconnected, underfunded, but undeniably exhilarating happenings.[93]

THE DECLINE OF THE LOFTS

Jazz performance in lofts began to decline around 1978. Their demise was brought on by numerous factors, the most pressing of which was the steady rise in rents throughout lower Manhattan. Some musicians connected this rise to new political regimes, as demonstrated in an interview with Sam Rivers in the 1990s: "The political establishment was changing in New York. Mayor [Edward] Koch came in and that was a serious problem. After that it was all over, pretty much. The rent for [Rivbea] got so exorbitant that I just didn't feel there was any need of going on any longer, so I moved out."[94] Koch, who took office in 1978, was indeed known for promoting land use policies that favored the middle and upper classes; he was once even quoted as saying, "If you want to live in Manhattan south of Ninety-sixth Street, you've got to pay for it."[95] Other musicians have pointed to national economic changes that followed the presidential election of Ronald Reagan in 1980. As most lofts could only operate through maintaining low overhead costs, rising rents quickly had dire effects on the scene.

Koch's policies undoubtedly exacerbated the situation, but the origins of lower Manhattan's rent surges had begun far earlier than many accounts recognize. As far back as 1974, a *New York Times* article titled "SoHo a 'Victim of Its Own Success'" chronicled the changes taking place since the area's rezoning in 1971. Even then—*before* the mid-decade zenith of the jazz lofts and *four years before* Koch took office—resident artists complained loudly about the drastic rent hikes: "Artists who came to SoHo for its exceptionally large, cheap living and working space saw rents and cooperative prices soar, since the zoning change provided no controls . . . Can artists still afford to live in SoHo? 'Not if they live solely by their art, unless they're quite well established,' said [Charles] Leslie, head of the SoHo Artists Association]."[96] With the exception of those who had formed resident co-op organizations as a way to combat these changes, many tenants saw their costs skyrocket. Since the rezoning had legalized private residence in the neighborhood, landlords no longer needed to bargain with tenants to compensate for illegal leases. The area also attracted new waves of middle-class residents who were drawn to the area's increasingly chic reputation and were willing to pay for it.

For this reason, Sharon Zukin has argued that in many ways the legalization efforts spearheaded by SoHo artists ultimately had the opposite effect from what they intended. The biggest problem was that the artist movement itself had been fundamentally enabled by the deep uncertainty in the real estate market, described in the previous chapter. The 1971 rezoning and the 1973 designation of the area as a landmark neighborhood—both seen as major victories for artists—suddenly eliminated this uncertainty, allowing the market to stabilize quickly. Although the outcome was not exactly what real estate developers had hoped for, the newfound stability gave them time to regroup and devise new strategies for extracting profit within a new legal climate. Since the neighborhood's exterior facades were now protected by preservation laws, they adjusted their focus toward converting older buildings to new uses.

Tapping into the newfound cachet of an aestheticized "loft lifestyle," developers began marketing new high-priced apartments inside of loft buildings—a move clearly echoing what artists had been doing for over a decade. But where the earlier artists' conversions had consisted of huge spaces in airy, unpartitioned floors, this later wave of commercially developed "loft apartments" usually carved those floors into multiple, smaller units. Such spaces advertised themselves as lofts (and charged considerably more as a result), but often differed little from smaller apartments in other parts of the city. Since the new preservation laws only protected the facades of the buildings, such internal renovations were entirely legal within this new climate.[97] In 1975, the city council accelerated the process further by amending the city code to give tax incentives to developers involved in the residential conversion of older buildings.[98]

The timeline of these changes is important; they were taking place just as the jazz lofts entered their most successful period, from 1974–76. This point underscores the spatial and temporal disconnects between the visual artist loft movement and the jazz lofts. While the former peaked in SoHo in the late 1960s, the latter was based primarily in the surrounding neighborhoods (especially NoHo and the Lower East Side) and crested in the mid-1970s. Their location just outside of SoHo may have been a key factor that allowed the jazz lofts to thrive for several years after the rezoning.[99] As the central battleground for the visual artist movement, SoHo had received the most attention in the press as a newly fashionable neighborhood. Even today, the phrase "SoHo loft" continues to carry a high degree of cachet. As a result, it is likely that many developers focused their efforts there in the immediate aftermath of the rezoning. It would be several years before such price increases began affecting the surrounding areas where most jazz lofts were located.

With rents on the rise by late decade, the economics of running a loft became much more daunting, causing palpable tension within the scene. A possible sign of things to come took place in the summer of 1977, when a dispute erupted between Sam Rivers and Stanley Crouch. At the time, Crouch was booking concerts at the Ladies' Fort, a loft located just a block away from Rivbea on Bond Street. In the early summer, Rivers was preparing to stage his annual summer festival. As had been the case since 1973, the event was supported through grant funding, allowing Rivers to offer a guaranteed fee to each musician. After the schedule was announced, however, Crouch began booking many of the same artists for a concurrent festival at the Ladies' Fort, capitalizing on the proximity of the two venues. All told, Crouch's program included seven leaders already booked to perform at Rivbea. At the Fort, however, artists were promised no guaranteed payments, but played for a percentage of door revenues.

Crouch argued that sufficient audiences existed to support both festivals, likely assuming that their confluence (which also coincided with the week of the Newport Jazz Festival) would attract extra attention for all parties. Rivers, however, became livid over the situation, which he saw as splintering an already small audience. He argued that Crouch's move demeaned artists by requiring them to play for the door, thereby undermining Rivbea's efforts to provide fairer wages.[100] When the festivals began, both were met with disappointingly small turnouts, further exacerbating the conflict. Things reached a boiling point halfway through the week with Rivers deciding to cancel the remaining concerts, a decision he announced in a strongly worded statement read on radio station WKCR.[101] Rivbea continued operating until early 1979, but the incident reveals the onrush of economic challenges that soon forced most lofts to close their doors.[102]

A second factor that hastened the decline of the lofts is that musicians themselves began to express dissatisfaction with the loft model. Somewhat ironically, many of the most pointed critiques came from alumni of Chicago's AACM, the organization that had provided a key inspiration for many organizers. Despite their prominence in the scene, many Chicagoans were sharply critical of both the lofts' economic model and their cultural connotations, which failed to fulfill the AACM's mission of presenting events in settings that were "designed to magnify the importance of creative music."[103] As Lewis argues, the informal nature of the lofts seemed like little more than "the new jazz club, inheriting from its predecessor minimal infrastructure and the related discourse of 'intimacy.'"[104] A perceived ghettoization of black artists in loft and nightclub settings was also framed as "a kind of unwanted surveillance of the black creative body" that was used to deny black artists access to concert halls and other formal opportunities.[105]

The occasional use of the term "loft jazz" as a genre description caused further consternation, as it was seen as illogically grouping musicians into a category associated with low-income performance. Saxophonist Hamiet Bluiett has related: "I never really liked the term and neither did a lot of the musicians; it's like naming the music after the buildings. I realize that it's a promotional kind of label, but you have to remember that what we're playing is musician's jazz, not building jazz."[106] The growth of such critiques in the late 1970s made the appearance of the newer, nonloft presenting organizations a welcome addition. As lofts closed, a wave of new presentation opportunities began arising in more formally administered spaces like Joseph Papp's Public Theater and The Kitchen (a topic taken up further in chapter 8). Not only did such spaces offer higher payments, but their emphasis on tracing the confluence of African American, Euro-American, and global experimentalist traditions was a closer match with the AACM ethos of putting pressure on insidious racialized boundary policing that can too often impede artistic mobility.

What becomes clear at this point is that the liberatory rhetoric that mobilized early loft organizers in the wake of the NYMJF had become less persuasive by the end of the decade. A number of factors fueled this disenchantment. First, the politicized intent of self-ownership as a form of empowerment gradually dissolved as musicians abandoned collectivism in favor of starting their own independent initiatives. Rather than framing grassroots production as a matter of mutual benefit, this instead yielded infighting due to escalating competition between artist-organizers. Second, the years of financial struggle that characterized much of the loft era may have exhausted the movement's early enthusiasm and corroded any hope for the lofts to erect an alternative, musician-run industry structure. Third, musicians' exposure to higher profile opportunities in Europe and from grant-funded initiatives in the United States presented an alternative that seemed preferable to low-profile, low-status, low-pay affairs in lofts. Fourth, the perception of genre policing that conceived "loft jazz" or "loft musicians" as a distinct category seemed to preclude the possibility of breaking out of the lofts to pursue higher profile opportunities. By the late 1970s, these concerns had largely stripped the movement of its earlier associations with musical, social, political, and industry critique.

The evolving interpretations of loft performance by musicians and nonmusicians alike create distinct challenges for historical interpretation. I suggest that the period is best understood not as a musical style or even a type of venue, but rather as an interrelated set of presentational practices. Common themes included: (1) musician-control over economics and performance environments, (2) circumvention of conventional music industry channels such as nightclubs and commercial record labels, (3) various forms of political consciousness, often connected to racial identity and economic inequality, (4) desire for involvement with the local community and/or the development of young musicians, (5) collaboration across artistic media, (6) avant garde and/or experimentalist artistic practices, (7) incorporation of non-Western sources in both music and imagery, and (8) the realization of such practices on a highly localized level *without* the formation of large collectives. This last point—emerging out of the context of New York real estate, described in the previous chapter—is a primary structural factor that distinguished the loft movement from earlier collectives.

Thinking of loft performance in terms of such practices, rather than in the more limited terms of genre designation or physical surroundings, also allows us to note the key conceptual connections between events occurring in lofts and closely related activities in other types of spaces. To be sure, the musician-organizing impetus was not restricted to former industrial buildings; events also took place in parks, churches, community centers, marches, political rallies, and even at traditional nightclubs. It is a mistake to disconnect these activities from performances in literal lofts alone. The impact of the movement lies not in a single type of architectural space, but in the explosion of self-produced programming that characterized New York in the period.

While the lofts had mostly dissipated by the early 1980s, their impact would be felt for decades. Many artists who began their careers in the lofts still continue to carry the scene's organizing impetus into the twenty-first century. Events like the Sound Unity Festivals of the mid-1980s and today's annual Vision Festival serve as critical extensions of the period's organizing ethos.[107] The venues themselves may have disappeared, but their legacy of empowered self-production in alternative spaces continues to exert a powerful influence on the New York avant garde.

PART TWO

TRAJECTORIES

4

FREEDOM

A seemingly endless stream of commentators have likened jazz with the ideal of freedom. It is an undeniably attractive metaphor, capable of evoking notions of individualism, democracy, virtuosity, experimentalism, social protest, American identity, African American identity, global liberation struggles, and a host of related themes. A typically poetic formulation can be found in a passage by Robert O'Meally: "This equation of jazz and America is easy enough to figure: Jazz is freedom music, the play of sounds that prizes individual assertion and group coordination, voices soloing and then (at their best) swinging together, the one-and-many *e pluribus unum* with a laid back beat."[1] Perusing recent book titles, one finds plenty of further examples: *Freedom Sounds; The Freedom Principle; Freedom Is, Freedom Ain't; Jazz as a Metaphor for Freedom; Let Freedom Swing.*[2] The trend is not limited to authors, either. Artists from Duke Ellington to Thelonious Monk to Sonny Rollins have issued statements on the subject, usually boiling it down to the premise, "Jazz is freedom."[3] While each iteration may express slightly different nuances, it is clear that the equation of jazz and freedom has long been a powerful tool for conveying the music's importance within American culture.

With such saturation, it would be easy to imagine that this linkage of jazz and freedom was read into the music from the time of its birth. A closer examination, however, reveals that this was not strictly the case. The popularity of the term seems to have exploded around the mid-1950s. A few numbers can help to illustrate this point. In the nearly three decades between the birth of jazz recording in 1917 and the end of 1955, the word "freedom" appeared in the titles of new recorded jazz compositions just four times.[4] It's a strikingly small number, especially when one considers the importance of liberation narratives (especially the biblical story

TABLE 1 Jazz Works with Titles Including the Word "Freedom," 1917–1965

Artist / Bandleader	Title	Year
Songs with "Freedom" in Title, 1917–1955		
Bing Crosby	"Song of Freedom"	1942
John Kirby	"Freedom Blues"	1946
Benny Goodman	"The Freedom Train"	1947
Lennie Tristano	"Freedom"	1947
Songs with "Freedom" in Title, 1956–1965		
Donald Byrd	"The Jazz Message (With Freedom for All)"	1956
Sonny Rollins	*The Freedom Suite*	1958
Johnny Dankworth	"Freedom Walk"	1960
Don Shirley	"Freedom (I'm on My Way)"	1960
Charles Mingus	"Cry for Freedom (Prayer for Passive Resistance)"	1960
Max Roach	*Freedom Now Suite*	1960
Art Blakey	"The Freedom Rider"	1961
The Jazz Crusaders	"Freedom Sound"	1961
Grant Green	"Freedom March"	1961
Oliver Nelson	"Freedom Dance"	1961
Josh White	"Freedom Road"	1961
Chico Hamilton	"Freedom Traveler"	1962
Charles Mingus	"Freedom"	1962
Oscar Peterson	"Hymn to Freedom"	1962
Shirley Scott	"Freedom Dance"	1963
Kai Winding	"March to Freedom"	1963
Billy Taylor	"Freedom"	1963
Shorty Rogers	"Freedom's Coming"	1963
Kenny Burrell	"Freedom"	1964
Ray DeFade	"Ride for Freedom"	1964
Art Blakey	"Freedom One Day"	1965
Jazz Workshop–Ruhr Festival	"The Freedom"	1965
Eddie Harris	"Freedom Jazz Dance"	1965
The Interpreters	"But Then It's Freedom"	1965
Danny Richmond	"Freedom Ride"	1965

of Moses in Exodus) in the African American spiritual tradition.[5] But in the ten-year stretch that followed, between 1956–65, the word appears in a startling twenty-four compositions (see Table 1). Several of these led to seminal recordings in the jazz canon, including Sonny Rollins's *Freedom Suite,* Max Roach's *We Insist! Freedom Now Suite,* and Eddie Harris's "Freedom Jazz Dance." The trend has shown no signs of abating; another thirty-eight pieces appeared by 1975, and the tendency continued steadily into the 1980s, '90s and '00s. Although such a measurement is far from scientific,[6] this unmistakable eruption at a specific historical moment speaks to a new set of signifying links connecting jazz and freedom—links that have become deeply ingrained in jazz commentary ever since.

But what did artists mean when they referenced freedom, and why did the term take on such importance at this particular moment? Interestingly, scholars have offered a range of interpretations. Historians of cultural diplomacy have pointed to the international use of jazz as a metaphor for American democracy during the Cold War.[7] Social theorists and ethnomusicologists have emphasized the role of African American political activism as a guiding force, echoing the growth of the civil rights and black power movements.[8] Journalists and historians have focused on the development of new musical techniques that point to aesthetic usages of the term, especially within the emerging avant garde subgenre of "free jazz."[9] Strong evidence can be cited in support of all three approaches (and, undoubtedly, many others), yet it is notable that they reflect very different ideals of what freedom signified at the time: freedom as America, freedom as protest, freedom as aesthetic exploration.

Rather than picking a single narrative, the key to understanding the period's burst of interest in freedom is to recognize its deep *overdetermination*—the ways in which these definitions overlapped, contested, and reinforced each other all at once. By the early 1960s, the term was capable of performing a wide range of conceptual work. Declaring that one's music expressed freedom could be an assertion of national pride, of revolutionary commitment, or of artistic experimentalism. But most importantly, it could mean all three, producing a rich multivalence that was deeply attractive to many artists. Musicians used "freedom" as a sort of discursive bridge, capable of mapping musical practices onto social values in multiple directions. Though there was near universal agreement on its attractiveness, musicians deployed the term for a wide array of descriptive and aesthetic purposes.

This multiplicity inevitably led to disputes over the most (or least) productive meanings of freedom, both inside and outside of jazz. As Scott Saul has observed, "Everyone aspired to freedom, but few agreed on the correct definition of the term, the limits that kept freedom from shading into anarchy or self-indulgence, and the enslaving power that freedom asserted itself against."[10] Among jazz artists, such debates continued throughout the 1960s.[11] Notably, the decade even saw the emergence of deep fractures in all three of the models named above: romantic celebrations of Americana cracked beneath increasing social protest over the Vietnam War and racial inequality; discord erupted in the civil rights movement regarding integrationist versus black nationalist strategies; and jazz underwent ongoing dispute over the artistic viability of avant garde styles. These growing divisions speak to another reason behind the explosion of "freedom" titles at this time. By referencing freedom, artists were not merely adding their voices to a harmonious chorus of camaraderie. They were also staking claims to particular ideals of freedom, drawing upon the term's powerful aura on behalf of their own individual musical and/or social visions.

. . .

Nowhere were these issues more apparent than in the loft scene, an environment characterized by the tension between solidarity and fragmentation. In an echo of the divisions arising in the aftermath of 1972's National Black Political Convention,[12] musicians found themselves in a setting where freedom remained a compelling ideal, but participants expressed divergent views about what it meant or how to obtain it. Like so many topics within the lofts, these discussions are difficult to characterize as a unified movement. However, their constant recurrence in accounts of the period offers a testament to their importance for loft artists.

This chapter will delve into several discourses of freedom, exploration, and control as articulated by artists of the loft period. I refer to these as "freedom dreams," a terminology I borrow from Robin D.G. Kelley.[13] In addressing this topic, I am less concerned with the fact that the many loft initiatives did not fully realize the sweeping social/political/cultural revolutions that their organizers envisioned. As Kelley observes, "By such a measure, virtually every radical movement failed because the basic power relations they sought to change remain pretty much intact."[14] Rather, I argue that the centrality of certain freedom dreams constituted a mobilizing force that subtended the loft movement from its inception, and that has continued to animate subsequent musician-organized initiatives. Understanding the significance of the period therefore requires close engagement with these motivations, regardless of their ultimate triumphs or shortcomings.

The topic of freedom—as well as related terms such as liberation, empowerment, and consciousness—recurred frequently in my interviews with loft artists. Though their positions were often informed by social activism, not all usage of the term was political. Philosophical and spiritual implications were also probed, pushing against the boundaries separating music, politics, faith, and various alternative lifestyles. In the absence of a unified vision, I propose to consider freedom dreams in terms of their fluid and evolving meanings at the time. Among other advantages, this shift allows us to move beyond oversimplified historical models that narrowly graft musical styles onto specific brands of revolutionary politics.[15] Black power, cultural nationalism, Afrocentrism, liberal integrationism, third world solidarity, and other social viewpoints all came up in my interviews, but no single orthodoxy dominated. It often seemed that artists enjoyed occupying a position one step removed from such debates, precluding the need to hem closely to any hard-line stance. Many participated in a range of diverse, and sometimes conflicting, movements.[16] Instead of political ideologies directly determining aesthetic practice, they appeared as constituent parts within larger, multifaceted freedom dreams that sought to remake the urban landscape/soundscape in many directions at once.

The sections below consider several recurrent subcategories of freedom dreams. The first looks at various modes of self-creation, a topic that arose in reference to both individuals and organizations. Musicians used many techniques for constructing and performing new identities, including African/internationalist naming practices and the production of handmade instruments. In doing so, they advanced visions emphasizing (self/collective) control over performative and economic resources. The second section deals with models that strived for freedom through forms of social transgression and/or transcendence. Conceived in terms of expanding consciousness, these activities entailed the exploration of diverse spiritualities, drug use, and "off-the-grid" cooperative living strategies.[17] Finally, the third section focuses on the development of the improvisational style known as "energy music," which engendered a radical reconception of musical freedom by pursuing total improvisation with minimal predetermined elements. The genre's emergence in New York provides telling insights about the stylistic fallouts resulting from urban geography, especially in comparison to other avant garde styles that sprang up in other parts of the country.

Several of the accounts below draw from two overarching vocabularies. I refer to these as collectivism and communalism. By collectivism, I point to strategies influenced by civil rights and black power doctrines, in which artists sought to build unified movements to present a centralized aesthetic and/or political agenda. Communalist approaches, on the other hand, channeled 1960s counterculture by eschewing social hierarchies in favor of fostering open, anticapitalist centers for sharing resources and pursuing alternative lifestyles. If the former emphasized discipline and self-control to articulate a vision of freedom based on empowerment, the latter focused on boundary transgression, transcendence, and liminality in the interest of cultivating an open sense of sharing and *communitas*. I see these as two distinct philosophies of freedom that undergird many of the examples outlined below. The two directions could perhaps be understood within a long-standing philosophical distinction between "freedom to" and "freedom from."[18] Collectivism desired the *freedom to* achieve respect and professional opportunities by building support and advocacy networks within a cultural milieu that could be indifferent at best, hostile at worst. Communalism sought *freedom from* that milieu by building alternative social and artistic domains that were self-cultivating, meaningful, and did not rely on outside support.

While these vocabularies provide a useful heuristic, I don't wish to impose them as a blunt binary. Quite the opposite: the fluidity of loft practices disrupts any attempts to draw overly rigid delineations. Despite occasional rifts that arose between musicians advocating one approach over the other, many artists moved freely between the two, incorporating, adapting, or combining their principles in creative ways. A particularly noteworthy demonstration was offered to me by several musicians (described further below) who juxtaposed philosophies from black nationalism and the 1960s counterculture—movements that historians have sometimes characterized as incompatible and/or hostile to one another.[19] Rather than trying to lump each freedom dream into ready-made categories of "collectivist" or "communalist," each should be understood as a creative strategy for navigating between these two discursive threads. While this doesn't erase their importance, it does demonstrate that, for many artists, the lines were not as sharply drawn as we might assume.

NAMING AND UNNAMING, BUILDING AND REBUILDING: FREEDOM DREAMS OF SELF-CREATION

As mixed-use performance spaces, jazz lofts inherently blurred the lines between performance and everyday life. The usually firm demarcations between, say, a stage and a living room, or a customer and a houseguest, became somewhat tenuous in a loft environment. Many accounts describe elements of domestic life creeping into the performance sphere, a topic addressed further in chapter 6. Conceptual slippage took place in the other direction as well, with aspects of performance moving offstage and into other environments, ranging from fluxus-style happenings to park concerts to protest marches. If urban disinvestment left lower Manhattan as an empty canvas, artists explored countless approaches to filling it.

As presentational practices became more malleable, so did understandings of individual and group identity. I have found it useful to interpret such developments as part of a broader impetus that manifests through various forms of *self-creation*. I use this phrase instead of the more commonly found "self-determination" to draw attention to the many connections between aesthetics and identities, rather than focusing on political economy alone. Unquestionably the most direct example of self-creation can be seen in the loft venues themselves, those physical spaces where musicians circumvented commercial channels in order to reclaim economic and aesthetic control over their performance environments. But closer analysis reveals that many other spheres of the loft enterprise were animated by conscious acts of self-creation. Here, I focus on two: re/naming practices and the invention of handmade instruments.

Perhaps no self-creative act combines personal identity and public performance more forcefully than the adoption of new names, a practice that became increasingly common among jazz artists of the 1960s and '70s. Such acts have a long history within African American culture, a topic that has been theorized by literary historian Kimberly Benston. Self-naming was pivotal, for example, in many early slave narratives, wherein individuals took new names in a conscious effort to distance themselves from the identities of their former masters.[20] Its potency lies in the radical deconstruction and regrafting of relationships between past, present, and future. In the wake of emancipation after the Civil War, renaming acted as a vivid metonym for the promises and challenges faced by African

Americans, as individuals grappled with ways of re/constructing identities as free citizens. In Benston's words: "For the Afro-American, then, self-creation and reformation of a fragmented familial past are endlessly interwoven: Naming is inevitably genealogical revisionism."[21]

Benston situates the power of naming practices within three interrelated processes: naming, unnaming, and renaming. The third of these he also calls "(re)baptism" in order to emphasize the spiritual significance of identity construction. None of these processes are inherently positive or negative. For example, unnaming—viewed in terms of its liberatory potential by freed slaves—is also found in the acts of erasure employed by masters to suppress African languages and cultural practices. The invention of the term "nigger" constitutes a simultaneous naming and unnaming through a "mechanism of control by contraction; it subsumes the complexities of human experience into a tractable sign while manifesting an essential inability to *see* (to grasp, to apprehend) the signified."[22] The key to naming narratives, therefore, is not a conflict between these three processes, but rather a struggle regarding who is granted control over them. The power to name, unname, or rename oneself therefore functions as a powerful tool of liberation.

The 1950s and '60s saw several radical deployments of naming practices, especially among civil rights and black power activists. The best-known example is undoubtedly that of Malcolm X, whose substitution of a mathematical variable for his surname provides a conspicuous commentary on the tragic unknowability of African ancestry in the aftermath of the slave trade. This choice overtly implies the absent presence of an African past, as well as the conscious jettisoning of a "white slavemaster name."[23] Alternatively, the variable can also be read as a distinctly postmodern gesture. Like Ralph Ellison's narrator in *Invisible Man*, the suggestion of variability connotes the possibility of self-creative potential outside the ascriptive power of external forces.

The example of Malcolm X also points to the growing influence of Islam in African American re/naming practices of the mid-twentieth century. These connections have taken on a number of evolving associations over time; the use of Arabic names, for example, was interpreted quite differently in various decades.[24] One anecdote told by Dizzy Gillespie relates how during the 1940s some musicians took on such names (with varying degrees of religious adherence) as a way to distance themselves from black identity:

> "Man, if you join the Muslim faith, you ain't colored no more, you'll be white," they'd say. "You get a new name and you don't have to be a nigger no more." So everybody started joining because they considered it a big advantage not to be black during the time of segregation ... Musicians started having it printed on their police cards where it said, "Race," "W" for white. Kenny Clarke had one and he showed it to me. He said, "See nigger, I ain't no spook; I'm white, 'W.'" He changed his name to Arabic, Liaqat Ali Salaam.[25]

The relationship between Arabic names and black identity shifted dramatically in the 1950s. This was due primarily to the growing visibility of the Nation of Islam (NOI), a sect that overtly linked the faith with African identity and nationalist politics. In this new context, taking a Muslim name was reconceived as a potent *affirmation* of black identity that acted in tandem with religious conversion. As a caveat, it is important to note that not all Muslim converts (particularly within jazz) were members of the NOI.[26] Nevertheless, the group's visibility as a flashpoint for confrontational politics led to a dramatic change in how Arabic names were perceived within American society at large. What had once implied a distancing from black identity gradually came to stand as a militant claim for black agency.

Other political figures engaged in re/naming practices that drew directly from African sources. Cultural nationalist leader Maulana Karenga (né Ron Everett) derived his name from the Swahili words for "master teacher" and "nationalist," and encouraged members of his US Organization to take on their own Swahili names.[27] Stokely Carmichael renamed himself Kwame Ture as an homage to African political leaders Kwame Nkrumah and Sékou Touré, a move that echoed his political shift toward Pan-Africanism in the late 1960s.[28] Everett Leroy Jones—who had already changed the spelling of his name to the French "Leroi"—managed to find a middle ground between Muslim and African re/naming strategies. Jones explored a series of religious systems in the late 1960s, including Yoruba, Sunni Islam, and Karenga's hybridized synthesis of Muslim and African practices called Kawaida. He eventually assumed the Arabic Ameer Barakat, which translated to "Blessed Prince."[29] Later, after urging from Karenga, he chose to "Swahilize" it to Amiri Baraka.[30] The close connection between the Arabic and Swahili versions not only speaks to their historical connections, but also demonstrates a fluid nonequivalence that individuals like Baraka interrogated as part of an effort to re/construct old and new visions of black identity.

Re/naming practices among loft musicians mirrored many of the above tendencies with a few noteworthy variations. A number of musicians took Arabic names in the period, an act which was frequently associated by observers (sometimes incorrectly) with NOI teachings on black identity and political militancy. Such associations had the tendency to be somewhat flattening; they failed to account, for instance, for those who practiced forms of Islam that did not share the NOI's politics. Bassist Hakim Jami cited his name as a professional liability among industry representatives who uncritically linked Islam with militant politics:

MH: Was there a lot of racial tension during the loft period?

HJ: Mmm hmm [agreement].

MH: Tell me about it.

HJ: Let me see, how can I approach that? In my dealings it was racial and religious. So I had the racial thing, which was appearance—my being black—and religious because of my name. It came down to gigs. They wouldn't let you play on record dates, or they wouldn't offer you a record date . . . With musicians, there was a lot of us that changed our names and got no action [work]. Look at Kiane [Zawadi]! He's a hell of a euphonium player. The best I've heard, and I played euphonium! . . . But if you had a different type of name or different affiliations that were not according to Hoyle, then they [mistreated] you.[31]

It is notable how Jami's discussion of religion surfaced in response to a question about race relations during the period. While I would not suggest that his faith should be understood in political terms (Jami was quite careful to distinguish the two), his statements demonstrate how divergent discourses of religion, race, and politics became conflated in complex and sometimes unexpected ways. Often these connections were used as a tool for personal empowerment, but in some situations they could also be a professional liability.

Interestingly, other musicians took on Arabic or Arabic-sounding names without ever converting to Islam. Percussionist Ali Abuwi (né Oliver Anderson), for example, was not Muslim, but took on the name Ali as a phonetic transformation of his birth name (Oliver became Ollie became Ali). The last name "Abuwi" was Yoruba derived, and was bestowed upon him by his drum teacher Vera Kuza.[32] Drummer Rashid Bakr (who now performs as Charles Downs)[33] adopted his name purely as a tribute to his favorite percussionist Rashied Ali.[34] And trumpeter Ahmed Abdullah (né Leroy Bland) attended a mosque briefly, but soon converted to Buddhism, a faith he has continued to practice ever since.[35] He continues to use the Arabic name professionally and was later given the additional names of Solomon and Melchizedek, both of which are derived from Hebrew but have significance in Muslim theology. He has used these later names for a number of professional projects.

By drawing attention to Arabic naming practices among non-Muslims I do not intend to impugn the seriousness of the many musicians who did (and do) practice the faith. Rather, the tendency shows how secular re/naming coexisted alongside religious re/naming, with the lines between them often blurred. The hybridized name of Ali Abuwi, like that of Baraka, serves as a particularly strong example by combining Muslim and non-Muslim signifiers. When describing his name's meaning, Abuwi pointed to both components (Ali and Abuwi) as inspired by a connection to Africa and the rejection of slave identity:

MH: What was the significance of [your name]?

AA: The significance was [having] an African name. [My birth name of] Anderson, that's a slave name. We were on the plantation owned by the Andersons. We had to change that up. Oliver was my given name and they called me Ollie. That changed into Ali instead of Ollie . . . Those were transformations that I had nothing to do with! It wasn't me! But that's the way things used to work in those days! This was not related to Islam in that sense.[36]

Despite having no connection with religion, it is telling how Abuwi's adoption of the Arabic homonym "Ali" functioned as part of a secular rebaptism to exorcise his slave identity. The observation that this change was initiated by others in his circle demonstrates that this linkage was not merely a personal or idiosyncratic choice, but was representative of larger dialogues circulating among musicians.

African-derived appellations were adopted by numerous musicians as well. These occasionally involved wholesale name changes like that of Juma Sultan (né Edward Lewis) or Alan "Juice" Glover's adoption of the Yoruba name Akinjorin Omolade. At other times African names were taken on as supplementary honorifics added to Western names. Examples include saxophonist Makanda Ken McIntyre and West Coast trumpeter Mugo Eddie Gale. Several musicians from Chicago's AACM also employed this approach, including Muhal Richard Abrams, Amina Claudine Myers, and Famoudou Don Moye.[37] Still others took honorifics from other languages and world cultures, such as Leo Smith's adoption of the Rastafarian "Wadada" or Joseph Jarman's later use of the Japanese "Shaku Gyo." An explicitly cross-cultural example can be found in Kalaparusha Ahrah Difda (Maurice McIntyre), who created his name from a combination of African, Indian, and Arabic sources. The practice of renaming was not limited to only black musicians. Drummer Bob Moses adopted the spiritual name "Rakalam," while Burton Greene was given the Hindu honorific "Narada."

In contrast to these examples illustrating a movement away from European and/or slave identities, other musicians employed a different, somewhat contradictory strategy to naming. Perhaps following the lead of earlier avant gardists like Charles Mingus, John Coltrane, Ornette Coleman, and Cecil Taylor, musicians who kept their birth names often leaned toward more formalized versions, rather than shortened or diminutive forms. Earlier jazz's preference for hip, familiarized nicknames like Charlie (Parker, Christian, Rouse), Jimmy (Blanton, Smith, Heath), and Tony (Williams, Scott) gave way to Charles (Tyler, Tolliver, Brackeen), James (DuBoise, Newton), and Anthony (Braxton, Davis, Coleman). Although this move could be interpreted as acting in opposition to African and international naming practices (moving toward—rather than away from—Europeanized forms), I would instead suggest that both strategies worked toward a similar goal of emphasizing autonomy and gravity within one's professional identity.

This dual movement away from using casual nicknames in professional contexts points to two major themes from the period.[38] The first (reflected in the use of European/formalized names) is an engagement with practices of concert music, a theme stressed by George Lewis in his study of the AACM.[39] This included not only musical approaches, but also applications for support by arts patrons, recognition by cultural commentators, and calls for improved performance conditions. The second (illustrated by African/internationalized names) underscores a liberation impetus that looked to global freedom struggles for personal and aesthetic inspiration. These two impulses may seem quite distinct from one another, but it is crucial to recognize that they were not mutually exclusive, and often commingled on the concert stage. The performance practices of the Art Ensemble of Chicago, for example, were striking in their sonic and visual juxtapositions of African and European signifiers. Such work comprised a dual movement both toward and away from European cultural logics, perhaps dismantling them in the process. The lack of contradiction was further demonstrated in the naming practices of musicians who used *both* internationalist honorifics and formalized forms, such as AACM founder Muhal Richard Abrams. The duality of naming practices that used either African / internationalizing or European / formalizing strategies can also be noted in the names of bands. Some used appellations that highlighted African / Muslim / Internationalist themes (Aboriginal Music Society, Ju-Ju, Dance of Magic, Muntu, Revolutionary Ensemble, Third World Energy Ensemble, Abdullah) while others highlighted more formal / intellectual / modernist connotations (Melodic Art-Tet, Musical Directions Ensemble, Other Dimensions in Music, The Music Ensemble, Interface).[40]

The importance of naming as part of a self-conscious identity creation was emphasized dramatically during an interview I conducted with multi-instrumentalist Cooper-Moore (né Gene Ashton). As we sat down, I asked what I felt would be a fairly innocuous question to get the conversation flowing. Instead, he took things in a very different direction, offering a brief lesson on performative identity construction:

> MH: So you were born in Virginia?
>
> CM: That's what most people believe. People get all serious about this, but I think it's show business.... You go from place to place. It's like being in a carnival or circus. Everywhere you go you can reinvent yourself for that audience. That's how I think. I'm a creative person. That's what I do. Look at Sun Ra. [Some] people think if you do that you're cheapening yourself, but I don't think it's that at all. It's all about who's in front of you at the moment. Not any kind of legacy or any of that. [*Lengthy pause.*] Yeah, I was born in Virginia. That's the truth.[41]

Though Cooper-Moore was kind to ultimately acquiesce in his too-literal interviewer's request for a birthplace, his preamble speaks to the potential of re-creating identities both inside and outside of the act of musical performance. Through creative action, one's identity becomes part of a larger desire for socio-aesthetic mobility—the possibility of creating / performing / embodying new visions of self and community. Rather than discarding the logic of the commercial ("it's show business"), Cooper-Moore, evoking the role of the trickster, inverts it.[42] Where some avant garde improvisers decried show business's fixation with image as a restriction that limited black artistry, Cooper-Moore locates the performer's power in his / her mastery over the world of images. This mutability gives the artist the ability to constantly shift forms and re-create his/her identity through a distinctly Ellisonian invisibility.

Cooper-Moore's personal and professional emphasis on self-creation pervaded many facets of our discussion. The choices he makes, however, are not merely intended to enact a fragmented, postmodern concept of malleable identity. Rather, he uses performance as a vehicle for re/constructing relationships between personal, familial, and cultural pasts, while opening new possibilities for the present and future. This multitemporal orientation is demonstrated, for example, in his own choice of name, which derives from the maiden names of his two grandmothers. He chose this as a constant self-reminder to be a moral person ("You don't be bad in front of your grandmothers!"[43]) while also striving to "follow your bliss," a concept coined by writer/philosopher Joseph Campbell and imparted to Cooper-Moore by drummer Jimmy Hopps.[44]

Perhaps the most visible enactment of Cooper-Moore's self-creation lies in his work as an inventor and builder of handmade instruments, a skill he began cultivating in his loft during the 1970s. He was not alone in this pursuit; instrument building was a frequent, if not pervasive, practice in the lofts. Using found materials from the neighborhood, he built dozens of idiophones, flutes, drums, strings and, later, electronic instruments. Some observers have compared his creations to African instruments, yet Cooper-Moore himself stresses their American origins:

> My thing is that all the elements [of my instruments] are in the culture that I'm from. I don't have to go outside to Africa or Arabia.... People can say, "Well, this is [African]." No. These are all instruments that you find in America that slaves and black folks and the culture create. Whether it's the mouth-bow, or the diddly-bow, the banjo, everything! These are all instruments from African-American culture. My thing is: these are the tools that my ancestors used; these are the tools that I use to create the music of my time.[45]

Juma Sultan, who also built drums and wind instruments in the 1970s, articulated a similar connection in his work:

> After the emancipation, African Americans were allowed to make cigar box banjos. [My desire to build instruments] came from my concept that a borrowed instrument never finishes a song. I don't care if you use a kitchen pot or a washtub bass! A borrowed instrument never finishes a song ... But if you have your own instrument, it's *your* instrument. Whether you bought it, made it, stole it. It's your instrument. It's your ax.[46]

In both cases, the artist-artisans employ language that contextualizes ownership and individuality ("my time," "your instrument") within a longer tradition of African American musical practices. Like the naming narratives examined by Benston, the construction of new sonic tools becomes connected to processes of "genealogical revisionism" that connect with the past while articulating new identities in the present.

As the examples above make clear, neither naming practices nor instrument building were isolated to loft performers. Both connected with long-standing traditions, drawn most frequently from African American culture. Such efforts are best considered alongside other forms of de- and reconstruction that took place in the lofts, including the repurposing of space and the exploration of extended musical form. Taken as a whole, self-creative practices encouraged a critical revaluation of the most basic bulwarks of musical, environmental, and social structure, from the diatonic scale to the name on a birth certificate. Freedom dreams of self-creation highlight the possibility of reformulating each of these structures, breaking them down and reconstructing them into new forms of poetic self-imagining.

BORDERS ARE BORING: FREEDOM DREAMS OF TRANSGRESSION AND TRANSCENDENCE

In their broadest sense, self-creative practices can be situated within a politics of empowerment informed by collectivist ideals. Other perspectives from the period, however, reflect a preference for more loosely structured communalist paradigms derived from 1960s counterculture movements. Todd Gitlin has described the counterculture's ideology as "tr[ying] to combine two impulses at once—the libertarian and the spiritual."[47] Both impulses spilled into the lofts, with artists seeking a release from societal structures and restrictions (transgression) alongside forms of intellectual and spiritual enlightenment (transcendence).

Importantly, these desires did not necessarily come at the expense of a focus on racial politics or cultural identity. Contrary to histories that primarily emphasize points of division between black nationalists and "hippie" counterculturalists, the lofts provide numerous examples of both ideals coexisting, often in the same individual.[48] Dave Burrell expressed it in this way:

> You wanted your identity. You wanted black is beautiful. You wanted to comb your hair out and show your pretty blackness . . . [But] it wasn't that you were now saying, "Since I'm Afrocentric, I hate white people." It wasn't that at all with artists. Maybe with the Panthers it might have been. But with artists, it was "I'm Afrocentric and I like to have friends from everywhere to get with me and be free." Like Woodstock. So the Woodstock "be free and get everybody together" [philosophy] was also in the jazz thing.[49]

Connections manifested in various ways, including spiritual beliefs, alternative lifestyles, quasi-legal "off-the-grid" economics, and experimentation with forms of altered consciousness. Pianist Burton Greene summed up the attitude through a personal mantra that he applies to political, musical, and metaphysical concerns: "Borders are boring."[50]

Transcendent spirituality was a recurrent theme throughout my interviews with loft artists. A number of musicians related anecdotes in which musical performance coincided with powerful moments of religious clarity or revelation. Many accounts involved shared moments of transcendence within a group setting:

> *Burton Greene:* We were playing [outdoors] and it was such a magic atmosphere. The sky was totally blue. It was summer ... All of the sudden I looked up and there was this one cumulous cloud in the middle of this blue. I just felt this universal spirit behind that cloud watching us. Everybody looked up at the same time, like on cue. We looked at each other and said, "Can you feel what's coming from that cloud?" "Yes, I do." It was supernal.[51]
>
> *Ali Abuwi:* I remember some amazing things that were happening with this music, spiritually. I remember we played in Central Park one time. There was about three or four hundred musicians on the stage ... We were supposed to stop at six or seven o'clock, but they couldn't stop it. Then they cut the lights out and we kept playing. It felt like we were actually lifting off of the stage. We were going someplace else. And I remember the police were scared to come up there. They didn't want nothing to do with this.[52]
>
> *Stanley Crouch:* There was a period when Billy Higgins had gone in the hospital in California to get a liver transplant ... One night at Sweet Basil, Cedar Walton, David Williams, and Kenny Washington were there playing. Suddenly Higgins walks in! Nobody knew he was out of the hospital, nor in New York.... So Higgins got up and [sat in] ... He was playing so good I thought to myself at one point, "Every drummer in New York needs to be here tonight!" When the music was over I looked around and they all were in there! I started walking around and asking the guys. They said, "Well, something just told me to come down here." Then I realized that on a certain level it's not something you can measure. It's not something that can be proven. But I think that sometimes there's something spiritual connected to every art that tells the people that need to learn, "You need to go over there."[53]

Without appealing to any specific religion, these excerpts describe musical performance as a force that prompts, facilitates, or reflects moments of spiritual exaltation. Though I spoke to many artists who adhere strictly to a particular faith, such accounts were almost never conveyed in parochial terms. To the contrary, several seemed to go out of their way to use neutral language such as "creator" (rather than God or Allah) and "spiritual" (rather than religious). These substitutions may aim to portray such events as shared moments of togetherness—a desire to draw people in, rather than to push them apart with denominational boundaries.

Several musicians described pursuing forms of spiritual pluralism that embrace a diverse spectrum of beliefs. One example was Abuwi, who self-identifies as a follower of Yoruba religious practices. Despite his personal devotion, during our interview he described performing and seeking spiritual communion with artists of many different faiths. He framed this as a form of pan-spirituality: "I think it was, like, all of the above. That's kind of almost another religion that brings in all of the cultures, all of the religions as one."[54] Juma Sultan—a devout Christian who conducts ministry work in the Hudson Valley—conveyed a similar sentiment:

> I don't even differentiate between church music and secular music at this point in my life. It depends on where you're coming from . . . It doesn't make any difference if I'm playing a love song or I'm in church playing with a choir. There's no difference in the music. Personally, my life and my music are consecrated. People can call it a higher power or anything. I call it God.[55]

The desire for spiritual openness was also expressed by trumpeter Ahmed Abdullah, a follower of the Buddhist practice of *Nam-myoho-renge-kyo*. After exploring numerous religions early in life, he found many doctrines too restrictive for the life of a musician. The attraction of Buddhism, for Abdullah, was rooted not only in its doctrines, but also its amenability to a range of lifestyles and viewpoints.[56]

In the late 1960s, connections between music, altered consciousness, spiritual practices, and communal togetherness were theorized in anthropologist Victor Turner's model of *communitas*. Turner defined *communitas* as a deep connection forged between individuals who had been stripped of the structural inequalities characteristic of social life. Turner initially developed the concept to characterize the heightened liminal states associated with sacred rituals, but later examined how it could apply to other types of social institutions as well. The so-called "hippie" movement of 1960s counterculture was one of several groups that Turner discussed in this regard:

> The "sacred" properties often assigned to *communitas* are not lacking here, either: this can be seen in [hippies'] frequent use of religious terms, such as "saint" and "angel," to describe their congeners, and in their interest in Zen Buddhism. The Zen formulation "all is one, one is none, none is all" well expresses the global, unstructured character applied to *communitas*. The hippie emphasis on spontaneity, immediacy, and "existence" throws into relief one of the senses in which *communitas* contrasts with structure.[57]

For Turner, the use of the arts—whether in or outside the context of ritual—plays a key role in generating the "surplus of signifiers" that is conducive to the production of *communitas*.

The desire among many loft artists to pursue heightened consciousness and nonhierarchical spaces of togetherness makes *communitas* a useful model for thinking about the period's communalist freedom dreams. Turner's stress on the elimination of social hierarchies, for example, exhibits parallels with certain descriptions of the loft community. One instance came in an interview with reed player Rozanne Levine, who criticized the hierarchical "star system" employed by the commercial entertainment industry and contrasted it with loft approaches:

> It seems like there's always this push to pick a very few people to make [into] stars that they can put them out there and sell zillions of whatever. The loft scene was very diffuse and it was very group-oriented. People weren't wanting to be stars. It was about the music. So much of this marketing is about pulling somebody out . . . The loft scene wasn't conducive to that at all. I think that's why it was kind of ignored.[58]

Levine's statements echo a 1972 document written by the organizers of the New York Musicians' Jazz Festival, which promised: "Our organization will function free from separative classification. No person shall have any superior status or hold any arbitrary positions of power over another."[59] The decidedly anticapitalist undertones of many statements may also reflect Marxist ideologies that had become prominent in certain circles of black nationalism.[60]

A second, equally compelling application of *communitas* may also apply the concept to moments of liminal transcendence experienced within the act of musical performance itself. Notably, this idea was advanced independently in two different ethnomusicological studies of the New York avant garde, written forty years apart. The first was a master's thesis by Kali Z. Fasteau (née Susan Lévi-Fasteau), a multi-instrumentalist who attended Wesleyan University in the late 1960s.[61] Drawing from Turner's etymological homology of the words "existence" and "ecstasy," she theorizes the act of producing sound as a form of religious ritual that she dubs the "Religion of Ecstasy." Fasteau's thesis argues that by pursuing a creative life in which cultural production exists outside of capitalist workflows, loft music-making was inherently threatening to hegemonic power structures, a factor that continually reinforced their marginality.[62] Although the thesis may somewhat overstate the extent to which the lofts succeeded in erasing social hierarchies (especially regarding race, class, and gender),[63] it provides an ambitious attempt to connect aesthetic practices, social politics, and ritual acts through then-contemporary anthropological theory.

A more recent application of Turner appears in A. Scott Currie's 2009 dissertation on New York's Vision Festival, an artist-run event that regularly features former loft musicians.[64] Currie combines Turner's focus on transcendent liminality with psychologist Mihaly Csikszentmihalyi's related theory of psychological "flow states."[65] Defined as the "optimal experience" of intense and fulfilling absorption in an intrinsically rewarding activity, flow provides a model of heightened consciousness that—unlike Turner—applies primarily to individual (rather than group) experience. Underscoring jazz's duality as simultaneously individual *and* collective, Currie states that performance rituals facilitate multiple levels of heightened experience:

> In the avant-garde jazz improvisational contexts typical of Vision Festival performances, the simultaneous achievement of individual flow states by multiple musicians playing in the same group tends to "liquify" social structure on the bandstand, giving

rise to a complex ensemble dynamic that generalizes flow in the direction of communitas. In such situations, musicians collectively retain the "merging of action and awareness" and "loss of self-consciousness" even as the "goal-directed, rule-bound action system" (Csikszentmihalyi 1990: 53, 62, 71) gives way to a less structured, multi-directional or "polytelic" field of symbolic action characterized by intense, ludic interplay focused above all on maintaining individual and ensemble flow.[66]

Currie further contends that these effects expand beyond the bandstand, and can be seen within the festival's structure as a densely programmed, week-long, multisensory event that can be readily "associated with interdisciplinary modes of presentation characteristic of liminal ritual."[67] The aspects that Currie cites—interdisciplinarity, restructuring of the artist-audience relationship, the creation of cohesive communities—all possess strong antecedents in the activities of the lofts.

The most explicit reference to ritual acts that I encountered among my interviews came from filmmaker McClinton Karma Stanley. During the 1970s, Stanley recalled working with loft musicians on multimedia productions called "ritual theater" that stitched together acting, music, and dance. Their motivation was explicitly rooted in exploring African identities:

> Ritual comes from Africa. That was the first theater in Africa. It was all the ritual. Theater was developed out of the ritual in Africa. Their theater was ritual. Even the ceremonies and all of that. It was done in ritual format. It was dance, song, movement. A lot of spiritual connecting. It had a multifunctional thing. It became a spiritual connection and it became an entertaining thing, too, because we had the music and we had the dance . . . In the true African tradition it was all related. It was all intertwined. It wasn't separate. Everything was done through the power of the ritual.[68]

Stanley's description provides a remarkable chain of equivalences between practices and identities: Ritual = Theater = Dance = Song = Spirituality = Entertainment = Africa. In doing so, it combines a Turnerian ritualistic surplus of signifiers with a black cultural nationalist-tinged philosophy of African aesthetics that demands that art be "functional, collective and . . . committed" to community uplift and revolutionary action.[69]

Discussions of spiritual and quasi-spiritual forms of heightened experience sometimes overlapped with other approaches to expanding consciousness. In some cases this included the use of narcotics. One musician cited this connection in reference to one loft that specialized in psychedelic experimentation:

> The Center for the Exploration of Consciousness . . . was on West 27th Street. Steve Birnbach ran that. He was real good friends with Jeanne Lee so he had many concerts of the Galaxy Dream Band there. He had these incredible art exhibits. He was also a photographer and he was into psychedelic art and psychedelic thought and consciousness-raising. He had workshops there for paranormal experience and extrasensory perception. [He invited] Stanley [Stanislav] Grof and other people who

were studying parapsychology. Since there was LSD around [they studied] the facts of drug or nondrug paranormal experiences. There was music and art and workshops and good smoke (laughs). For a while that was a really good center for music and this intermingling of the arts. He had really big audiences.[70]

The association of mind-altering substances with transcendent states and/or spiritual revelations appears in a number of cultures, but received a great deal of attention in the United States during the 1960s. Countercultural icons like Timothy Leary promoted the role of drugs as a religious sacrament that facilitated spiritual understanding and communal togetherness.[71] While such ideas are not often associated with the jazz avant garde, quotes like the one above suggests a more nuanced story. The reference to Grof—a psychiatrist who researched the therapeutic use of LSD—demonstrates a direct point of engagement between the two movements.[72]

Experimentation with drugs in the lofts was highly contested among the musicians that I interviewed. Some saw them as an aid to artistic work and facilitator of a friendly, communal ambiance. At least one loft was financed in large part through marijuana sales conducted by one of the primary organizers. A regular visitor recalled the drug as a welcome aspect of the space's communal culture: "Cats was hanging out. You could play and get your buzz on and just hang out. Whatever you wanted to do. It was very loose and very free. A jam session was liable to happen at any time. Could happen in the afternoon or whatever . . . It was really a community place in that sense, for musicians."[73] The organizer himself reminisced about how he agreed with this assessment at the time, saying, "I thought selling pot was doing people favors." Later in life, he rescinded this notion: "Things change as you go. When you get grandchildren you say, 'Is pot really good for my grandson?'"[74]

It is worth pausing to reflect upon the sensitivities surrounding drug use in the lofts.[75] Such concerns are understandable; jazz writing has a long, disquieting history of fetishizing drug use (among other sensationalistic details), particularly within biographies of black artists. I have no wish to perpetuate such tropes. And, of course, all of this must be read against the deep-rooted racial disparities embedded in American drug policy, unequal enforcement patterns, the prison complex, and media depictions of drug abuse, all of which remain highly prejudiced against minority (especially black) communities.[76] The jazz world of the 1970s—like the decades that came before and after it—was deeply impacted by these inequalities.

At the same time, avoiding the issue may risk enacting a different kind of double standard. Scholars of the 1960s counterculture exhibit few reservations about framing drug use as a spiritual, political, or philosophical practice among (often white) hippie-era counterculturalists. The doctrines of drug advocates like Leary, Abbie Hoffman, or members of the Youth International Party (aka the Yippies) continue to be seriously engaged—if not always agreed with—in scholarly treatments. This level of sincere consideration is too often not afforded to black artists, for whom the topic more frequently carries associations of ignorance, addiction, or criminality. The challenge, then, is how to confront the presence of drugs in ways that: (a) do not simply reinforce negative stereotypes, (b) avoid whitewashing the issue in order to paint a more heroic or family-friendly portrait, and (c) grapple with the agency of black and/or jazz artists within a wave of revolutionary philosophies sweeping through American youth culture of the 1960s and '70s. Loft musicians were certainly no more involved with drugs than their countercultural peers, and many suffered the same tragic consequences of drug addiction—as well as the threat of greater legal punishment.

It is equally important to note that not all musicians partook in this aspect of the scene. Many rejected drugs entirely and bemoaned their destructive impact on the community. This was most often expressed when discussing musicians who suffered or died from crippling addictions. Some accounts distinguished between drugs that were seen as less harmful (marijuana, sometimes LSD) and those that were seen as more addictive and dangerous (heroin, cocaine).[77] In one conversation, I was surprised to hear a musician casually discussing a restaurant where he would get "great smoke" mere minutes before complaining about how the Lower East Side became more dangerous with the arrival of "the druggies" in later years.[78] The distinction was sometimes framed in terms of different substances' perceived effects on creativity and social cohesion. Marijuana was often depicted as relatively harmless and conducive to communal experience and artistic work. At the other end of the spectrum, one former cocaine addict described his years of addiction as being especially painful because his life became "the opposite of a creative existence."[79] If the positive aspects of drug use were affirmed as supplements to a psycho-spiritual freedom dream, the forced servitude wrought by addiction served to repudiate any such romantic associations.

Speaking in the late 2000s, most of my consultants renounced all forms of drug use. Nevertheless, confronting the complicated social economies of the lofts requires engaging with the role that they played at the time. A particularly revealing story involved a loft organizer who was arrested on a drug distribution charge in the late 1970s. The prosecution had an ironclad case that could easily have resulted in a decade-plus jail term. The defense, however, produced a laundry list of letters from community members that praised the charitable outreach programming that had been sponsored by the loft. Rather than allowing the accused to be portrayed exclusively as a menace, this tactic presented the jury with a complex individual who contributed both positively and negatively to a range of social economies. The artist was sentenced with probation, after which he turned away from drug dealing altogether.[80]

. . .

A final approach to enacting transgression in lofts was through various forms of "off-the-grid" living. Several of my interviews included stories about how, despite the lack of money circulating in the lofts, musicians managed to survive through a combination of communal sharing and/or resourceful ploys to obtain free or low-cost amenities. The appeal of living off-the-grid was no mere celebration of squalor, but was embraced as an anticapitalist critique of city power structures—a critique that arguably began with the simple act of illegal residence in abandoned lofts. Such accounts once again drew from 1960s counterculture. Similar philosophies, for example, were reported by sociologist Lewis Yablonsky in his ethnography *The Hippie Trip*:[81]

> The American competitive system of free enterprise is clearly rejected by the hippie movement. The Diggers' [a community-action group] effort at barter and trade, rejecting the use of money wherever possible, is a concrete part of this reaction-formation situation.
>
> Affluence is consciously and often methodically replaced by poverty in the hippie movement. As one young lady in the East Village told me, "I joined the hippie scene because I wanted to experience the emotion of poverty." She came from an extremely wealthy family in the Midwest.[82]

Yablonsky's none-too-subtle last sentence points to a social tension embedded in this element of counterculture movements. The impression that participants came from middle- and upper-class backgrounds made their efforts vulnerable to accusations of slum tourism rather than authentic social critique. This frequently caused tension with economically marginalized minority groups in many locales, including the East Village.[83]

Musicians regularly recounted to me their lack of income during the loft years. These stories were sometimes presented as parables of sharing that closely echoed countercultural ideals. Like Yablonsky, saxophonist Mark Whitecage referenced the community services provided by the Diggers: "There was a group of guys called the Diggers. They'd set up a kitchen in Tompkins Square Park, and if you were hungry, you'd just go eat. There was a restaurant called the Paradox on 6th street. If you needed a bowl of rice and didn't have any money you could go in there and they'd give you a bowl of brown rice. I mean, it was human!"[84] Food was also given away or sold cheaply at some loft venues, including 501 Canal Street and the Ladies' Fort. Bassist Hakim Jami, who ran the Ladies' Fort after Joe Lee Wilson relocated to Europe, described how food fulfilled multiple roles:

> HJ: None of us [loft organizers] charged musicians. Musicians were always there. And in my place I always had food because I was right off the Bowery.
>
> MH: Even when people were just coming for rehearsal you'd give them something to eat?
>
> HJ: Oh yeah. I kept beans and rice. That's all it would be sometimes . . . When I bought the club from Joe Lee, he said, "Hakim, whatever you do, don't get rid of the popcorn machine!" I said, "Why? What the fuck does the popcorn machine have to do with any of this?" He said, "[Selling popcorn is] how I pay the rent! . . . "
>
> [Our food was] all organic. The beans, popcorn, salt. Being that I opened around midnight, a lot of my clientele were vegetarians. That was one of the only spots they could get organic food until eight o'clock in the morning.[85]

Jami's statements speak to the dual importance of food as both a shareable resource and a potentially profitable asset. This again underscores a blurring of boundaries between domestic and commercial space. The emphasis on organic ingredients and vegetarianism may also reflect the influence of the counterculture.[86]

Musicians also related stories about unconventional strategies for gaining access to resources. Several related how the unregulated character of loft spaces allowed them to obtain and/or steal various public utilities. Greene, for example, jovially portrayed how he would manipulate the gas meter inside Studio We:

> We had all kinds of tricks [to save money]. Con Ed had these big industrial heaters. They used a lot of gas, which was a lot of moola. So through the grapevine we [learned] that the gas comes in and the meter runs this way. So we'd get a nice smooth pliers and around the sixteenth of the month [we would] turn the meter around so that it ran the other way... Oh man, we had fun!... One guy forgot to do it and at the last minute he blew the meter back to less than it had been before the last month!... Oh, the stories, man![87]

Cooper-Moore told similar tales, casting his own efforts in terms of economic necessity. For him, learning ways to circumvent utility payments was simply another part of the quasi-legal economics of loft living:

> Having a building was very interesting [in terms of] economics. [For instance,] you don't let Con Edison into your building because they'll want to read the meter. We didn't have a meter, we jumped the line. Economics! You have Ma Bell put in a pay phone in the hallway downstairs. Then you jump the line and have an extension all the way upstairs so you have your own phone upstairs. But it's all for their quarter... Economics! We didn't have the money. We were struggling! So to make phone calls we got them to put it in for free... It was years and years and years before the electric company [found out].[88]

There was often a palpable degree of nostalgia in the retelling of such tales. Such actions were not depicted merely as petty crimes, but also as youthful forms of social protest against city power brokers. The destructive urban policies of disinvestment and benign neglect that had decimated much of lower Manhattan created a distinctly anti-establishment bent among downtown artists. Sultan explained the attitude with an analogy to farming debates near his current home in upstate New York: "It's like you have the small farmers here in New York going against the major growers. The laws were shaped to only enable the big organizations. But the little guys, we were growing organic too! We're using the old-fashioned way instead of the chemicals for fast growth."

Other musicians told tales of economic hardship in ways that underscored the struggle of creative life, drawing from the trope of the starving artist. Violinist Billy Bang, for example, recalled how when he and William Parker performed in the band The Music Ensemble, their intense practice regime left little time for outside work, necessitating that they seek other ways of finding sustenance:

> We used to rehearse all day, until three, four, five in the morning. Then William [Parker] and I would walk . . . back to the East Village, because we rehearsed on the west side. A bakery would be open and they'd throw out the bread from yesterday, so we would get that bread. Then one of the guys that worked with William worked in a cheese place and he gave us some cheese. It was HARD, man. But we were making it work. We never quit. That's the thing.[89]

Sultan also recalled scavenging for discarded food, a practice he characterized using the countercultural vocabulary of "dumpster diving."[90] It is easy to view such activities in terms of the small-scale protest strategies advocated by countercultural dissident figures like Abbie Hoffman. In 1971's *Steal This Book,* Hoffman advocated dumpster diving alongside other strategies for free living and social protest, ranging from publishing leaflets to assembling makeshift weapons.

Ideologies aside, a more direct economic explanation for such efforts can provide some much-needed context. Specifically, the low cost of loft living disincentivized full-time work, which was difficult to find anyway in the city's flagging economy. With shelter provided at low rent, utilities available through cunning or theft, and food obtainable through sharing, conserving, or even dumpster diving, the cost of living in lower Manhattan was exceedingly low, especially for a major urban center. Part-time work, supplemented by various forms of austerity and resourcefulness, was often enough to sustain a stable life. For artists, this surplus of free time could be devoted to developing one's work and/or collaborating with others.[91] Such a system might not have been ideally suited for courting social respectability, cultural capital, or public recognition, but it did facilitate a vibrant atmosphere brimming with jam sessions, rehearsals, and performances.

To summarize, while my consultants did not express uniformity on issues of spirituality, drug use, or off-the-grid economics, each was a palpable factor during the loft era. Unlike collectivist strategies that stressed control, public engagement, and social protest, these transcendent/transgressive practices stemmed from the counterculture's libertarian-spiritual axis. Such threads are made even more concrete when one considers the direct connections between loft organizers and the counterculture mecca of Woodstock, New York, which will be explored further in chapter 5.

ATOMIC BALMS: FREEDOM DREAMS OF SONIC ENERGY

One of the more controversial topics among musicians of the 1970s was the occasional tendency of journalists to use "loft jazz" to designate a specific musical genre. The notion was roundly rejected in both commentary from the period and among musicians with whom I spoke in the late 2000s. With the exception of a few venues that used the term for advertising purposes, I encountered no instances of musicians defending it as a meaningful musical descriptor.[92] Instead, artists often pointed to a variety of playing styles that were heard in the lofts. Trumpeter Roy Campbell—a major voice in avant garde groups like Ensemble Muntu and Other Dimensions in Music—recalled how he received his earliest musical training through New York's Jazzmobile program with bebop legend Kenny Dorham. In contrast to accounts that associate lofts exclusively with the avant garde, Campbell pointed to a wide spectrum of coexisting approaches: "Everybody respected each other ... The beboppers and hard boppers respected the avant garde cats. We would all hang out together. It was like a U.N. of all the jazz musicians."[93]

Several lofts worked to promote a sense of unity across genres. One illustration took place in 1975, when Studio We became instrumental in resurrecting the career of 80-year-old big band legend Sam Wooding. In the 1920s, Wooding had been among the first wave of African American bandleaders to tour Europe, including a historic trip to Russia in 1926. After retiring for several decades, he resumed performing in the early 1970s, cofounding a big band with vocalist Rae Harrison. Studio We became a crucial supporter of his return, hosting numerous performances at the loft, as well as producing higher-profile concerts at Cami Hall and the Brooklyn Academy of Music.[94] In a radio interview, Harrison expressed the band's enthusiasm about collaborating with an organization run by black artists: "We've been wonderfully blessed by being presented by the We Studio. This is wonderful because they're black people just like us. I'm very proud of them and so is Sam." Wooding echoed the sentiment when responding to a question about why young musicians were opening their own venues: "Why did the young men go into this thing? I have one answer: it was the lack of opportunity of black men to do things that they wanted to do. That's the reason why they're taking it on for themselves."[95]

Even within the category of "avant garde jazz," many different stylistic variants could be heard in the lofts. In a radio interview, composer and pianist Anthony Davis rejected the umbrella term of "free jazz" to describe the period's diversity of coexisting approaches:

> [Free jazz] really came in the '60s. I think there was a different response in the '70s in that we were turning toward more structure. [For example], the Art Ensemble [of Chicago] was in the idea of using ritual and theater. Julius [Hemphill] did theatrical [multi-genre] things. I think what we were interested in is combining all the new gains in terms of freedom of improvisation, but bringing it into a more structured, coherent composition. And that was very exciting.[96]

Davis's comments run parallel to the writing of musicologist Ekkehard Jost. In the introduction to his landmark study *Free Jazz* (Jost's preferred term, despite Davis's reservations), Jost argues that the music did not constitute a genre in the same sense as earlier jazz styles:

> The conventions of harmonically and metrically confined jazz styles up to hard bop, could be reduced to a relatively narrow and stable system of agreements; therefore, analysis of a given style could concentrate on detecting and interpreting the congruities present in individual ways of operating within that system of agreements. With the advent of free jazz, however, a large number of divergent personal styles developed. Their only point of agreement lay in a negation of traditional norms; otherwise, they exhibited such heterogeneous formative principles that any reduction to a common denominator was bound to be an oversimplification. The initiators of free jazz drew widely different consequences from the renunciation of harmonic-metrical patterns, of the regulative force of the beat, and of the structural principles of the "jazz piece." As a result, the conventions that arose in free jazz with regard to instrumental technique, ensemble playing, formal organization, etc., were never as universally binding as those in traditional areas of jazz.[97]

If it seems that Jost is offering a negative definition (defining the genre through what it is not), his subsequent chapters provide crucial nuances that clarify his meaning. Far from abandoning structure, artists sought ways to rebuild it from the ground up. The remainder of the study presents Jost's analyses of several such reconstructivist musical strategies.

While no single avant garde approach dominated in the lofts, certain styles did become associated with musicians from particular regions of the country. This was especially true following the mid-decade wave of new arrivals from the Midwest and West Coast. A typical characterization can be found in a 1976 review of trumpeter Lester Bowie, written by Stanley Crouch:

> Lester Bowie is one of the exceptional musicians from the Midwest who have offered very interesting alternatives to the "energy" schools of the New York avant-garde. Like Archie Shepp (and Charles Mingus before him), as well as Sun Ra, another Midwesterner, Bowie, who is the regular trumpeter with The Art Ensemble of Chicago, prefers to use freely the *entire* tradition as a series of jumping off points rather than focus on the high speed fire that few other than Cecil Taylor can make interesting for more than a short time.[98]

Like much of Crouch's writing in the period, the piece displays a preference for players that drew explicitly from older jazz styles. Midwestern and West Coast musicians were seen as being more firmly rooted in such practices, which placed them in the favor of both Crouch and Gary Giddins, the two most prolific writers covering loft events. Crouch was far more critical of the dense, extended, free improvisations known as "energy music," which he associated with New York improvisers.

Such divisions should not be drawn too finely, as musicians frequently contradicted any facile reduction into regional tendencies. Plus, as trumpeter Ted Daniel pointed out, many of the so-called "New York" energy artists had roots outside the city. Their association with New York merely stemmed from having arrived before the mid-70s influx: "Before Chicago was the Cleveland delegation [in the late 1960s] . . . That was Bobby Few, that was Reverend [Frank] Wright, Charles Tyler, Larry Hancock . . . At one point there was a Detroit delegation with Donald Byrd and this one and that one. Then there's the Philly thing that came. It's always been like that because that's what New York *IS*."[99] Despite these caveats, the suggestion of a New York–centered school of "energy music" was not altogether unfounded, and may offer certain insights into the aesthetics of loft performance. A brief history of the term itself can offer some elucidation.

The earliest references to energy music appear in mid-1960s texts by Amiri Baraka and Archie Shepp. In several articles published in the collection *Black Music*, Baraka uses the term to depict both musical techniques and meta-musical goals pursued by avant garde artists. Here, the creation of physically forceful sounds is linked to both spiritual pursuits and African American history, a construct that Baraka labels "the black spirit-energy sound."[100] Connections to spirituality appear in interviews with John Coltrane and Albert Ayler from the same period, who similarly highlighted religious associations in their work.[101]

In 1966, Shepp offered a more precise musical description of energy music in a *Down Beat* essay titled, "A View from the Inside." Where Baraka had used the term somewhat generally, Shepp uses it to suggest a specific playing style, exemplified primarily by saxophonists:

> The predominant styles on alto among the so-called avant-garde players are those of the post-Ornette players (these labels aren't meant to be hard-and-fast subcategories) and those whom I would term "energy-sound" players . . . Among the latter I would cite Giuseppi Logan, Marshall Allen, and Carlos Ward . . . The thing that [energy players] seem to bring to the music is an enormous quantity of energy and formidable abilities to create sound textures. At times I have the feeling that they haven't quite solved the problem of channeling all the energy or of how to turn some of those textures into lines, but this may be simply a difference in interpretation and, as is probable, will resolve itself through the synthesis of the two existing approaches.[102]

In contrast to usages that present the term merely as a vague synonym for "free jazz," "avant garde," or the "new thing," Shepp's more specific formulation gradually became the more common one used by musicians. Energy music tended toward high textural density, freely improvised structure, lengthy performances, avoidance of consonance or a steady pulse, timbral exploration via extended instrumental techniques, and extreme volumes (both high and low). The primary blueprints can be found in the music of Albert Ayler (for example, his album *Spiritual Unity*) as well as post-1965 John Coltrane (*Ascension, Live at the Village Vanguard Again*).[103] Ornette Coleman's album *Free Jazz* was also cited as an influence, but much of Coleman's other work during the 1960s leaned away from energy approaches by retaining an emphasis on melody, 4/4 swing feel, walking bass lines, and ensemble roles from earlier jazz styles.[104] As such, it is not surprising that Shepp's definition positions Coleman as the antithesis of the energy approach, while still acknowledging his importance to the new music.

A second quote from Shepp describes the style through the use of visual metaphor: "The idea is similar to what the action painters do in that it creates various surfaces of color which push into each other, creates tensions and counter tensions and various fields of energy."[105] Like the work of artists such as Jackson Pollock, energy music fills the aural canvas with interweaving and contrasting lines, minimizing distinctions between musical sections, but participating in a perpetual play of dense sonic interaction. To extend the metaphor further, we might say that energy music is not synonymous with the jazz avant garde in the same way that Pollock's style is not synonymous with postwar abstract expressionism. Alternative approaches—say, the more spare work of a Braxton or a Rothko—confronted the same aesthetic terrain but produced a very different set of results.

Energy approaches continued to play an important role in New York as the lofts rose to prominence. Certain groups, such as Ted Daniel's Third World Energy Ensemble and the group Kuntu, openly embraced the word in their names and press materials.[106] Others hesitated to identify themselves as purely energy players, since, as Shepp predicted, they combined aspects of energy music with preplanned compositional structures. Several of my consultants recalled the prevalence of the energy aesthetic in both public and private sessions during the period. For example, Cooper-Moore conveyed the playing style of his band Apogee by saying, "At that time it was just—BLOW. Blow until you stop blowing . . . Whoever is in the audience, they [either] get it or they don't get it. But basically—BLOW. Just blow."[107]

Similar recollections were offered by Greene, who detailed how the physical nature of energy music took a toll on many musicians' bodies:

> We exploded out of those closed forms, but I exploded my back, my teeth, everything. A lot of cats couldn't put back the pieces. Look at Marion [Brown]. Poor Marion. He's in a nursing home. He's in and out of consciousness. One foot was taken away because of diabetes. All kinds of cats. David Izenson had a heart attack chasing after his bass, which was stolen in a taxi cab. A lot of cats [have died]. Two thirds of that ESP [Records] catalog is gone![108]

Echoing the peaceful language of Coltrane and Ayler, Greene went on to note that the inspiration for the style was not anger,[109] but a healing impetus that aspired to new forms of consciousness through trance-like repetition:

> BG: There's kind of a myopic illness of people who cannot deal with the dynamics of what we were doing. We dealt with an atomic BALM. They believe in atomic bombs, but not atomic balms. The artist must show that the energy is greater

in the creativity than it is in the destruction . . . It was an explosion of consciousness. You were there or you were not there . . . Conscious repetition builds creativity in anything. If you're consciously repeating yourself, you'll explode. It's centrifugal energy. But that can be in a creative sense. It doesn't have to be a bomb! It can be a balm. That's what we did. We focused on one thing. If you focus long enough, it creates heat! That's what the caveman did when he created fire. We did that with the music. It exploded.

MH: But it wasn't about anger.

BG: No! But we didn't realize that the electric cord had to be as strong as the electricity. Otherwise you short circuit. So I lost my teeth and my lower back. I had to go to Romania to rebuild myself.[110]

Greene's description of exploring consciousness provides another link connecting energy practices with the earlier discussion of transcendent experience through spiritual practices and liminal states of *communitas* and flow.

In terms of economics and urban ecology, the lofts provided an ideal environment for energy music to prosper. The open format of loft events ameliorated presentational concerns over set length or volume, while a surplus of informal playing opportunities gave ample occasion for groups to experiment with extended form. The commercially uncompromising nature of the style—referenced by both Cooper-Moore and Greene—was a small obstacle, since the low overhead of the lofts did not force them to rely on attracting large audiences. And because musicians themselves controlled the spaces, events had no requirement to meet the commercial tastes of club owners, the cultural ideals of arts funders, or to sell enough tickets to offset an independent space rental. In this way, the off-the-grid nature of loft economics was key to enabling the development of an overtly anticommercial musical style.

This was not the case in other cities, even when experimental work was fostered by the creation of collective organizations. Even the most successful collectives could not match the lofts in their sheer number of readily available opportunities. Instead, collectives emphasized strategies of professionalization, precision, and control that allowed them to produce fewer, but often more deliberately planned, presentations. Such an atmosphere undoubtedly disincentivized the development of energy approaches. If, for instance, a band had only an hour to perform each month at a collective-sponsored concert, it would behoove them to craft a tight, well-defined set to present their work. This was especially evident in the artists of Chicago's AACM, who became renowned for developing meticulous compositional structures that interfaced with both African American traditions and Euro-American experimentalism. By contrast, in the lofts—where time and space limitations were minimal—organizers instead benefitted from staging a constant stream of performances, making the extended exploration of energy approaches a viable option.

This is not to say that nightly energy sessions ever provided an especially effective business model. To the contrary, many described how when the Mid/Western musicians arrived, their greater savvy in crafting and promoting their events offered them a significant advantage over New York artists. As described by Whitecage:

> The Chicago guys studied the business. They wanted to do business. We [New York players] were more nonchalant. We wanted to play. We opened our doors and hoped somebody would come, but we just put out a few posters and stuff like that . . .
>
> I remember when Anthony Braxton hit town. The next day you'd see "Anthony Braxton at Town Hall." Posters, this big on every wall! They just blanketed the whole town. It must have cost them a few thousand dollars . . . But all of the sudden everybody knew who Anthony Braxton was.
>
> Me and Jimmy [DuBoise] and Juma [Sultan], we were just playing the music. We weren't taking care of business all that well. They were.[111]

Despite the fact that the stated goals of the AACM mirrored many concerns of New York organizers, the former group's more thorough planning in regard to presentational style, compositional practices, and business strategies helped them to gain rapid exposure and find resonance with the press. But, as noted in chapter 3, this success also occasionally drew resentment from other factions in the New York scene.

CONCLUSION: FREEDOM'S CONTEXTS AND CONTESTS

Rather than writing off the tension between New York and Mid/Western artists as a form of petty infighting, it is more fruitful to consider it in terms of differing investments in communalist versus collectivist freedom dreams. Many New York organizers—empowered by the easy accessibility of low-rent lofts—tended to draw from communalist vocabularies that conceived of freedom in terms of isolationism, the construction of new types of social relations, and the exploration of experimental practices free from outside assessment or rebuke. The off-the-grid loft economy allowed artists to explore uncompromising musical practices that ran parallel to other forms of heightened experience. Energy music was the clearest example of such a focus. The style discarded many traditional musical structures, but its surplus of sensory signifiers was designed to promote heightened experiences of liminality, flow, and *communitas*.[112]

But communalist isolation came at a cost. By removing themselves from public channels, loft organizers sometimes impeded their own efforts to act as effective advocates for industry and/or social reform. Their activities—vibrant though they were—made little impact on larger debates (even in the jazz press), because they lacked sustained contact with those debates. This is especially evident when considering the relative dearth of loft coverage in national jazz publications prior to the Mid/Western arrivals. Thus, while it can be argued that the lofts promoted a high degree of freedom for individual artists, a lack of external engagement made it impractical as a strategy for mounting effective social critique.

On the other hand, collectivist enterprises like the AACM emphasized a greater degree of control over their actions, largely through strategies of ownership and local organizing. Such approaches were inevitably more restrictive on the individual level. Members of collectives had to abide by numerous bylaws and design public presentations in line with an overall organizational mission. Yet through such control, collectives were better situated to deploy a unified message, pursue concrete goals, and promote the performances of their members. Consciously or unconsciously, control strategies may also have been reflected musically through increased emphases on both compositional structure and attachment to earlier musical styles. These tendencies were evident in the work of artists from collectives like the AACM, BAG, UGMAA, and CBA. Their discipline in regard to business practices also aided the groups in attracting audiences, obtaining grant funding, and promoting journalistic and scholarly coverage of their activities. If the loose, communal structure of the lofts facilitated unfettered artistic freedom, the disciplined engagement of collective approaches was more suited to courting cultural recognition and developing effective advocacy.

Considering the numerous contradictions between the two models, it is no wonder that the sides exhibited occasional tension. The haphazard organization of many lofts was a natural point of criticism from Midwest collectivists, while the business focus of the collectives was sometimes blamed for disrupting efforts at open egalitarianism.

What is more surprising, however, is how frequently individuals shifted between these two ideals, and how friendships and collaborations developed across conceptual lines. The diffuse structure of the loft landscape allowed them to coexist in a tenuous duality, making music together in an ongoing dialogue over the very freedom of "free jazz."

5

COMMUNITY

It is October 2009, and I am sitting across from multi-instrumentalist and instrument-maker Cooper-Moore in his Harlem apartment. We are drinking green tea and discussing his former residence in a loft called 501 Canal Street. Though he's a torrent of energy on stage, his conversational style is gentle and quietly confident. As we talk, it becomes clear that his memories of the loft era are somewhat less romantic than those of some of his contemporaries.[1]

Cooper-Moore moved to New York in 1973 after several years of study at Boston's Berklee College of Music. Earlier that year, his band Apogee—a leaderless collective that also included saxophonist David S. Ware, drummer Marc Edwards, and bassist Chris Amburger—had traveled from Boston to open for Sonny Rollins at the Village Vanguard. They received a positive response and decided to permanently relocate, testing the waters of the New York jazz landscape. As the group focused on working as a unit, they began searching for a building where they could live and rehearse together. During the summer, Cooper-Moore found one: a four-story residential structure that had been unoccupied for forty years. By August, they had moved in.

Each member of the group occupied a single floor. Ware lived on the second (along with fellow saxophonist Alan Braufman), Cooper-Moore and his family took the third and Amburger the fourth. For a time, a small, unfinished room above the top floor was occupied by drummer Jimmy Hopps, who heated the unit in the winter by warming a brick on a hotplate. The only unoccupied unit was the first floor storefront, which the musicians converted into a rehearsal and performance space. By the following summer, their activities had gained enough attention to be profiled in two separate newspaper pieces, one a survey of active jazz lofts[2] and the other a concert review titled "Taking Chances at 501 Canal."[3] The rent for the entire building was $550 per month, split evenly among the residents.

On the surface, the group's arrival narrative is similar to those told by other loft organizers. An initial desire for space culminates in finding a mostly abandoned structure. The space is then repaired by the artists themselves (Cooper-Moore details his painstaking efforts to repoint the brickwork) and transformed into a multi-use venue for public and private events. But unlike several of my consultants who framed such efforts through the lens of empowerment and self-sufficiency, Cooper-Moore's account is geared more toward the negative factors that made such arrangements necessary in the first place:

> You're talking about a scene at a particular time that was difficult. It was *very* difficult in New York in the seventies. [The city was] bankrupt. Have [your other interviews] talked about that? . . . I've heard no one talk about the fact that economics in the city for people who *had* venues was very, very, very difficult.
>
> Everyone wants to talk about artists and self-determination and stuff, but sometimes you do what you have to do because that's the only way to do it.[4]

Such statements should not imply that Cooper-Moore is unsympathetic to concerns of political control and artistic enfranchisement. Quite the contrary—as we talk more, he relates the many ways that he has been active in such efforts since the mid-1960s. Instead, Cooper-Moore's point is that by placing too much attention on narratives of empowerment, historians risk misrepresenting the period as a whole. At best, such efforts create overly romanticized stories. At worst they threaten to overlook the stark political and economic disparities that necessitated loft activities in the first place.

Later in our interview, I ask Cooper-Moore how he would characterize the loft community. His response is telling:

> CM: The loft thing was less conducive to community, I think.
>
> MH: *(audibly surprised)* Less conducive?
>
> CM: *(surprised at interviewer's surprise)* Yes.
>
> MH: I'm not being incredulous, but—
>
> CM: Well look where they were. It's not going to be like here [in Harlem]. I mean, I know my super, I know all the supers. I know everybody that moves in. I know everybody in my building . . .
>
> MH: It's interesting to me because some of the people I talked to talk about the Lower East Side having so many musicians that a certain kind of community emerged.
>
> CM: That's true, but I'm not talking about that kind of community. I'm talking about the kind of community where we can talk to each other about sanitation not picking up the garbage. Or the homeless guy down there needs some help, we've got to get him some social services. Or the fact that my son was walked

into every store around here and I said, "This is my son. If you ever see him out here doing anything or he needs some help, you help him . . ." *That* kind of community, you know what I mean?[5]

Cooper-Moore's interpretation runs counter to the many affirmative portrayals I encountered, but he was not the only musician to express such views. These less-idealized accounts were usually not in direct opposition to positive appraisals, but must be situated alongside them in subtle ways. It is clear, for instance, that Cooper-Moore does not dispute the importance of community bonds, but merely defines the term "community" differently from some of his peers. Here and elsewhere, the ways that a speaker theorizes the meaning(s) of community act as key factors in how they assess the successes and failures of the loft period as a whole.

This point is emblematic of a larger issue surrounding the significance of community in the lofts. In both archival and interview sources from the period, the concept of community (like the term "freedom") is appreciably overdetermined. Though it is constantly invoked, participants define the term in myriad ways, leading to a dizzying collection of symbolically delimited social formations. Taken as a whole, their descriptions offer a telling window into the malleability of the term itself, which operates not as a transparent referent, but as a fluid set of discursive structures that are deployed for particular social, cultural, or aesthetic functions.

. . .

This chapter will analyze the multiple meanings of the term "community" as it has been applied to the loft movement. Expanding upon insights from recent scholarship on musical collectivities, I argue that a nuanced understanding of the term must contend with its semantic fluidity and multiplicity as adopted by a group under study. The discussion will proceed in three sections. First, I offer a brief review of scholarly models of musical collectivity, with special attention paid to recent approaches that allow for flexible conceptions of group membership. The second, and longest, section describes a range of depictions of community that I observed among former loft artists and organizers, with an eye toward unraveling the symbolic boundaries of loft collectivities. Drawing from interview and archival material, I identify four overlapping boundary discourses that recurred most often, which I refer to as discourses of pay, play, place, and race. By focusing on a contested discursive landscape (rather than a rigid structural model), I strive to maintain the messy and sometimes contradictory ways that the term is used in practice. The third section takes a brief detour to consider contrasting portrayals that framed the lofts as spaces of isolation and loneliness, revisiting the description offered above by Cooper-Moore. Here, I question how the social structure of the lofts could produce an alienating environment for certain participants, even as it built strong social networks for others.

The final section attempts to synthesize insights derived from the first three. Taking the musicians' boundary discourses as a starting point, I revisit two scholarly models of collectivity alluded to earlier: actor-network theory and the so-called "scenes perspective." The latter requires a bit of terminological clarification. Although throughout this book I have frequently followed the parlance of musicians by using the term "loft scene" to refer generally to the totality of loft practices, my usage in this last section draws from a more specific definition theorized by scholars of popular music. In exploring these models, I do not seek to anoint any single approach as more insightful than another, but rather to ask how each perspective can add additional clarity to the musicians' accounts.

MODELING COLLECTIVITY IN AN ERA OF FRAGMENTATION

Although the vast majority of musical studies engage with some type of community, it is only relatively recently that music scholars have begun to problematize the term itself. Part of this shift stems from a gradual increase of ethnomusicological research conducted in urban areas. As Adelaida Reyes Schramm observed in the early 1980s, city life tends to be characterized by multiple layers of heterogeneity (economic, racial, ethnic, aesthetic, institutional, etc.), creating an interweaving context that complicates attempts to identify distinct, circumscribed groups.[6] On one hand, the density of urban populations ensures that many residents never meet face-to-face, making it difficult to posit a community based on geographic proximity. On the other, city residents group themselves into countless smaller collectivities that may be based on any number of criteria (work, religion, hobbies, etc.).[7] These collectivities are rarely discrete; a single person may consider him/herself to be a member of several different communities.[8] Such insights have given rise to numerous models to account for porous boundaries and/or degrees of fragmentation within social groups.

Though we might be tempted to associate these polyvalent conceptions of collectivity with the rise of postmodernism in the 1980s, such themes have been prominent in African American letters since the late nineteenth century. The best-known early example is W. E. B. Du Bois's theory of "double consciousness," published in 1903. Du Bois coined the term to describe African Americans' ever-present and unavoidable awareness of the oppressive gaze of white eyes. Black citizens were forced to simultaneously view themselves as American and as Negro, overlapping collectivities that were difficult to reconcile under oppressive social conditions.[9] Although his text is primarily concerned with fragmentation within the individual psyche, Du Bois's model hinges on issues of community belonging, social exclusion, and symbolic boundary formation, all of which loomed large as the nation struggled to define itself in the postbellum era.[10]

The decades that followed gave rise to a slew of literary interrogations of fragmented identity and community belonging. The themes loom large in the work of authors like James Weldon Johnson,[11] Jean Toomer,[12] James Baldwin,[13] and dozens of others. Perhaps the pinnacle of such literature arrived in 1952 with Ralph Ellison's *Invisible Man*. Throughout the novel, Ellison's unnamed narrator drifts from community to community, finding himself repeatedly typecast in various reductive stereotypes of black masculinity. Only at the book's conclusion does he come to terms with his own fragmented identity, realizing that his ability to move undetected between social spaces constitutes a form of power that he dubs invisibility.[14] Like earlier texts, Ellison's work reveals how individual identities and the borders delimiting communit(y)/ies cannot be simplistically reduced to binaries of black and white, thereby exposing the disruptive impact of racial reductivism on American social dynamics.

Such nuances were not lost on musicians. A salient example can be found in an interview with Duke Ellington from 1964. At one point, the interviewer asks about the process of writing "the music of your people." The phrasing is intended to reference Ellington's suite *My People,* composed the previous year for an exposition titled "Century of Negro Progress." The interviewer likely expected Ellington to answer in reference to the African American community—a topic that he had broached in the past. Instead, the maestro took the conversation in another direction:

> Let's see. My people. Now which of my people [do you mean]? I mean, I'm in several groups. I'm in the group of the piano players. I'm in the group of the listeners. I'm in the group of people who have general appreciation of music. I'm in the group of those who aspire to be dilettantes. I'm in the group of those who attempt to produce something fit for the plateau. I'm in the group of . . . oh yeah, those who appreciate Beaujolais [laughs]. And of course I've had such a strong influence by the music of the people. THE people. That's the better word. THE people rather than MY people. Because THE people are MY people.[15]

A standard interpretation of such a quote might point to Ellington's ongoing quest to overcome categorical distinctions, a common theme in his interviews and writings. Yet beneath this surface, Ellington's answer points to a fluid conception of group dynamics that knowingly subverts the interviewer's intent to reduce his identity to race alone.

But despite its centrality to American intellectual history, race is merely one sphere in which uncritical ascriptions of "community" can have a flattening effect. This shortcoming has led a number of music scholars to abandon the term altogether, instead developing alternative languages for thinking about social collectivity. Advocates for such efforts argue that the term carries too many prior associations, assuming classical anthropological divisions such as geography, religion, commerce, or familial ties. It fails, however, to address the diverse forms and processes of group membership that have come to characterize an increasingly interconnected modern life, especially in urban settings.

A 2011 article by Kay Shelemay surveys a number of proposed alternatives.[16] One approach abandons community in favor of the term "subculture," a concept pioneered by Dick Hebdige and applied in ethnomusicology by Mark Slobin.[17] Subcultural approaches identify particular groups—often youth movements—whose collectivity is defined in opposition to a larger cultural mainstream. A second approach, pioneered by sociologist Harold Becker, has been to examine "art worlds," a concept that situates art as a social product requiring not only the labor of artists, but also wide-ranging "support activities" provided by funders, producers, writers, listeners, friends, and so on.[18] A third, drawing from Becker but also upon aspects of social network theory, is Ruth Finnegan's concept of "musical pathways." Finnegan also emphasizes art as the product of social forces, but moves away from the stable images of Becker's "worlds" in favor of a more fluid understanding of movement within and across a complex network of collectivities.[19] Lastly, studies of musical "scenes"—initiated by Barry Shank, Will Straw, and Andy Bennett—describe collectivities that are defined by their systems of articulation (how a scene is defined) and processes of differentiation (how it is distinct from other scenes).[20] Straw argues that such an approach is especially well-suited for analyzing popular music, in which global processes create an endless variety of new opportunities for cross-fertilization and change.

Shelemay goes on to identify shortcomings in each model, contending that none suffices as a wholesale replacement of community. In the end, she argues against searching for alternatives and instead proposes a reconceived model of community based around three interrelated processes: descent (communities grounded in notions of shared identity), dissent (communities grounded in opposition or resistance to an existing power), and affinity (communities formed around shared tastes or preferences). Allowing for overlap between these categories permits such a model to account for transformations in musical meaning across time and space. In addition, retaining the term "community" provides the benefit of being legible to those outside of the academy—including the groups under study—without becoming weighed down in technical jargon.[21]

What becomes clear in such a review is that while each model has been applied fruitfully in various contexts, the choice of theoretical lens (community, subculture, art world, network, scene, pathway) carries the potent consequence of limiting the types of stories that scholars are equipped to tell. Is a given collectivity an object or a process? A collection of individuals or a coalescence of ideas? Is it defined by a relationship with an exterior or through its own internal regulations? But where Shelemay depicts such limiting functions as an impediment to developing a broader meta-language, I would propose that these divergences create the exciting potential of telling *multiple* stories, each of which explores a particular aspect of a group's social dynamics. In pursuing several avenues at once, it becomes possible to craft the sorts of rich, polysemic narratives that so often characterize the lived experience of social discourse.

COMMUNITY IN THE LOFTS: PAY, PLAY, PLACE, RACE

The jazz lofts present a unique case study for modeling how multiple definitions of community can arise within a single locale. Insofar as "loft jazz" constituted a social collectivity (and some might deny that it did), it arose as a new phenomenon during the 1960s and '70s. Unlike traditional communities, its emergence was not defined by any long-established historical continuity; on the contrary it came about in reaction to highly specific historical and economic contexts. As described in the preceding chapters, the loft movement possessed an extraordinary degree of internal fragmentation, even when compared to contemporaneous musician-run movements. Unlike the city-wide jazz collectives established in 1960s Chicago and St. Louis, the lofts were a dispersed collection of mostly unaffiliated individuals and organizations. Although organizers often faced similar challenges and concerns, it would be a mistake to ascribe the lofts with a single unified mission. Instead, they developed within a diverse web of motivations, influences, and professional strategies.

Despite this diversity, loft musicians repeatedly appealed to images of community as central to their work, even while disagreeing sharply about how such communities might be defined. Conceptualizing the possible meanings of "loft community" therefore requires sifting through a range of intertwined and/or conflicting interpretations. Following the work of Anthony Cohen, I have found it useful to think of these descriptions in terms of how and where they locate the "symbolic boundaries" that define loft collectivity.[22] In other words: what is the basis upon which membership in, or exclusion from, the community is established?

During the course of my fieldwork, four boundary discourses appeared most frequently. These focused on economics, musical practices, neighborhood involvement, and racial identity, or what I call discourses of pay, play, place, and race. It is important to note that these constructions did not receive equal emphasis from all participants. To the contrary, most of my interlocutors combined, omitted, contested, or stressed particular facets when relating their memories, as will become clear in the descriptions that follow.

(1) Communities of Pay

Pay discourses arise when musicians identify economic strategies as the distinguishing feature of loft community. Such models present the lofts as a socioeconomic critique of the jazz industry, especially nightclub performance. These statements can take a number of forms. Some overtly accuse club owners and impresarios of underhandedness (critiques of practice), while others criticize an industry structure in which nonartist businessmen profit excessively from the labor of underpaid musicians (critiques of structure). The lofts are framed as offering a potential corrective by providing both literal and conceptual stages for protest. Organizers sought to effect change by building an alternative economy in which performers would retain greater control over the presentational and economic aspects of their work. Since most of the small cover charges at loft events (usually a suggested donation of between one and three dollars) went directly to musicians, artists were perceived as receiving direct remuneration, even if this meant that the venues had fewer resources to spend on promotion or production costs. The simplicity of the arrangement—ten audience members produce ten cover charges—also helped avoid exploitation on the part of venue managers.

By highlighting the importance of industry protest, pay discourses depict the lofts as a type of dissent community emerging in opposition to a common foe. A prime example can be seen in a 1973 essay written by drummer Rashied Ali: "Fellow musicians . . . I appeal to you not to be taken in by the exploiter . . . Exploiters is about getting rich, [amassing] fame and fortune, and doing it off our blood and sweat . . . We've got to really bring this shit to a screeching halt. We have to start getting a little more control over our product."[23] The call for an economically delineated dissent community is evident throughout the passage. Ali even goes so far as to refer to the music itself as "product," language that displays an atypical degree of commodification but belies the primacy of financial control within his message.

Economics were sometimes described as influencing other aspects of the loft experience as well. Pianist John Fischer, for example, felt that the removal of industry middlemen was as attractive to audiences as it was to performers:

> It meant that the artists were going to give you what they really wanted you to hear, not what the producers allowed them to do. That's a very key point. This was where you did what you wanted to do without anybody judging you or telling you, "You can't do this. You can't do that. It's not commercial!" The artistic decisions were made by musicians and composers. That's extremely attractive to people.[24]

Fischer's point conflates economic concerns (pay discourses) with aesthetic ones (play discourses, see below), drawing on notions of artistic authenticity to legitimize loft practices. Whether or not this was always accurate, his implication is that eliminating middlemen removed the threat that commercial motives might water down performances.[25] Others emphasized how conducting business among fellow musicians encouraged a high degree of trust and camaraderie, even when resources were scant. As James DuBoise described: "When I did Studio We, I got to be really known with the musicians because that's who I was dealing with, and I was dealing *fairly*. In other words, I wasn't dealing politically. If you could do it, you could play."[26] This connection between fair business practices and feelings of togetherness demonstrates a distinct blurring of the lines between employee, employer, collaborator, colleague, and friend.

Describing the lofts in economic terms was especially common during the earlier half of the 1970s. As noted in chapter 3, it was during these years that participants and reporters were most likely to characterize the lofts as a unified movement. Economic struggle often sat at the center of such narratives. An informational brochure released by the Jazz Composers Orchestra of America (JCOA) around 1972 referenced this aspect:

> Jazz has always suffered from lack of organized effort. For a musician to dirty his hands with business was considered a sure sign of his inconsequence as an artist. Thus, conditions affecting musicians in general were neglected, while everyone sought his own personal glory and fortune. Now that people are becoming aware that their own well-being is finally tied up in the well-being of others, some of the leaders in the new jazz are starting to form organizations that will benefit a greater number of musicians.[27]

This perspective can be traced back to the mid-60s activities of the Jazz Composers' Guild, the collective from which the JCOA sprang. The reference to a growing organizing impetus emerging in the early 1970s is significant, and is echoed in other accounts. Such statements foreground efforts to create a stable economic groundwork to support avant garde work, an ideal shared with the collectives of the Midwest.

Considering loft communities in economic terms also helps to explain the exclusion of certain musicians from being commonly labeled as "loft artists." This includes several major figures in the development of avant garde jazz, some of whom lived in lower Manhattan at the time. Most striking in this regard is Ornette Coleman, who—despite his early adoption of the loft model at Artist House—was classified by several of my consultants as more of an "ardent supporter" who generally kept his involvement at arm's length. Coleman did not perform in lofts frequently and was, for Sultan, more of an inspiration than an active member of the community.[28] Cecil Taylor occupied a similar role. He actively recruited loft players into his bands, including David S. Ware, Marc Edwards, Rashid Bakr (Charles Downs), and William Parker, but did not generally perform publicly in lofts and is usually not associated with them. Saxophonists Archie Shepp and Pharoah Sanders were comparably positioned. Both hired band members from the lofts and occasionally performed in them, yet neither tends to be described as full-fledged members of the scene.

The common link connecting these "outlier" artists may be their position as avant garde improvisers who achieved success through more conventional channels, including commercial recordings and concert appearances. Their commercial successes should not be read as a tacit acceptance of industry practices; during the 1960s, Taylor and Shepp were among the most vocal critics of the jazz industry, especially nightclub economics.[29] Yet by the 1970s, these artists' higher level of prominence meant that they had less need to participate in grassroots efforts. Without direct involvement in the economic struggles that exemplified loft practices, they were one step removed from the community, as defined by pay discourses. This was the case despite their close physical proximity (Coleman and Taylor both lived in lower Manhattan), musical affinity, and abundant professional relationships with loft artists.

(2) Communities of Play

Play discourses describe loft collectivity in terms of musical practices. This criterion stresses the act of performance as the defining factor of community membership. Connections with audience members or other external supporters are here relegated to the background. Play discourses were sometimes linked to economics by conceiving of lofts as sites where musicians could pool their collective energies toward financial gain. At other times, however, they focused on creating welcoming, open, and often *noncommercial* spaces to gather and collaborate, with no money changing hands.

Communities of play are generally described in one of two ways: (1) those that eschew genre boundaries and portray lofts as open sites of inter-genre, cross-cultural togetherness, or (2) those that highlight the primacy of the avant garde. Musicians highlighting the first of these categories—open-genre play spaces—often pull from communalist philosophies of 1960s counterculture. Just as the previous chapter described how countercultural philosophies influenced conceptions of freedom, here we find an instance where these same philosophies affected ideas about open acceptance, communal living, and cooperative economics.

In this case, the influence may be even more direct, as a number of early loft players had previously been involved in artists' colonies near the counterculture mecca of Woodstock, New York.[30] In the late 1960s, several future loft participants spent time at a settlement called Group 212 Intermedia Workshop. Group 212 brought together artists from several disciplines and provided basic housing and food. In return, the artists' only obligation was to develop their own work and present public programs in the area. Multimedia collaborations were especially encouraged and the atmosphere led to a great deal of experimentation. Members of the group were central to organizing the influential "Sound Out" festivals of 1968, which were an important precursor to the better-known Woodstock rock festival in 1969.[31]

One musician who spent time at Group 212 was percussionist Ali Abuwi. While in residence, Abuwi collaborated with Juma Sultan to form the Aboriginal Music

Society, a hybrid organization that combined the activities of a band, a traveling jam session, and a concert presenting organization. The group would later move to New York and become involved, among other projects, in building a recording studio inside of Studio We.[32] When I spoke to Abuwi about the lofts, he emphasized a multicultural form of communalism that appears strongly influenced by his time in Woodstock. For him, loft performance was less about financial motives and more about creating inclusive environments of musical togetherness without economic, social, or cultural hierarchies:

> With musicians, we come at things a different way from other people. I can play with anybody in the world, not speaking the same language or dealing with the same culture, but we can sit down and play music and communicate with each other . . . Anywhere I've gone in the world, if I'm down and out or I need something or whatever, when I play music or tell people I'm a musician, doors open up. And other musicians say, "Come on. We've got this for you. We'll do that for you. You can sleep here. I'll feed you. Let's play together." There's another spirituality there . . .
>
> [Political and economic factors eventually pushed the lofts out because] it was too—[*pauses*]. I was going to say community, but it was too communist. It was too communal. Not in the sense of the political communists, but it was too communal. It was too happy.[33]

The description echoes a central imperative of 1960s counterculture movements, described by Todd Gitlin as an effort to "'create a soulful socialism' (communes, shared housekeeping, and vanguards 'who lead by virtue of their moral and political example' rather than by manipulation)."[34] Music provided the discursive space through which this social harmony was enacted, strengthening bonds among participants.

The excess of free services provided by loft organizers also speaks to anticapitalist motivations. It was common at most lofts, for example, to not require other musicians to pay cover charges and some also provided free food. Several loft organizers, such as percussionist Warren Smith, described making their lofts available as free temporary living spaces for musicians who were new in town or down on their luck.[35] The use of lofts for rehearsals—though occasionally conducted as paid rental—was also regularly offered free of charge. Musicians' abundant memories of camaraderie and pervasive day-and-night musical activity were strongly facilitated by this spirit of openness and sharing of resources.[36]

But open communalism was only one way of framing the lofts as communities of play. A second sense describes the lofts as foregrounding specific musical styles. Despite numerous examples of mainstream and Latin jazz being performed in the lofts,[37] most concede that the spaces were predominantly associated with the avant garde. Stanley Crouch remembered little overlap between straight-ahead and avant garde audiences:

SC: I started to notice that the jazz audience wasn't really interested in that kind of playing. What I mean is if a musician decides to embrace a certain kind of avant gardism, then the musician has to satisfy himself with the same kind of audience that goes to an art gallery. So there's a certain kind of pretentious and snooty quality that really is not characteristic of the jazz audience. It's characteristic of bohemian-derived avant garde audiences.

MH: And you didn't see a lot of crossover?

SC: No.

MH: There weren't a lot of people like yourself who were going both ways?

SC: No.[38]

Avant garde–focused accounts of the lofts were often conflated with the goal of presenting music that was shunned from commercial clubs, a formulation again linking pay and play discourses. In this light, the primacy of the avant garde appears partially as a side-effect of economic structures rather than an aesthetic rejection of straight-ahead styles—an attitude I did not encounter among my interviews. On the contrary, many musicians self-consciously positioned their work inside of a larger jazz tradition, even as they sought to expand the boundaries of free improvisation. Concerts like Studio We's "Pianists in Focus"—which presented artists from four different eras of jazz—or projects like Arthur Blythe's *In the Tradition* represented modern styles in the context of an evolutionary chronology of black music.[39] In this sense, the characterization of lofts through avant garde play discourses can be seen not as a rejection of the past, but as an effort to embed experimentalist practices within a larger historical narrative.

(3) Communities of Place

A third discourse emphasizes the role of geographic place, particularly the Lower East Side of Manhattan. This framework foregrounds efforts to integrate musical activities with the concerns of other neighborhood residents. Musicians sought to promote such bonds through a wide range of activities, including public concerts, educational programs, and local political activism. Place discourses run counter to characterizations of the lofts that portray a detached esotericism that appealed mostly to white and/or middle- and upper-class aesthetes.[40] Rather, many participants made overt efforts to connect their musical goals with the concerns of local residents, thereby implanting their work as a vital part of the neighborhood fabric.

One strategy to bond with local neighborhoods was to stage concerts in public venues and gathering places. These often included city parks, which were used with increasing frequency after the 1972 New York Musicians' Jazz Festival (Fig. 10). Presenting outdoor concerts brought the music to unfamiliar audiences who might not otherwise attend loft events. The tactic also carried several pronounced benefits: (1) the presence of permanent stages or bandshells often made setup

FIGURE 10. Pharoah Sanders performing at Marcus Garvey Park. July 7, 1972. Photo by Bunny Brissett. Image courtesy of the Juma Sultan Archive (Print 129).

relatively easy, (2) their outdoor location made them highly visible, and (3) the lack of a cover charge made them financially accessible for all who wished to attend.

The rise of park concerts by loft artists also coincided with bureaucratic shifts that bolstered city support of such activities. Between 1967 and 1970, New York's Department of Cultural Affairs (DCLA)—which administered performing arts as well as museums, zoos, and other public spaces—was folded into the city Parks Department.[41] The move was intended to streamline and expand cultural offerings for city residents, especially those that could be offered at low or no cost. The musicians' efforts were ideally timed and perfectly suited to this new organizational structure, especially since it required minimal financial investment from the city. For much of the decade, the Parks Department generously granted low-cost permits and occasionally offered additional funding, equipment, or support staff for jazz events.

One musician to make substantial use of these new opportunities was bassist Steve Tintweiss. In the early 1970s, Tintweiss established an organization called the New York Free Music Committee (NYFMC) that specialized almost exclusively in park performances.⁴² The events were funded primarily by small DCLA grants that he obtained each year. NYFMC events specialized in juxtaposing widely contrasting genres of radical music. Tintweiss would gleefully present free improvisation alongside punk rock and new wave, two other burgeoning movements coalescing around the Lower East Side. One such concert paired guitarist and instrument-maker Emmett Chapman (inventor of the Chapman Stick) with the first headlining appearance of the germinal new wave band Blondie. Tintweiss saw such efforts as effective in promoting multiple genres to new audiences while also creating opportunities for dialogue between musical communities.⁴³

A close friend of Tintweiss, James DuBoise also made frequent use of parks for Studio We events. After the dissolution of the New York Musicians' Jazz Festival,⁴⁴ the loft launched its own summer park series in 1974, presented in collaboration with the New York Musicians Organization (NYMO). Their efforts were not limited to lower Manhattan, but staged concerts in all five boroughs of the city. During their early years, these endeavors were strongly supported by DCLA, though DuBoise recalled this support gradually fading over time:

> Our park concert series was one of our most successful events. I would usually do five in each borough . . . At that time the Parks Administration was so amazed at what we were doing that they ordered show-mobiles [mobile stages] for us. That's a lot of money that they spent! . . . Plus you had to have three people working on it, and they would always get them to us for free. The first eight or nine years we had a good time, because I could give a concert anywhere! But later the political stuff got into it. To do a park concert now, you'd be surprised what you have to go through. You have to get insurance and pay a lot of money upfront. To do the same concerts I used to do for free!⁴⁵

The series was successful in attracting funders and collaborating organizations, who appreciated the organization's ambition to provide free performances. Testament to the concerts' strong local impact can be seen in letters of support written by local politicians (Fig. 11).

In addition to parks, musicians produced events at all manner of neighborhood-oriented spaces, a fact that speaks to the semantic inadequacy of the term "loft scene." Though this search for alternative venues was largely prompted by a lack of nightclub and concert opportunities, many musicians also expressed a desire to present their work as a form of local outreach. As William Parker described:

> Our idea was that the music [should go] where the people are. You take the music to the people. Play at a concert hall one day and then you go do a concert on somebody's lawn or house the next day . . . There's nothing wrong with a concert hall, but at the same time in the community we have barber shops, we have community centers, we have kids playing basketball on the basketball court. Let's do a concert on the basketball court, that's my philosophy.⁴⁶

CITY OF NEW YORK
PRESIDENT
OF THE
BOROUGH OF RICHMOND

ROBERT T. CONNOR
PRESIDENT

BOROUGH HALL, STATEN ISLAND, N.Y. 10301

June 18, 1974

Mr. Juma Sultan
Director
New York Musicians Organization
193 Eldridge Street
New York, New York

Dear Mr. Sultan:

This will acknowledge your letter of June 12, 1974, apprising Borough President Robert T. Connor of the free park concerts in the five boroughs of New York City, conducted by your organization.

The Borough President recalls the pleasure and enjoyment experienced by our constituents here on Staten Island who attended these concerts, and he is most grateful that you plan to continue them, particularly on Staten Island, and wishes to express his support and endorsement of this program.

I am enclosing a copy of a letter that we are sending to the New York Musicians Trust Fund, c/o Local 802, for your information.

Thanking you for your interest in the cultural arts of Staten Island, and looking forward to enjoying your concerts, I remain

Sincerely yours,

Ralph J. Lamberti
Deputy Borough President

Enc.

FIGURE 11. Letter of support for Studio We park concerts, from the office of Staten Island Borough President Robert T. Connor. Image courtesy of the Juma Sultan Archive (F0020.08).

Flyers and advertisements from the period speak to the prominence of such practices (Figs. 12–15). Performances were staged at churches such as Washington Square Methodist Church and St. Mark's on the Bowery; community centers like the Bronx River Neighborhood Center, Third World Cultural Center, the Harlem Cultural Council, and the Olatunji Center; community museums like the Storefront Museum, New Muse Community Museum, and the Studio Museum in Harlem; and a variety of other spaces including libraries, health food markets, bookstores, and craft shops.

Outside of producing concerts, another form of local outreach was to offer free or low-cost educational workshops. One noteworthy example was a short-lived music school organized in 1972 as a joint venture between Studio We, Studio Rivbea, NYMO, and Archie Shepp's Black Artists for Community Action. For a five-dollar registration fee, students could choose from an impressive schedule of classes taught by prominent musicians like Jimmy Garrison, Sam Rivers, Dave Burrell, Frank Foster, and Joe Chambers. Shepp himself offered a special one-time lecture titled "Revolutionary Concepts in the Arts."[47] Registration forms show that the program attracted at least eighty students (mostly between ages twenty and thirty), but faltered when the organizers were unable to secure necessary funding.[48] Other initiatives achieved greater longevity, including perennial workshops organized by Jazzmobile, the Collective Black Artists, and Henry Street Settlement. Studio We also briefly offered language classes in Zulu, Xhosa, and Sesotho taught by South African drummer Paul Makgoba.[49]

The importance of place discourses in defining loft collectivities is further evident in the common phenomenon of creating maps of loft locations. During the course of my research, I encountered such mapping in two forms. First, a startling number of my consultants extemporized verbal maps of the lofts during the course of our conversations. Spaces were introduced in terms of their location and proximity to one another, as in the following example from Parker:

> [Saxophonist Alan Glover] lived in a Firehouse on Avenue C and 11th Street. Down the block, Wilbur Ware lived. Andrew Hill lived across the street. Charles Brackeen lived on 10th Street. Rashied Sinan lived on 10th Street. Frank Lowe, Kappo Umezu, Ahmed Abdullah [all lived in the neighborhood] . . . There was a place on Second Avenue called Sunrise Studios run by Mike Mahaffay. The Ladies' Fort was run by the singer Joe Lee Wilson. That was on Bond Street. Studio Rivbea, named after Sam and Bea Rivers, was at 24 Bond Street. Later on Ali's Alley opened up . . . Everywhere you looked there was a place because all the musicians lived down here.[50]

Numerous illustrated maps of loft locations appeared as well, including a *New York Times* graphic produced to accompany a feature on the 1977 Jazz Loft Celebration.[51] In later years, maps have provided central images in several historical

FIGURE 12. Poster template for trumpeter Eddie Gale featuring tagline "Community Learning is 'Truth.'" Image courtesy of the Juma Sultan Archive (F0007.04, F0156.21, F0113.08, F0007.17).

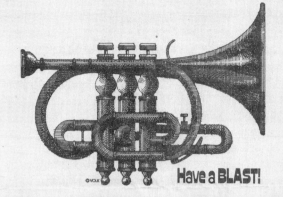

On
WEDNESDAY
MARCH 19, 1975
7:00 p.m.

ADMISSION FREE !

The New York Public Library
COUNTEE CULLEN REGIONAL BRANCH
104 West 136th Street
New York, New York 10030
212-281-0700

presents

THE MODERN MUSIC
of

ANDREW CYRILLE
and
MANO
with

DAVID S. WARE - Tenor Saxophone
TED DANIEL - Trumpet
DONALD SMITH - Piano
STAFFORD JAMES - Bass Violin
ANDREW CYRILLE - Percussion

##
This concert is made possible with a grant from the Office of
Manhattan Borough President, Honorable Percy Sutton, and the Music
Performance Trust Fund with the cooperation of Local 802, A.F.M.

FIGURE 13. Flyer for Andrew Cyrille and his band Maono at Harlem's Countee Cullen Library. Image courtesy of the Juma Sultan Archive (F0007.04, F0156.21, F0113.08, F0007.17).

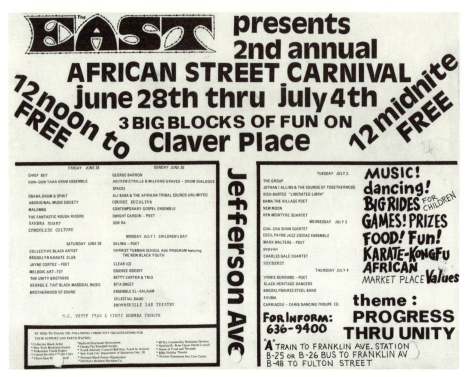

FIGURE 14. Flyer for African Street Carnival (featuring several avant garde jazz groups) held at the influential Brooklyn cultural center The East, a community-oriented space. Image courtesy of the Juma Sultan Archive (F0007.04, F0156.21, F0113.08, F0007.17).

projects such as the WKCR Loft Radio Festival, which created T-shirts featuring a map with the most prominent lofts (Figs. 16–19; see pages 114–17).[52]

The significance of these maps derives from the surprising frequency with which they appear. Maps and mapping narratives are deployed in order to convey an intoxicating vibrancy, established through the sheer density of musical activity packed into a small geographic region. Similar to depictions of 52nd Street in the 1940s, the physical proximity of the lofts allowed listeners and performers to travel easily from one space to the next, creating an image of constant activity, movement, and interaction.[53] As a form of place discourse, this saturation is framed as central to constructing social bonds by bringing participants (both performers and listeners) together on an ongoing basis.

(4) Communities of Race

The fourth, and most controversial, boundary discourse was that of race. In race discourses, loft practices are overtly connected to concerns of the black

FIGURE 15. Flyer for William Parker's Aumic Orchestra at the Bronx's Third World Cultural Center, a community-oriented space. Image courtesy of the Juma Sultan Archive (F0007.04, F0156.21, F0113.08, F0007.17).

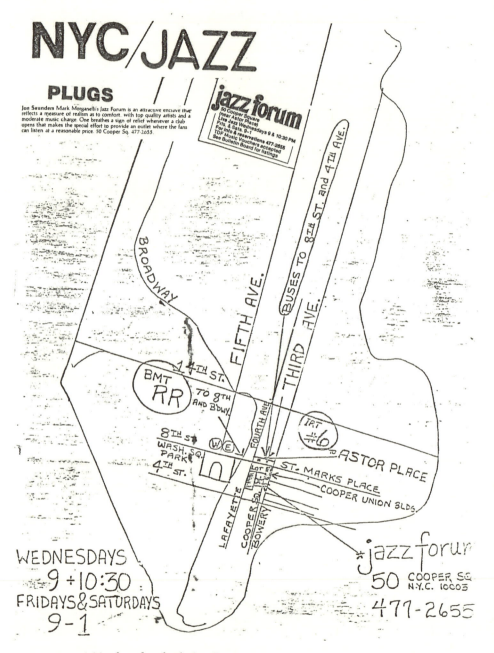

FIGURE 16. Map from flyer for the Jazz Forum.

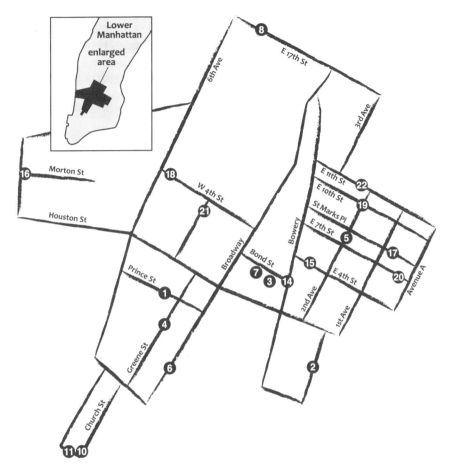

FIGURE 17. Map created for liner booklet for Muntu box set (Design by Jeff DiPerna and Oskar Anosovas, NoBusiness Records, 2010).

community and/or civil rights movement. As with pay discourses, such models were more common in the early years of the 1970s, when lofts were more likely to be described in the vocabularies of black nationalism—especially efforts to promote black-owned business practices. Take, for example, the following excerpt from a 1973 press release for the New York Musicians' Jazz Festival:

> Since the emergence of the jazz music form from our native African culture, and the subsequent jazz variations of spirituals, gospel, swing, avant garde and etc., the Black musicians, composers, and writers have been the victims of a paternalistic system of exploitation that is unequalled in human debasement and neglect. The creative talents and genius of Black musicians has been used and abused as a foundation for massive empires of wealth for all hierarchy involved, except the Black musicians . . .

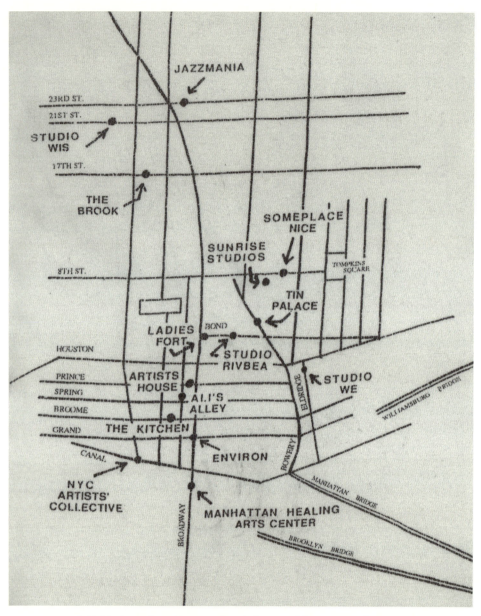

FIGURE 18. T-shirt image featuring map of jazz lofts, created for WKCR Lofts Festival, 1993.

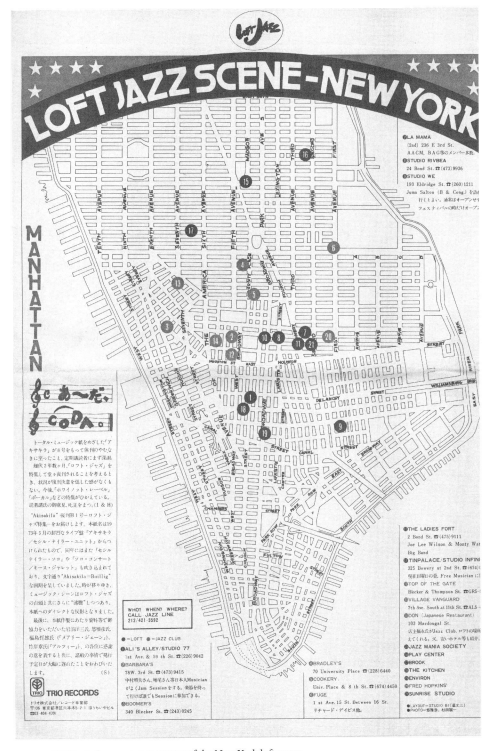

FIGURE 19. Japanese map poster of the New York loft scene.

> This is a new era for the Black Man. The hierarchy is served notice that a Black musician is a Black Man first and a Black musician second.[54]

Such overt statements leave little doubt regarding the centrality of racial concerns for some artists.[55] Here, the dominance of industry forces is not cast solely in economic terms (as in pay discourses), but is placed in a broader social context of racial discrimination and the restriction of opportunities for African Americans. Following nationalist logic, black ownership is promoted as a strategy for closing ranks in an effort to escape a vicious cycle of subjugation, which the authors trace to the earliest emergence of African American music.[56]

Speaking in the late 2000s, most of my consultants hesitated to identify with the types of militant positions represented in the excerpt above, though they acknowledged that such positions were a strong presence during the period.[57] Several black artists recalled experiencing internal tension between their own personal connections with white colleagues and the structural critiques being leveled by political movements. Warren Smith offered a thoughtful account of an incident in which one organization that he was involved with voted to exclude white members:

> I didn't have a hard time adjusting to integration, but I was what you would call a Black Nationalist, politically speaking. So when this whole thing came about [to eject white members], I didn't like the fact that there were vital white people in the organization being excluded on that basis. But I didn't disaffiliate myself with it because of that, because I felt that [black artists] did need to unite and do some things together.[58]

White musicians also related feelings of tension between personal and structural concerns. Many expressed support with the goals of black nationalism, while simultaneously registering resentment when they were, to borrow a phrase from Ingrid Monson, "made to stand symbolically for the whole history of white racism."[59] John Fischer, the Belgian-born pianist who ran the loft Environ, recalled—with no evident bitterness—that he sometimes encountered an understandable reticence from musicians who worried that he was unfairly profiting from black music.

> I got washed over by all of these black musicians who weren't very friendly to white people. Not because they didn't want to be but because of circumstances being what they are. Nobody in their environment trusted any white producers because they had been taken advantage of for decades. And here's John Fischer saying, "Listen, all I need is a small deposit for the use of the space and you get the rest of the gate, or 80% of the gate."[60]

Over time, Fischer was able to develop trust within this community, and his loft ultimately became a key home for concerts by members of the AACM. Later in our interview, he described the overall tenor of the period as multicultural: "The really talented creative musicians didn't fall into the racial trap. [*pause*] Maybe a little, you know, because that was the proper thing to do. It was sort of expected. But they were far more intelligent and far more aware that this is an international thing."[61] Fischer's comments are telling in that they reject race as a determinant of community membership but still recognize the deep intersections between jazz performance and racial politics. Far from offering simplistic narratives of color-blindness or power-evasiveness,[62] many of my consultants—both black and white—expressed awareness and solidarity with nationalist concerns, while simultaneously struggling to come to terms with their own positionality within racially fraught power structures.[63]

At other lofts, a concern with black identity was an ever-present theme. For organizers like Sultan, this motivation informed many activities, even when it was not overtly stated:

> What happened was that [Studio We] had a strong nucleus [of black leadership]. It was almost unspoken. When we formed the New York Musicians Organization, I don't remember any discussion where we talked about precluding whites from the organization. It was open to all. But it was predominantly a black organization. I don't remember one discussion about that . . . That's the way we did way back then. We weren't thinking about excluding, we were thinking about including.[64]

Here, the centrality of blackness is described not as a contested argument that required constant reaffirmation, but as an underlying premise that guided the group's activities. For Sultan, this tacit acceptance of black primacy eliminated the need for any overt race restrictions, such as those imposed by all-black organizations like the AACM, BAG, or the Collective Black Artists. Despite a widespread concern with racial empowerment, I encountered no instances of any lofts restricting the participation of nonblack artists. Yet far from implying a utopian image of color-blindness, the statements of Sultan and others emphasize an ongoing engagement with racial discourses on an everyday level, deeply impacting how artists envisioned themselves as a form of dissent community.

Taken as a whole, discourses of pay, play, place, and race constitute a four-part framework of symbolic community boundaries that were articulated by my consultants. As noted at the outset, these categories were not mutually exclusive, and often jostled against one another in manifold ways. Some musicians, for example, spoke of the lofts as spaces that provided jobs for avant garde artists, an argument emphasizing pay and play. Others spoke of helping black musicians connect with local neighborhoods, an approach stressing place and race, and so forth. Rather than encountering a single basis for defining loft collectivity, musicians invoked a range of visions that circled around these four discursive axes.

PARABLES OF UNCOMMUNITY

In contrast to the preceding frameworks focusing on how participants came together, a handful of individuals described experiences in which the lofts impeded *any* formation of community bonds. In certain cases, the living and working in a loft could generate feelings of separation, isolation, and loneliness. DuBoise, for instance, spoke of how his work as an organizer often pulled him away from some of his closest associates: "Sam [Rivers] would never come over to Studio We to play because he had his own place. Before that, Sam and I did concerts together, with me producing the concert. But there was harmony [between our efforts]."[65] DuBoise's final qualifier ("there was harmony") echoes the thoughts of other organizers I interviewed, who generally denied the presence of competitive bitterness between spaces.[66] Instead, it is the *structure* of the scene itself that appears to have acted as the primary catalyst for imposing distance between artists. Part of the issue stems from a factor that we might call the "organizer's dilemma," in which the time spent producing events forces musicians to neglect their own art and/or connection with the scene. This difficulty was referenced in a number of my interviews, and eventually pushed several participants away from event production altogether.[67]

My most extended discussion regarding isolation came during the interview with Cooper-Moore that began this chapter. A few years after moving into 501 Canal, Cooper-Moore enjoyed an impressive degree of independence, both artistically and financially. Exclusively a pianist at the time (he would begin building other instruments in 1974), living in the loft provided the opportunity to practice music to his heart's content, often for hours every day. If he wished to appear publicly, it was a simple matter of setting up a concert in the first-floor performance space. His financial situation was stable as well; not only did he share in the low overhead costs enjoyed by other loft residents, but his living expenses were funded by a generous patron.[68] In short, Cooper-Moore enjoyed many of the ideals strived for by the founders of the loft movement: artistic opportunity, financial independence, and living quarters that were shared with like-minded artists.

Despite this seemingly idyllic setup, Cooper-Moore found himself growing increasingly depressed. Looking back, he cited two primary reasons for his despondency. The first related to the slow dissolution of the band Apogee, which performed less frequently as the months wore on. David S. Ware and Marc Edwards had begun playing in Cecil Taylor's band, a prestigious and better-paying gig that left them less time to devote to the collective. Meanwhile, Chris Amburger was continually on tour with the Buddy Rich and Woody Herman Orchestras, and would eventually move out of 501 Canal entirely. Though newer residents like Alan Braufman, Tom Bruno, and Ellen Christi kept the space musically active, the initial dream of Apogee moving to New York to live and work together was quickly dissolving. Cooper-Moore was the last member clinging to this dream.

Compounding this disappointment was Cooper-Moore's isolating routine as a loft organizer, which in many ways was built into the structure of the loft lifestyle itself. The ongoing requirements of the building ate up a great deal of his time, while the ownership of his own rehearsal and performance space removed the necessity to network widely in the city's music scene. At one point during our discussion, he told me, "[Having a] space was limiting. When you've got a space like that, it becomes very inward because you don't have to go out there and hustle some club owner to get a gig. You put your gig on!" This statement strongly conveys the double-edged sword of loft social structure. On one hand, foregoing the need to "hustle" club owners was empowering, but on the other it bred isolation by removing the necessity to develop robust social networks. Perhaps most striking is the fact that Cooper-Moore's isolation was not a product of exclusion *from* a unified group of "loft musicians," but rather was a factor *built into* the very structure of loft practices. This situation creates something of a paradox; despite the rhetoric surrounding self-ownership as a form of coming together, the era's emphasis on *independent* action simultaneously entailed an element of pulling apart, as musicians retreated to develop their own private venues.

The sociomusical ecologies of the lofts were capable of producing both valuable benefits and thorny obstacles, depending on how one chose to navigate their waters. On the positive side, loft participation provided a powerful networking opportunity for performers, allowing artists to meet and collaborate in a supportive atmosphere. According to bassist Hakim Jami, "If you wanted to network, all you had to do was come into one of those places. None of [the lofts] charged musicians. Musicians were always there."[69] Warren Smith reminisced about how his welcoming philosophy at Studio WIS helped create bonds between older and younger participants. Such connections proved to be valuable for several of Smith's students from the State University of New York at Old Westbury, including Craig Harris and Knoel Scott, both of whom went on to work with the Sun Ra Arkestra.[70]

For organizers like DuBoise and Cooper-Moore, however, the administrative responsibilities of running a venue sometimes generated the feeling of being, in Cooper-Moore's phrase, "a slave" to those spaces.[71] The scene's vibrancy became difficult to access when one became tethered to a single building. Despite heroic portrayals of empowered musician/organizers, the devotion and time commitment entailed in organizing work often hampered those individuals from reaping the benefits of the very musical community that they helped to create.

NETWORKS AND SCENES: RECONSIDERING TWO ALTERNATIVE MODELS

Armed with the preceding overview of musicians' perspectives, it is now useful to reconsider some of the scholarly models outlined above. Most importantly, I question how these various models might account for (a) a context in which the symbolic boundaries of loft collectivity shared no single criterion, but rested upon four contested axes of group identity, and (b) the contrary reporting of isolation that impeded certain participants from feeling *any* sense of group cohesion, even as their actions placed them squarely within the movement. Two models in particular—analyses based on networks and scenes—seem to offer potential insights.

Describing the lofts as a network can help to explain both the independence of various spaces/individuals as well as the forms of connectivity that linked them. Importantly, network theory does not initially presume the presence of a discrete social group. Instead, it examines the presence of separate nodes and the nature of connections between them. The content of both the nodes and the connectors changes depending on what kind of network is under consideration, as well as what branch of the theory is being employed. Early models of social network analysis[72] theorize these nodes as individuals, with ties created by bonds such as kinship, friendship, or professional association. A more recent model was proposed in the 1980s with the development of "actor-network theory" (or ANT) by social scientists Bruno Latour, Michel Callon, and John Law. This approach attempts to consider not only human actors, but also the roles performed by material objects (tools, media, machines, etc.). Individuals are still seen as being connected to one another, but are also linked to and by these various technologies, which can be as simple as a chair or piece of paper. All of these elements—both human and nonhuman—are termed "actors"[73] within the theory and are considered crucial to the functioning of the system as a whole.[74]

ANT's insistence on the agency of nonhuman actors represents its most significant—and also its most controversial—move. Critics have charged that the approach ignores and/or degrades human volition by placing people on the same level as inanimate objects.[75] But proponents counter that the theory makes no such claim, and that recognizing the interrelationships between humans and nonhumans need not imply that all rest on equal footing. Instead, they argue that considering the specific affordances of material things allows us to craft more precise accounts of how networks function: how meaning is produced, how goals are achieved, how dominance is enacted, etc. Neither does ANT deny the existence of social categories or power structures; to the contrary, one of the field's best-known early articles expressly set out "to study the role played by science and technology in structuring power relationships."[76] It does, however, perceive such categories as *emergent*, arising out of a matrix of constantly evolving bonds rather than as preexisting ontological superstructures that govern human action. For all of these reasons, Benjamin Piekut reminds us that ANT is not a theory in a strict sense at all. It is instead a methodology that provides a "starting point for an inquiry into the alliances, creases, and asymmetries of the real world, always encountered *in medias res*."[77]

Illuminating the exchanges between human and nonhuman actors offers particular benefits in analyzing the lofts, in which networks materialized with clear connections to certain types of physical space. To be sure, the ties between musicians were undoubtedly essential and manifested through shared goals, musical practices, and organizational philosophies. But equally important were the linkages between individuals and the loft buildings themselves, through which the emergent technologies of postindustrial urban repurposing tangibly altered the city's sociomusical landscape. The physical presence and financial obtainability of crumbling, abandoned factories made new demands upon—and opened new conceptual vistas for—the figures who occupied and utilized them. For organizers, individual investment (what Latour terms "enrollment") in developing a given space simultaneously entailed an implicit investment in the network more broadly. This role necessarily differed from that of other actors, such as musicians with no organizational ties to any one venue. According to the theory, a network will remain coherent only as long as actors (both human and nonhuman) accept their roles and continue to "perform" the required social connections.[78] In this way, the network must be constantly reinvented and reaffirmed by its participants. When the integral connections break down—as the boundary discourses of the lofts began to do in the 1980s—the network dissipates. It is instructive to note that in the lofts this breakdown involved not only the choices of human actors, but also changes in the nature of the spaces themselves, which became exponentially more expensive due to gentrification. This was crippling to the movement, since the spaces' affordability constituted a key component in their function as a usable technology for jazz performance.

Thinking in terms of actor networks has the advantage of being able to structurally account for certain differences between loft activities and the citywide collectives of the Midwest. While the motivations animating each movement were similar (structural inadequacies impeding the professional development of avant garde improvisers) and they enrolled a similar population of human actors, the two networks manifested quite differently. The contrast is particularly stark in regard to their varying degrees of centralization—a term that refers to a network's tendency to cluster around one or a few nodes. The AACM, for example, functioned as a single central node that connected many of Chicago's African American avant garde artists. By contrast, the lofts formed as independent entities within a much more diffuse network. An ANT approach can suggest a possible explanation by highlighting the (nonhuman) influence of available, low-cost buildings. New York's glut of space made self-presentation a considerably simpler affair, largely negating the need for a powerful parent organization. As a result, no single group succeeded in creating a long-term musicians' coalition—though several tried. Detractors of loft strategies would claim that this decentralization came at a heavy price. With an audience dispersed among dozens of competing nodes rather than coalescing around a single point of convergence, performances within the network were generally small, sparsely attended, and lacked the organizational backing made possible by a larger, more centralized group.

Network models also allow us to consider the ramifications of social capital theory, a field with roots in sociology and economics. Here, scholars attempt to reconceive features of social life (networks, participation in common endeavors, shared values, trustworthiness, etc.) as resources accumulated for the betterment of an individual or group.[79] Theorists differ on how such resources can be accumulated and deployed, but share a concern with how social capital can be exchanged for other types of capital, including physical, cultural, human, or financial capital.[80] Such exchanges can be difficult to quantify, especially since maintaining particular types of social relationships can sometimes seem to work against an individual's best interests. However, viewing such relationships as a long-term investment in social capital reconfigures the action as one in which the individual stands to benefit at a later time through an accumulation of resources and support structures.[81]

Applying this framework to the lofts provides a useful way to consider a range of interactions between varying modes of capital. The network's myriad personal and professional connections between participants gave rise to a range of informal support systems, which, in turn encouraged further participation. Financial capital may have been scarce, but musicians had ready access to other resources including physical capital (semi-abandoned buildings), social capital (friendship, support networks), and, for a time, cultural capital (recognition from listeners, critics, and arts organizations). For certain organizers like Cooper-Moore, however, the structure became somewhat distorted. Here, a time-intensive investment in physical capital (maintaining 501 Canal) allowed him to cultivate a degree of cultural capital (critical recognition for public concerts at the loft), both valuable commodities within the network. However, his heavy time investment precluded him from developing social capital (interacting with other artists), an oversight that ultimately led to feelings of social isolation. By contrast, other members of Apogee made less of an investment in the physical capital of 501 Canal, instead developing sturdier social and professional networks throughout the city.

A very different calculus can be seen in the example of Warren Smith. Rather than positioning Studio WIS as an influential public venue, Smith's loft focused largely on rehearsals and informal gatherings.[82] He cultivated an open environment, giving out keys to musicians and encouraging ongoing activity, even when he wasn't present. As a result, WIS functioned primarily to foster social capital among artists, rather than to promote public performances (cultural capital) or to make a profit (financial capital).[83] Although his loft was never as publicly visible as many others, during our interview Smith expressed none of the feelings of isolation reported by Cooper-Moore.[84]

A final model for reconsideration is the "scenes perspective," developed most notably by Barry Shank, Will Straw, and Andy Bennett. As noted above, the analysis of scenes arose as a reaction against earlier models of community that overstressed conventional demographic features such as race, class, or local origin.

Recognizing that contemporary movements often cut across such lines, a scenes approach attempts to locate the generative structures that define social relations within and between groups. These "systems of articulation" and "processes of differentiation" need not remain static, and often shift in different settings and musical contexts.[85] As such, particular musical practices may come to represent very different things in different times and spaces.

Considering the lofts as a musical scene emphasizes the period's profound reassessment of spatial and musical meanings. It provides a compelling model for tying together the four boundary discourses delineated above. Instead of viewing these as delimiting the borders of a social group, the discourses of pay, play, place, and race can instead be conceived as the primary systems of articulation that define the scene from the ground up. This need not discount the importance of other sociohistorical processes (including stylistic development and urban ecologies), but instead recognizes the lofts as a collectivity that cuts across them in myriad ways.

It is no accident that this terminology matches the most frequent designation used by musicians: it is far more common to hear one refer to the "loft scene" than to the "loft network" or "loft community." Indeed, it has been the primary term that I have employed throughout this book. A scenes perspective offers the clearest way to characterize the elusive malleability of loft practices. The lofts were not an organization, nor a movement, nor an ideology, nor a genre, nor a neighborhood, nor a lineage of individuals. They were, instead, a meeting point, a locus for interaction. I mean this not only in terms of their presence as physical spaces, but also in their role as what Straw refers to as "cultural space[s] in which a range of musical practices coexist, interacting with each other within a variety of processes of differentiation, and according to widely varying trajectories of change and crossfertilization."[86] Loft performance did not define one's identity; nearly every musician I spoke to bristled at the idea of being referred to as a "loft artist." Instead, lofts provided a stage upon which various identities could be enacted in dialogue with a shared set of central concerns.

A scenes approach may also provide the most legible narrative of the demise of the lofts in the early 1980s. At this point, all four systems of articulation became highly unstable, threatening the coherence of the system. The economic aspirations of creating an alternative economy (pay) lost credibility as rents rose and organizers found it difficult to stay afloat. Musical practices as a defining factor (play) began breaking down in two directions. On one hand, the new decade saw heightened factioning between straight-ahead and avant garde styles, spurred, in part, by the contentious rhetoric surrounding a new generation of neotraditionalist musicians such as Wynton Marsalis.[87] This growing rift obstructed the feasibility of developing harmonious, open play communities. On the other, the association of lofts as the focal point of the avant garde became more tenuous as newer lofts (such as the Jazz Forum) began specializing in straight-ahead styles, while avant garde activities shifted to nonloft venues like the Public Theater. Neighborhood concerns (place) were constantly in flux as gentrification sped up in lower Manhattan, displacing older populations and pushing many artists out of their spaces. Finally, racial factors (race) were altered by both a steady movement away from 1960s-style nationalist rhetoric, as well as the rise of a new generation of white avant gardists like John Zorn and Eugene Chadbourne. Viewed in total, the end of the loft scene was caused by more than only a rise in rents, though it undoubtedly played a major part. Instead, a gradual breakdown of all four systems of articulation undercut the very basis of the loft enterprise. Once these systems failed to hold meaning, the scene essentially ceased to exist.

CONCLUSION: MOVEMENT IN CONCERT

The frequency with which loft musicians evoked images of community speaks to the concept's importance within the era. Yet such discussions also display a telling diversity regarding what these concepts of community mean/t in practice. Individuals invested very differently in particular aspects of the overarching loft enterprise, with no single vision seizing a dominant role. The decentralized nature of loft practices found many musicians following similar paths, but often without the need for close coordination of their activities or overt articulation of guiding philosophies. Instead, communities arose in various guises that played out in a multitude of discussions, a central yet contested aspect of the period's significance.

But recognizing the term's multiplicity need not reduce the notion of loft community to a purposeless mélange of deconstructed discourses. As outlined above, common goals, narratives, and debates provided critical pillars that give a degree of order to a disjointed collectivity. The discursive categories of pay, play, place, and race functioned as central axes of engagement, without providing a single, settled model of community structure. Instead, collectivity appears as a complex amalgam of individuals and worldviews, which may be conceived through various theoretical lenses: for instance, an interconnected actor network or a conceptually emergent musical scene. For all its lack of cohesion, loft musicians' ongoing investment in discourses of community highlights an underlying ideal that continually strived for harmony and communal uplift—a vision, however tenuous, of making music together.

6

SPACE

Descriptions of early loft conversions in New York tend to follow a familiar pattern. I refer not only to the jazz lofts, but to the larger phenomenon of transforming old industrial spaces for residential use. A 2010 *New York Times* profile of two longtime SoHo artists, Elizabeth Weatherford and Murray Reich, exhibits several of the most recurrent themes.[1]

The stage is often set by alluding to the industrial origins of the building being converted, harkening back to a storied industrial past ("[Reich] was approached by a friend. Would he like to join three families who were buying an old garment factory . . . ?"). The neighborhood's history in the early twentieth century is referenced obliquely, suggesting that the departure of industry created an empty void for the artists to fill ("That was the late 1960s, a time artists were colonizing the empty cast-iron buildings south of Houston Street.") This account is generally supplemented by enumerating the structure's remarkably low price ("We put down $10,000 and got a mortgage of $26,000 . . . Sounds cheap, right?") and its deplorable condition upon moving in ("Rats scurried about as if they owned the place . . . The rackety boiler reminded Mr. Reich of a 19th century steam engine. Heat, hot water and electricity were sometime things.") But in the end, the new residents fashion a miraculous rebirth, powered by a combination of elbow grease and pioneer spirit ("Sleeping on mattresses and living like vagabonds, the couple gradually transformed the old loft . . . Together they covered the original floor with lengths of pine and refinished the floor-to-ceiling columns—actually pine tree trunks—left over from the loft's industrial days.") With the transformation complete, the metamorphosed space emerges triumphantly as an ideal and awe-inspiring home, the perfect emblem of urban repurposing in the postindustrial city.[2]

Such narratives are undeniably attractive in their rosy neatness, and similar details crop up in nearly every retelling of the loft movement. When examined more closely, however, such accounts reveal telling omissions, especially in regard to issues of class, ethnicity, and local land use patterns. Consider, for instance, the prehistory of 193 Eldridge Street, which would later become the home of the jazz loft Studio We. Its origins can be traced to the spring of 1893, when the building was first erected by a man named Nicholas A. McCool. A builder by trade, McCool was the son of an Irish immigrant, Nicholas McCool, Sr., who had amassed a sizeable fortune in real estate and the construction trades.[3] The younger McCool followed in his father's footsteps, and eventually began purchasing properties of his own. That March, he acquired a lot at the corner of Eldridge and Rivington for a sum of $25,000.[4] He then submitted plans to the Department of Buildings to tear down the existing structures on the lot and replace them with a six-story brick building with a tin roof (not technically a loft), to be used as factory space. The projected construction cost was $12,000.[5]

McCool would not retain ownership of the finished building for very long. By early 1894, it had been sold, and three years later, McCool would land in jail for perjury connected to a major counterfeiting case.[6] This was actually his second major run-in with the law; he had previously been arrested for forging a promissory note in his mother's name.[7] Under new ownership,[8] the building was soon filled with a variety of businesses. Over the next fifty years, tenants would include machine shops, furniture dealers, breweries, and wholesalers dealing in commercial fixtures. Tailors were the most common tenants, however, with over eight separate businesses listed in city directories between 1899 and 1910.[9]

Eldridge Street sat in the heart of the Lower East Side's Jewish community. The area was home to huge populations of migrants from Eastern Europe, who had begun moving to the city around the 1870s.[10] Around the turn of the century, 193 Eldridge's first-floor storefront even housed the Jewish congregation Ache Josef.[11] Many of the surrounding buildings were tightly packed tenements, a common sight throughout the neighborhood. Up the block at 201 Eldridge, for example, the 1905 New York State Census registered eighty-seven residents squeezed into a single five-story structure, nearly all of whom listed a birthplace in Eastern Europe.[12] As a commercial building, 193 Eldridge was not technically designed for residents, but a handful of people lived there nonetheless, including several who worked as watchmen for the commercial tenants.[13] In 1902, one such resident was 67-year-old Alter Guloff, who migrated to New York five years earlier and worked as a watchman for a tailor.[14] Guloff's wife, Pearl, had remained in Russia, but in 1899 he received word that she had died, leaving him to care for their two daughters, Malke (age 9) and Jennie (age 2). By September of 1902, Alter decided he was unable to provide for them, and applied to have the girls committed to the New York Hebrew Orphan Asylum. At least one of them remained in the orphanage until 1912.[15]

The building served in a variety of roles during the decades that followed. In the late 1940s, it became home to the Pakistan League of America, which promoted Pakistani culture after the country's independence in 1947. By the 1950s and '60s, however, it underwent a steady drop in tenancy, a fate shared by numerous structures in the neighborhood. Its location was a mere two blocks from the path of the massive proposed highway known as the "Lower Manhattan Expressway," a project that was a major cause of disinvestment in the decades after the war.[16] By the time pianist Burton Greene arrived in late 1960s, the building was in severe disrepair and was filled with squatters and drug addicts sleeping in the stairwells. Although the musician-occupants would go on to do extensive work to improve the space in the ensuing years, Studio We maintained a reputation as a somewhat "wild and woolly" venue throughout the loft era.[17]

Seen in this detail, the standard three-part heroic structure of loft conversion—grand industry → willing abandonment → miraculous resurrection—only holds in its most basic form. Each stage is complicated by numerous factors that temper attempts at romanticism. In the first stage (industry), the space appears not as a quaint holdover from the simpler times of small-scale production, but as a calculated risk by developers—in this case, criminals—devoted to extracting as much profit as possible from a limited space. The original owner buys, builds, and sells almost immediately, and what follows are decades of cramped tenancy by the neighborhood's community of recent immigrants. The sweatshop-like conditions that characterized loft manufacturing during this time disturb narratives of a noble, bygone age of industrial primacy.

In the second stage (abandonment), the building's slide into disuse does not occur solely because previous tenants chose to move on to greener pastures. While the exodus of commerce is part of the story, residents were also gradually pushed out due to citywide policies (detailed in chapter 2) that allowed large swaths of the city to fall into disrepair. These policies were explicitly designed to benefit white-collar workers and suburban commuters at the expense of the area's prior residents. Thus, artists did not simply arrive into an empty void that no one wanted, but an area that had been systematically ravaged. It is worth remembering that the presence of artists had long been met with mixed reactions from older residents, many of whom were still working to save the neighborhood from its reputation as a lost cause suitable only for artist occupancy or corporate redevelopment. Instead, these communities endeavored to "[resist] the fatalist construction of their community and the landlord actions that furthered urban despair."[18]

Finally, the concluding stage (resurrection) must also be seen as steeped in social class and economics. By the mid-1970s, the growing popularity of loft living meant that neighborhoods like SoHo were already becoming too expensive for their previous residents, artist and nonartist alike.[19] Artists regularly relate this fact with understandable bitterness, protesting that they were pushed out of a neighborhood that had only become desirable because of the improvements that they had implemented.[20] But even their outcries must be taken with a grain of salt, in light of the older historical communities (often severely marginalized) that populated the region before the artists arrived.

I don't present this background to impugn the progressive, revolutionary ideals espoused by many jazz loft organizers. Rather, the goal of this chapter is to situate their efforts within a broader discussion about the meanings of place and space in 1970s New York. I seek to explore the strange constellation of events that led to a musical movement being named after a type of architectural space. While the moniker "loft jazz" was (and continues to be) abhorred by some musicians, others described how the unique environment of the lofts afforded new modalities of performing and listening. It is worth remembering that unlike the first wave of visual artists' lofts in SoHo, many of the jazz loft venues were not technically housed in structures that would be considered "lofts" in a strict architectural definition. Several were in former tenements, apartments, or commercial retail spaces instead. In referring to the movement as "loft jazz," then, participants were not simply claiming connection with certain types of space, but with a larger ethos of reclamation, repurposing, and the cultivation of new communities.

So what is significant, then, in the term "loft" within "loft jazz"? Why did this word come to define a music genre, an artistic movement? Whereas the sections above have focused on the emergence of lofts within the landscape of the city, the sections to follow step inside the walls to explore the spaces themselves (Fig. 20).

INDUSTRIAL PLACES AND IMAGINATIVE SPACES

Industrial nostalgia is rampant in architectural descriptions of loft conversions. Consider the following example, taken from a recent trade press handbook on architectural design: "For many people, there is nothing new that can match the stories told by a cracked and stained concrete floor, or the romance of years' worth of chips and dings in walls and doors. Rough elm floors, original iron window frames and radiators, concrete or timber pillars, brick walls, even wheezing old cage elevators (properly restored, of course), are what bring a twinkle to a buyer's eye and an extra zero to the price when it comes to lofts."[21] In such accounts, the allure of the spaces is not measured in terms of amenities, but in more ephemeral "stories" and "romance." The imagined history of an industrial past is not only fetishized, it is monetized, as developers charge higher prices for property that is cracked, stained, rough, and wheezing. As we might expect, however, the spaces shown in the photos accompanying this narrative do not appear even remotely run-down. To the contrary, glossy pages radiate with multimillion-dollar renovations that only occasionally retain a rusty beam or exposed pipe (properly restored, of course). These extravagant spaces—the subject of dozens of coffee table

FIGURE 20. Performance at Studio We. L–R: Hakim Jami, bass; Mark Whitecage, alto saxophone; James DuBoise, trumpet; Shelly Rusten, drums. Photo by Jeannette Hamblin. Image courtesy of the Juma Sultan Archive (Print 86).

books and interior design blogs—are a far cry from the original DIY artist lofts of the 1960s and '70s. By the late twentieth century, old buildings had become big business.[22]

By far the most detailed account of industrial nostalgia in loft spaces is offered by sociologist Sharon Zukin, whose rich analysis is worth recounting at some length. Zukin argues: "The changing appreciation of loft buildings also reflects a deeper preoccupation with space and time. A sense that the great industrial age has ended creates melancholy over the machines and factories of the past."[23] She cites this appreciation as a pivotal component in the creation of a chic "loft lifestyle." For Zukin, the burgeoning aesthetic appreciation of lofts reflected broader transitions taking place in the decades after World War II. These changes are typically summarized through the rubric of "post-industrialism," an economic theory that was just beginning to gain traction during the loft era. In his landmark 1973 study *The Coming of Post-Industrial Society,* sociologist Daniel Bell projected that modern nations would gradually move away from economies based on material production and toward knowledge production and service industries such as finance, education, and the sciences.[24] At the time the book was written, the United States had recently become the first nation in which the service sector comprised more than half of the national economy.[25] Bell correctly predicted that other affluent nations would follow suit, with traditional manufacturing increasingly outsourced to less developed nations. In New York, these changes became visible in the evolving landscape of lower Manhattan during the period that manufacturing left the area. Zukin traces how the exploding appeal of expensive upper-class loft conversions mirrored the city's socioeconomic changes on both structural and aesthetic levels. Prosperous members of the new service classes literally began living inside of the hollowed corpses of dead industry, and they reveled in the process.

Given the frequency with which one encounters such nostalgia in architectural literature on lofts, one might expect similar themes to permeate the accounts of the jazz artists who inhabited them. Surprisingly, I have not found this to be the case during my interviews with former loft jazz musicians. Descriptions of the industrial fixtures arose quite rarely, and when they did they usually passed quickly. None of my consultants echoed the rhetoric of figures like Andy Warhol, whose famous studio "The Factory" used industrial space as a both a literal workshop and as a conceptual metaphor for the impersonal nature of modern artistic production.[26] Instead, their stories tended to concentrate primarily on the transformative work that musicians undertook in order to impart *new* meanings into spaces that they conceived as empty vessels, a subject taken up further below. This gap suggests a striking discrepancy between the way that industrial memory resonated—or failed to resonate—among various waves of residents, buyers, and commentators.

A significant aspect of this divergence revolves around issues of class privilege. As Zukin points out, "Only people who do not know the steam and sweat of a real factory can find industrial space romantic or interesting."[27] This observation may help to shed light on the absence of nostalgia in many accounts by artists, many of whom came from decidedly working-class backgrounds. For these occupants, the challenges of living in these unfinished spaces often greatly outweighed any appeals to nostalgia. As visual artist Richard Kostelanetz writes, "Though the presence of artists made SoHo loft living seem romantic, especially to publicists who lived elsewhere, lofts posed problems unknown in, say, residential apartment buildings or even brownstone duplexes."[28] For outside onlookers and high-income residents who could afford to pay contractors for repairs or renovations, it was easy to maintain an air of detached romance from the distant specters of industry. But for many artists, these origins were not selling points to be fawned over, but shortcomings to be endured.

Rather than leaning on industrial nostalgia, whenever I would ask musicians for physical descriptions of loft spaces, the most common adjectives that came up were terms like raw, big, or empty. John Fischer characterized Environ as "one huge square room with only two sets of columns and a lot of empty space."[29] Dave Sewelson recalled visiting the Brook and finding it to be "like a loft—big wood floor in a big space."[30] Hakim Jami remembered the appeal of the Ladies' Fort not as being rooted in any features inherent to the space, but in the musicians' ability to "build us a recital hall with *our* specifications. Then we've *done* something."[31] Over and over, such descriptions depicted the structures as large, affordable, and open, but said little else about their fixtures or décor. While it might be easy to chalk up a lack of detail to fuzzy memories, the openness and rawness of the spaces was consistently presented as one of their most valuable qualities. The power of lofts, in other words, was less about fetishizing any particular elements, and more about reimagining space as a blank slate, an empty canvas that allows for the creation of new types of experiences.

We might think about these priorities in terms of a familiar dichotomy drawn by cultural geographers: the distinction between place and space. While the two terms are often conflated in common parlance, a delineation between them has been traced as far back as ancient Greece.[32] Simply put, space generally refers to an open, abstract grid, an unfilled medium that stretches out indefinitely but can be carved into smaller units. Place connotes an actual set of objects at a location and a particular moment in time. A single lot of real estate marked off on a map represents a way of thinking in terms of space; the home that sits on that lot, filled with sofas, appliances, family photos, and the like, refers to a specific place. Geographer Yi-Fu Tuan outlines some of the basic ramifications of the demarcation:

> Place is security, space is freedom: we are attached to the one and long for the other.[33]

> "Space" is more abstract than "place." What begins as undifferentiated space becomes place as we get to know it better and endow it with value . . . From the security and stability of place we are aware of the openness, freedom, and threat of space, and vice versa.[34]

To take an example from jazz, then, when clarinetist Perry Robinson describes the loft movement as simply, "People coming together in a space to try new things," we might think of this as a fairly literal use of the term "space."[35] Like Tuan, Robinson invokes "space" not for the comforts nestled into the familiar, but for the opportunities enabled by the new.[36] It provides a stage for improvisation in every sense of the term (musical, social, and otherwise). We might further think of this framing as related to meanings proposed by Michel De Certeau, who argues that "place" instills a way of thinking that focuses on fixity and death, while "space" is characterized by movement, transition, and the changing relationships between objects: "In short, space is a practiced place."[37] In this context, space—as openness and possibility—also becomes deeply liberatory, a sentiment that ties in closely with the musicians' related principles relating to issues of freedom and self-determination.

The tendency to value the lofts' potentialities as space has often emerged as an alternative to narratives of industrial nostalgia. In the words of architect Henry Smith-Miller, who moved into his first loft in 1972, "We couldn't afford nostalgia. The reasons were tectonic and economic. The only thing that was luxurious about a loft then was space. If there was stuff there, you just left it. I had a printing press that was too heavy to throw out. But I didn't want it."[38] Similarly, my conversations with musicians almost never veered toward attempts to hold on to vestiges of the past. Instead, what emerged over and over were stories about altering and renovating the spaces to make them usable: James DuBoise talked in some detail about fixing the roof at Studio We; Cooper-Moore about sealing cracks in the walls at 501 Canal; Hakim Jami about applying polyurethane to the floors of the Ladies' Fort.[39] Despite the major role of historic preservationists in protecting the buildings in the area, historical fidelity was almost never cited as a central goal. Instead, descriptions emphasized forward motion, repair, and improvement.[40]

The sense of possibility also informed the types of events that were held in loft venues. Outside of music concerts, jazz lofts were often used for dance productions, art installations, gallery showings, or educational programs. A flyer from 1975, for example, shows Studio Rivbea hosting a multimedia exhibit by filmmaker Karma Stanley titled "Sun Station, Black Light." The event featured music, visual art, and projected excerpts of two of Stanley's films—one about the aftermath of the Nigerian Civil War and another titled "Streets of Harlem."[41] John Fischer was similarly interested in developing multisensory experiences:

> You could do any number of things with a space. You could have jugglers, you could have clowns, you could have dancers, you could have musicians, you could have discussions. Name it. My thing was to have a material that would work on your senses. So I served ice cream that was a mixture of vanilla and anchovies. Then I served coffee that was made with soy sauce. I just offered the kinds of foods that shocked you because they didn't taste like you expected them to.[42]

It was these types of projects that inspired Fischer to name his loft Environ, which expressed his hope to offer an environment to house different types of experience. Dave Burrell voiced a similar sentiment more succinctly: "Once you had a space, it could be anything."[43] Or, as Cooper-Moore put it: "The building, the loft, the space—it was a tool. It was the way we could [become something else] because we weren't pressured . . . It was about developing. The good and bad."[44]

The open possibilities of loft space also allowed musicians to develop new performance paradigms that combined the conviviality of the jam session, the sonic reverence of the concert hall, and the politics of self-empowerment. Many of my consultants, for example, drew sharp delineations between listening to music at a loft versus listening at a nightclub. Poet Steve Dalachinsky was one of multiple audience members who described how he found lofts to be more comfortable because they didn't serve alcohol, eliminating pushy waitstaff or distracting sounds from the bar. He then went on to argue for a certain *un*importance of place in performance venues, saying, "You see those ten people in the front row? They don't give a fuck about the club [environment]. They just want to hear the music."[45] This ideal of erasing distractions and focusing on sound alone moves firmly away from a nightclub model, and toward the rhetoric of the concert hall. The latter foregrounds the value of "quiet and attentive listening,"[46] a modality that has been lionized in Western art music since the nineteenth century.[47] Yet the loft setting's small scale and tendency to attenuate the distance between audiences and performer (more on this below) marks them as distinct from the concert hall as well. Perhaps the house concerts and salons of the European bourgeoisie might imply a different kind of parallel, yet the loft movement's political focus on self-ownership, DIY aesthetics, and revolutionary politics would draw sharp contrasts in such a comparison as well.

In all of these ways, loft spaces provided more than a simple repackaging of prior performance models. Much like the open studios movement of SoHo visual artists, lofts provided a type of third space, an alternative to the tightly policed venues of high culture (the museum / the concert hall) or to commercial enterprises that seemed to underscore financial concerns (the gallery / the nightclub). In doing so, artists emphasized the pliability of space and the capacity to devise new paradigms of working, performing, and living, as we'll see below.

FIRE MUSIC IN THE HEARTH

While references to the industrial past were relatively rare in the loft jazz scene, allusions to domestic imagery were substantially more frequent. Take, for instance, the following excerpt from a newspaper description of the loft Jazzmania:

> It's easy to feel at home in the fourth-story loft where the Jazzmania Society holds forth . . . In subdued but cheerful lighting, a crowd of predominantly young couples, middle-aged groups, and a few singles were seated on casually placed divans, chairs and pillows. There were high beams overhead and red carpeting underfoot. Near the snack bar several windows overlooked Madison Square. A ladder rose to a mini-loft, a cozy roost for balcony listeners . . . The choice spot, if you really want to get into the

Jazzmania spirit, is the long, low couch against the brick wall, near a crackling fireplace and the bandstand.[48]

Notice how the author luxuriates in the presence of furnishings associated with the home: divans, pillows, carpeting, a cozy roost, a crackling fireplace. The cultivation of a warm, welcoming ambiance was common in many venues, and it was often lauded as a meaningful part of the loft experience. Cost was undoubtedly a factor in such decorating choices; a mismatched collection of pillows and couches was cheaper to assemble and maintain than a uniform set of restaurant-style fixtures. Nevertheless, most accounts portrayed such furnishings not as a concession, but as comfortable, original, and inviting.

Furnishings were not the only factor that could impart a sense of home. Other depictions pointed to domestic atmospheres emerging through social relationships, citing attributes like the presence of spouses and children, the sharing of food,[49] or the close interaction between artists and listeners. Studio Rivbea was by far the most frequently mentioned loft in this regard, and many accounts particularly highlighted the presence of the entire Rivers family. Saxophonist Rocco John Iacovone—a regular at Rivbea and a member of Sam Rivers's large rehearsal band—provides a representative portrayal:

> The loft itself was two stories. The street level was where [Sam] lived with his family. Then you'd go down a flight and that's where the rehearsal place was. [Bea] would make big vats of soup. With the two or three bucks [the audience] paid to get in, they'd get a bowl of soup. No alcohol ... There was a family atmosphere, definitely. There was a warm atmosphere. Sometimes you'd see the kids running around. You felt like, yes, this is family. But you didn't feel like you were intruding because there was a completely different space upstairs.[50]

Iacovone's account speaks to the type of blurred (if not totally eliminated) boundaries between public and private space that were characteristic of loft homes. As Zukin describes: "Living in a loft is a little like living in a showcase. Because of the structure of many small industrial buildings, most lofts are entered directly from the elevator. So guests penetrate immediately into the living area. This contrasts with the gradual transition between 'outside' and 'inside,' and public and private space, in a typical home."[51] Unlike earlier paradigms of home design—in which small rooms were cordoned off for specific uses—lofts emphasized openness and transparency, razing walls on both literal and figurative levels. The dissolution of lines between public and private becomes especially salient in a space like Rivbea. Even though the performance area was physically set-off from the living quarters, domestic life nevertheless continued to bleed into the space, as testified by Iacovone's description of a family milieu without intrusion.

Motifs of domesticity came up repeatedly in my interview with bassist William Parker, who was a young musician in the 1970s and played at dozens of loft spaces.

When we spoke, his depictions of many of them employed language that subtly suggests domestic tranquility: "It was comfy"; "It was a nice homey place"; "It was warm in the winter and hot in the summer. It was a nice feeling"; "It was very soft. They had rugs and . . . drapes all over the place. And a lot of kids."[52] The friendly relationships that the spaces fostered also encouraged musicians to stop by at any time of the day or night to play or talk: "There'd always be something happening there . . . Sometimes [we would be] sitting outside from four o'clock in the morning until the sun would rise, talking about music."[53] For Parker, the welcoming loft atmosphere created porous boundaries between his professional and personal relationships, allowing for a continuous flow of musical life.

The loft setting also promoted a higher degree of socializing between artists and listeners. As David Kreuter, a regular visitor to Studio Rivbea, related: "There was a distinction between performer and listener, which has to exist in order for live music to be successful. But there was a definite approachable thing happening with the musicians. It wasn't like they would play their instruments and then go away. There was nowhere to go!"[54] The lack of a backstage area meant that the open rooms had to serve musicians and audiences simultaneously, another example of how the elimination of walls worked to reconfigure social roles. Kreuter become particularly friendly with the bassist Sirone after seeing him play in loft settings, and the two remained in touch for years afterward. Another example was related by Madeleine Kamber, an avid listener who attended a concert at the Jazz Forum during a visit from her native Switzerland in the early 1980s. At the show, she struck up a friendship with dancer Pat Hall and her husband percussionist Warren Smith. Soon thereafter, Kamber helped organize a series of workshops for the couple in Europe, sparking a lasting friendship. The next time she visited New York, she and her husband were invited stay at Smith's loft, Studio WIS. While there, she met a succession of musicians who came by the space to perform and rehearse, leading to further acquaintances.[55]

Listeners often interacted with other listeners as well. Bruce Gallanter—who would later go on to own the record shop Downtown Music Gallery—remembered how he would regularly go to shows with a few friends, but also got to know others who frequented the scene: "It was kind of like a communal thing. It was like a family." Likewise, Steven Koenig recalled attending loft shows as a teenager, where he eventually met the legendary jazz fans Stephanie and Irving Stone. Born in the early 1920s, the Stones were the city's most ardent and ever-present supporters of experimental music starting in the 1970s. They were regular fixtures at loft events, especially after Irving retired from his job as a statistician for the New York State Housing Authority.[56] Despite the fact that Koenig was much younger, he reminisced about becoming friendly with the couple after repeatedly running into them, and he holds fond memories of riding the train back to Brooklyn together after performances.[57] Intergenerational camaraderie even extended down to the very youngest listeners at loft concerts. Musician Ras Moshe recounted stories of being taken to loft events as a young child by his father, saxophonist Jacob Burnett. As he recalled: "The musicians were always very nice to children. It was a very free creative music. The audience was a mixture of a lot of different people. People from the community and people from everywhere. The music was a uniting force in many regards."[58] Moshe's recollections echo a plethora of narratives that mention the presence of kids, usually the children of the organizers or artists.

Viewed as a whole, these various markers of domesticity provided yet another way of distinguishing the loft experience from that of a nightclub. They even served to demarcate lofts from other musician-run spaces like Ali's Alley, which featured table seating and a full bar. Despite the musician-run venue's location inside the home of drummer Rashied Ali, its function as a gathering space for musicians, and the building's history as a former manufacturing loft, many of my consultants (including Ali himself) took pains to remind me that the space was not a loft, but a club.[59] By replacing markers of domesticity with the trappings of more commercial presentations, Ali positioned his space outside the category of "lofts" entirely, again demonstrating that the term implied much more than a nod to architecture.

The cultivation of a family-friendly atmosphere—especially through the presence of children—serves as another crucial contrast between the two types of venues. Nightclubs tend to be adult-oriented, often explicitly prohibiting children and relying on the sale of alcohol to remain profitable. Within jazz, their value as performance spaces has been a subject of considerable debate. While some accounts have praised nightclubs as cultivating a desirable environment of closeness and intimacy,[60] others have critiqued them for undermining the importance of the music in various ways. Nightclubs have often been typified by male domination and/or heteronormative sexual pursuit, illicit drug use, and a damaging commercialization. By the 1970s, such critiques were sometimes informed by racial consciousness as well, as when saxophonist Archie Shepp rebuked the tendency to ghettoize jazz into alcohol-centered venues, saying, "[W]e are forced into stereotypes when a black child has to learn about black music in a bar."[61] The domesticized reconfiguration of loft venues offered something of an antithesis to the nightclub format: audiences of all ages were welcome, alcohol was absent, and attention shifted from commercially profitable styles toward more experimental genres.[62]

GENDERED SPACES

The spatial reimaginings enacted by loft performance were also deeply intertwined with issues of gender. By far the most illuminating account of gender discourses in New York jazz of the period appears in Valerie Wilmer's landmark 1977 work, *As Serious as Your Life*.[63] In a section titled "Woman's Role," Wilmer compiles a wealth of interviews on the subject, often revealing troubling power disparities. In many of the comments—particularly from male musicians—the role of women is described primarily as providing support (financial, familial, sexual, and spiritual) for their male partners. Domestic work and child-rearing are among the most commonly cited duties, implicitly placing such labor in juxtaposition to the presumably male vocation of music-making. At least two of Wilmer's female informants even describe being pressured to abandon their own performance careers at the insistence of male partners.

Wilmer strongly defies such stereotypes in a subsequent chapter chronicling several female musicians in the scene, including Lynda Sharrock, Barbara Donald, Monette Sudler, Carmen Lowe, Moki Cherry, Mary Maria, and Kali Z. Fasteau. But this chapter, too, is peppered with stories about female players being summarily dismissed as incompetent, or being forced to undergo harsh hazing rituals before gaining the acceptance of male colleagues. While Wilmer's overall impression points to a community that remained structured by deep-rooted patriarchy, she is also careful to provide numerous counterexamples of male and female artists expressing more progressive views. The section even concludes on a hopeful note, expressing optimism that women were beginning to take powerful steps "towards their liberation within the hitherto-male dominated art form."[64]

Wilmer's account is most legible in relation to contemporaneous gender discourses emerging out of black cultural nationalism, a movement that is cited at several times during her text. Black feminists scholars since the 1970s have offered extensive critiques of the gender politics expressed by early nationalist authors like Amiri Baraka and Maulana Karenga.[65] In an article from 1970, for instance, Baraka writes:

> We talk about the black woman and the black man like we were separate because we have been separated . . . We were separated by the deed and process of slavery . . .
>
> But we must erase the separateness by providing ourselves with healthy African identities. By embracing a value system that knows of no separation but only of the divine complement the black woman is for her man. For instance we do not believe in the "equality" of men and women. We cannot understand what the devils and the devilishly influenced mean when they say equality for women. We could never be equals . . . nature has not provided thus. The brother says, "Let a woman be a wo-man . . . and let a man be a ma-an . . . "[66]

Such arguments often purported to uplift black femininity by promoting women's pivotal contribution to a larger liberation struggle. This contribution, however, was too often limited to domestic responsibilities, a role that was portrayed as aligning with traditional African family structures. As Patricia Hill Collins and others have noted, such ideals arose as part of a more widespread glorification of the figure of the black mother—an image that was frequently transferred onto the entire ancestral homeland as "mother Africa." Yet Collins also notes that such depictions can carry insidious consequences. Not only do they limit women's agency to a tightly circumscribed arena, they do so by overtly controlling her reproduction and sexuality, placing it entirely in the service of a male struggle for power. This process can further serve to negate any contributions from women audacious enough to step outside of this constricted role:

> With so much vested in glorifying the mother, Black women who fail to fulfill these functions can only face censure. A distinction can be made between those women who uphold the values of the nation but do not adhere to them and those women who, by refusing [the] protection [of men], challenge the premises of the system. Within this framework, Black gays, Black lesbians, and Black women who embrace feminism all become suspect, because each group in its own way challenges the centrality of motherhood for Black families, communities, and ultimately the Black nation.[67]

Collins is one of many feminist authors to reject such ideas. Writing in the early 1980s, bell hooks similarly rebuked the notion that anything distinctly African could be found in maintaining misogynist value systems: "Although Baraka presents this 'new' black nation he envisions as a world that will have distinctly different values from those of the white world he is rejecting, the social structure he conceived was based on the same patriarchal foundation as that of white American society."[68] With these contexts in mind, Wilmer's accounts of women being pigeonholed into certain roles is reflective of larger debates that were taking place, particularly within radical political movements. Women who sought to pursue their own music may have therefore been seen as similarly "challeng[ing] the premises of the system," and were continually faced with various forms of censure and dismissal.[69]

Wilmer does not take up the issue of space directly, yet the strict division between home and performance spheres underlies much of her discussion. This is especially true in her chapter "It Takes Two People to Confirm the Truth," which explores the social role of musicians' wives.[70] In many of her interviews, the home is represented as a female space of repose, where musicians come to recharge and recover from the exhaustion of artistic creation.[71] The spaces of performance (including bandstands, rehearsals, and tours), on the other hand, are framed as loci of homosocial male inspiration and triumph, but also as spaces that breed frustration and disappointment due to the inequities of the music industry. The degree to which the two spaces are separated is quite striking. Wilmer notes, for instance, that even in instances when wives actively managed their husband's business concerns, "The idea of a wife or any woman being involved to the extent of following them on gigs or turning up at rehearsals is generally considered restricting. These are times when they want to relax in their all-male environment."[72] This separation does not, however, preclude the possibility of sexual conquest in the aftermath of a performance. Instead, liaisons that begin on the bandstand are marked off as firmly outside of the domestic realm, a factor that sometimes crops up as a justification for infidelity. As one wife puts it, "If you have a husband that goes on the road for two and a half months in Europe, for you to sit home and imagine that there's not other women involved, I think that's just crazy."[73] The fact that multiple male musicians insisted that their wives abandon musical careers further underscores a deep-seated desire to cordon off separate domestic and performance domains.[74]

With this in mind, the tendency of loft venues to blur the lines between these spheres may have carried numerous ramifications. Rather than demarcating the performance space as one of exclusive male dominance, in which women appear only as sexual objects, the act of performing (in) the home worked to unravel commonly held associations. This change not only impacted musicians, but also affected the way listeners experienced lofts, as evidenced in another description of Studio Rivbea, written by reporter Susan Mannheimer:

> The audience can sit on the floor, on pillows, low mattresses, park benches—anywhere. (The relaxed atmosphere and similar seating arrangements are also features of Artist's [sic] House, etc.) In between sets, the people can wander upstairs, talk with musicians, read "Swing" magazine (in Japanese), look at the photos and paintings lining the walls, and just feel good ... The presence of young children is an added stimulant and another bonus is that women can feel free to come unaccompanied, without having to be paranoid about the traditional attitudes still prevailing concerning women who go to hear jazz alone.[75]

Mannheimer's statement connects the cultivation of a domestic atmosphere—especially epitomized by the presence of children—to a reassessment of her own feelings of safety as a woman attending a jazz concert. Although the account does little to transgress conventional gender roles (femininity remains tied to domesticity and the family, for example), it does imply that the lofts' blurring of the home/gig binary subtly began to undermine the gendered meanings affixed to particular types of spaces. This observation by no means negates the problematic views that remained all too common in the period. It may, however, support Wilmer's underlying hope that a shift in the scene's constructions of gender was slowly beginning to be take shape.

CONCLUSION: BUILDING FROM SCRATCH

Of all the musicians I interviewed, perhaps none embodied the tension between domestic place and emancipatory space more fully than percussionist Hetty Fox. Among jazz devotees, Fox is best known for touring Europe with Ornette Coleman's band in 1974. Prior to that, however, she was an active presence in the early loft movement, working closely with the organizers of Studio We and leading an all-female band called Presearch.[76] Her introduction to issues of urban reclamation and activism, however, began a few years earlier, and several miles north from the downtown center of loft activity.[77]

Born in 1937, Fox is a lifelong native of the Bronx, where she grew up on a tiny one-block-long street called Lyman Place. She remained in the neighborhood through her early adulthood, earning a bachelor's degree in psychology from Hunter College and briefly teaching elementary school near her childhood home. In the early 1960s, she left for California to pursue a doctorate in sociology at Valley State University (now Cal State Northridge), and she remained on the West Coast for nearly a decade. While there, she became deeply involved in social justice causes, including a series of protests by Valley State's Black Students' Union. This activism ultimately led to the university establishing a Department of Afro-American Studies in 1969, part of an early wave of such departments being formed throughout the nation.[78] When she returned to New York City in 1970, she was shocked to find her old neighborhood quite different from what she had remembered:

> When I came back home, I saw signs of deterioration going on, which was very disturbing... This area [the South Bronx] was ground zero for the greatest loss of housing that the whole United States ever experienced... Fires were all over the place; I could hear the fire engine going almost every night. I had to sleep with my boots on practically. You never knew when you might have to jump up and fight, or jump up and run. What the heck is going on here?!...
>
> The whole place smelled like—I don't know, old coffee? Bleach? Gas leak? Everything smelled different... It seemed so dead. People were riding the subway like they were zombies. It was scary. I did not know what was going on or what was wrong. I could sense that *something* was terribly wrong. The whole dynamic in the city of New York seemed to be just flat.[79]

Much like the problems plaguing the Lower East Side, the main culprit of this disruption was a highway construction project conceived by Robert Moses. The Cross-Bronx Expressway was built between 1948 and 1953, but its impact would be felt for decades.[80] Over 60,000 residents were displaced by the construction alone, while areas surrounding the corridor experienced precipitous drops in property values. Middle-class flight followed, leading to a wave of property abandonment. Slumlords who held on to their buildings often resorted to arson for profit, hiring "rent-a-thugs" to burn them down for insurance money. Other fires were caused by outdated electrical systems in vacant properties, with equally devastating results. By the mid-1970s, 43,000 housing units in the South Bronx had gone up in smoke, a number that corroborates Fox's recollections of wailing sirens.[81] Disinvestment by private business was followed by the removal of city services, further exacerbating the neighborhood's downward spiral.

Fox was crushed to see her neighborhood in such disrepair. In fact, much of her professional life throughout the forty years since has been devoted to revitalizing the area by setting up a community center on the same block in which she grew up.[82] But when I spoke with her about her memories of the period, I was somewhat surprised to find her describing how her initial despair was also accompanied with a strange sense of possibility:

> I said, "Oh look at this! We have a fresh, clean slate here!" So now you have to shift gears. You can't talk about how you're going to maneuver around the things that are in place. They all disappeared! So now we have to ask what we want to see grow here. What do we want to see happen? . . . [A] lot of things didn't have to be knocked down here because they were *falling* down . . . Here we had an opportunity to build from scratch.[83]

Fox's reaction exemplifies a strange double-edged sword of urban reclamation in the loft period. On one hand, the fact that large swaths of the city had been allowed to sink into disrepair was a tragic reminder of deep-rooted economic inequities and the government's lack of concern for lower-income residents. Yet at the same time, the rash of abandonment was precisely what allowed a wave of forward-thinking artists to take up these spaces, allowing them to reimagine their surroundings in creative and revolutionary ways. The challenge of, in Fox's words, "building from scratch" was both a cause for mourning and a deeply empowering prospect, especially for artists who were invested in ideals of self-creation.

Later in our interview, Fox offered a brief but telling non sequitur. In the middle of discussing loft events, she abruptly changed the subject to the topic of graffiti, specifically when it began blanketing New York in the late 1970s and '80s:

> [Graffiti] first began to appear on the subways especially. People were outraged! . . . They're riding up and down the subways paying their fare and sitting there like zombies. But I'm riding the subway and I see this artwork starting to splash about. I look and I say, "Oh my god! Look at that! That's fantastic." Little old ladies are on the subway saying, "This is terrible! How dare these children, these wayward juvenile delinquents come up and do this. Vandalism! How dare they!"
>
> And then I said, "Look at this! These people are complaining. The art woke them up. It gave them a stroke of life that they don't even understand. Their complaining is like a rush of blood into their veins that literally woke them up! This is fantastic! They are alive! They're able to function!" I thought it was the most fantastic thing in the whole world. These kids are actually disobeying ALL of society . . . but they splashed color, design, shape and energy [throughout the city].[84]

Fox was the only artist I spoke with who raised the topic of graffiti, and at no point did she link it explicitly with jazz performance. Yet I find that this unexpected interjection offers a unique way of thinking about relationships between art, consciousness, and urban space. Fox's enthusiasm for graffiti stems from a renewed sense of possibility that it invokes. While she does not read any specific message into the artwork, she sees it as conveying new ways of viewing the world and reclaiming the spaces that surround us. The lofts ventured toward similar goals, as musicians occupied crumbling structures in an effort to assert ownership, pursue self-determination, and explore new models of creativity. Her reference to the disgust of "little old ladies" alludes to the inherent political resonance of such acts. In her example, the subway car is doubly repurposed—first as an art object and second as a battleground for ownership, aesthetics, and the fate of a city in decline.

It is in this sense that space was central to the loft movement. Despite occasional criticism by musicians who argued that talking about buildings diminishes the importance of "the music itself,"[85] the act of converting dusty old structures into vital sites for community-building and experimentation constituted a critical aspect of the loft era's musico-political enterprise. At their best, lofts did not merely sustain drowsy nostalgia for the past, but spurred boundless visions of possible futures.

7

ARCHIVE

August 3, 2009: After a lengthy drive on winding roads, I arrive at Juma Sultan's home in the tranquil mountains of Kerhonkson, New York. It is only my second time here, although we have been in touch extensively about the project we plan to carry out together. For the next five months, I will be working with Juma to study his extensive archive of loft tapes and documents, as well as interviewing him about his perspectives on the period. I pull into his driveway just after noon, which is the time we had set to meet.

Juma is running a few minutes late, so I am welcomed into the house by his wife Mariyah, who kindly offers me a drink and a helping of the salad she made for lunch. I have known Juma for over five years, but this is my first time meeting Mariyah. A few minutes into our conversation, she begins asking a series of questions relating to the research I have planned. Her questions start casually, but soon grow increasingly specific about the exact details of my arrangement with her husband. It becomes clear that Mariyah is deeply skeptical about my presence, and she expresses her fear that I am here simply to exploit Juma's resources for my own gain, without giving anything back to him or the black community. She notes that he has been taken advantage of in the past by unscrupulous collectors, especially in relation to his career with Jimi Hendrix. I assure her that I don't intend to profit economically and that my goal is to *collaborate* with Juma to increase the visibility of his project. She remains hesitant. By the time Juma arrives fifteen minutes later, Mariyah is scrutinizing a research agreement that I had sent several weeks earlier, noting places where the language would need to be changed, as I frantically scribble down her requests.

The tone shifts quickly after Juma's entrance. Though we continue discussing the agreement for a few more minutes, he reassures her about my presence, explaining *that he has known me for a number of years and is familiar with my research. He agrees with several of Mariyah's suggestions about the research agreement but disagrees with others, ultimately deciding he would like to give it more thought before signing a final document. In the meantime, he proposes that we proceed with the plan that we had discussed. Within minutes we are in his barn beginning the process of sorting and cataloguing that would occupy much of our time in the months that followed.*

Looking back on this episode, I found it to be a jarring start to my fieldwork, and I remained deeply shaken throughout my early weeks in Kerhonkson. After long planning and preparation for a project that I envisioned as supporting an underacknowledged community, it was upsetting to be immediately accused of ill intentions and profiteering. But as time passed, I began to appreciate the appropriateness of this beginning, which seemed fitting for a project saturated with issues of ownership and control over historical legacy. On the one hand, Juma's generosity reflected an eagerness to build a collaboration governed by ideals of community, trust, and friendship. On the other, Mariyah's wariness drove home the degree to which questions of economics and authority continued to resonate in very real ways. I would encounter similar reactions (on both sides of the spectrum) from many other musicians in the months that followed. Some embraced the project with open arms, happy to share their time, memories, and resources. Others were more reluctant, worried that I would get the details wrong, or simply use their stories to promote myself as a scholar. Such skepticism was beneficial; it constantly reminded me of the ethical aspects of historical inquiry.

The work we began that day was geared toward reaching into the past, but it often seemed as though that past was reaching back to us. Many documents made explicit reference to preserving materials for future generations, seeming to foretell some future act of reconstruction that we now found ourselves performing. Fragments of half-discarded messages and aborted organizational systems would reveal themselves briefly before receding into the collection's copious sprawl. They appeared as clues from the past to aid unknown figures in an unknowable future, a future in which I now found myself.

I reached out with Juma, toward Juma, and we tried to decipher the messages of both.

TAPE / PAPER / HUMAN: ARCHIVAL ETHNOGRAPHY IN THREE MEDIA

Loft jazz artists were prolific self-archivists. Throughout my interviews, musicians repeatedly wanted to show off personal collections of tapes, flyers, newspaper clippings, and other materials. Bassist Hakim Jami, a loft regular and latter-day owner of the Ladies' Fort, proudly brought out a scrapbook of photos, flyers, and articles that he has carefully laid out in plastic-lined pages. Pianist John Fischer, former manager of Environ, stores his materials in large cardboard boxes in the basement of his Tribeca home. Bassist William Parker keeps his in several file drawers inside his East Village apartment, while percussionist Warren Smith installed built-in shelving to hold the cassettes that he recorded at Studio WIS. Perhaps the most spacious storage space I found was the one maintained by visual artist Jeff Schlanger, who keeps materials in a free-standing building behind his home—a repurposed train station in New Rochelle. In addition to providing studio space to develop new pieces, the structure holds dozens of cabinets filled with Schlanger's paintings of live performances dating to the mid-70s. Through these and many similar examples, it becomes clear that an archive like Juma Sultan's cannot be considered in isolation, but as part of a more widespread phenomenon.

How should we read this move toward self-documentation? The goal of this chapter is to consider this question through the lens of a decidedly different sort of "archival turn" that has emerged in the humanities over the past few decades. In that time, a number of theorists have begun to question the nature and authority of archival knowledge, which previously stood as the *sine qua non* of historical scholarship. Rather than simply treating archives as politically neutral repositories of unadorned fact, this new wave began interrogating the ways that archives (especially large state and institutional holdings) are deeply implicated in issues of power and control over the creation of knowledge. Seemingly innocent processes of curation, preservation, and research were reconceived as moments at which ideologies asserted themselves through choices over what is worth saving and what is not. Archives not only inform what is written, they establish *what is possible* to write. They also dictate what is impossible and therefore suppressed.[1] Changes to the archive—whether by including new sources or by revising the way we interpret old materials—therefore carry the potential to drastically revise the way we think and write about the past.[2]

The decentered nature of private archives offers a unique opportunity to reevaluate the empirical framework underlying jazz history. Whereas the field has traditionally relied primarily on a combination of oral history and commercially published sources, a shift toward private artifacts compels us to rethink our most basic historiographic values. As an alternative to focusing on public narratives (including the triumphs of a small cadre of "great men"), private collections allow us to take a broader view that considers the community underpinnings of musical scenes. While these everyday social resonances might not have been useful to commercial presenters—especially during the nadir of jazz's market influence in the 1970s—they remained deeply meaningful for the participants themselves. In tracing them, it becomes possible to write alternative histories of where the music went after the record companies stopped calling.

The insight that archives possess the power to change history was not lost on loft artists. As outlined in chapter 1, many musicians envisioned their archiving as part of a larger mission to re/claim control over their careers and legacies.[3] The value of self-controlled archives sat alongside that of other types of musician-run institutions: performance venues, record companies, artists' collectives, and so on. Brent Edwards has referred to these practices using the term "autoarchivization," the purposeful establishment of archives of the self. Drawing parallels with postcolonial literature, Edwards ties the practice to longer activist streams from throughout the history of black radicalism.[4] We might think of it as a sort of conceptual precursor to autobiography through which the individual asserts control over her/his own historicization. In the face of a historiographic hegemony designed to write particular types of stories (be they colonialist, ethnocentric, masculinist, neoliberal, or otherwise), the creation of private archives provides the groundwork for alternative modes of historical writing. This concern with contesting certain narratives while enabling others therefore situates the practice as a distinctly activist enterprise.

In striving to build a collaborative project that highlights the agency of musicians, I designed my work with Sultan as an "ethnography of the archive," a phrase that has been invoked repeatedly in recent literature.[5] Scholars like Nicholas Dirks have used the expression to reference the goal of interrogating how the power dynamics underlying archival knowledge are the result of social processes.[6] Archives are not inherently oppressive or hegemonic, but their existence does rely on choices made by individual figures operating within complex, and often unequal, social milieus. Illuminating an archive's hidden logic requires reconceiving it as a social entity, in which patrons, administrators, research subjects, and archivists (dead or alive) are equally implicated. The tools of ethnography—including a reflexive gaze back upon our own subjectivity as researchers—provide a model for theorizing archival work as a constantly negotiated, multiply mediated social practice. Taking this idea further, Kate Eichhorn has critiqued certain scholars of the archival turn for treating the archive primarily as a site for "stag[ing] encounters with the past," which she argues, "emphasize the archive's status as a historiographic rather than a preservationist technology."[7] In other words, by treating the archive as fading fragments of an irrecoverable past, we lose track of the fact that the *practice* of archiving is resolutely oriented forward toward users in the future. Eichhorn addresses this problem by conducting her own ethnographies with feminist archivists curating new types of collections with the hope of inspiring future scholarship.

My own collaboration with Sultan follows Eichhorn by employing the ethnographic practice of participant observation in the archive. For five months I worked closely alongside him as a sort of employee/consultant/researcher, assisting him in cataloging his materials, digitizing tapes, developing an inventory, and writing grant applications. As a result, my accounts do not rely solely on a close reading of the artifacts themselves, though this has certainly been a part of my approach throughout this book. Instead, they were developed in dialogue with living human actors. I do not mean to imply that my collaborators would necessarily agree with my interpretations. Nor should it insinuate that I, nor Sultan, nor any other participant, has authoritative claims upon historical truth. Any such claim would miss the point; Sultan's stated goals of raising awareness about the lofts make no attempt to mask the project in an illusory objectivity. Instead, they rely upon the potential of physical objects to advance specific narratives, namely those that affirm the significance of himself and his loft colleagues. The accounts that emerge from the archive are—like all ethnographic accounts—deeply situated in a particular place, time, and system of values.

With these issues in mind, let us enter the Sultan Archive, engaging with the artifacts and actors within. The analysis that follows is structured in three sections, corresponding to different substrates within the archive upon which traces of the past are inscribed. The first examines tape recordings, exploring how the loft generation's explosion of amateur recording arose from a series of overlapping motivations. The second turns to written documents, asking how paper archives unavoidably reproduce the logic of certain types of "paperly" activities. The final section considers the human archive, embodied in the memory and agency of Sultan himself. In lieu of framing the human witness and the material artifact as distinct realms of remembrance, I consider them in constant dialogue, mediating and remediating one another in an ongoing dance of co-creation. By juxtaposing these sites of inscription (which, as we will see, overlap extensively), I aim to consider how theorizing private preservation gives us new ways to think about the loft era, as well as music historical research more broadly.

I. Tape / The Archive We Hear

It is always the tapes that get mentioned first. Over and over during my interviews, conversations would turn to sound recordings, often captured and saved by the musicians themselves. The trope of the "lost tape" is all-too-common among producers of historical reissues.[8] Indeed, it was referenced directly in a fundraising video that Sultan released in 2007: *The Lost Archive of Juma Sultan*.[9] I can't claim detachment from this romantic pull of the tapes; the mysterious allure generated by the video was a major factor that had drawn me to Sultan's in the first place. Long before my first trip into the mountains, I watched as the camera panned desperately across crumbling boxes like a landscape of ruins—a window into the past, a resonant tomb.[10] I imagined how my work would cut through dust and oxide, allowing dormant soundscapes to reassert themselves and take their rightful place in jazz history. But like many archivists before us, Sultan and I soon learned that the transposition from the material to the historical would not be quite so simple.

When I arrived, the tape collection consisted of 433 items, stored primarily on open reels (374 items) with the remainder on cassettes (59 items). The reels were stored in their original cardboard boxes, which, in turn, were housed in larger cardboard moving boxes, all of which were slowly disintegrating. Like all of Sultan's materials, they resided on the ground floor of Sultan's barn, an unfinished space with exposed beams and floorboards, shrouded in Tyvek homewrap. The tapes varied widely in terms of how much contextual information was present. Some had meticulous notes (dates, locations, personnels, etc.). Others had no information whatsoever. The majority lay between these poles, offering fragmentary, oftentimes cryptic messages: "AMS Shaki Edress"; "Bay's Wedding"; "Side I ENDS on Christmas Prayer." Most of the tape boxes were also assigned handwritten numbers (sometimes several) etched in various colors of ink. These seemed to be lingering vestiges of organizational systems, but Sultan only vaguely recalled the details. Our early hopes of finding a written catalog never materialized. Adding further frustration, once we began listening we found that a few of the reels had been misfiled or mislabeled, forcing us to ignore the annotations entirely and attempt to identify the performances by ear.

Though we lacked the resources of formal libraries, we used what we had available and began taking steps to make the tapes usable. We started by transferring the reels to covered, acid-free archival crates, which had been purchased the previous year with a grant from the National Endowment for the Arts. Unable to decipher the old numbering systems, we established a new one, affixing labels with new accession numbers to the spine of each item. We used these numbers to create a catalog spreadsheet, in which we transcribed all data written on the tape boxes (even when it was found to be inaccurate). After consulting with specialists in tape preservation, we borrowed a small collection of playback and transfer equipment, while also seeking guidance about how to assess the stability of each item.[11] We operated with a general strategy of "do no harm." Any items that seemed fragile were set aside for fear of doing irreparable damage. These preparations occupied us for approximately the first two weeks of our time together.

With a basic system in place, we finally began the time-consuming process of listening, annotating, and creating digital transfers of each item, using Sultan's ear and memory to flesh out the catalog information. The decision to make digital copies was made for reasons of both preservation and usability. Having reference copies allowed us to listen repeatedly without damaging the original tape, while also ensuring that a second copy existed in the event of damage to the original. As we lacked an archival-quality hard drive (we would obtain one much later on), we compensated by making redundant copies. After burning each item to disc using a CD recorder, we transferred the WAV files to three separate hard drives: one remained with Sultan, one traveled back to Boston with me, and one was sent to Stephen Farina, a communications professor at Clarkson University with whom Juma had collaborated in the past.[12] The CD-R copies were then used as a tool for quick reference. I should be clear that none of this work was done to the kinds of exacting standards recommended by professional archives.[13] We were well aware of this, yet also recognized that the limited timeframe of my fieldwork was a significant opportunity to advance both Sultan's goals and my own. Neither one of us wished to squander it by waiting for more ideal circumstances that might never arrive. Instead, we made do with the limited resources we had available, an approach not unlike that of the original loft organizers in the 1970s. Over about five months, we managed to go through about one-third of the tapes using this strategy.

Amateur Recordings: Priorities, Motivations, Deployments. Our long process of listening gradually suggested insights about the priorities that informed Sultan's recording practices during the loft years. The tapes hinted at distinctions about which types of sounds were deemed worthy of recording and which were not. We noticed, for example, a clear emphasis on recording music and music alone, a detail that is not quite as trivial as it might seem. Excerpts of stage announcements, audience banter, or conversations were purposely omitted from most items. In such cases, the recorder would audibly cut off as each piece concluded, restarting again only when the next selection began. Sultan described this choice as being rooted in economics. By cutting out banter, musicians could maximize the storage capacities of tape stock. Economic concerns manifested in other ways as well. In addition to recording over some reels multiple times, a handful of the tapes were made on discarded reels that musicians had found in the garbage outside of local television and radio stations.[14] A few times, glitches in the recording process resulted in faint echoes of older material remaining audible underneath the newer performances, sonic residues of the loft strategy of creative repurposing.[15] Sultan's collection is hardly unique in its fiscal concerns. Difficult decisions are inherent in the practice of building any archive. To echo an observation from Michel-Rolph Trouillot about historical inscription more broadly: "Something is always left out while something else is recorded."[16] Storage is never infinite; choices must always be made.

But the recordist's decisions to omit nonmusical sounds had noticeable repercussions for Sultan and myself. As we labored to reconstruct contextual details in the face of limited data, spoken interludes (such as introducing the band during a performance) became essential pieces of the puzzle. Our ears would perk up whenever a song came to a close and the bandleader began to speak, only to turn away frustrated when the recording cut out. The situation reveals a disjuncture in the archival priorities valued by the recordists (Sultan and his associates in the 1970s) versus those of the catalogers (Sultan and myself in 2009). Where the former wanted to direct all available resources to the preservation of musical performance, the latter placed a much greater emphasis on context and metadata. These constitute very different strategies for constructing aural-historical narratives.

At the same time that we pursued our technical tasks, I also engaged Sultan in a series of conversations (some formal, some casual) about his motivations for building the archive and his goals for the future. I was particularly curious about what prompted musicians in the lofts to record themselves in such a widespread and systematic way. Part of the story was technological, as the 1960s had seen an explosion in the sales of amateur recording equipment. Tape historian David Morton has described how prior to this time, tape technology had been limited mostly to educational and military settings, with the necessary equipment being too expensive for most home users. The situation changed with the introduction of cheaper, transistorized recorders in the late 1950s, which in turn was followed by further advances such as the 8-track and the cassette. By the late 1960s, sales of tape recorders in the United States were approaching ten million dollars per year with the home market leading the charge.[17] Sultan himself was a part of this wave, obtaining his first recorder (a Uher brand unit) around this time.

In light of the long history of records as a central locus of jazz practice, it is perhaps no surprise that musicians would embrace the opportunity to create their own recordings. Yet as Jonathan Sterne cautions, the mere existence of a new technology is not enough to guarantee its adoption.[18] To gain traction, it must fill some cultural need, whether or not it is explicitly acknowledged by users. The most significant question, therefore, revolves less upon the mere *fact* of recording, and more about the social and professional functions that it fulfilled. In my interviews with Sultan, he identified at least four overlapping motivations that animated his efforts as a recordist: pedagogy, commercial use, historical preservation, and sonic experimentation.

By "pedagogical use" I mean the use of tapes in musicians' attempts to improve their musical skills through autodidactic learning strategies. Sultan cited this as his first inspiration for recording himself in the 1960s: "My [initial] motivation [for recording] was a learning process . . . I'd listen back and say, 'Okay, next time we play I'm gonna do it better.' That's really what my motive was in the beginning. I used to practice by myself and put it on tape. I'd listen to it and then [record] over it, fifty times on the same tape! Things of that nature, just to see if I was developing."[19] Such techniques were used in group rehearsals as well, which would be recorded and listened to together to promote discussion and development. A large percentage of the tapes in Sultan's collection consist of rehearsals taped for such purposes. Tape therefore acted as a supplement to other forms of autodidacticism that were common among avant garde improvisers.[20]

Commercial motivation could take a number of forms, which only sometimes involved actively publishing and selling records. Recordings could also be used for purposes like compiling demos to send to record companies or concert promoters. Several tapes in Sultan's collections are marked as "samplers" of his band Aboriginal Music Society, made up of short excerpts dubbed from other tapes.[21] In some cases, tapes recorded for other reasons could also be repurposed for commercial use. This tactic can be seen in a memo from the mid-1970s detailing plans for an upcoming radio appearance to promote Sultan's New York Musicians Organization (NYMO). The memo requests that the recipient (Sultan's collaborator Ali Abuwi) locate and bring along eleven tapes that the group had recorded at a festival the previous year.[22] Though the reels were initially recorded simply to document the event (no plans for commercial release were in place), they were easily repurposed as marketing tools to help promote future NYMO events.

The goal of historical preservation is the one that aligns most closely with common conceptions of the archive. Performances were preserved simply because the musicians believed their work had historical importance and could provide valuable lessons for future artists, activists, and fans. Sultan recalls being encouraged in this direction by older musicians, such as alto saxophonist Sonny Simmons:

> [My attitude toward recording] shifted when I started playing with other people and I said, "Oh man, that didn't sound that bad! Next time I'm gonna bring my tape recorder! I'm gonna see if I can save some of this stuff!" After a few years I figured out that I was documenting it, so I took on the term documentarian. Sonny [Simmons] was saying "Someday this stuff is going to be worth something!" I got encouragement from older musicians in that area. "It's good that you young boys are doing this." That kind of stuff.[23]

These comments further demonstrate how the goals of historical documentation and economic advancement could be intertwined. Sultan diligently recorded the more high-profile events that he produced, such as the 1972 New York Musicians Festival. As part of the proceedings, he assembled a team of recordists and filmmakers to capture performances throughout the city, with the hope of creating a documentary titled "The New Music Scene in New York." Though the final film never materialized, a handful of the source recordings remain in Sultan's collection.[24]

Finally, tapes could be used as experimentalist compositional tools to explore new combinations of sound. I use the term in the manner suggested by Benjamin Piekut who (paraphrasing Michael Nyman) defines experimentalism as a practice that focuses on "fluid processes instead of static objects; antiteleological procedures instead of goal-driven works."[25] This category frequently overlaps with pedagogical uses, but a crucial delineation can be drawn based on the role that recording plays in the musical process. Tapes I refer to as pedagogical are often explicitly teleological, as they were intended for review, critique, and self-improvement. Such use promotes the gradual development of specific musical goals, geared toward reproducibility and technical facility. Those that I refer to as experimental foreground unplanned musical happenings designed to generate and/or capture an irreproducible moment. The tape itself becomes the only goal of recording, whereas in pedagogical use the main goal is to improve future performances. A prime example can be heard on tape number T0163 in the Sultan collection. Recorded outdoors in Woodstock during the late 1960s, the recording consists entirely of Sultan and one or two associates playing sparse improvisations to the accompaniment of a lake filled with croaking frogs.[26]

Slippage between these four categories was, and remains, frequent. Material once intended for pedagogical use could later be deemed strong enough to put on a commercial record; tapes made to document live events could be overdubbed into experimental audio pastiches; and any material can potentially be repurposed by historians. In this respect, the *deployment* of archival materials becomes as crucial as their *inscription* in establishing the living significance of an artifact. When I spoke with musicians and collectors about how the tapes should be used today, I received a wide range of responses that largely mirrored the original motivations cited for recording them in the first place.

This ongoing elision between diverse forms of deployment—especially in regard to the relationship between the commercial and the historical—complicates certain assumptions about the ontological status of archival objects. Writing about corporate, administrative, and state archives, Sven Spieker posits three locations that traditionally define the life of documents: the office, the archive, and the registry. The office refers to where documents circulate while they are still in use, the archive to where they go once they are out of circulation. The registry occupies a liminal space between the two, where items are sorted and prepared for their final resting place in the archive. In such a model, the document enters the archive only at the point at which it is no longer needed—when it has essentially become garbage. In relation to the office, the archive is not where things go to be remembered, but to be forgotten.[27]

Such a model fails to account for an archive like Sultan's in that it assumes a sharp separation between the categories of "circulating" and "archival." The private archive suggests the potential to transcend this distinction by allowing objects to function in multiple modalities at once, oscillating between old and new uses. The goals of such archives—especially when they remain in the hands of their original founders—need not be directed only toward future historians' efforts to (in Spieker's somewhat sarcastic phrase) "turn garbage into culture."[28] Just as often, materials—especially recordings—can continue to function in their original roles, in some instances at the same time that they are being refashioned as historical objects.

The practice of repackaging archival tapes as commercial records provides a familiar example. Musicians regularly use their collections as source material to produce and market new releases of never-before-heard performances.[29] In one sense, the tapes' ongoing commercial viability underscores a connection to their original function. The usage is unequivocally nonarchival (in the sense described by Spieker) in that it indicates an ongoing form of circulation. It simultaneously embraces and eschews its own designation as archival, intimating new possibilities for what/where an archive might be. The fact that such initiatives also connect to loft-era ideals of ownership and self-production lends further credence to such a reading. But on the other hand, an alternative reading might suggest that the presentation of such releases as "historical," "archival," or "from the vaults" tells of a discrete change in the perceived status of the materials among consumers. They imply the possibility of two distinct—but by no means mutually exclusive—modes of listening: the appreciation of music as an aesthetic object in the present (music *qua* music, music as beautiful), and the appreciation of music as a window into the past (music *qua* artifact, music as data).

The Master and the Outtake: Sonny Simmons's Archival Presence. With these issues in mind, let us examine a selection of tapes to ask what stories they can tell. Our example returns once again to alto saxophonist Sonny Simmons, a frequent collaborator of Sultan's and one of the most heavily represented artists in the collection. The two met in the early 1960s, when a young Sultan approached Simmons after hearing him play a concert in Los Angeles. Simmons had already developed a strong professional reputation, both as a leader and through his experience as a sideman with Eric Dolphy. The two struck up a quick friendship over a shared set of musical and political interests, and they remained in contact during the years that followed. One recurring topic of discussion was a vision for creating pan-nationalistic forms of black music, which they referred to using the term "aboriginal." This wasn't intended to refer to any particular aboriginal groups, but stemmed from a broader search for the origins of African diasporic artistry. Sultan explains his use of the word as deriving from the terms "abba" (father) and "origin."[30] Simmons ended up referencing the idea in his composition "Aborigine Dance in Scotland," which he recorded with the Elvin Jones / Jimmy Garrison Sextet in 1963.[31] Sultan embraced the idea even more wholeheartedly a few years later when he formed his performance group "Aboriginal Music Society."[32]

Simmons relocated to New York in 1966, joined by his wife and trumpet collaborator Barbara Donald. Sultan (playing mostly bass at the time) followed soon thereafter, along with drummer Paul Smith. On the East Coast, the four musicians began rehearsing together frequently, referring to their ensemble as "The Depth Probers." They were periodically joined by a tenor saxophonist named Brian Ross (who went by the nickname "Nairb"). The group rehearsed in numerous spaces throughout lower Manhattan, including the art gallery True Creation from Vibrations, and Sultan's small basement apartment on 3rd Street. Though Simmons chose not to use them for his first two albums on the ESP label, the ensemble (minus Nairb) is heard on the album *Manhattan Egos* from 1969.[33] Sultan and Smith also performed separately as a rhythm section duo, jamming with other musicians on the scene. The crest of their activities came right around the time Sultan also obtained his first tape recorder, which resulted in several hours of rehearsal recordings.[34]

By showcasing the process of free improvisation within amicable extended sessions, these rehearsals offer a window into the everyday musical practices of the early loft era. They differ in critical ways from the polished works that appear on commercial records. This point becomes especially apparent when comparing pieces available in both rehearsal and album formats. Take, for instance, the piece "Zarak's Symphony," which Simmons included on his 1968 album *Music from the Spheres*.[35] The album version begins with a tricky, angular head with multiple shifts in meter, feel, and tempo (see example 1). The form is a modified AABA, with a mostly triple-meter A section, a Latin jazz bridge, and a free rhythm interlude in between. The melody is followed by a blistering solo by Simmons, who plays quite freely despite the rhythm section (Jim Zitro, Juney Booth, and Michael Cohen) initially maintaining a triple-meter pulse. The time slowly begins to become more flexible over the course of the piece's three solos, with Simmons followed by Donald's bebop-inflected trumpet and Cohen's piano. A brief, dissonant shout chorus kicks off the most unfettered playing on the track, an ecstatic "energy music" improvisation performed by the entire ensemble. The uproar eventually fades into a short bass solo, which sets the stage for the return of the piece's head. All told, the full track clocks in at just under thirteen minutes.

Within Sultan's collection are several Simmons rehearsals of the very same piece, spread over three different tapes from the late 1960s. Instead of the group from the album, we instead find the full Depth Probers lineup of Simmons, Sultan, Donald, Ross, and Smith. Several of the members appear to be learning the piece, as the sessions include multiple repeated runs through the difficult melody line. Although much of the conversation between playing is cut out, a few takes focus simply on the head alone. The tape cuts off after each time through, perhaps to allow the musicians time to listen to the recording, discuss the performance, and make additional tweaks (as usual, the recordist declined to record these nonplaying sections of the rehearsal). Once the group decides to embark on a full take, however, all interruptions cease. The musicians launch into an extended thirty-minute version of the piece, with the bulk of the time devoted to solos with the full ensemble.[36]

Thus far, none of this should seem all that surprising to anyone with even minimal experience with musical rehearsal. The tapes simply appear to document a band practicing a new piece, honing it until it becomes polished enough to present in concert or on record. The repeated emphasis on the head (the section requiring the most coordinated technical precision) would undoubtedly support such a

EXAMPLE 1. Sonny Simmons, *Zarak's Symphony (Head)*.

reading. The extended solos in the full archival take can similarly be heard as a process of collective development, with the group gradually coalescing around a unified sound within the context of the piece's overall texture. Listening to the tapes in this way would therefore present the rehearsals as a teleological progression leading up to a finished product, a model that essentially falls in line with a fairly conservative "work-centric" concept of musical production. The notion of the musical work—a definitive, reified version of a musical object—is most often associated with the role of the score in Western classical music, a model that has been extensively problematized by musicologists such as Lydia Goehr.[37] Although some scholars have argued that the improvisatory nature of jazz recording inherently upsets the work concept,[38] others like Tony Whyton contend that in jazz it is often transferred onto recordings, which carry the potential to become similarly canonical. This is especially palpable when recorded versions are re-created by subsequent performers, the main example discussed by Whyton.[39] But even without such reanimation, a more subtle version of the work concept is enacted whenever we conceive of a recording as being a definitive version. The record industry's practice of privileging a single "master take" provides one such example. In the case of Simmons, a teleological understanding of the relationship between the album (commercial) and rehearsal (archival) versions of "Zarak's Symphony" suggests a similar type of understanding. Here, the work is represented by the album version of the piece, an authoritative document frozen in wax, sold to consumers, circulated globally, and entered irrevocably into Simmons's discography. The private sessions represent nothing more than early, unfinished drafts.

But is this the only possible interpretation? Contrast this example with another set of archival recordings, this time of Simmons's "Seven Dances of Salome" from the album *Manhattan Egos*.[40] Unlike "Zarak's Symphony," the piece has no tricky unison heads for the ensemble to master. Indeed, there is no pre-composed melody at all. Its structure is little more than a predetermined texture and harmonic palette. Simmons's English horn and improvised vocalizing are juxtaposed against the hand drums of Sultan and Voodoo Bembe (possibly a pseudonym for the flautist Bembe Shaki). The improvisations focus on variants of the harmonic minor scale in an effort to evoke a soundscape of the Middle East (Sultan referred to them as "Mohammedan" scales.)[41] Beyond this, no other elements are predetermined. Sultan recalled regularly holding such extended sessions in this format, and the archive houses at least six tapes along these lines, totaling over two hours of material.[42] The longest such exploration continues for over an hour without interruption. The commercial version, by contrast, lasts a mere seven minutes.

If the "Zarak's Symphony" rehearsals can be imagined as primarily teleological, the "Salome" tapes are trickier to theorize in this way. Although the sheer quantity of the latter tapes gives them a larger footprint in the archive, the recordings offer little sense of gradual development or honing. There is no stopping and starting, no repeating difficult sections, no gradual improvement in feel or texture. Rather, they appear to be convivial extended sessions for the pleasure of making music together. Viewed in this way, the album version is not an apotheosis of everything that came before. It is merely a fragment, a tiny window into a joyous extended exploration that the two musicians shared over many separate sessions. Reading backwards, it becomes possible to reframe the extended archival take of "Zarak's Symphony" in a similar light. In numerous ways, this longer take less resembles the streamlined album version than it does other extended blowing sessions found in Sultan's collection. Several other tapes of the Simmons band feature completely free improvisations that last thirty minutes or more.

Thinking of the album as a window rather than a final product also coincides with other descriptions of loft music-making. As noted earlier, one of the more striking aspects of the loft movement was its radical dedication to the pleasures of extended improvisation, whether in public, semi-public, or private settings. This has been a major musical legacy of the lofts as well: speaking generally, the New York school of "energy music" players tended to move away from work-oriented ideals, emphasizing instead the affective potentials of minimally planned collective improvisation. From this perspective, the sessions captured on Sultan's private tapes are not merely a developmental step progressing toward a more finished work, but a window into an artistic community that placed tremendous value on these very sorts of informal gatherings. The epistemological status of the rehearsal / recording binary is therefore inverted. The commercial album, for all its polish, appears as little more than an overmediated remnant that distorts a scene's sociomusical values in order to conform to technological limits and capitalist strictures. The real aesthetic essence of music-making—an intimate, co-creative, real-time process—always supersedes the frozen, declawed product of the final recording. The master is always an outtake.

But in the end, this reading, too, falls flat by relying on an overly narrow epistemology. To simply invert the binary of what constitutes the music's "true" essence misses the point. A more nuanced reading recognizes that loft artists engaged in diverse activities to advance a variety of musical, social, and economic goals. Some of these goals were explicitly tied to capitalist advancement, particularly in their calls for self-determination via musician-owned venues, record labels, and businesses. Others were less profit-oriented, and focused more on building egalitarian communities in private settings. These multiple objectives present no contradiction, but rather highlight the musicians' roles as resourceful agents navigating a complex network of overlapping musical terrains. Each performance context forced them to employ different strategies and set new priorities. A recording date offered a discrete set of affordances and limitations (including technological, social, and economic considerations). A private session offered another. A nightclub yet a third. And so on. The fact that musicians approached each situation differently should not be seen as conceding some mythical ideal of artistic purity. Instead, it demonstrates the radical agency of artists to continually reimagine their musical practice and craft performances that respond (as improvisation always must) to the environment at hand.

Rather than offering a story about truth, here the archive speaks to the multiplicity of artistic life. It reminds us, to quote Jed Rasula, that "[A]ll the little stories do not so easily add up to a big story. The megascopic aggregate of all the little stories is not a story at all, but a *big picture,* an image of totality that masquerades as explanation."[43] The lofts were not well suited to the tidiness of linear narratives; they instead provided an artistic village in which music was folded into the fabric of the everyday. It did not offer a sequence of legendary moments, but a neighborhood of nurturing spaces. By eluding and eliding the forced chronology of commercial discography, the loft archive sheds light on a richer canvas.

II. Paper / The Archive We Read

Sultan's paper holdings are sequenced in 256 separate folders, most of which contain no exterior marks. The material is widely varied, blending personal and professional concerns. Much of it stems from Sultan's activities between 1972 and 1976, during the height of his time with NYMO. Working alongside trumpeter James DuBoise during these years, Sultan produced ambitious festivals at locations throughout the city. These activities generated a steady stream of documents: funding requests, event schedules, press announcements, brochures, internal memos, and so on. The folders have moved through several locations in the intervening decades, but have not undergone any systematic processing, resulting in a fairly haphazard arrangement. Very little was thrown out, leaving multiple photocopies of certain documents. These duplicates sometimes make it difficult to differentiate originals from copies, or rough drafts from final versions. If we found an unmarked budget, it might be an early projection, a working draft, a final tally, or a report to send back to funders. Ambiguity over such details often made it challenging to interpret the significance of particular items.

For all the value that it preserves, the paper archive can create insidious distortions. Consider the case of a collective named "Intramedia, Inc.," an organization that led a brief but busy existence in early 1975.[44] It was founded by a group of college students from the City University of New York and New York University who wished to advocate for an increased minority presence in the media. Sultan (though unaffiliated with either university) became a member early in the group's existence and preserved a wealth of organizational documents including meeting minutes, grant proposals, and correspondence. With nods to Marshall McLuhan and Karl Marx, Intramedia defined its organizational mission as follows: "In this rapid moving age when the media is the message, it is imperative that minorities be involved in those processes. The media is a tool through which we learn of ourselves and our environment... Often, the communication arts fail to relate [to] minorities as individual entities. As a result, certain ethnic groups are alienated from themselves and attempt to conform to other cultures, totally unaware of their own."[45]

Fueled by a strong sense of purpose, the students generated an enormous amount of paperwork in a relatively short time. By March, a lengthy constitution and set of bylaws had been prepared and distributed, with annotations made by a lawyer.[46] Plans were drawn up for a multimedia festival to begin in June, with programs on the following themes: Third World Women (6/4/75), Third World Liberation (8/29/75), Black Arts in America (10/19/75), The Theatre Ritual (12/26/75), Black in America (2/15/76), Black Culture: A Historical Perspective (3/17/76), and The Black Male (6/25/76). Proposed guests included star performers like Stevie Wonder, Nancy Wilson, Earth Wind and Fire, and McCoy Tyner, alongside academics and social activists.[47] The group also developed proposals for a massive multimedia archive and information center, slated to hold a library, film and video production sites, a movie theater to present films by minority artists, and classroom facilities for a media training program. Budget projections ranged from $300,000 to over $1 million, depending on the document.[48] To validate their efforts, the group established an advisory council of local media professionals, including a reporter from the *New York Daily News* and a professor of communications at Rutgers University.[49] They were prolific writers; Sultan's collection houses dozens of documents such as pitches for radio and television shows, meeting minutes, and funding proposals. By sheer volume, the Sultan Archive contains more material about Intramedia than nearly any other organization, with the lone exception being Sultan's own activities with NYMO. Looking at the documents in isolation, one might assume that the Intramedia project was one of the most significant episodes in Sultan's life, if not in the loft scene more generally.

But oral history tells a very different story. By Sultan's recollection, none of the group's projects ever got off the ground.[50] At the time of their founding in the early spring, the students generated copious amounts of prose espousing revolutionary ideals. As a paper presence in the archive, their concern with formal structure and articulating clear goals gives them the appearance of tight coordination, especially in comparison with the more casual documents written by some of Sultan's other affiliates. But before any of the projects took shape, the group's fervor seemed to dissipate. Perhaps not coincidentally, this took place right around the end of the academic year. In the absence of any actual programming, Intramedia's organizational prowess turns out to have been little more than a façade. In the end, many of Sultan's other, less text-oriented projects succeeded in producing far more actual programming than Intramedia would ever muster.

This disjuncture highlights the nontransparency of archival preservation. Archival holdings do not offer unmediated connections to the past, but emerge tautologically from processes geared toward *generating the types of artifacts* that the archive is best-equipped to preserve. A collection designed to hold paper, for example, tends to overemphasize groups that are more skilled in generating paperwork. As always, the archive preserves too much and never enough.

Paper Identities and the Office. As others have observed, the gaps and omissions in an archive can reveal as much as the materials that are present.[51] One conspicuous absence in Sultan's papers is a dearth of direct musician-to-musician correspondence. The gap could perhaps be partially explained by the nature of the loft neighborhood. The geographic proximity of musicians (along with, obviously, the presence of telephones) likely meant that personal contact did not need to rely on the mediation of the written word. Likewise, there is very little paper documentation of any music that was performed (whether through sheet music, set lists, rehearsal schedules, descriptions of pieces under development, etc.). Sultan's artistic proclivities may have contributed to this absence as well, since his own musical approach leaned heavily toward improvisational formats involving minimal pre-composed elements. Archives kept by those who focused more on written composition might be more likely to house materials of this type. Saxophonist Sam Rivers, for one, penned a wealth of compositions during the loft area, resulting in a sizable sheet music library that became the basis for many of his ensembles later in life.[52]

If Sultan's papers contain little in the way of personal correspondence or musical practice, what do they contain? Primarily, the documents trace the development not of individual identities but of *organizational* identities, with NYMO being the most pervasive. This corporate underpinning of the paper archive is an important detail. In almost every case, the documents generated by NYMO (grant applications, budgets, press releases, etc.) were tools for engaging with legal or corporate entities. We might say that the medium of paper functioned as a type of mechanism, an instrument designed to meet a set of standards and/or trigger specific effects within a system.[53] For this reason, paper—like any archival presence—cannot be read as a straightforward reflection of reality. Paper emerged primarily at those moments when musicians needed it in order to interact with, and benefit from, particular types of power structures. The politics of arts funding is a key linchpin. For many funders, it was (and is) only through acts of writing that an organization can exist in a formal sense, an overtly graphocentric way of adjudicating the value of social groups. Obtaining state and private grants requires facility with myriad paper technologies: incorporation papers, program proposals, press releases, projected and finalized budgets, mission statements and organizational philosophies, final reports, press kits, letters of support, lists of past events, and so on. These are the exact type of materials that are heavily represented within the Sultan archive. In the eyes of arts funders, it was not enough to merely play together, live together, or act together; jazz collectives could only exist by writing themselves into being.

Sultan's paper archive therefore tells a story of organization-building. In doing so, it presents a narrative that is somewhat richer than the offhand accounts of lofts as low-budget, pieced-together affairs that relied on little more than word-of-mouth and a makeshift stage (not that these didn't exist—more on this topic follows shortly). For the more formally administered spaces, the broader goals of self-actualization necessitated a great deal of proficiency in the "paper logics" of the American office of the 1970s.[54] I use this phrase—rather than more familiar terms such as "literacy" or "writing"—to highlight the fact that deploying the *mechanism* of paper required more than the ability to generate prose, though this was obviously a crucial factor. To be effective, documents had to follow standardized templates, display certain types of graphics, exist in the correct number of copies, be arranged in a specific order, and arrive in the hands of the proper person at the appropriate moment in time. We might think of these factors as the recombinatory dynamics of paper, which were every bit as crucial as expository elegance.

An illustration of the contingencies of paper can be seen in an episode from 1975 in which Sultan and DuBoise sought to apply for a grant from the National Endowment for the Arts. According to a letter written later by Sultan, the group had made both written and telephoned requests for the application materials, but they never arrived. As the deadline drew near, the musicians decided they wouldn't have time to submit the application by mail, so Sultan embarked on an overnight drive to Washington DC (the trip was delayed further when Sultan fell asleep behind the wheel and ended up in an accident in Harve de Grace, Maryland).[55] He eventually arrived in Washington and obtained the form, which he and DuBoise subsequently rushed to complete and send off before the April 15 deadline. Later in the month, however, the two noticed several errors in their hastily prepared application, and sent a follow-up letter to make the corrections and explain the cause of the delay.[56] At each stage in the story, the efficacy of paper relies not only on the content of what is written, but also on the bureaucratic contingencies of formatting and location. The musicians were initially unable to complete the application because: (a) they did not have the relevant paper form, and (b) without the form they didn't know the correct format to follow in their application. The contingencies of the deadline (the moment when the paper must be in the proper hands) results in a frantic journey and a hastily prepared document. This, in turn, requires the creation of a second document to correct the initial errors, which—being sent after the deadline—is further required to offer an account of its own tardiness.

To state the matter more simply: the effective use of paper required a well-organized and labor-intensive office structure. The time and energy that this demanded was not lost on musicians, nor was the fact that not everyone on the scene was equally adept at handling bureaucratic responsibilities. One early NYMO document consists of a handwritten list of musicians named as "People who can deal with the press," implying an opinion that engaging with reporters required levels of articulateness, savvy, and willingness that not all possessed.[57] Musicians who were known to have office skills would be in high demand, occasionally more than they bargained for. During our interview in 2009, James DuBoise described how he eventually became so bogged down with organizing duties that he stopped playing the trumpet altogether for a few years. His focus on administration ultimately led to a long career serving on selection committees for the New York State Council on the Arts. John Fischer was similarly sought out for his organizational prowess, which he honed by staging art happenings and bread-baking festivals in the 1960s. Fischer had no plans to manage a loft until he was approached by the brothers Darius, Danny, and Chris Brubeck, who had just moved into a large space on Broadway and were interested in holding concerts. Having little interest in the administrative details, the brothers enlisted Fischer, who proceeded to transform the space into one of the more prominent loft venues of the time. The Brubecks remained largely behind-the-scenes and were infrequently seen at the space, partially due to an extensive touring schedule with the Two Generations of Brubeck band. From their more stable financial position, the decision to secure the assistance of Fischer allowed them to focus their energies on their musical activities.

Such divisions of labor were not uncommon in the lofts, despite the common rhetoric of the spaces being "artist-organized." While musicians generally received the most credit, a number of venues delegated certain tasks to underrecognized support figures, leaving the artists free to focus on their craft. A number of women took on essential behind-the-scenes roles, an often overlooked detail that reveals gender disparities in regard to labor and prestige. At Studio Rivbea, Bea Rivers was in charge of most of the space's administrative and financial oversight, while her husband Sam scheduled the musicians and pursued his own artistic projects. Of all the lofts, Rivbea was among the most successful at courting grant funding for their annual summer festivals, a testament to Bea's productivity and efficacy.

Similarly, in the early years of Studio We, Sultan and DuBoise enlisted the help of Dr. Hetty Fox, a percussionist and community activist with a doctorate in sociology. Fox assisted in the office work of Studio We from roughly 1972 to 1974. Though she would later characterize her contributions as little more than "typing," her skill is evident in the documents from these years, which rank among the more professionally prepared materials in the collection.[58] Her background in academia may also have helped her contribute to the many mission statements and grant funding templates that the Studio generated around this same time. Several spouses of musicians also helped with various day-to-day tasks in the lofts, including DuBoise's wife, Andrea, and John Fischer's wife, Francis. Fischer further recalled how Francis helped financially support their family while he pursued grants to advance his career as a sculptor and pianist. Such support continues a long tradition of jazz spouses acting as crucial, overlooked partners who are necessary to artistic production, a phenomenon that has been documented by Robin Kelley.[59]

But arguably the loft period's most striking female administrator was Cobi Narita, a Japanese American organizer who was appointed executive director of the Collective Black Artists (CBA). Her story is unique enough to warrant a brief detour.

Born in California in 1925, Narita's family spent years detained in a California internment camp during World War II. In a recent autobiographical essay, she traces her love of organizing to this time, describing a camp-wide newsletter that she published to keep occupants informed of marriages, births, and other announcements.[60] She remained in California throughout her early adulthood, holding numerous office jobs to provide for her seven children. A lifelong jazz lover, she also volunteered at the Los Angeles nightclub Memory Lane, where she met a steady stream of musicians passing through town. She moved to New York in 1969 and grew increasingly involved in the jazz scene, first as a fan and later as a volunteer. Before long, she worked with Jazz Interactions, Inc., an organization that produced concerts and maintained a telephone hotline promoting jazz events.[61]

The same year that Narita arrived in the city, a group of New York artists established the CBA, a collective designed to offer performance opportunities and professional support services to black artists. Early CBA initiatives included newsletters, flyer distribution, educational workshops, professional training seminars, and the formation of an 18-piece orchestra called the CBA Ensemble. Over time, the group's programs had expanded to a degree that they required a director with experience in fundraising and managing an office. Narita's professional background made her well suited for such a role, and she was officially appointed as the group's executive director in 1974.

The disjuncture of installing an Asian American female as director of a black organization did not go unnoticed by the membership. Narita would later characterize her time with the CBA as follows:

> They needed someone to help them get funding and I had a track record of being able to do that. The first year, I was able to get them $110,000 for their projects, which was a pretty big amount. Even though I was Executive Director, I only took a half salary. I wanted most of the money to go to the orchestra and its projects . . . The three main directors were Reggie Workman, Jimmy Owens, and Kenny Rogers, the ones who ran the orchestra. They were the ones who hired me. Two and a half years later they were also the ones who fired me—they really thought a male black person should be in that job; it just looked better than an Asian woman. I couldn't believe it. Later, they came to me and said that letting me go was the worst mistake they ever made.[62]

Looking back, perhaps it isn't surprising that Narita's race and gender became a point of contention. The episode speaks to the too-frequently gendered nature of black liberation movements of the 1960s and '70s, in which, to quote Angela Davis, "some black activists ... confuse[d] their political activity with the assertion of their maleness."[63] Indeed, it seems more unusual that she was ever appointed in the first place. Yet the choice becomes more legible alongside the parallel organizational positions held by other women during the same timespan. In this light, it becomes part of a larger trend of women administrators working behind-the-scenes to advance the goals of musician-organized groups. Narita's account of her departure speaks to the power structures underlying the episode; her firing was not the result of any professional failing, but was based on the fact that her highly visible position undercut the group's rhetoric of (black and/or artist and/or male) self-determination. Narita would go on to launch a series of subsequent organizations, including the Universal Jazz Coalition, the New York Women's Jazz Festival, and the performance venue Cobi's Place.

Narita's administrative expertise was a boon to the CBA, which saw the height of its activities during her tenure. And while her contributions do not really manifest themselves in the realm of discography, they leave a larger mark in the paper archive. In the Sultan archive, the CBA materials that have been preserved date largely from Narita's tenure, and show deployments of paper that far outstrip many other organizations. In addition to mailings promoting their own activities, the CBA offered a low-cost service in which they would also circulate flyers for other musicians and organizations (with a CBA notice added to the top). The creation and distribution of paper notices is therefore not merely framed as a method for promoting themselves, but as a service offered as part of the group's larger mission. The group's newsletter *Expansions*—of which Sultan saved the 1974/75 "souvenir" edition—sits among the most professionally designed magazines distributed by any jazz collective, with dense photo spreads accompanying descriptions of CBA programming. But most of all, Narita's success in fundraising may stand as her most foremost accomplishment during her time with the CBA.[64] In each of these achievements, Narita's facility with paper and the mandates of the office were what constituted her legacy within the musicians' movement.[65]

But the CBA is not the only organization that leaves traces in the paper archive. The documents in the Sultan collection reveal the enormous breadth of organizing activities that animated 1970s New York. In pamphlets, newsletters, invitations, meeting minutes, and other materials, the archive paints a picture of dozens of organizations of all sizes and orientations. We encounter the ghosts of groups with names like Poettential Unlimited, Brooklyn Musicians Registry, Afrikan Carnival Association, Community Crossroads, Menwem Writers Workshop, Consortium of Jazz Organizations, Storefront Museum, Black Theater Alliance, and many, many others. Some of these were groups that Sultan was directly involved with for a good number of years; others were simply one-off mailings. The most coherent trend is a consistent desire to connect artistic practice to broader streams of cultural and political activism, especially in regard to African American communities.

FIGURE 21. Page from packet of materials sent by Nation Time Productions. Circa 1971. Image courtesy of the Juma Sultan Archive (F0143.04).

To take one example, culled from a faded, typewritten cover page of a promotional packet for a theater production company:

> We, of "NATION TIME" Productions, being of African descent, believe in the traditions of our ancestors. We also believe in the judgment of our present-day prophets and seers. We further believe in the reason of our selves / the people / the community / each other. We are the same people . . .
>
> We do not believe in "art for the sake of art." We believe that "form follows function"; that creativity springs from need; and that design or motif are expressions directly related to and coming from our own life-style. We are not singing and dancing in the abstract; as it were. We are, in fact, "saying something."[66]

The message is signed with a set of six Egyptian hieroglyphs, spelling out the first name of the company's director, Kimako Baraka (Fig. 21). The packet ends with a final page listing the seven principles of Kwanzaa.[67]

It is difficult to give a sense of the totality of the archive through a single document. Yet by dwelling in Sultan's paper collection, I was struck by how consistently such messages appeared, how powerfully the "Black Arts Imperative" permeated the collection as a mobilizing force. The place where this message asserted itself most clearly was in the paper artifacts emanating from dozens of arts organizations grappling with such issues. While such sentiments may not have been universal throughout all of the city's musicians, their importance in Sultan's orbit is preserved unmistakably in word and image, through ink and paper.

The Historicity of Flyers. Not all activities in the lofts were carefully planned by organizations with a formal office. Both the glory and curse of the loft era is that so much music was played without official sanction or detailed planning. The ease of obtaining space in Lower Manhattan meant that musicians could stage events with minimal preparation and infrastructure. Often all that was needed was an empty room. Not surprisingly, such performances are conspicuously elusive within the paper archive, as they generate a minimum of written documentation. In many cases, only a single document survives: the flyer.

Flyers provided the simplest, cheapest, and most widely-used method for artists to promote self-produced events. The materials often took on an unabashed DIY aesthetic, pasting together photos, hand-drawn illustrations, and printed or handwritten texts. The arrival of low-cost copy shops like the Village Copier allowed musicians to print hundreds of copies for less than five cents each.[68] They would then post them throughout the neighborhood using wheat paste. Violinist Jason Kao Hwang remembered the impact of this as a young NYU student in 1975: "If you wanted to figure out what you wanted to do on any particular night, you would just look at the local lamppost and there were tons of flyers." Hwang recalled attending numerous events he learned about through flyers, which helped him become acclimated to the New York scene. Later, he began promoting his own concerts in the same way: "There was a certain point where there were so many flyers that you would go out at, say, six o'clock and put up your flyer. By the time you walked from Avenue A all the way to Hudson and then came back, the flyers you put up at six were already covered up by someone else. So then you'd have to put yours back up!"[69] Hwang's account of jockeying for space speaks to the sheer density of flyers at the time. In a setting where many events were put on with minimal funds, flyering was significantly cheaper than other forms of publicity, such as purchasing small ads in local newspapers or coordinating direct mailings.

This volume of production leaves its mark on the archive as well. Several musicians showed me thoughtfully preserved collections that they saved in boxes or scrapbooks. Whenever it was possible throughout my interviews, I would try to arrive with photocopied flyers of Sultan's, which tended to elicit wistful smiles and spark reminiscences about the events in question. William Parker is one of a number of musicians who has amassed an extensive set that documents his career dating back over forty years. The collection served as a vital resource for discographer Rick Lopez, who has assembled a detailed online sessionography chronicling every performance throughout Parker's prolific career.[70] When a hard copy of the sessionography was published in 2014, it featured numerous reproductions from Parker's collection.[71] Such recycling is not uncommon; flyers are frequently used as artwork for recent reissues and archival recordings, where they offer a visual flavor of the period. A few nonmusicians are equally enthusiastic about amassing them, with loft habitues like Irving Stone and Jim Eigo compiling sizable collections.[72]

In many instances throughout my interviews, flyers seemed to take on an almost talismanic importance. They were second only to tapes as the preferred medium for tapping into the auratic power of the past. I believe that the source of this power lies in the multiple registers in which flyers speak. On the level of positivist history, they record basic personnels, dates, and place data for events that are sparsely recorded elsewhere. They can simultaneously help inform social histories by sketching the flows of musical practice across a changing landscape of DIY urban repurposing. As visual artworks, they document the graphic styles (in terms of both fine art and design) that accompanied the music. For fans, flyers exist as tangible objects that connect us to a romantic past, conjuring images of secret underground events attended by a select few. For musicians, they serve as something between a family photo album (directed inward, to preserve personal memories) and a professional portfolio (directed outward, to demonstrate experience and creative output).

In each of these capacities, the flyer—like the archive itself—provides a way to attenuate loss. It works to circumvent death by carving out an exterior location of memory, etched upon materials that survive, almost accidentally, beyond the context of their creation. Its archival function relies upon the two crucial moments of transformation alluded to earlier by Spieker: the shift from circulation to obsolescence, and from obsolescence to the archive.[73] The moment a performance takes place, its flyers immediately transform from pieces of functional publicity to scraps of garbage. They are torn down at the next available opportunity, without a hint of remorse or regret. Their very effectiveness relies on this renewal; the space must be cleared to promote the next event. The decision to preserve a flyer, then, is the archival move *par excellence:* the conscious conversion of one type of functionality to another. It is, to again use Spieker's phrase, a literal move to transform "garbage into culture."[74] Such an action takes on marked significance in environments like the lofts, in which these disposable, photocopied bits of debris often provide our only link to the events that they record.

The impulse toward preserving flyers for loft artists therefore provides evidence of a desire to be "documented"—quite literally, to have their legacies inscribed upon paper. As with tape, to create a presence in the paper archive is to make oneself available to the enunciation of future histories.

III. Human / The Archive That Speaks Back

We conclude with a consideration of Sultan himself, the human presence who is author, subject, and object of his own collection. How do we account for Sultan's continued presence as living repository? He founded the archive, he administers the archive, but he is also, inescapably, an artifact within it. His memories provide crucial contexts and details that are not recorded in any other source. But, like any archival medium, they are also inherently fallible. Many times throughout our time together, Sultan's recollections would clash with details given in other materials we unearthed, requiring adjustment, reassessment, or an acceptance of uncertainty. His annotations were invaluable, but never absolute.

In considering Sultan as a presence in his own collection, I hope to accomplish two goals. First, I aim to frame the human presence in the archive not as unimpeachable truth (the mode of naïve oral history), nor as irreparably distorted (the mode of naïve document-based history). Instead, I place it within a larger network of meanings that are continuously transferred between various sites of inscription, all of which are incomplete. By taking this approach, I have no intention of dehumanizing the collector as some sort of agentless, inanimate storage medium. Quite the opposite—by creating exterior sites for recording traces of the past, the *practice* of archiving is profoundly human. It engenders new types of objects that are capable of speaking back to us and remembering what we cannot. This observation feeds directly into my second goal: foregrounding the complex intimacies involved in conducting collaborative ethnography with a (self-)archivist. As I indicated in the introduction to this chapter, my time with Sultan at times felt like a journey we embarked upon together, encountering unexpected objects that continually forced us to reevaluate our perceptions of the past. The feeling was no accident—it is the archive functioning exactly as it is designed to.

The Terms of Engagement: History, Memory, and the Archive. The relationship between human actors and archival collections has long been a central concern for librarians. Many archives, of course, begin in the possession of individuals who accumulate and arrange materials based on their own personal (and often idiosyncratic) preferences and associations. When such holdings are donated to institutional repositories, these preexisting frameworks can yield distinct challenges. The thorniest decision is whether to reorder the materials to correspond with the organizational system of the library, or instead to maintain the original order established by the donor. The latter approach—a principle known by the French term *respect des fonds*—tends to be preferred, and has become an important tenet of archival theory throughout the past century. This point underscores a broad professional awareness that the logic by which a collection is organized constitutes a key component of its meaning and value. The broad acceptance of this principle, however, does not mean that librarians always agree on how it should be defined; debates over the precise scope of *respect des fonds* have animated many of the major paradigm shifts that have occurred in archival science since the late nineteenth century.[75]

More recently, historians and philosophers writing in the wake of the archival turn have contemplated the topic of human archives very differently. For some, such as Jacques Derrida, the most basic definition of the archive entails a movement toward exteriorization. It emerges only at that moment when memory/knowledge/power moves outside of the sole possession of an individual and becomes inscribed/impressed upon an exterior surface. In the most conventional sense, this move involves some sort of transcription into some form of media, be it the written page, the photograph, or the visual artifact. Archives therefore act as a mechanical supplement to memory, but in doing so they simultaneously destroy and replace it.[76]

Exteriorization can function in a variety of ways. For Spieker, the decisive moment for corporate archives is not that of inscription, but rather the acknowledgment that materials are no longer in circulation. If we imagine a business document—say, an invoice—we see that the item has a unique corporate function from the moment it is created (a record of a transaction, a promise of moneys paid, a deadline, etc.). It is only *after* these functions are exhausted that such a document may be reassigned to the archive, a site where it takes on a new set of affordances.[77] Exteriorization thus occurs through the process of reassignment, the moment when the material is transferred, physically or conceptually, to a distant location. The gravity of exteriorization can perhaps also be projected onto anxieties over *respect des fonds*. The instant when materials are transferred from the private collector to the institutional repository acts as a liminal, exteriorizing moment that is easy to imagine as the archive's crucial (re)birth. What had previously been personal *becomes* archival at the moment it exits the realm of the private and enters the public institution.

But readings that place the archive as antithetical to private, interior, or community-based meanings have also been contested. Often, such discussions pivot on the relationships between the terms "history" and "memory," a distinction that has been blurred in a great deal of recent literature. The issue has been notably contentious for writers engaging with subaltern archives emerging from the ashes of colonial regimes. In the introduction to a compilation of essays about archival practice, Antoinette Burton discusses one such example regarding debates over the status of archival "facts" that emerged in South Africa's Truth and Reconciliation Commission after the fall of apartheid: "Such a project was and is tied to 'making public memory, publicly,' and as such it often pits conventional forms of knowledge about the past (History) against the claims of groups who have typically been disenfranchised by dominant regimes of truth but who are also seeking political rights—in ways that endanger the status and livelihoods of some, traumatize others, and make visible the extent to which national identities are founded on archival elisions, distortions, and secrets."[78] Burton's scholarship has been influential in recognizing the hegemonic power of state archives to limit the types of histories that are possible to write. In this example, the shift from history to memory acts as a powerful weapon for disenfranchised communities to push back against state-sanctioned narratives. Memory—both individual and cultural—becomes a critical tool for self-assertion and justice.

But this distinction need not imply that memories and archives are always at odds. A very different picture emerges in literature documenting subaltern archives, in which disenfranchised groups compile material to promote alternative accounts of the past. Here, archives serve as a crucial supplement to memories, both by providing documentary validation and by creating long-term repositories for recollections transcribed in interviews and recordings. It is this type of function that is conveyed by David Scott in an essay about his experiences with the Marcus Garvey collection at UCLA: "I gradually came to realize that embedded in the seemingly quotidian construction of this archive ... there was an activity of thinking and imagination that opened out vast possibilities not just of memory but of *counter*-memory: the moral idiom and semiotic registers of remembering against the grain of history of New World black deracination, subjection and exclusion."[79] Scott's formulation in terms of "counter-memory" rather than "counter-history" is pivotal to his argument. Conceiving of such narratives as memories alludes to the more malleable quality of such truths before they stultify into the domain of accepted "facts." Memories may be fallible and subject to interpretation, but they are remarkably resilient and potent, often providing the groundwork for larger notions of tradition and community. In this sense, memories act with considerable force on the individuals who access them, resisting attempts at historical erasure.

By examining the interplay between memory, history, and the archive, subaltern archival theorists like Burton and Scott challenge models that would stress a clear line between fuzzy memories and hard "facts." In doing so, they reinsert human bodies as storage media (and not only as detached authors) that are integral to re/constructing our stories about the past. Yet the past is not the only temporality in which the archive operates, nor in which its creators reside. How can such lessons be applied in cases where the human is not a figure to be coaxed out of dusty pages, but a living, breathing presence who walks the stacks alongside us?

Working Alongside the Archive. In Sultan, we encounter a unique collection of archival issues. His multiple roles as administrator, curator, annotator, and subject of his collection create deep cuts in the binary associations inflecting most archival work: interior/exterior, circulating/noncirculating, memories/records, original intent / archival function. These factors are not only of theoretical importance, but they deeply alter the way users must engage with the collection. I learned this repeatedly throughout my time with him.

The first thing one encounters is that the human and the material coexist in constant dialogue. As Sultan and I sorted through the materials together, there were innumerable instances where human and nonhuman memories corrected, disputed, reinforced, or supplemented one another. The most basic examples involved simple annotations, which we would often make while listening to tapes from the collection. Sultan would offer his remembrances of the music we heard, in varying degrees of detail. I would note these recollections in catalogs that we compiled. On a few occasions, I also tape-recorded our annotation sessions together. If I found a separate paper document that offered further details, I would also add this information to the catalog. Both the catalog and the interview recordings were duplicated and added to the archive as well, providing yet another layer of mediated memory. In the end, our catalog included information culled from all three of the media discussed herein: the sounds of the tapes, the writings from documents, the memories of the archivists.

In countless cases, Sultan's recollections provided invaluable corrections and contextual details. In addition to making factual annotations, they were crucial to me in assessing the significance of particular materials, as demonstrated by the above example regarding Intramedia, Inc. In other cases, though, the dialogue moved in the opposite direction, with archival materials speaking back to Sultan and altering his recollections. During our tape annotations, for example, there were some occasions in which Sultan identified specific musicians by ear as being present, only to be contradicted minutes later by a spoken announcement from the band leader. This happened with enough frequency that we eventually chose to make data fields in the catalog to list the sources of each piece of information. For instance, if a certain saxophonist was listed, we would note whether this information was gleaned through annotations on the tape box, ear identifications by Sultan, cross-referencing with other documents, or through another source altogether. On still other occasions, the tapes acted as a catalyst for further remembrances that had been long dormant. During another of our tape review sessions, the sound of a performance space sparked a series of ruminations about a studio space that Sultan had not thought about in years (and which had not previously been listed on the tape box).[80]

Nothing in this account should be read as an indictment of Sultan's memory. Such episodes merely reinforce the most basic purpose of the archive. As a technology of preservation, it offers a supplement or a prosthesis, designed expressly to store those things that memory cannot (say, the sound vibrations produced by ninety minutes of music). But Sultan's presence also teaches us that the archive can never be a replacement. His contextual annotations offer alternative wisps of the past that eluded the mechanisms of paper and tape. In the end, we see messages running in multiple directions between human and nonhuman, with neither subservient to the other. Memory is never comprehensive, but neither is the archive. Instead, memories continually augment the media in the archive, even as those media simultaneously supplement our memories—a dialogue that is forever incomplete and constantly under revision.

Sultan's dialogue with the archive extends beyond the level of individual artifacts. It also informs the larger logic that organizes the collection, such as decisions about which materials are/are not included, as well as how they are arranged. It is worth noting that the repository officially designated as "The Juma Sultan Archive" does not contain every tape he ever recorded. Instead, it is consciously limited to his jazz career, beginning in Woodstock in the late '60s and continuing through the loft scene. If one proceeds to the very top level of the barn, one can find additional crates filled with tapes documenting his later musical projects, when he returned to Woodstock to focus primarily on gospel music. Prior to about 2007, all of these materials (jazz, gospel, and otherwise) were stored together, without any differentiation between them. Sultan only started separating out the jazz tapes after he began to be approached by scholars with an interest in the period, including myself. For better or worse, the desires of the searchers has had a palpable effect on the type of archive that has emerged. As much as I tried to defer any decisions about the archive to Sultan, like any ethnographer, I cannot pretend that my presence had no impact. One can easily imagine that the collection would look quite different if he had been contacted by, say, a writer interested in the musical history of the Hudson Valley. In such a scenario, Sultan's 1960s free jazz might sit comfortably alongside his gospel work in the 1980s, while his foray into lofts remained in the attic collecting dust.

Additional organizational choices were made for other reasons, which carried direct ramifications during our time together. Early on, Sultan informed me that as I explored the archive, I might come across items relating to the guitarist Jimi Hendrix. Sultan was a member of Hendrix's bands for several years leading up to the guitarist's death in 1970, and to the general public this remains his largest claim to fame. To this day, Sultan appears regularly at rock conventions that publicize his connection to the guitarist—he even signs photos of the band's legendary 1969 performance at the Woodstock Festival. Were I to come across any Hendrix-related material, Sultan asked that I remove it from the collection and place it in a separate area for him to relocate. While the request was partially guided by a desire to focus the scope of the collection, his more direct motivation was financial. Unlike most loft materials, Hendrix artifacts carry considerable sales potential for collectors or memorabilia dealers. My introductory tension with Sultan's wife Mariyah—referenced at the beginning of this chapter—was deeply colored by previous experiences in which collectors had robbed Sultan of Hendrix material. Since then, he has been especially wary with such items. On the few occasions I found such materials, I immediately put them aside in deference to Sultan's request.[81]

Such actions unquestionably alter the resultant logic of the archive. Imagining future researchers, the presence of Hendrix in an archive of loft jazz would immediately alter the types of stories it becomes possible to tell—what Michel Foucault referred to as the archive's "enunciability."[82] In particular, Hendrix's presence may signal a closer connection between the activities of 1960s rock counterculture with those of the jazz avant garde, a largely unexamined connection that I began exploring in chapters 5 and 6. To physically excise such materials enacts a palpable erasure. Still other relationships could be obscured or emphasized by the reordering of materials, which Sultan and I did several times throughout the cataloging process. While the library community tends to shy away from such reordering in deference to *respect des fonds,* the situation seems considerably different when the materials remain with their original collector. Should Sultan himself be required to abide by *respect des fonds,* maintaining whatever relationships were present at an earlier moment? Or, are his alterations, excisions, and adjustments of inherent interest simply because of his privileged position as both subject and object of the archive?[83]

As an outsider in the collection, the nebulousness of such questions did little to alleviate my own apprehension over *respect des fonds.* On a few occasions, Sultan would finish looking over a certain document or tape and proceed to casually refile it in an entirely different place from where he found it. When this happened, I would pipe up as the nervous archivist, asking if it would be permissible to leave the object in its original location, both to aid in our ongoing cataloguing efforts (I feared having to process the same materials multiple times), as well as to maintain the original relationships between items. Sultan generally obliged, as we had developed a strong collaborative relationship by this point. Nevertheless, such experiences often made me question the nature of my own human presence in the archive's order. Perhaps I was overstepping my bounds by impeding the organic evolution of an archival logic guided by Sultan alone. I felt a palpable discomfort with my own actions at such moments: who was I to protect materials from their owner?! My only justification was that I imagined my actions as maintaining the archival logic of an earlier period, in effect privileging the choices made by Sultan in the late 1970s over those made by Sultan in the late 2000s. This is not to say that I was correct in doing so; who knows whether both Sultans would have made the same choices?

The crux of this tension lies in the transition between objects in circulation and artifacts in the archive. Unlike Spieker's corporate examples—in which archiving is crisply delineated by the act of physical rehousing—Sultan's materials have gone through no clear-cut process of exteriorization. Their designation as "archival" therefore remains disconcertingly ambiguous, determined more by use than by any formal decision. But in some cases, Sultan's own use of the materials seemed to *reject* the archival designation by treating them as objects still in circulation, still retaining traces of their original nonarchival functions. When he requested the Hendrix materials be set aside, for example, he did so not for historiographic reasons, but because he saw the potential to profit through active commercial value. In another way, Sultan's casual relationship with the order of the collection might stem from the same idea. When he picks up a document or spools a tape, he does so with an ease and familiarity that stray far from the protocols of strict preservation (e.g., wearing gloves or separating materials by media). For him, to use the materials is simply a part of his ongoing life as a musician and activist. They are not delicate relics in a mausoleum, but comforting mementos in his home. In a conventional model, the moment that they *become* archival is, as it were, the moment they are frozen—where their importance as a snapshot of a bygone era outweighs their potential for active and/or familiar use.

This factor underscores the discrepancy between my own neuroses about organization and Sultan's more comfortable relationship with the materials. From my perspective, the very act of traveling to an archive had largely predetermined my relationship with the materials before I even arrived. I was at an archive because I had been told (or told myself) that I was coming to an archive. Once I arrived, it was my duty to preserve the collection in its original state and order. For Sultan, there was no such arrival. The archive has always existed alongside him, often literally inside his home. The only transformation—minor but not totally insignificant—was the appearance of a researcher with a particular agenda and set of interests. This was not a moment where interior became exterior—the standard archival move—but where exterior became interior: the arrival of a foreign entity unavoidably altering the status of archival relationships. If anything, Sultan was more keenly aware of this potential than I was; the possibility that my presence could help advance his mission was the primary reason that I was invited in the first place. Subsequent grant applications regularly referenced my presence there, as well as other external support from Clarkson University and the National Endowment for the Arts. For funders operating in a traditional archival paradigm, the presence of outsiders validates the archive by locating its reach beyond the private sphere, into the exterior world. For Sultan and me, struggling to make sense of the messages within, the distinctions were far less clear.

The tension between circulation and the archive may also underlie Sultan's decision to maintain private control over his archive for so long, rather than donating it to an institutional collection. To donate a private collection is no small matter; it is a deliberate choice to take documents out of active circulation and irrevocably redesignate them as archival objects. I raised the topic when speaking with Annie Kuebler of the Rutgers Institute of Jazz Studies, an archivist with extensive experience corresponding with musician donors. In addition to financial negotiations, Kuebler described how the process is fraught with complex emotions:

> A person's archive, it's their past ... The definition of an archive is all these things that are no longer being used [for their original purpose. The musician is] not *using* the

material anymore. He doesn't *need* the business records. He doesn't really *need* the recordings . . . So it's all past. It's all dead. It's no longer in use. It's no longer viable for his daily life. But what does that say about him? [The musician thinks:] "If this *stuff* is considered historic, what does that say about me? That my time is over?" These are the kind of issues that come up.[84]

In the lofts, these emotional concerns are heightened by the link between musician-organized activities and narratives of self-empowerment. Despite the efforts of libraries to maintain collaborative relationships with their donors, the choice to surrender ownership is a monumental and often irreversible decision that radically alters the relationship between collector and collection. It prefigures the death of the collector by severing the cord between human and material memory.

The example of the Sultan archive demonstrates how divisions between human and nonhuman media are not always as clear-cut as we might imagine. Instead, objects and their humans constantly rub against one another on both factual and emotional levels. Sultan requires the supplement of the archive just as the archive requires the supplement of Sultan. Their mutual reliance generates a feedback loop that expands the scope of the archive even as it reinforces its inadequacy, an ongoing improvisation that undergirds the production of knowledge itself.

CONCLUSION: WHERE IS THE ARCHIVE OF JAZZ?

If the present chapter has diverged somewhat from the loft era, per se, it has done so with the intention of asking broader questions about the practice of jazz research, as well as archival history more broadly. Where is the archive of jazz? How does our delimitation of data pools curtail or empower the types of histories that we are able to write? What role do musicians play in establishing or pushing back against these archives, thereby reclaiming a degree of agency in the way they are represented?

The archives that inform our histories have migrated several times throughout the history of jazz scholarship. Early writers relied extensively on testimonies provided via oral histories, transcribing spoken recollections into engaging narratives. By the 1960s, commercial recordings assumed pride of place, led by the analytic approach of writers like Gunther Schuller. Concurrently, the growing field of discography sought to systematize reference materials on recorded sounds, reinforcing the historiographical primacy of the jazz record. By the 1980s, a generation of trained historians such as Lawrence Gushee and Lewis Porter began crafting more rigorously documented histories that used a previously untapped cache of paper sources, ranging from contracts to newspaper accounts to birth records. The growth of the "new jazz studies" in the 1990s found scholars employing new theories of social history, while simultaneously reengaging with living artists through ethnography. None of these strains fully supplanted those that preceded them, which continued to exist as parallel streams. Today, examples of all of these approaches—oral history, discography, music analysis, positivist history, critical theorizing, ethnographic engagement—can be seen in books and articles that appear every year. At their core, the distinction between them lies in the types of archives that they draw from, as well as the disciplinary tactics they employ to engage with those archives.

It is in this sense that private archives matter for jazz studies, especially in regard to the music created in the loft era. In a period saturated with self-organizing and amateur production, private materials offer both new documentary data and novel ways to think about how we write about jazz. As a direct effort to reclaim control over the substance of history, loft archiving provides a means by which musicians continue to promote the values that informed them in the 1970s. A private archive is more than the sum of its artifacts, it is also the thrust of its intention—a tool in a process of self-affirmation that has animated musician activism for half a century.

The archive is a storehouse, but it is also a mechanism. A mine, but also a pickaxe.

8

AFTERMATHS AND LEGACIES

> *This is probably as good a time and place as any to report that loft jazz no longer exists. Actually, it never existed, not as a distinct variety of jazz with a sound and style of its own. But during the last few years, when a new generation of jazz musicians arrived in New York and gave a number of concerts in lofts, it was a convenient term. Under the cloak of loft jazz some excellent young musicians established reputations and new jazz in general received a great deal of badly needed attention. But the musicians were always quick to point out that they did not play something called loft jazz, they played jazz and, since most night clubs and concert halls then were not receptive to their music, they played in lofts.*
>
> —ROBERT PALMER, *NEW YORK TIMES*

The opening paragraph of Robert Palmer's column of January 26, 1979, is as close as anyone came to writing an official obituary for the loft scene. The catalyst was the recent closure of Studio Rivbea, which had quietly shut down in the preceding months. Although Sam and Bea Rivers would stage one final festival that summer at Joseph Papp's Public Theater, the shuttering of their Bond Street venue marked, for Palmer, the end of the lofts' position at the center of the New York jazz avant garde.[1] In their place appeared a wave of new performance initiatives at theaters and nightclubs, with Papp's series "Jazz at the Public" among the most prominent. Though the lofts may have died, Palmer was optimistic that the music itself would live on in other venues.

Upon closer examination, the vanishing of the lofts may not have been quite as conclusive as Palmer makes it seem. If the precise definition of a "jazz loft" was vague in the early years of the movement, it became even more ambiguous during the late/post loft years of the late 1970s and early '80s. The designation "loft" remained in use to refer to a motley assortment of venues, ranging from small concert halls to commercial nightclubs. Several spaces continued operating into the 1980s, but many bore distinct differences from the early paradigm of converting one's homes into a performance space.

These later examples generally departed from the 1970s lofts in one of two ways. On one side were venues that emulated more formal concert presentations. Spaces like the Kitchen, Roulette, the Experimental Intermedia Foundation, and Soundscape employed more tightly organized presentational approaches than had been common in many lofts. Each of these venues pursued fundraising opportunities to support their work, rather than merely staying afloat by maintaining low overhead costs.[2] Their bookings also extended far outside of jazz: the former three often presented composers from New York's downtown new music scene, while the latter also featured folk and art traditions from around the world. Writers sometimes seemed unsure how to categorize such venues, which drew from certain aspects of the lofts (intimate spaces, blurring of lines between performer and audience) while eschewing others (low pay, insufficient funding, flawed acoustics). In the end, they were described in myriad ways: sometimes as lofts,[3] but other times as concert venues that improved upon the loft model.[4]

A second departure came via loft venues that moved further in the direction of commercial nightclubs. One example of this was the Jazz Forum, which was run by trumpeter Mark Morganelli and operated in two locations from 1979–83. The space departed from most other lofts by concentrating primarily on mainstream jazz, featuring artists like Woody Shaw, Barry Harris, and Tommy Flanagan. Its first incarnation at 50 Cooper Square functioned similarly to most other early lofts. Morganelli lived in the unit along with several other musicians, and the minimal rent allowed him to program a busy schedule while maintaining low-ticket prices (between three and five dollars).[5] When Morganelli was evicted in January 1981, he took it as an opportunity to expand into a new location at 648 Broadway. The new space was much larger, but at nearly triple the rent, costing $1,400 per month in contrast to the $550 he paid previously. To compensate, ticket prices crept toward ten dollars, and waitresses were hired to sell refreshments. In the spring, Morganelli built a 30-foot oak bar so that he could sell beer and wine. Later, when finances became more dire, they expanded to a full liquor selection. All this was done despite the fact that they had no alcohol license of any kind.

Morganelli was not the first presenter to smudge the boundaries between loft and nightclub approaches. As noted in chapters 3 and 6, Rashied Ali had undertaken similar efforts at Ali's Alley since the early 1970s. But unlike Ali, Morganelli did not shy away from the term "loft." To the contrary, he saw the Jazz Forum's loft identity as a valuable attribute that helped it stand out from other clubs that employed the same artists:

> MM: We had lounge areas where you could sit on a sofa and hear Art Blakey and the Jazz Messengers. I mean, where does that happen?! ... People would come early and scope out their [spot]. "This is where I'm sitting!" It was very, very comfortable ... I guess the camaraderie and the laid-back nature of the vibe and the ambiance created a very warm and inviting atmosphere for both

> listeners and players. People were able to try out new ideas and compositions and arrangements ... Chet Baker comes off the elevator one day and he and I start playing together. This is the kind of stuff that would happen! ...
>
> MH: You talk about wanting a loft for straight-ahead jazz, despite the fact that a lot of the [artists] were also playing at clubs.
>
> MM: Yeah, but they could really stretch out at my place! There was no curfew. We don't have a big payroll. People were partying back then in the loft—they weren't partying sitting in a club in full view of somebody during the Rockefeller drug laws. It was a very different scene.[6]

Morganelli's description is a powerful example of how by the late 1970s the appeal of the loft aesthetic had extended beyond pure economic necessity. Far from being an inferior alternative for musicians who were shunned by conventional venues, for some the loft setting had become attractive to the Jazz Forum's musicians *in spite of* and *in addition to* club opportunities.

What becomes clear in both of these directions (the grant-supported presentation of spaces like the Kitchen, and the nightclub model of the Jazz Forum) is that by the early 1980s, the perception that lofts offered a radically different approach from concert halls and clubs had begun to break down. Instead, a somewhat defanged loft aesthetic was now used to simply supplement these two models. Loft-esque trappings could offer a degree of added value, but the approach ceased to provide an alternative to other presentational logics, or a substantive critique of them. Interestingly, this shift tended to overemphasize the physical elements of the spaces themselves, rather than the movement's earlier ethos of experimentalism and self-determination.[7]

Within a few years, two primary narratives emerged as the most common historical frameworks for discussing the 1970s loft period. The first, which I call the romantic narrative, drew on the ideals of self-ownership and anticapitalism cited by early loft organizers. An example can be found in a *New York Times* article from 1979:

> The scenario runs something like this: during the early 1970's, a new generation of original, exploratory jazz players arrived in New York. They found that the avant garde of the 60's—players like Archie Shepp and Dave Burrell—hadn't yet been accepted into the musical mainstream, a situation that seemed to leave little room for the younger musicians. But they were resourceful, self-reliant people, and they began organizing their concerts, in lofts and galleries and small halls. They drew crowds, they got reviews, they began recording, they solidified their individual reputations. And collectively, they helped open up the jazz world in New York, which had been confined for too long to a handful of nightclubs and to concerts run by a very few promoters.[8]

During much of the 1980s, however, many writers seemed reluctant to describe the lofts in such idealistic terms. As most of the lofts had only recently closed down, it might have seemed somewhat naive at the time to argue for their viability as a form of industry protest.

What appeared more frequently in these early post-loft years was what I refer to as the teleological narrative. In these accounts, the loft model is portrayed as being inherently flawed, especially in regard to the practice of paying artists based on door profits. The movement is therefore depicted as a necessary but unfortunate step in developing an audience for the new music. Once the music started to become accepted in higher-profile spaces like clubs and concert halls, it was inevitable that the lofts would become obsolete. As one reporter described it in 1983:

> [T]he 1970's avant-garde *has* come up from the underground. Players who performed in lofts 10 years ago, for audiences that were sometimes outnumbered by band members, are now drawing crowds to club engagements. And all of a sudden, the classical-music world has stopped condescending to jazz. This season, improvised music is showing up at such unexpected venues as Carnegie Recital Hall, the Brooklyn Academy of Music and even the New Music America festival in Washington, D. C.[9]

Subsequent scholarship has problematized this notion that black experimentalism was unreservedly accepted in concert venues.[10] Yet in the early 1980s, these inroads often seemed like a step in the right direction. The failure of the lofts to provide lasting gains for either organizers or musicians made the period deeply vulnerable to criticism during this time, especially once artists began to see more profitable opportunities arise both at home and abroad.

Many musicians who had previously performed in lofts became vocal critics of the practice. George Lewis, for example, describes the phrase "loft generation" as "a term whose ephemerality the musicians are no doubt quite grateful for today."[11] He particularly references the disdain that members of Chicago's AACM had for the phrase "loft jazz," which he argues constituted a constricting designation that restricted the professional opportunities of musicians who sought recognition as concert artists. Despite praising the high quality of much music performed in the lofts and giving organizers credit for providing "entry-level support for an emerging multiracial network of musicians," Lewis's analysis ultimately sees loft practices as misguided and lacking the seriousness of more formal collectives.[12]

Although Lewis's role as a participant grants him a more direct perspective than my own as a researcher, I find his characterization of musicians being unwaveringly critical of lofts to be somewhat overstated. In my own interviews, a number of musicians offered memories that were decidedly more mixed. By no means were they uncritical, but many tempered their critiques with recollections of deeply inspiring aspects of the scene. These included the development of strong musical and social networks, the pervasiveness of performance opportunities, and the feeling of empowerment that surrounded self-production. Far from encountering only resentment, my conversations tended to evoke a range of sometimes conflicting valences and appraisals.

In print, one example can be found by examining statements made by saxophonist Chico Freeman, an AACM member who came to New York in 1977. Lewis mentions Freeman as a typical representative of musicians' disdain for the "loft" designation, citing a 1980 interview in which Freeman said, "I don't know where it came from, somebody came up with this term 'loft jazz.' Not just me, but every musician who was involved in it vehemently opposed that."[13] But a single quote only tells part of the story. Contrast this statement with another that Freeman offered six years later: "Remember the period of all the loft concerts, back in the '70's? People were playing in all sorts of different combinations; it wasn't really about one guy hiring a group of sidemen to play his own compositions. It was a good period, the music was changing and evolving."[14] Here, Freeman is more generous in characterizing what he saw as virtues of the loft period, highlighting the scene's communal spirit. While this does not negate his criticisms, it does provide an important counterpoint.

An even more dramatic example can be heard in a 1994 radio interview with saxophonist David Murray, conducted as a part of a loft radio festival produced by Columbia University's WKCR-FM. Early in the interview, Murray comes out as highly critical of the loft moniker:

> *Interviewer:* So when you came [to New York], was it the lofts that attracted you? Writing about them and playing in them? You knew about the loft scene?
>
> *David Murray:* Well, to me there was nothing magical about the buildings themselves. I want to make that distinction. We would do very creative ensembles in all of these lofts and personally we resented the fact that they would call us "loft jazz" musicians. Say, for instance, I do a quintet there and it was beautiful music. Then the next day it would say, "Loft Jazz Artists Strike Again!" instead of saying, "David Murray Quintet Strikes Again." I thought that was absurd, and I still do. And I resent the fact that I'm actually called a "loft jazz" musician . . . I don't consider myself a "loft jazz" musician now. That's why I'm here stating my case. I felt it was necessary. I feel like I've transcended that. A lot of people that were lumped into that "loft jazz" business didn't flourish as well as I have. Maybe that grouping might have been one of the reasons of their demise. I don't know. I tend to think so.[15]

This opening salvo seems to take the somewhat timid student interviewer by surprise, especially in the context of a festival that was largely celebratory of the loft enterprise. Rather than engage with the criticism, she proceeds gamely with her set of prepared questions, attempting to draw out the positive aspects of Murray's experience: "What musical influences have you pulled out of the loft scene?" "So the lofts were very important? They were a major musical outlet?" "In terms of your playing today, is there anything the lofts were invaluable for?" The open-endedness of the questions eventually leads Murray to reminisce about the fruitful aspects of the period:

> Interviewer: Do you think more great players came out of the '70s loft period because they had a chance to develop in public?
> David Murray: Certainly. I think the loft period was a golden period for that reason. There were a lot of players like myself who were trying to play past their influences and play right through them . . . I think the loft jazz period was good because all of these forces were fighting to be heard.[16]

By the end of the interview, even Murray seems to acknowledge the significance of the spaces themselves and their potential for cultivating musical community. When asked for his final thoughts on the period, Murray pauses before saying, "I have an idea. They keep creating these clubs in Japan. They want to make a replica of the Vanguard and a Sweet Basil and this club and that club. I think they ought to have a re-creation of loft jazz."[17] In distinct contrast to his introductory statements that there was "nothing magical about the buildings," his concluding thoughts go so far as to suggest a physical re-creation of lofts to pay tribute to the period's vibrancy.

These examples should not be read as an attempt to catch artists in a contradiction (a kind of "gotcha" scholarship). To the contrary, the statements entail relatively little contradiction at all. Instead, they rely on coherent and common patterns for characterizing the period. Both Freeman and Murray are critical of reductive commentaries that subsumed individual creation under a vague rubric of "loft jazz," a term that seemed to imply a limited cultural and economic viability. On the other hand, both artists also acknowledge the strong social networks that were fostered within musician-organized venues, a factor contributing to the rise of a "golden period." Such assessments demonstrate the types of complex memories often evoked by the loft era, in which musicians look back fondly on certain aspects of the period, even while recognizing distinct failings in others.

SHIFTING HISTORICAL LEGACIES SINCE THE 1990S

Teleological narratives emphasizing the failure of the lofts dominated much journalism written in the 1980s. Starting in the 1990s, however, a handful of outlets began portraying the loft era in a more favorable light. One strong example was the aforementioned loft radio festival produced by WKCR-FM in 1994. Organized by station programmers (and recent Columbia graduates) Ben Young, Sarah Schmidt, and Jennifer McNeeley, the germ of the festival was formed when the station recorded a memorial service following the death of saxophonist Charles Tyler. According to Young, a eulogy given by Phil Schaap (the station's most prominent programmer) set the idea into motion:

> Phil [Schaap] was asked to give a eulogy for Charles Tyler because they knew each other . . . Somewhere in his discourse he said the following: "When they tell the history of this music, they'd better leave a lot of room for the lofts." . . . I want to say that on the way back from that event [we started discussing a festival]. McNeeley was undoubtedly the first person to ask, "Shouldn't we have a lofts festival?" or something like that. And it was the nature of how the vibe [at the station] was that we all said, "Yeah, of course we should! Let's do it."[18]

Starting in late 1993, the station began recording dozens of interviews with organizers and participants. The festival aired in January of 1994, culminating with two nights of concerts featuring former loft artists.[19]

Over the course of the festival, the station also aired several hours of unreleased private tapes of loft performances, one of the first efforts to showcase the wealth of private archival materials kept by artists.[20] The tapes became a key part of the festival's on-air interviews. Student DJs used the recordings to prompt musicians' memories and convey the sonic atmosphere of the loft period. Speaking in 2012, Young recalled that some of the musicians were astonished by the level of enthusiasm expressed by the station's student programmers, most of whom were too young to have been present at the lofts themselves.[21]

A few years later, a second venture commemorated the lofts through the medium of live performance. In 1998–99 the loft scene was featured in the ongoing concert series "Lost Jazz Shrines," a multicity venture that paid tribute to historical centers of jazz activity. In a group of concerts that year titled "The Loft Scene," the series honored three spaces: Studio Rivbea, Ali's Alley, and the Ladies' Fort. Press materials steered away from criticisms and toward more romantic narratives, with statements like, "Never before or since has the jazz cutting edge, also known by that disreputable term the jazz 'avant-garde,' found a more agreeable home than was afforded . . . during [the loft] period."[22] One of the organizers of the series was publicist Jim Eigo, who had been a devotee of loft concerts in the 1970s and obsessively collected flyers and ephemera.[23]

In the years that followed, Eigo would also be involved in two CD releases that paid further tribute to the lofts. In 1999, he produced the first reissue of the classic *Wildflowers* recordings, documenting the Studio Rivbea Summer Festival in 1976. The following year, he served as executive producer of a box set of recordings made in the 1950s–60s loft of painter David X. Young.[24] The trend of using private recordings made by musicians as source material for commercial records has continued strongly into the new millennium. A slew of such releases have hit the market since 2000, including lavishly constructed box sets on boutique labels (such as the Ayler

Records box set of Jimmy Lyons[25] or the NoBusiness Records collections of Ensemble Muntu and William Parker[26]) as well as independently produced CDs from artists like Alan Glover, Ted Daniel, and Cooper-Moore.[27] Extensive liner notes (often employing versions of the romantic narrative) accompany much of this output.

Alongside these releases, a second trend has been the incorporation and/or transformation of private collections into academic or institutional archives. The Collective Black Artists, Irving Stone, and Vision Festival Collections all currently reside at the Rutgers Institute of Jazz Studies, while a large cache of recordings from Soundscape has been donated to WKCR. Columbia University now holds a collection of over 400 hours of tape recorded by Karl Berger at his Woodstock-based Creative Music Studio, and NYU houses several collections related to downtown performance traditions of the 1970s and '80s. Perhaps the best-publicized collection is Duke University's somewhat confusingly titled *Jazz Loft Project,* which does not chronicle the 1970s loft scene of lower Manhattan, but an earlier space owned by photographer and jazz aficionado W. Eugene Smith (described in chapter 2). Smith's loft in New York's Flower District became a vital meeting place and jam session venue for jazz artists from 1957–65. Smith meticulously documented the events that transpired, taking roughly 40,000 photographs and recording 1,740 reels of audio.[28] The directors of the Duke archive have done extensive work across media to promote the collection including an extensive website, lavish coffee table book, and a ten-part radio documentary on NPR that aired in 2009. As of this writing, the organizers are also preparing a documentary film chronicling the project.[29]

Taken together, these varied activities (festivals, concert series, record releases, institutional archives) reveal two themes. The first is a pendular swing away from teleological narratives that frame the lofts as a failure, and toward a renewed historical engagement with the lofts as centers for musical experimentation and as sites for enacting artistic self-determination. The second is a growing tendency to ground historical initiatives in the period's copious musician-owned collections of tapes and artifacts.

In light of my own research's connection with one such archive, during my interviews I often asked musicians how they felt private archives ought to be used in the twenty-first century. Their answers generally referenced one of the two dissemination strategies listed above: commercial releases or institutional archiving. Those who stressed commercial release emphasized the importance of wide distribution and equitable remuneration for living artists. James DuBoise argued that releases should be done by "some noticeable record company . . . [who will] do the contracts right and won't overstep their bounds."[30] Ted Daniel, who has released a number of loft tapes on his Ujamaa label, described how archival projects have become an essential aspect of his recent output: "That's why I have music coming out today, because I'm releasing music from that period!"[31] Ali Abuwi went so far as to express surprise at the very suggestion that private tapes could be used for any purpose other than commercial releases or personal mementos. When I raised the possibility of depositing tapes in university archives, he responded: "When you say 'archive' that's just putting it together for history right? . . . Boy! We're all elders now, man! I don't know!"[32]

Other musicians seemed more amenable to the idea of institutional deposits, expressing a desire to have the materials stored safely at a university or library. Some affirmed how working with a fully functioning archive could bolster preservation efforts. Steve Tintweiss described how he wished to set up an arrangement to house his tape collection at a local university, which would allow for archival-grade digital preservation.[33] Others observed that such arrangements would make more materials more widely available, allowing their contents to be more thoroughly absorbed into music histories. Ahmed Abdullah, who developed his early love for jazz by borrowing records from his local library, favored depositing materials at publicly open institutions that can be accessed by all.[34] In all of these cases, musicians made direct associations pointing to the historiographic potential of physical artifacts to revise common constructions of jazz history.

LIVING VISIONS

Yet artifacts only provide part of the story. The 1990s expansion of loft interest was bolstered further by the growing prominence of a community of improvisers with direct ties to the period. The most notable of these was bassist William Parker. Born in the Bronx, Parker was a young musician in the early 1970s, and the dynamic atmosphere of the lofts was central to his early development. Over the course of the decade, Parker played in a string of important ensembles (Ensemble Muntu, The Music Ensemble, Commitment, Other Dimensions in Music) before gaining international exposure as a member of Cecil Taylor's band in the early 1980s. Parker also self-produced dozens of concerts of his own music, continuing the practice long after the lofts closed their doors.[35] His most ambitious efforts came in 1984 and 1988, when he collaborated with dancer and choreographer Patricia Nicholson (who is also Parker's wife) and German bassist Peter Kowald to produce the Sound Unity Festivals, two massive events that showcased improvisers from New York and Europe.[36]

From 1993 to 1995, Parker, Nicholson, and several dozen others came together to form the Improvisors Collective, a group designed to encourage multidisciplinary collaborations between musicians, dancers, poets, and visual artists.[37] Many of the group's core members had been active participants in the loft scene, and the venture was strongly motivated by the period's spirit of togetherness and cooperation. As Nicholson explains: "[During the early 1990s], no one was seeing each other. This was a way to bring back the sense of community that existed during the loft era."[38]

Soon after the collective dissipated, Nicholson would go on to launch the annual Vision Festival in 1996.[39] Occurring each summer in many different types of venues (churches, synagogues, community centers, theaters), the festival has grown into a leading international showcase of the jazz avant garde. Although its participants hail from across the globe, New York–based artists from the loft period have long provided the core of Vision programming. As of this writing, the festival has just completed its twenty-first year, making it by far the longest-lived artist-run festival in the history of jazz.

Vision is by no means alone. Throughout New York, many of the most vibrant places to hear avant garde jazz are found in venues, festivals, and concert series programmed by artists. One particularly prominent space is The Stone, a small gallery in the Lower East Side founded by saxophonist John Zorn. Born in New York, Zorn moved to lower Manhattan in the mid-1970s just as the lofts were entering their peak. The Stone features a schedule that is entirely curated by artists, usually in residencies that last between one and two weeks. It came up numerous times in my interviews, often described as providing a feel that evokes the 1970s lofts, especially in regard to its layout (a single austere room, musicians on the same level as the audience), lack of food or drink, and an atmosphere in which listeners and performers interact in close contact. The venue even takes its name from the late couple Irving and Stephanie Stone, two legendary audience members who were regular attendees at loft events.

It would be too simplistic to lump all of these projects together as direct progeny of the lofts. Each initiative arose from a unique set of circumstances and aesthetic goals. It is, however, notable how so much of the New York jazz avant garde continues to revolve around musician-organized practices, which often share many of the concerns noted throughout this book. These include: (1) an ongoing concern with ideals of freedom, both as a musical value and a political program for self-determination; (2) a community-oriented focus, aimed at bringing together artists and listeners; (3) efforts to build and/or repurpose spaces for cultivating artistic practices; and (4) relying on a combination of cooperative DIY practices and funding through grants and city arts programs. Through the efforts of artist-organizers, New York has continually managed to maintain an active and intergenerational community of improvisers, many of whom hold direct ties to the loft era.[40]

POSTSCRIPTS AND PROLOGUES: LOFT LEGACIES AND THE ARCHIVAL FUTURE

I conclude this book in the same place that it began: in the archive of Juma Sultan. As of this writing, the future of the Sultan archive is uncertain, but signs are promising. Starting in 2012, Sultan began receiving preservation assistance from individuals at Columbia University, including Brent Hayes Edwards, Ben Young, and several undergraduates from campus radio station WKCR. I had met with Edwards and Young a number of times throughout my research, primarily to discuss other historical initiatives related to the lofts.[41] Some of these conversations eventually blossomed into the WKCR / Center for Jazz Studies Oral History Project, which remains ongoing and has documented numerous figures from the period. Once my fieldwork was over, the Columbia team expressed interest in continuing the work that Sultan and I had begun. Expanding upon the catalog that we developed, they created digital transfers of another hundred tapes, and have continued annotating them through ongoing consultation with Sultan.

Most recently, the Columbia libraries are looking into purchasing the materials from Sultan to give them a permanent home. As of this writing (March 2016), the archive has been professionally appraised and the two parties are in the final stages of negotiating a purchase price. If this arrangement were to take place, the material would be significantly easier to access, and would enjoy a level of preservation far beyond what Sultan can provide in the mountains of Kerhonkson. It is hoped that such acquisition—along with Columbia's aforementioned Creative Music Studio archive—would provide a sort of seed collection to attract further archives in the future, particularly from artists. Such a site is sorely needed to provide a long-term solution for musicians who hold onto irreplaceable private artifacts (a box of tapes, a scrapbook of flyers), but don't know the best way to preserve or disseminate them for future generations. It would unquestionably make Columbia the premier research site for studying New York's jazz avant garde of the 1970s.

It remains to be seen if this transaction is ultimately consummated. While the prospect offers many benefits, the politics of ownership have always been central to Sultan's archival work, and he wants to be very sure the materials will be afforded the proper care and respect before making a final decision. For my part, I have strived to remain impartial, offering advice when asked and pledging to support any efforts that emerge.

The collaboration between Sultan and Columbia, like the other legacy projects surveyed here, bodes well for future scholarship. As jazz studies has moved away from heroic stories of musical triumph, a new wave of historians and fans have begun to appreciate the significance of experimentalist practices that surface within local musical networks. The loft scene provides one such example, and its influence continues to resonate. The period's multiplicity of goals, values, and practices—so difficult to shoehorn into a single, tidy narrative—provides fertile ground for historians. There are always other perspectives to explore, other avenues to meander down. This book has followed a few, but countless others remain, tucked into the secluded corners of lower Manhattan and beyond.

The lessons of the lofts remain relevant today as well. Faced with a musical technoscape in which sharing is effortless but making a living is harder than ever, waiting around is no longer a viable strategy. Heeding the call of previous generations of organizers, we must instead construct our own pathways. We pursue freedom by remembering art's potential for resistance and transcendence. We build communities by finding like-minded spirits. We carve out spaces where we can gather to work, live, and play. We build archives that will carry our stories forward. These goals might sound idealistic, but perhaps that should be expected from a loft movement that strived to reimagine both sound and city. As William Parker put it: "I think it was the greatest period ever. I don't think there was anything bad about the loft period. Maybe I'm looking at it with rose-colored glasses, but there's nothing wrong with rose-colored glasses. I love rose-colored glasses."[42]

. . .

In one of our very first recorded interviews, Juma and I chatted while listening to one of his tapes. The music was a duo rehearsal featuring him and saxophonist Sonny Simmons, which we would later label T0120. As we listened, he mused about the creative impulse that guided them, even during informal rehearsals:

> JS: You can either read [the music], or you can *bring something* to it . . . You bring your expression into it—even written music. Somebody could come with an idea and you might say, "That's a good groove, man. But I'm not going to play that all night!" That was the attitude.
>
> MH: So [it was about] constantly reinterpreting and communicating?
>
> JS: Exactly. Exactly. And respecting one another. [Respecting] that each one could bring in their contribution.[43]

As I listen back to this exchange several years later, the lesson seems to be about more than the sounds revived from a forty-year-old tape. It was about our relationship as well, framed through the broader values of the loft era. It summoned a commitment to the uncompromising. An ethics of collaboration. A desire to keep moving forward, while leaving our ears open to the wisdom of those before us. A vision that continually imagines worlds that are different from the one we currently inhabit. A provocation to never stop searching for the spaces where we may craft our song together.

ACKNOWLEDGMENTS

This book has been in the making for nearly fifteen years. If I had to write a myth of origin, it would probably begin in 2002, when I took a seminar on "Jazz and Politics" at Columbia University, taught by Robin D.G. Kelley. The class sparked my first engagement with the impact of musician-run organizations as incubators for artist empowerment and political activism. I continued exploring this subject in the years that followed, both inside the academy (while pursuing degrees at Rutgers and Harvard) and out (through working for New York's Vision Festival). No matter where I went, each thread seemed to circle back to this fascinating set of activities in New York in the 1970s. It seemed like everyone talked about it, but an extended study had yet to be written. I soon learned the challenges involved, and could never have completed this project without the invaluable help of dozens of colleagues, mentors, and friends.

I begin by extending my deepest thanks to Juma Sultan, without whom none of this would have been possible. Juma's ongoing efforts to preserve materials from the loft era are nothing short of Herculean; they will benefit scholars for generations to come. His guidance and support were constant reminders of why this work is important, and I hope the text does justice to his vision. But Juma has been more than that to me. He is an inspiring model of kindness, dedication, and generosity. He constantly thinks of others first, and he's never too exhausted to do a good deed for another person. During our time working together, he often had to step away to provide counseling for local individuals. Some of this he did through his job at a local Christian ministry, but many times it was simply part of his tireless devotion to helping those in need. When I got married in 2012, I was tremendously touched that Juma drove the four hours from Woodstock to Boston to attend, only to turn around and drive four hours back for a gig that he had agreed to play in New York. I've simply never met a person who so powerfully embodies selflessness, self-assuredness, and a community focus all at the same time. I consider myself very lucky to have him as a friend. This book is, in large part, dedicated to him.

ACKNOWLEDGMENTS

I extend enormous gratitude to my mentors at Harvard University, where much of this research was conceived. None was more essential than my advisor Ingrid Monson, a constant source of inspiration. I can't thank her enough for her unwavering ability to make time for graduate students, even when her obligations pulled her all over the world. Dr. Monson's writing, teaching, and mentorship have provided my most valued lessons as a scholar. Kay Kaufman Shelemay has been another powerfully influential guide, not just for me but for generations of ethnomusicologists. She provided essential methodological training, a keen critical eye as a reader, and much-needed professional guidance. A truly heartfelt thanks also goes to my classmates at Harvard, for sharpening my critical tools and creating such a warm environment in which to work. I would not be the person I am today without Meredith Schweig, Andrea Bohlman, Glenda Goodman, Corinna Campbell, Katherine Lee, Jack Hamilton, Danny Mekonnen, and many others. Thanks also to members of the "Mnemonic Deep" reading group on archival theory, including Matthew Battles, Brigid Cohen, Stephanie Frampton, and Hannah Marcus. And extra special thanks go to study motivators / partners-in-crime Peter McMurray and Emily Richmond Pollack. So many of the pages of this book would never have been written if not for our time together in the world's most secluded (and high-ceilinged!) reading room.

I am grateful to my new colleagues at the University of Pittsburgh, who have provided as supportive an atmosphere as a junior faculty member could hope for. Over the past year, it has been an honor and a joy to work with Geri Allen, Aaron Johnson, Deane Root, Andrew Weintraub, Eric Moe, Mathew Rosenblum, James Cassaro, Adriana Helbig, Gavin Steingo, Neil Newton, and all other members of the faculty. I am equally grateful to the Pitt administration, particularly Dean John Cooper for his tremendous support of jazz studies. The university library system has also been an invaluable source of help, especially Ed Galloway and Miriam Meislik. I wish every early career scholar could find themselves in an environment as positive and encouraging as I have been so lucky to find at Pitt.

Several individuals from other institutions were pivotal to the growth of this research. Deep gratitude goes to Brent Hayes Edwards of Columbia University for providing invaluable feedback and contributing his profound knowledge of the loft period. From our first meeting, Dr. Edwards's insight and encouragement convinced me that he would be an essential ally in developing this project, and I truly cannot wait to read his own forthcoming work on the subject. I extend my thanks to Ben Young, formerly of Columbia's WKCR-FM, who is always exceedingly gracious in sharing his expertise to any and all music lovers. Also at WKCR, I offer my ongoing gratitude to the incomparable Phil Schaap, who first inspired me to pursue a career in jazz scholarship. The faculty and staff of Columbia's Center for Jazz Studies, particularly Robert O'Meally, were also deeply influential during my time at Columbia.

Teachers and colleagues during my master's studies at Rutgers were additional sources of help and training. None has been more supportive than my advisor and friend Lewis Porter, who helped mold me into a professional researcher and is always willing to talk and write recommendation letters for former students. Henry Martin was key in developing a theoretical understanding of the jazz tradition, while John Howland helped introduce me to more recent theoretical developments in the "new" jazz studies. My colleagues in the program again pushed me to bigger and better heights, especially John Wriggle and Ricky

Riccardi (the other two-thirds of the "power trio") and Todd Weeks. The staff of the Rutgers Institute of Jazz Studies, under the direction of Dan Morgenstern, were pivotal in helping to navigate their tremendous holdings, while also instilling a deep interest in archival processes. Vincent Pelote, Ed Berger, Joe Peterson, Tad Hershorn, and the late Annie Kuebler were especially wonderful and I continue to treasure them.

Outside of Columbia and Rutgers, I am also thankful for the feedback provided by Scott Currie, Michael Veal, Travis Jackson, Mark Laver, Jason Stanyek, Steven Isoardi, Christopher Wells, Darren Mueller, Nicholas Gebhardt, and Ed Hazell, among many others. My research would not have been possible without the visionary work of Stephen D. Farina and Johndan Johnson-Eilola of Clarkson University. They were the first scholars to spearhead the development of the Juma Sultan Archive, and contributed tireless energy, loving devotion, and countless hours of work to the materials. Their efforts developing the collection's public face at www.jumasarchive.org are especially appreciated.

Many influences came from outside the academy as well. A tremendous source of motivation came from my colleagues at the Vision Festival, where I worked in various capacities from 2001–6. None was more inspiring than Patricia Nicholson Parker, the festival's perennially under-recognized founder and guiding light. I have never known a person with more energy, dedication, and belief in a cause than Patricia. She managed to turn a Lower East Side festival run on $5,000 and elbow grease into the world's premier presentation of the jazz avant garde. If critics only knew how much of the festival is enabled by her efforts alone, she would win every award, every year. Todd Nicholson, a brilliant bassist who—along with Patricia and myself—made up the entire Vision staff at the time, also deserves praise and thanks. The musicians I met during my time at the festival (many of whom are interviewed in the present volume) taught me about the importance of dedication to one's art and devotion to self-production practices. For all of their help, special thanks go to William Parker, Roy Campbell, Cooper-Moore, Rob Brown, Matthew Shipp, festival volunteers James Keepnews, Bill Mazza, and Richard and Roberta Berger, and friends Ras Moshe and John Rogers.

Several generous benefactors provided crucial financial assistance throughout the research process. I was deeply humbled to receive the H. Earle Johnson Book Subvention from the Society for American Music, and I extend enormous thanks to society president Charles Hiroshi Garrett and prize committee chair Julie Hubbert. My period of fieldwork at the Juma Sultan Archive was made possible by a grant from Harvard's Charles Warren Center for Studies in American History, as well as additional support from the University of Illinois at Urbana–Champaign's Kate Neal Kinley Prize. Additional funding during earlier stages of writing was offered by the Harvard Music Department's Buttenweiser Dissertation Fellowship, the William Mitch Scholarship, the Wesley Weyman Award, and the Richard F. French Prize Fellowship.

My endless thanks also go out to the wonderful staff at the University of California Press for believing in this project when it was little more than a twinkle in the eye of a young graduate student. I couldn't ask for a more incredible team than my fabulous editor Raina Polivka, editorial assistant Zuha Khan, project editor Rachel Berchten, marketing manager Aimee Goggins, editorial director Kim Robinson, and major gifts officer Anh Ly. I am enormously grateful to copyeditor Paul Tyler for his meticulous work on the manuscript, and to Alexander Trotter for preparing the index. I extend special thanks as well to the wonderful

Mary Francis for her initial enthusiasm for the project and invaluable guidance during its early stages.

I conclude by thanking my family, who have been a rock throughout my life. First and foremost I thank my beloved wife Charlene Kim, who has been remarkably understanding about book-related stress, even when it has coincided with other stresses such as wedding planning and pregnancy. Charlie was my first, last, and best editor at every stage of this process. As I write these words, we are preparing to have our first child, and I can't imagine a more amazing person with whom to share this next adventure. My siblings Chris and Patrick Heller have also been invaluable sources of support, as have my sister-in-law Shia and my niece Ayla and nephew Devin. And of course, thank you to Kim Oma and Tubby for making our home complete.

Lastly, I can never offer enough thanks to my parents. My mother Kathleen Heller is, quite simply, a saint, who has stood by my music work—as well as *all* of our family's diverse interests—throughout my life. As I prepare to enter parenthood, I hope I have absorbed even a fraction of your patience and love. Finally, I wish to remember my father Richard Heller, who helped instill deep-seated passions for both music and writing. Dad, I wish you could have been here to see this project reach completion, and I dedicate this book to you.

NOTES

CHAPTER 1

Epigraph: Sven Spieker, *The Big Archive: Art from Bureaucracy* (Cambridge, MA: MIT Press, 2008), 4.

1. Juma Sultan, interview with author, December 17, 2009, digital recording, Kingston, NY.

2. Letter from unknown sender (likely Juma Sultan) to Volunteer Lawyers for the Arts, incomplete, November 19, 1975, Juma Sultan Archive, F0096.02, Kerhonkson, NY.

3. George Lewis, *A Power Stronger Than Itself: The AACM and American Experimental Music* (Chicago: University of Chicago Press, 2008).

4. Benjamin Looker, *BAG: "Point from Which Creation Begins"—The Black Artists' Group of St. Louis* (St. Louis: University of Missouri Press, 2004).

5. Steven Louis Isoardi, *The Dark Tree: Jazz and the Community Arts in Los Angeles* (Berkeley: University of California Press, 2006); Horace Tapscott and Steven Louis Isoardi, *Songs of the Unsung: The Musical and Social Journey of Horace Taspcott* (Durham, NC: Duke University Press, 2001).

6. Broad characterizations about the lofts are necessarily vague. In regard to dates, loft concerts began as casual affairs in the 1960s, but picked up steam as advertised professional events in the 1970s. The decline of the scene began near the end of 1978 with the closing of Studio Rivbea. Other closures followed soon after. By about 1980 most of the major lofts had shut down or vastly reduced their public offerings. For a more precise historical chronology, see chapters 2 and 3.

7. For a critique of such designations, see Lewis, *Power Stronger Than Itself,* 351–53.

8. Such shifts can be noted in the work of many recent scholars, including Paul Berliner, Scott DeVeaux, Brent Hayes Edwards, Krin Gabbard, Robin D. G. Kelley, Ingrid Monson, Eric Porter, Ronald Radano, Guthrie Ramsey, and Sherrie Tucker, to name just a few.

9. Rasula argues that the historical value of recordings is obscured by the fact that their circulation relies on mechanisms saturated with economic and sociopolitical fallout, including corporate promotion and distribution, perceptions of marketability, the social identities of artists (especially their race and gender), the state of the recording industry at particular periods, and the dominance of particular urban centers. In the end, Rasula stops short of suggesting that scholars abandon recordings as essential source material. Instead, he reminds us that recordings—like any historical text—must be treated critically and not taken as unproblematic and/or objective starting points for analysis. Jed Rasula, "The Media of Memory: The Seductive Menace of Records in Jazz History," in *Jazz among the Discourses,* ed. Krin Gabbard (Durham, NC: Duke University Press, 1995).

10. I use Christopher Small's term "musicking" to encompass the roles of listeners, supporters, dancers, producers, and others participating in the musical life of a community. See Christopher Small, *Musicking: The Meanings of Performing and Listening* (Hanover, NH: University Press of New England, 1998).

11. For more extended critical analysis of how the jazz canon has been constructed see Scott DeVeaux, "Constructing the Jazz Tradition," *Black American Literature Forum* 25, no. 3 (1991); Krin Gabbard, "The Jazz Canon and Its Consequences," in Gabbard, ed., *Jazz among the Discourses*; Catherine Gunther Kodat, "Conversing with Ourselves: Canon, Freedom, Jazz," *American Quarterly* 55, no. 1 (2003).

12. Barry Dean Kernfeld, "The Bop Revival," in *The Blackwell Guide to Recorded Jazz* (Cambridge, MA: Blackwell, 1995); George Wein and Nate Chinen, *Myself among Others* (Cambridge, MA: Da Capo Press, 2004), 404–5.

13. Henry Martin and Keith Waters's popular textbook *Jazz: The First 100 Years* provides an example. After structuring earlier chapters around particular decades and styles (swing, bebop, hard bop, etc.), the 1970s are represented only with a chapter called "Jazz Rock, Jazz Funk, Fusion." Musician-organized groups such as the AACM and BAG are discussed only in reference to the 1960s avant garde. Henry Martin and Keith Waters, *Jazz: The First 100 Years,* 3rd ed. (Boston: Cengage Learning, 2010).

14. Take, for instance, the following passage from the introduction to a textbook chapter titled, "Confusion and Fusion: From the '70s to the '80s," by Frank Tirro: "Rock 'n' roll and free jazz had attacked the mainstream music and threatened the old guard. These sounds so pervaded the music of young jazz musicians that [Sonny] Rollins and others foundered directionless in a turbulent sea. They had paid their dues and were ready to reap their rewards, but what they knew and what they believed in were no longer of value, or so it seemed . . . By the end of the decade, the leading figures would find satisfactory and satisfying answers. But at that moment, it seemed to many that jazz would not survive." Frank Tirro, *Jazz: A History,* 2nd ed. (New York: Norton, 1993), 406–7.

15. Ken Burns's ten-part documentary *Jazz* is perhaps the most extreme in this regard. The final episode, which covers the years 1961–2000, devotes practically no time to new musical movements of the 1970s, with the exception of five minutes about fusion (all on Miles Davis), two minutes on the Art Ensemble of Chicago, and five minutes to cover (somewhat pejoratively) the entire career of Cecil Taylor. By contrast, the episode includes approximately forty-three minutes on the later careers of Duke Ellington, Louis Armstrong, and Dexter Gordon. It also includes a two-minute eulogy on the death of jazz in the 1970s, which precedes a discussion of the rise of the neoclassical movement of the 1980s.

Ken Burns, Lynn Novick, and Geoffrey C. Ward, *Jazz* (Washington, DC: PBS DVD, 2000), DVD.

16. Joachim-Ernst Berendt and Günther Huesmann, *The Jazz Book: From Ragtime to the 21st Century*, 7th ed. (Chicago: Lawrence Hill Books, 2009), 32–34.

17. To take two clear examples, locally based studies such as William Howland Kenney's work on Chicago and Thomas Brothers' scholarship on New Orleans reveal how each city existed not as a homogeneous stepping-stone toward an inevitable musical (r)evolution, but as fragmented communities that developed in diverse and idiosyncratic ways. William Howland Kenney, *Chicago Jazz: A Cultural History, 1904–1930* (New York: Oxford University Press, 1993); Thomas David Brothers, *Louis Armstrong's New Orleans* (New York: W. W. Norton, 2006).

18. Looker, *BAG: Point from Which Creation Begins*; Isoardi, *Dark Tree*; Lewis, *Power Stronger Than Itself*.

19. Other work to benefit from geographically grounded analysis includes the above-cited examples of Thomas Brothers and William Howland Kenney, as well as Patrick Burke, *Come On In and Hear the Truth: Jazz and Race on 52nd Street* (Chicago: University of Chicago Press, 2008).

20. Several groups tried to position themselves in such a role during this period, including the Jazz Composers Guild, the New York Musicians Organization, and the Collective Black Artists, but none managed to form a citywide coalition on the scale of Chicago's AACM or St. Louis's BAG.

21. For an overview of deconstructive approaches to historiography, see Alun Munslow, *Deconstructing History*, 2nd ed. (New York: Routledge, 2006).

22. For a more detailed account of Sultan's life and work with the Aboriginal Music Society, see Michael Heller, liner notes to Aboriginal Music Society, *Father of Origin*, Eremite Records MTE-54/55/56, 2011, 2 LPs, 1 compact disc.

23. Albums recorded at Studio We include: Ted Daniel, *In the Beginning*, recorded April–May 1975, Altura Records ALT 1, 1997, compact disc; Steve Reid, *Nova*, Mustevic MS-2001, 1976, LP; Kappo Umezu, *Seikatsu Kōjyō Iinkai*, recorded August 11, 1975, Self-released, 1975, LP.

24. Aboriginal Music Society, *Father of Origin*; Aboriginal Music Society, *Whispers from the Archive*, Porter Records PRCD4070 / PRLP027, LP and compact disc.

25. For example, analyses that draw crude equivalences between certain playing styles with certain political views.

26. Ingrid T. Monson, *Freedom Sounds: Civil Rights Call Out to Jazz and Africa* (Oxford: Oxford University Press, 2007), 23–28.

27. Gabriel Solis, *Monk's Music: Thelonious Monk and Jazz History in the Making* (Berkeley: University of California Press, 2008), 1–16, 28–60.

28. David Scott, "Introduction: On the Archaeologies of Black Memory," *Small Axe*, no. 26 (2008): xiv.

29. Antoinette M. Burton, *Dwelling in the Archive: Women Writing House, Home, and History in Late Colonial India* (New York: Oxford University Press, 2003).

30. Lewis, *Power Stronger Than Itself*, xxvii.

31. Ahmed Abdullah, interview with author, November 11, 2009, digital recording, Brooklyn, NY.

32. Cooper-Moore, interview with author, October 16, 2009, digital recording, New York, NY.

33. This issue is taken up further in chapter 8.
34. Billy Bang, interview with author, July 27, 2010, digital recording, Bronx, NY.

CHAPTER 2

1. As just one example, the New Grove Dictionary of Jazz mentions lofts in the entries of thirty separate musicians. The entry for "Loft Jazz," however, consists of a single, somewhat misleading sentence: "Loft Jazz: A term sometimes applied to the styles of free jazz which were performed in lofts in New York in the mid-1970s." "Loft Jazz," in *The New Grove Dictionary of Jazz*, 2nd ed., edited by Barry Kernfeld. *Oxford Music Online*, accessed February 13, 2012, www.oxfordmusiconline.com/subscriber/article/grove/music/J273300.

2. George Lewis, *A Power Stronger Than Itself: The AACM and American Experimental Music* (Chicago: University of Chicago Press, 2008), 88–89.

3. Brian Priestley, *Mingus: A Critical Biography* (London: Quartet Books, 1982), 46.

4. Lewis, *Power Stronger Than Itself*, 90.

5. Scott Saul, *Freedom Is, Freedom Ain't: Jazz and the Making of the Sixties* (Cambridge, MA: Harvard University Press, 2003), 125–26; Michael Heller, "So We Did It Ourselves: A Social and Musical History of Musician-Organized Jazz Festivals from 1960 to 1973" (MA thesis, Rutgers University, 2005), 15–17.

6. Quoted in Saul, *Freedom Is, Freedom Ain't*, 125.

7. Scott Saul's account of this event places it on the day after the festival. However, Gene Lee's contemporary reporting cites the final performances taking place on that afternoon. I have chosen to use Lee's chronology, due to its closer proximity to the event (Gene Lees, "Newport: The Trouble," *Down Beat*, August 18, 1960, 22).

8. Heller, "So We Did It Ourselves," 33–35.

9. Several excellent accounts of the guild's activities have been published. See Benjamin Piekut, *Experimentalism Otherwise: The New York Avant-Garde and Its Limits* (Berkeley: University of California Press, 2011); Ben Young, *Dixonia: A Bio-Discography of Bill Dixon* (Westport, CT: Greenwood Press, 1998); Christopher Backriges, "African American Musical Avant-Gardism" (PhD dissertation, York University, 2001); Heller, "So We Did It Ourselves."

10. Rob Backus, *Fire Music: A Political History of Jazz* (Chicago: Vanguard Books, 1976), 71–72.

11. Coltrane expressed admiration for the project, but declined to participate. Young, *Dixonia*, 178.

12. Lewis, *Power Stronger Than Itself*, 91.

13. Lewis, *Power Stronger Than Itself*.

14. Benjamin Looker, *BAG: "Point from Which Creation Begins"—The Black Artists' Group of St. Louis* (St. Louis: University of Missouri Press, 2004).

15. Steven Louis Isoardi, *The Dark Tree: Jazz and the Community Arts in Los Angeles* (Berkeley: University of California Press, 2006), 97.

16. Two other factors should be noted in passing. One relates to the visionary leadership that animated and inspired these groups, especially that of Muhal Richard Abrams in Chicago and Tapscott in Los Angeles. A second would be the vastly different settings of mid-1960s New York, Chicago, St. Louis, and LA, each of which presented unique challenges for musicians.

17. Per the group's bylaws reprinted in Lewis, *Power Stronger Than Itself,* the group's only restriction was that in AACM-sponsored concerts, "The majority personnel . . . must be AACM members in good standing" (117). Members performing in other, non-AACM concerts presented no problems for the organization (121).

18. Though this was true throughout the 1960s and '70s, Isoardi notes that in later decades the Arkestra would accept more Latino members, and in the 1990s collaborated with several white artists as well. Isoardi, *Dark Tree,* 96–97, 287.

19. Frank Kofsky, *Black Nationalism and the Revolution in Music* (New York: Pathfinder Press, 1970); John D. Baskerville, *The Impact of Black Nationalist Ideology on American Jazz Music of the 1960s and 1970s* (Lewiston, NY: E. Mellen Press, 2003); Philippe Carles and Jean-Louis Comolli, *Free Jazz—Black Power* (Paris: Galilée, 1979).

20. Lewis, *Power Stronger Than Itself,* 197–99.

21. Looker, *BAG: "Point from Which Creation Begins,"* 67.

22. Taumbu (né Hal Ector), quoted in Isoardi, *Dark Tree,* 96.

23. Kofsky's work is especially forward in such assertions.

24. Sharon Zukin, *Loft Living: Culture and Capital in Urban Change* (London: Radius, 1988), 30–31.

25. Ibid., 2.

26. Ibid., 14. See also chapter 6.

27. Ibid., 24.

28. Ibid., 44.

29. Robert Caro, *The Power Broker: Robert Moses and the Fall of New York* (New York: Knopf, 1974), 769–70.

30. Christopher Mele, *Selling the Lower East Side: Culture, Real Estate, and Resistance in New York City* (Minneapolis: University of Minnesota Press, 2000), 180–219.

31. Ann L. Buttenwieser, Paul Willen, and James S. Rossant, eds., *The Lower Manhattan Plan: Visions for Downtown New York* (New York: Princeton Architectural Press, 1966 [2002]). This document does not explicitly address LOMEX, which is mentioned only in passing as a project whose future completion was tacitly assumed (Pt. 2, p. 12). It also does not address proposals for a sports stadium, which are referenced in Zukin, *Loft Living,* 45.

32. Zukin, *Loft Living,* 44.

33. Ibid., 55.

34. Ibid., 114.

35. Mele, *Selling the Lower East Side:* 191–93.

36. Jill Jonnes, *South Bronx Rising: The Rise, Fall, and Resurrection of an American City* (New York: Fordham University Press, 2002), 117–26.

37. Ibid., 26.

38. Definitions of SoHo have changed somewhat over time. These boundaries signify the region named when the area was declared a landmark district in 1973.

39. Zukin, *Loft Living,* 121.

40. Ibid., 54.

41. "SoHo Wins Landmark Fight," *SoHo Weekly News,* October 11, 1973, 1.

42. Scott E. Brown and Robert Hilbert, *James P. Johnson: A Case of Mistaken Identity* (Metuchen, NJ: Scarecrow Press, 1986), 165–75.

43. Scott DeVeaux, *The Birth of Bebop: A Social and Musical History* (Berkeley: University of California Press, 1997), 202–35.

44. Linda Dahl, *Morning Glory: A Biography of Mary Lou Williams* (New York: Pantheon Books, 1999), 177–93; Stephanie Stein Crease, *Gil Evans: Out of the Cool: His Life and Music* (Chicago: A cappella, 2002), 124–45.

45. Barney Josephson and Terry Trilling-Josephson, *Cafe Society: The Wrong Place for the Right People* (Urbana: University of Illinois Press, 2009); Patrick Burke, *Come On In and Hear the Truth: Jazz and Race on 52nd Street* (Chicago: University of Chicago Press, 2008); Imamu Amiri Baraka, "New York Loft and Coffee Shop Jazz," in *Black Music* (New York: Akashic, [1967] 2010), 112–14; Young, *Dixonia*, 18.

46. Sam Stephenson, *The Jazz Loft Project: Photographs and Tapes of W. Eugene Smith from 821 Sixth Avenue, 1957–1965* (New York: Knopf, 2009).

47. Dan Serro, interview with author, June 28, 2010, digital recording, New York, NY.

48. Unlike the many stories that circulate about unscrupulous recordists who made tapes without permission, Serro was careful to note that he always tried to get clearance from musicians before recording them.

49. Serro, interview with author.

50. Ibid.

51. The space was not Serro's residence. Dan Serro, email correspondence with author, January 2, 2011.

52. Baraka, "New York Loft and Coffee Shop Jazz."

53. The fact that the concerts were open to the public is demonstrated by Baraka's reference to ads in the *Village Voice*. Ibid., 112.

54. Ibid., 98, 104.

55. Piekut, *Experimentalism Otherwise*, 106.

56. The space was just across the street from the building that later housed the Tin Palace and Studio Infinity.

57. Dave Burrell, interview with author, July 29, 2010, digital recording, Philadelphia, PA.

58. Mark Whitecage, interview with author, July 28, 2010, digital recording, Montville, NJ.

CHAPTER 3

1. Kiyoshi Koyama, "Ornette at Prince Street," *Swing Journal*, October 1969.

2. Ornette Coleman, interview with author, October 22, 2009, digital recording, New York, NY.

3. John Litweiler, *Ornette Coleman: The Harmolodic Life* (London: Quartet Books, 1992), 136–37.

4. Ornette Coleman, *Friends and Neighbors: Ornette Live at Prince Street*, Flying Dutchman FDS-123, 1970, LP.

5. Litweiler, *Ornette Coleman: The Harmolodic Life*.

6. Rashied Ali, interview with author, September 26, 2007, digital recording via telephone, New York, NY.

7. Juma Sultan, interview with author, September 11, 2009, digital recording, Kerhonkson, NY

8. Brent Hayes Edwards and Katherine Whatley, "'Ornette at Prince Street': A Glimpse from the Archives," *Point of Departure,* accessed March 9, 2016, www.pointofdeparture.org/PoD53/PoD53Ornette.html.

9. Burton Greene, email to author, January 19, 2010 (capitalization and punctuation in original).

10. Burton Greene, interview with author, February 27, 2010, digital recording, Cambridge, MA.

11. Biographical information culled from James DuBoise, interview with author, September 21, 2009, digital recording, Staten Island, NY; James DuBoise, radio interview with Ben Young, December 6, 1993, WKCR-FM, New York, NY.

12. Matt Edison, "History of the Pittsburgh Musicians' Union Local No. 471," University of Pittsburgh Libraries, Digital Collections, accessed December 15, 2011, www.library.pitt.edu/labor_legacy/MusiciansHistory471.htm.

13. Ingrid T. Monson, *Freedom Sounds: Civil Rights Call Out to Jazz and Africa* (Oxford: Oxford University Press, 2007), 42–54.

14. DuBoise, interview with Young.

15. DuBoise, interview with author.

16. History and funding proposal for Studio We, incomplete, 1974, Juma Sultan Archive, F0169.14, Kerhonkson, NY.

17. Daniel Carter, interview with author, October 29, 2009, digital recording, New York, NY.

18. Flyer for "Three Days of Peace between the Ears," 1970, Juma Sultan Archive, F0054.19, Kerhonkson, NY.

19. DuBoise, interview with Young.

20. George Frazier, "Newport: (1954—?)," *Boston Globe,* July 7, 1971. Wein corroborates this version of events in a dramatic passage of his autobiography. Despite these accounts, I question the exact coincidence of the song with the riot based on other contemporary reports, which have the riots peaking just after Warwick's set. The delicious irony of the rioting fans accompanied by Warwick's paean to peace and love might have led writers to employ a degree of poetic license. George Wein and Nate Chinen, *Myself among Others* (Cambridge, MA: Da Capo Press, 2004), 308; Ernie Santosuosso and Nathan Cobb, "Riot Threatens Early End to Jazz Festival," *Boston Globe,* July 4, 1971, 17.

21. Wein and Chinen, *Myself among Others,* 304–12.

22. Wein made the latter point explicitly in the festival's introductory press conference: "We will create the same kind of atmosphere for jazz in New York City that exists for classical music, ballet, and theater in Edinburgh and Salzburg." "Newport Jazz Festival Moves to NY," *New York Amsterdam News,* January 22, 1972.

23. Pop-oriented groups would begin to return by 1973.

24. A handful of avant garde performers were showcased, including Cecil Taylor, Pharaoh Sanders, Archie Shepp, and Ornette Coleman, who debuted his orchestral piece *Skies of America* at the festival. The bulk of the remaining schedule consisted of more straight-ahead styles. Burt Goldblatt, *Newport Jazz Festival: The Illustrated History* (New York: Dial Press, 1977), 275–78.

25. Hollie West, "From Newport to New York," *Washington Post,* January 5, 1972.

26. Wein and Chinen, *Myself among Others,* 379.

27. DuBoise, interview with Young.
28. Les Ledbetter, "Dissonants Hear Another Jazz," *New York Times*, July 6, 1972.
29. Ibid.
30. Rashied Ali, "Exploitation among NYC Musicians," personal collection of Rashied Ali, copy in possession of author (New York 1973).
31. Ali Abuwi, interview with author, September 24, 2009, digital recording, Brooklyn, NY.
32. Sam and Bea Rivers, radio interview with Ben Young, Jennifer McNeely, and Sarah Schmidt, January 9, 1994, WKCR-FM, New York, NY.
33. Noah Howard, interview with author, July 9, 2007, digital recording via telephone, Tervuren, Belgium.
34. Rashied Ali, interview with author; Ben Young, *Dixonia: A Bio-Discography of Bill Dixon* (Westport, CT: Greenwood Press, 1998).
35. Page from year-end report on NYMO activities, 1973, Juma Sultan Archive, F0248.03, Kerhonkson, NY. This copy of the list was reproduced in 1973 as part of an annual report disseminated to NYMO members. A copy of the original document from 1972 has not been found.
36. Jefferson and Moody's appearance is noted in the *New York Times*, which notes that their "services were donated with [Wein]." The exact details of the arrangement are not given. Les Ledbetter, "Street Fair's Wares and Music Attract Thousands in Harlem," *New York Times*, July 3, 1972.
37. Monson, *Freedom Sounds*, 280.
38. Monson also points out the openly discriminatory nature of business lending practices in the period (269).
39. Eric Porter, *What Is This Thing Called Jazz?: African American Musicians as Artists, Critics, and Activists* (Berkeley: University of California Press, 2002), 192.
40. Also known as "operational unity" this idea was borrowed from the cultural nationalist movement of Maulana Karenga. A major force behind the Gary convention was poet and activist Amiri Baraka, who was an adherent to Karenga's model at this time. Robert Charles Smith, *We Have No Leaders: African-Americans in the Post–Civil Rights Era* (Albany: State University of New York Press, 1996).
41. Ibid., 27–85.
42. At the group's very first meeting, AACM alums Leroy Jenkins and Anthony Braxton were brought in to discuss strategies for operating a collective. Robert Mike Mahaffay, *Free Life Loft Jazz (Snapshot of a Movement), Vol. 1* (Portland, OR: Mahaffay's Musical Archives [no catalog number], 2010), MP3 album download.
43. Digital Archives of Dave Liebman, accessed January 19, 2012, www.daveliebman.com/earticles4.php?WEBYEP_DI = 1.
44. Several organizational shortcomings are noted, for example, in Les Ledbetter, "29 Jazzmen in Rousing Jam Session on Mall," *New York Times*, July 11, 1972.
45. Drafts of the group's sample contract show extensive annotations made with saxophonist Archie Shepp. While Shepp was not a member of the organizing committee, the group incorporated Shepp's suggestions into subsequent versions. Contracts for New York Musicians Jazz Festival, Summer 1972, Juma Sultan Archive, F0075.12, Kerhonkson, NY.

46. Archival documents indicate that not every group paid the fee. Financial report and final budget of the 1972 New York Musicians' Jazz Festival, January 22, 1973, Juma Sultan Archive, F0070.14, Kerhonkson, NY.

47. The film never materialized, but some of the footage remains in the Juma Sultan Archive. Planning documents for documentary titled "The New Music Scene in New York City," circa 1973–74, Juma Sultan Archive, F0044.03–7, Kerhonkson, NY.

48. Michael Heller, "So We Did It Ourselves: A Social and Musical History of Musician-Organized Jazz from 1960 to 1973" (MA thesis, Rutgers University, 2005), 124.

49. Edwin Diamond, *Behind the Times: Inside the "New" New York Times* (New York: Villard Books, 1994), 187.

50. Chris Flicker and Thierry Trombert, "Newport Jazz Festival À New York," *Jazz Hot*, September 1972. Although the piece took its title from the Newport Festival, the magazine's cover read "New York Musicians' Jazz Festival," with no reference to Newport. The text discusses both festivals but with a clear preference for the NYMJF activities.

51. Announcement and Call for Participants for the New York Musicians' Jazz Festival, Spring 1972, Juma Sultan Archive, F0016.10, Kerhonkson, NY (emphasis in original).

52. Internal memo circulated with organizers of the New York Musicians' Jazz Festival, 1972, Juma Sultan Archive, F0108.22, Kerhonkson, NY.

53. A brief note on punctuation: in contrast to the NYMJF, which used the possessive apostrophe on the word "musicians," NYMO tended not to, instead simply using "musicians."

54. Les Ledbetter, "500 Jazz Artists Form New Group," *New York Times*, September 2, 1972.

55. Ibid.

56. Tom Johnson, "Free Jazz: A Scrawly Texture," *Village Voice*, September 14, 1972.

57. Teachers in the pilot program included Rivers, Sultan, and DuBoise, as well as Sonny Donaldson, Joe Chambers, Earl Cross, Frank Foster, Dave Burrell, Arthur Doyle, Beaver Harris, Phil Lasley, Robin Clark, and Jimmy Garrison. Archie Shepp was also scheduled to deliver a one-time lecture titled "Revolutionary Concepts in the Arts." Registration forms and informational materials relating to the Studio We School, Fall 1972, Juma Sultan Archive, F0017.02, Kerhonkson, NY.

58. Ali, "Exploitation among NYC Musicians."

59. Sam Rivers, Letter of resignation from NYMO, March 19, 1973, Juma Sultan Archive, F0248.09, Kerhonkson, NY. (Date absent on JSA copy, but present on another copy of the same letter from the collection of Rashied Ali.)

60. Letter from the board of directors of NYMO to Sam Rivers, written in response to his request to resign from the board. March 26, 1973, Juma Sultan Archive, F0022.49, Kerhonkson, NY.

61. Sultan even moved into Studio We during this period, allowing him and DuBoise to collaborate more closely.

62. Other funding during this period was obtained through Meet the Composer, the New York Department of Cultural Affairs, the New York Foundation for the Arts, the Bronx Council for the Arts and the NEA, among other organizations.

63. James DuBoise, letter to All States Management Corporation, February 19, 1975, Juma Sultan Archive, F0068.19, Kerhonkson, NY.

64. The Ladies' Fort, Studio WIS, and the Firehouse were run with vocalist Joe Lee Wilson, percussionist Warren Smith, and saxophonist Alan "Juice" Glover, respectively. All three performed in the 1972 festival. Sunrise Studios, which was organized with percussionist Mike Mahaffey, also became an important venue for Liebman and Richie Beirach after the two musicians left Free Life Communication in 1973.

65. Rivers, Letter of Resignation. Emphasis as in original. Both Sam and Bea also reiterated the importance of the festival in a 1994 radio interview. Rivers, interview with Young, McNeely, and Schmidt.

66. The festival ended on July 10; Rivbea's first concert in its new schedule took place on July 28.

67. Studio Rivbea Advertisements, *Village Voice*, from 7/27, 8/3, 8/10, 8/17, 8/24, 8/31, 9/7, 9/14, 9/21.

68. Studio Rivbea brochure and schedule, April 1973, Juma Sultan Archive, F0113.24, Kerhonkson, NY.

69. The most overtly political statements from Rivers about race came in a 1977 article in *Newsweek*, which describes Rivers as a deeply angry individual who "seethes with resentment" and quotes him saying, "There are no white men who have made any contribution to jazz ... But there sure are white men who have taken things from it. This music here is based on a life-style and that is black." The statement and the reporter's depiction are somewhat surprising, especially since Rivers's own ensemble at the time included white artists Barry Altshul and Dave Holland. I encountered no musicians from the period (white or black) who shared the authors' assessment of Rivers as an angry person. To the contrary, most described him as consistently gentle and welcoming. It is worth noting that the article appeared just a month after Rivers's highly contentious feud with Stanley Crouch, discussed further in this chapter. Hubert Saal and Abigail Kuflik, "Jazz Comes Back!," *Newsweek*, August 8, 1977.

70. Rivers, interview with Young, McNeely, and Schmidt.

71. NYSCA funding noted in ad from the *Village Voice*, July 5, 1973.

72. Rivers, interview with Young, McNeely, and Schmidt.

73. Various Artists, *Wildflowers: The New York Loft Jazz Sessions*, recorded May 14–23, 1976, Knitting Factory Works KCR 3037/39, 2000, 3 compact discs.

74. Its visibility was demonstrated strongly in 1977, when Douglas Records took out a full-page ad in the *Village Voice* to promote the set. The ad dwarfed those purchased by the loft venues themselves, which generally took up no more than one-ninth of a page. Advertisement for *Wildflowers, Village Voice*, July 4, 1977, 55.

75. Saal and Kuflik, "Jazz Comes Back!"

76. Alexandra Anderson and Robert Christgau, "Bebop to Anarchy," *Village Voice*, September 1, 1975.

77. Menu from Ali's Alley, date unknown, possibly 1976, Juma Sultan Archive, F0007.07, Kerhonkson, NY.

78. Ali, interview with author.

79. Alley's Bars flyer, 1980, Irving Stone Collection, Rutgers Institute of Jazz Studies, Newark, NJ.

80. See also chapter 6.

81. 501 Canal Street (located in a tenement building) provides an example of the former, while Ali's Alley demonstrates the latter.

82. Susan Mannheimer, "Jazz Lofts," *SoHo Weekly News,* April 18, 1974.

83. Anderson and Christgau, "Bebop to Anarchy."; Robert Palmer, "Jazz in New York's Lofts: New Music in a New Setting," *New York Times,* October 10, 1976; Stanley Crouch, "Jazz Lofts: A Walk through the Wild Sounds," *New York Times Magazine,* April 17, 1977.

84. Crouch, "Jazz Lofts: A Walk through the Wild Sounds," 40.

85. David Murray, radio interview with Paula Rich, January 6, 1994, WKCR-FM, New York, NY.

86. From Chicago's AACM came Muhal Richard Abrams, Kalaparusha Maurice McIntyre, Lester Bowie, Amina Claudine Myers, Henry Threadgill, Steve McCall, Fred Hopkins, Chico Freeman, Malachi Thompson, Iqua Colson, Adegoke Colson, George Lewis, and the members of the Art Ensemble of Chicago. From St. Louis came Julius Hemphill, Baikida Caroll, Charles Bobo Shaw, Joseph Bowie, Philip Wilson, Oliver Lake, J. D. Parran, Patricia Cruz, and Emilio Cruz. From LA came David Murray, Arthur Blythe, Butch Morris, Will Connell, James Newton, and Stanley Crouch (who was still actively performing as a drummer). George Lewis, *A Power Stronger Than Itself: The AACM and American Experimental Music* (Chicago: University of Chicago Press, 2008), 333; Benjamin Looker, *BAG: "Point from Which Creation Begins"—The Black Artists' Group of St. Louis* (St. Louis: University of Missouri Press, 2004), 222–25; Steven Louis Isoardi, *The Dark Tree: Jazz and the Community Arts in Los Angeles* (Berkeley: University of California Press, 2006), 143.

87. John Fischer, interview with author, November 12, 2009, digital recording, New York, NY.

88. Stanley Crouch, "Telescoping the Tradition," *SoHo Weekly News,* January 8, 1976.

89. Gary Giddins, "Blythe and Murray Tower over the Loft Underground," *Village Voice,* June 20, 1977.

90. Arthur Blythe, *In the Tradition,* recorded October 1978, Columbia Records JC36300, LP; Arthur Blythe, *Lenox Avenue Breakdown,* recorded 1978, Columbia Records JC35638, LP. This excludes Rivers's recordings for Impulse (a subsidiary of ABC), as Rivers was already a known figure from his 1960s recordings for Blue Note and his brief stint in Miles Davis's band.

91. Ted Daniel, interview with author, July 30, 2010 digital recording, Ossining, NY.

92. European presenters became especially enamored of loft artists during the period and offered considerably higher performance fees. The 1976 Berliner Jazztage went so far as to base their festival around a loft theme, presenting New York–based artists including Sam Rivers and Kalaparusha Maurice McIntyre. Programs from Berliner Jazztage, 1976, Juma Sultan Archive, F0245.03, Kerhonkson, NY.

93. One rare instance of cooperation took place in 1976 with the organization of the three-day New York Loft Jazz Celebration. For a single ticket price, audiences could travel between four different lofts: the Ladies' Fort, Sunrise Studios, Jazzmania, and Environ. These efforts at pooling resources succeeding in attracting greater press attention. The festival received a positive notice in the *Times,* and an even lengthier preview by Giddins in the *Village Voice.* When it was repeated the following year, the *Times* offered an even more lavish spread, including a map of the four venues and a grid schedule of events. Despite its success, the organizers made no move to form a permanent coalition. By 1978, an unexpected change of location for Environ and new ownership at the Ladies' Fort prevented the festival from continuing for a third year. John S. Wilson, "3-Day Loft Jazz Festival Veers to

the Avant-Garde," *New York Times*, June 6, 1976; Gary Giddins, "Up from the Saloon: Lofts Celebrate Alternate Jazz," *Village Voice*, June 7, 1976; Robert Palmer, "A Jazz Festival in the Lofts," *New York Times*, June 3, 1977.

94. Rivers, interview with Young, McNeely, and Schmidt.

95. Sharon Zukin, *Loft Living: Culture and Capital in Urban Change* (London: Radius, 1988), 20, 126.

96. Wendy Schuman, "SoHo a 'Victim of Its Own Success,'" *New York Times*, November 24, 1974.

97. Zukin, *Loft Living*, 30–57.

98. This adjustment was made to section J-51-2.5 of the city code. Ibid., 13.

99. Only a few of the jazz lofts were located inside SoHo proper. Ali's Alley, on Greene St., was aided by the fact that the building had become a co-op, sheltering Ali from arbitrary rent increases. He continued to live in the space until his death in 2009. Environ, located at two different locations on Broadway, was partially funded by Danny, Darius, and Chris Brubeck. The three brothers lived in the back of the space and had a steady income through touring with their father, Dave Brubeck, as part of the Two Generations of Brubeck Band. The third major space in the area was Coleman's Artist House, which was forced to close in 1974, just as many of the changes cited in the article were beginning to take place.

100. Robert Palmer, "The Pop Life: Alice Cooper Returns Snakes and All," *New York Times*, July 15, 1977, and "The Pop Life," *New York Times*, July 22, 1977.

101. J. R. Taylor, "In the Lofts: Bond Street Breakdown," *Village Voice*, July 18, 1977.

102. In retrospect, certain aspects of Rivers's complaints are a bit surprising. For one thing, Rivbea frequently offered musicians "door gigs" during other periods throughout the year, meaning Rivers was well acquainted with the economic necessity for such a model. For another, competition among concurrent summer festivals was an annual occurrence in the lofts, though perhaps nothing had been quite as egregious as Crouch's duplication. One could even argue that it was Rivers himself who initiated such splintering when he left the NYMJF to stage his own competing summer festival in 1973.

103. From the AACM's "Nine Purposes," outlined in their 1965 charter. Reprinted in Lewis, *Power Stronger Than Itself*, 116.

104. George Lewis, "Experimental Music in Black and White: The AACM in New York, 1970–1985," in *Uptown Conversation: The New Jazz Studies*, ed. Robert G. O'Meally et al. (New York: Columbia University Press, 2004), 69.

105. Ibid.

106. Palmer, "Pop Life," July 22, 1977.

107. Ebba Jahn, *Rising Tones Cross* (New York: FilmPals, 1984), DVD; A. Scott Currie, "The Vision Festival," in *Vision Festival: Peace*, ed. Patricia Nicholson (New York: Arts for Art, 2005). See also chapter 8.

CHAPTER 4

1. Robert G. O'Meally, *The Jazz Cadence of American Culture* (New York: Columbia University Press, 1998), 117.

2. Ingrid T. Monson, *Freedom Sounds: Civil Rights Call Out to Jazz and Africa* (Oxford: Oxford University Press, 2007); John Litweiler, *The Freedom Principle: Jazz after 1958* (New

York: W. Morrow, 1984); Scott Saul, *Freedom Is, Freedom Ain't: Jazz and the Making of the Sixties* (Cambridge, MA: Harvard University Press, 2003); Michael Zwerin, *Swing under the Nazis: Jazz as a Metaphor for Freedom* (New York: Cooper Square Press, 2000); Howard Reich, *Let Freedom Swing: Collected Writings on Jazz, Blues, and Gospel* (Evanston, IL: Northwestern University Press, 2010).

3. Ellington quoted in "Why Duke Ellington Avoided Music Schools," in *The Duke Ellington Reader*, ed. Mark Tucker (New York: Oxford University Press, 1993), 253; Monk quoted in "Golden Age / Time Future," *Esquire* 51, no. 1 (January 1959): 112; Rollins quoted in Ben Ratliff, *The Jazz Ear: Conversations over Music* (New York: Times Books, 2008), 41.

4. Numbers obtained from Tom Lord, *The Jazz Discography—TJD Online*, accessed July 30, 2013, www.lordisco.com. This number omits two recordings listed in Lord, both of which were pre-jazz pieces composed before 1917: The Deep River Boys' 1946 recording of the spiritual "Oh Freedom" and a W. C. Handy recording of his 1916 composition "Hail to the Spirit of Freedom," recorded in 1953.

5. A few isolated examples referencing freedom, including the previously cited quote from Ellington, do appear earlier, but not nearly as often as in the 1950s.

6. Three caveats in particular should be mentioned. First, this list cannot account for the changing nature of the recording industry and the documentation thereof. For instance, increased availability of low-cost recording equipment starting in the 1960s allowed for many more artists to record their work. The increase in numbers may therefore be partially affected by the sheer increase in the number of recordings made during those decades. Second, focusing on titles only does not account for pieces that reference freedom elsewhere in the lyrics. Third, focusing on a single word does not account for other, closely related words such as liberation, emancipation, equality, etc.

7. Penny M. Von Eschen, *Satchmo Blows Up the World: Jazz Ambassadors Play the Cold War* (Cambridge, MA: Harvard University Press, 2004); Lisa E. Davenport, *Jazz Diplomacy: Promoting America in the Cold War Era* (Jackson: University Press of Mississippi, 2009); Zwerin, *Swing under the Nazis*.

8. Frank Kofsky, *Black Nationalism and the Revolution in Music* (New York: Pathfinder Press, 1970); Imamu Amiri Baraka, *Black Music* (New York: Akashic, [1967] 2010); Saul, *Freedom Is, Freedom Ain't*; Monson, *Freedom Sounds*.

9. Litweiler, *Freedom Principle*; Ekkehard Jost, *Free Jazz* (New York: Da Capo Press, 1981).

10. Saul, *Freedom Is, Freedom Ain't*, 12.

11. Monson, *Freedom Sounds*, 238–82.

12. See chapter 3.

13. Robin D. G. Kelley, *Freedom Dreams: The Black Radical Imagination* (Boston: Beacon Press, 2002).

14. Ibid., ix.

15. As noted in chapter 2, several writers have taken this approach. See Kofsky, *Black Nationalism and the Revolution in Music*; John D. Baskerville, *The Impact of Black Nationalist Ideology on American Jazz Music of the 1960s and 1970s* (Lewiston, NY: E. Mellen Press, 2003); Philippe Carles and Jean-Louis Comolli, *Free Jazz—Black Power* (Paris: Galilée, 1979).

16. This is demonstrated, for example, by Horace Tapscott's Pan Afrikan Peoples Arkestra performing at both moderate and radical political events. Steven Louis Isoardi,

The Dark Tree: Jazz and the Community Arts in Los Angeles (Berkeley: University of California Press, 2006), 97. Similar contradictions are also discussed in Monson, *Freedom Sounds*.

17. Although the term "off-the-grid" was not common during the 1960s and '70s, I use it throughout this chapter in order to avoid the pejorative connotations of the more widespread contemporaneous term "drop out."

18. Isaiah Berlin, *Two Concepts of Liberty* (Oxford: Clarendon Press, 1958).

19. Saul's work is one example of a depiction that frames jazz artists and '60s counterculturalists as diametrically opposed. Saul, *Freedom Is, Freedom Ain't*, 16–17.

20. Quoted in Kimberly W. Benston, "'I Yam What I Am': Naming and Unnaming in Afro-American Literature," *Black American Literature Forum* 16, no. 1 (1982): 3.

21. Ibid.

22. Benston, "I Yam What I Am," 5.

23. Alex Haley, *The Autobiography of Malcolm X*, 2nd Ballantine Books ed. (New York: Ballantine Books, 1999), 203.

24. Later in his life, Malcolm X would also take on the name El-Hajj Malik El-Shabazz.

25. Bill Crow, *Jazz Anecdotes* (New York: Oxford University Press, 1990), 157.

26. Monson has pointed out that many Muslim jazz musicians were followers of the earlier Ahmaddiyah movement. Monson, *Freedom Sounds*: 147.

27. Scot Brown, *Fighting for US: Maulana Karenga, the US Organization, and Black Cultural Nationalism* (New York: New York University Press, 2003).

28. Robert Charles Smith, *We Have No Leaders: African-Americans in the Post–Civil Rights Era* (Albany: State University of New York Press, 1996), 29–30.

29. While Baraka stressed the significance of "discarding my 'slave name' and embracing blackness," the choice of name also connected with the royal references in his birth name; Le Roi, the king, becomes Amiri, the blessed prince. Imamu Amiri Baraka, *The Autobiography of LeRoi Jones / Amiri Baraka* (New York: Freundlich Books, 1984), 267.

30. Jerry Gafio Watts, *Amiri Baraka: The Politics and Art of a Black Intellectual* (New York: New York University Press, 2001), 310.

31. Hakim Jami, interview with author, October 1, 2009, digital recording, Brooklyn, NY.

32. Ali Abuwi, interview with author, September 24, 2009, digital recording from in Brooklyn, NY.

33. Throughout this chapter, I use the designator "né" to refer to the birth names that were later changed. I do this to indicate the past nature of the names, in deference to each individual's current choice of moniker. Bakr/Downs is a unique case in that he later reverted to his birth name, which he now uses in both professional and personal contexts. The omission of "né" here is intended to reflect this.

34. Charles Downs (Rashid Bakr), interview with author, October 3, 2009, digital recording, Brooklyn, NY.

35. Ahmed Abdullah, interview with author, November 11, 2009, digital recording, Brooklyn, NY.

36. Abuwi, interview with author.

37. See also George Lewis, *A Power Stronger Than Itself: The AACM and American Experimental Music* (Chicago: University of Chicago Press, 2008), 165.

38. The qualifier "professional" is important here, as many musicians continued referring to close friends and colleagues using nicknames.

39. Lewis, *Power Stronger Than Itself*.

40. It is notable, however, that venues generally did not use African-inspired names, but took their primary cue from the open-studios movement of the SoHo visual artists. This trend is especially evident in the prominence of the word "studio" in many venue names, such as Studio We, Studio Rivbea, Studio 77, Studio WIS, Sunrise Studios, and Studio Henry.

41. Cooper-Moore, interview with author, October 16, 2009, digital recording, Harlem, NY.

42. I intentionally position Cooper-Moore's move within the long tradition of trickster spirits in African American aesthetics. See Henry Louis Gates, *The Signifying Monkey: A Theory of Afro-American Literary Criticism* (New York: Oxford University Press, 1988), 3–43.

43. Cooper-Moore, interview with author.

44. Joseph Campbell et al., *Joseph Campbell and the Power of Myth* (New York: Mystic Fire Video, 2001), DVD.

45. Cooper-Moore, interview with author.

46. Juma Sultan, interview with author, July 26, 2010, digital recording, Kerhonkson, NY.

47. Todd Gitlin, *The Sixties: Years of Hope, Days of Rage* (Toronto: Bantam Books, 1987), 5.

48. For one example of a history emphasizing tension between the movements (and that also has connections to the jazz community), see accounts of Amiri Baraka's critiques of the hippie movement in Watts, *Amiri Baraka*, 235–26.

49. Dave Burrell, interview with author, July 29, 2010, digital recording, Philadelphia, PA.

50. Burton Greene, interview with author, February 27, 2010, digital recording, Cambridge, MA.

51. Ibid.

52. Abuwi, interview with author.

53. Stanley Crouch, interview with author, November 14, 2009, digital recording, Brooklyn, NY.

54. Abuwi, interview with author.

55. Juma Sultan, interview with author, August 21, 2009, digital recording, Kerhonkson, NY.

56. Abdullah, interview with author.

57. Victor Turner, *The Ritual Process: Structure and Anti-structure* (New York: Aldine de Gruyter, [1969] 1995), 115.

58. Rozanne Levine (with Mark Whitecage), interview with author, July 28, 2010, digital recording, Montville, NJ.

59. Internal memo circulated by organizers of the New York Musicians' Jazz Festival, 1972, Juma Sultan Archive, F0108.22, Kerhonkson, NY.

60. This reading is supported by the ensuing paragraphs of the document, which concentrate primarily on establishing black ownership in the jazz industry.

61. The thesis was never officially accepted by the Wesleyan Anthropology Department, a fact that Fasteau attributes to the department's conservative bent and to clashes with certain faculty members. Kali Z. Fasteau, email correspondence with author, June 21, 2010.

Though a full copy has not been located (Fasteau no longer has one, and none resides at Wesleyan), just under half of the text is preserved in the Juma Sultan Archive. Susan Levi-Fasteau (Zusaan Kali Fasteau), "Music: The Religion of Ecstasy" (incomplete copy), MA thesis, Wesleyan University, Anthropology Department, 1970 (not officially approved), Juma Sultan Archive, F0097.01, Kerhonkson, NY.

62. Levi-Fasteau, "Music: The Religion of Ecstasy," 65.

63. Levi-Fasteau's assertion, for example, that "within this society of musicians and artists, the distinctions of class, race, and sex, that form the basis for differentiation of roles and statuses in the larger society are absent" (16) reads more as a strived-for ideal than an accurate reflection of the scene as a whole, which continued to suffer from forms of structural inequality.

64. A. Scott Currie, "Sound Visions: An Ethnographic Study of Avant-Garde Jazz in New York City" (PhD dissertation, New York University, 2009).

65. Mihaly Csikszentmihalyi, *Flow: The Psychology of Optimal Experience* (New York: Harper & Row, 1990).

66. Currie, "Sound Visions," 385–86.

67. A. Scott Currie, "'The Revolution Never Ended': Improvisation, Interdisciplinarity, and Social Action on the Lower East Side," paper presented at the Annual Conference of the Society for Ethnomusicology, Philadelphia, November 17, 2011.

68. McClinton Karma Stanley, interview with author, March 13, 2010, digital recording, Brooklyn, NY.

69. Maulana (Ron) Karenga, "Black Cultural Nationalism," in *The Black Aesthetic*, ed. Addison Gayle, Jr. (New York: Doubleday, 1971), 33.

70. Interview with author, 2009, digital recording, name omitted to preserve anonymity.

71. Gitlin, *The Sixties*, 195–207.

72. Stanislav Grof, *Realms of the Human Unconscious: Observations from LSD Research* (New York: E. P. Dutton, 1976).

73. Interview with author, 2010, digital recording, name omitted to preserve anonymity.

74. Interview with author, 2009, digital recording, name omitted to preserve anonymity.

75. While the topic of drug use arose often during my interviews, two of my subjects requested not to be named in connection with the topic. These were the only such requests I received during my fieldwork. As a result, I have chosen to omit all names from this section.

76. Doris Marie Provine, *Unequal under Law: Race in the War on Drugs* (Chicago: University of Chicago Press, 2007).

77. Such distinctions were present in counterculture movements as well. See Lewis Yablonsky, *The Hippie Trip* (New York: Pegasus, 1968).

78. Interview with author, 2009, digital recording, name omitted to preserve anonymity.

79. Interview with author, 2009, digital recording, name omitted to preserve anonymity.

80. Interview with author, 2009, digital recording, name omitted to preserve anonymity.

81. At the time his account was being written, Yablonsky also served as doctoral adviser to percussionist Hetty Fox, who would later become an active participant at Studio We.

82. Yablonsky, *Hippie Trip*, 323.

83. Ibid., 308–9.

84. Mark Whitecage (with Rozanne Levine), interview with author, July 28, 2010, digital recording, Montville, NJ

85. Jami, interview with author.

86. Gitlin, *The Sixties*, 215.

87. Greene, interview with author.

88. Cooper-Moore, interview with author.

89. Billy Bang, interview with author, July 27, 2010, digital recording, Bronx, NY.

90. Abbie Hoffman, *Steal This Book* (New York: Pirate Editions, distributed by Grove Press, 1971), 11.

91. Mark Whitecage described how working a few days a month at a silkscreen shop was sufficient to pay his fifty-seven dollar per month rent in the early 1970s. The rest of his time could be devoted to music. Whitecage, interview by author.

92. Joe Lee Wilson's Ladies' Fort, for instance, referred to their annual summer festival as the "Loft Jazz Summer Festival" and used the term in flyers and newspaper advertisements. Studio WIS also used the term "Loft Music" at least once. (Various flyers, Juma Sultan Archive, F0007.15, F0114.12, F0137.01, F0215.03, Kerhonkson, NY.) The coalition of four spaces that convened for a joint festival in 1976–77 also did so under the title "Loft Jazz Celebration," though one of the organizers simultaneously critiqued the term in an interview with the *New York Times*. (Robert Palmer, "A Jazz Festival in the Lofts," *New York Times*, June 3, 1977.)

93. Roy Campbell, interview with author, October 2, 2009, digital recording, New York, NY.

94. Program for Sam Wooding Orchestra at Cami Hall, June 13, 1973, Juma Sultan Archive, F0054.11, Kerhonkson, NY; Concert Recording, Sam Wooding Orchestra at Cami Hall, June 13, 1973, Juma Sultan Archive, T0128, Kerhonkson, NY; Flyer for Studio We concert "Pianists in Focus," 1975, Juma Sultan Archive, F0007.23, Kerhonkson, NY.

95. Sam Wooding and Rae Harrison, interview with Lewis K. McMillan for syndicated radio program "Swinging with Lewis K. McMillan," June 9, 1975, sound recording in Juma Sultan Archive, T0114, Kerhonkson, NY.

96. Anthony Davis, radio interview on WKCR-FM, January 14, 1994, New York, NY.

97. Jost, *Free Jazz*, 9–10.

98. Stanley Crouch, "Telescoping the Tradition," *SoHo Weekly News,* January 8, 1976.

99. Ted Daniel, interview with author, July 30, 2010 digital recording, Ossining, NY.

100. Baraka, *Black Music*, 159.

101. The connection between energy and spirituality would also resonate strongly among European musicians in the decades that followed. Mike Heffley, *Northern Sun, Southern Moon: Europe's Reinvention of Jazz* (New Haven, CT: Yale University Press, 2005), 327 fn. 4.

102. Archie Shepp, "A View from the Inside," *Downbeat Music '66 (11th Yearbook)* 1966, 41.

103. Albert Ayler, *Spiritual Unity,* recorded July 10, 1964, ESP-Disk 1002, LP; John Coltrane, *Ascension,* recorded June 28, 1965, Impulse A95, LP; John Coltrane, *Live at the Village Vanguard Again,* recorded May 28, 1966, Impulse AS-9124, 1966, LP.

104. Ornette Coleman, *Free Jazz,* recorded December 21, 1960, Atlantic SD-1364, LP.

105. Archie Shepp, quoted in A. B. Spellman, liner notes to John Coltrane, *Ascension,* recorded June 28, 1965, Impulse A95, LP.

106. Press release for "Third World Energy" performance, May 28, 1975, Juma Sultan Archive, F0054.12, Kerhonkson, NY. Press information sheet about the ensemble Kuntu, date unknown, Juma Sultan Archive, F0075.09, Kerhonkson, NY.

107. Cooper-Moore contrasted this aspect of his past with his more recent approaches, which have moved away from energy approaches. Cooper-Moore, interview with author.

108. Greene, interview with author. ESP-Records was the most prominent label to record energy players from the mid-1960s on. Their catalog included Albert Ayler, Pharoah Sanders, Giuseppi Logan, Frank Wright, and many others who employed energy approaches.

109. Similar arguments against equating free jazz with anger have been made by scholars as well. See Mark Gridley, "Misconceptions in Linking Free Jazz with the Civil Rights Movement," *College Music Symposium* 41 (2007).

110. Greene, interview with author.

111. Whitecage, interview with author.

112. Currie, "Sound Visions."

CHAPTER 5

1. Except where noted, the information that follows is drawn from Cooper-Moore, interview with author, October 16, 2009, digital recording, Harlem, NY.

2. Susan Mannheimer, "Jazz Lofts," *SoHo Weekly News,* April 18, 1974.

3. Gary Giddins, "Taking Chances at 501 Canal," *Village Voice,* June 13, 1974.

4. Cooper-Moore, interview with author.

5. Ibid.

6. Adelaida Reyes Schramm, "Explorations in Urban Ethnomusicology: Hard Lessons from the Spectacularly Ordinary," *Yearbook for Traditional Music* 14, no. 2 (1982): 1–14; Ruth H. Finnegan, *The Hidden Musicians: Music-Making in an English Town* (Cambridge: Cambridge University Press, 1989).

7. As much of this chapter entails comparing different ways of theorizing social groups, I use the term "collectivity" as a neutral signifier to refer to any such model, including community, subculture, network, scene, etc.

8. Georg Simmel, "The Web of Group Affiliations," trans. Reinhard Bendix, in *Conflict: The Web of Group Affiliations* (New York: Free Press, [1955] 1964); Finnegan, *Hidden Musicians.*

9. W. E. B. Du Bois, *The Souls of Black Folk* (Mineola, NY: Dover, [1903] 1994), 2.

10. For an extended consideration of the relationship between double-consciousness and jazz, see Paul Austerlitz, *Jazz Consciousness: Music, Race, and Humanity* (Middletown, CT: Wesleyan University Press, 2005).

11. James Weldon Johnson, *The Autobiography of an Ex-Colored Man* (New York: Penguin Books, 1990); Kathleen Pfeiffer, "Individualism, Success, and American Identity in *The Autobiography of an Ex-Colored Man,*" *African American Review* 30, no. 3 (1996): 403–19.

12. Jean Toomer, *Cane,* Norton Critical ed. (New York: Norton, 1988); Jeff Webb, "Literature and Lynching: Identity in Jean Toomer's 'Cane,'" *English Literary History* 67, no. 1 (2000): 205–28.

13. James Baldwin, *Giovanni's Room* (New York: Delta Trade Paperbacks, [1956] 2000); Aliyyah I. Abur-Rahman, "'Simply a Menaced Boy': Analogizing Color, Undoing Domi-

nance in James Baldwin's 'Giovanni's Room,'" *African American Review* 41, no. 2 (2007): 477–86.

14. Ralph Ellison, *Invisible Man,* 2nd Vintage International ed. (New York: Vintage, 1995).

15. Duke Ellington, interview with Byng Whittaker, CBC-TV, September 2, 1964.

16. Kay Kaufman Shelemay, "Musical Communities: Rethinking the Collective in Music," *Journal of the American Musicological Society* 64, no. 2 (2011).

17. Dick Hebdige, *Subculture: The Meaning of Style* (London: Methuen, 1979); Mark Slobin, *Subcultural Sounds: Micromusics of the West* (Hanover, NH: Wesleyan University Press, 1993).

18. Howard Saul Becker, *Art Worlds* (Berkeley: University of California Press, 1982).

19. Finnegan, *Hidden Musicians.*

20. Barry Shank, "Transgressing the Boundaries of a Rock 'n' Roll Community," paper presented at the First Joint Conference of IASPM [International Association for the Study of Popular Music]-Canada and IASPM-USA, Yale University, October 1, 1988; Will Straw, "Systems of Articulation, Logics of Change: Communities and Scenes in Popular Music," *Cultural Studies* 5 (1991); Andy Bennett, "Consolidating the Music Scenes Perspective," *Poetics: Journal of Empirical Research on Culture, the Media and the Arts* 32 (2004).

21. Shelemay, "Musical Communities."

22. Anthony P. Cohen, *The Symbolic Construction of Community* (London: Tavistock, 1985).

23. Rashied Ali, "Exploitation among NYC Musicians," in personal collection of Rashied Ali, copy in possession of author (New York 1973).

24. John Fischer, interview with author, November 12, 2009, digital recording, New York, NY.

25. Fischer's model does not, for example, consider the possibility that artists might have *their own* commercial motives, especially since payment for performances was directly tied to audience turnout.

26. James DuBoise, interview with author, September 21, 2009, digital recording, Staten Island, NY.

27. Jazz Composers Orchestra of America Brochure, circa 1971–73, Juma Sultan Archive, F0150.02, Kerhonkson, NY.

28. Juma Sultan, interview with author, September 11, 2009, digital recording, Kerhonkson, NY.

29. See, for example, Shepp and Taylor's highly charged involvement in the panel discussion printed as "Point of Contact: A Discussion," *Downbeat Music '66 (11th Yearbook),* 1966.

30. Early loft-era artists to spend time in Woodstock in the late 1960s include Ali Abuwi, Barry Altshul, Karl Berger, Earl Cross, Barbara Donald, James DuBoise, Burton Greene, Eddie Heath, Rod Hicks, Sunny Murray, Ingrid Sertso, Sonny Simmons, Juma Sultan, Peter Warren, Mark Whitecage, and Philip Wilson. Berger and Sertso also founded the Creative Music Studio in Woodstock, which has presented programs in New York City and upstate since the early 1970s.

31. Burton Greene, interview with author, February 27, 2010, digital recording, Cambridge, MA.

32. Michael Heller, liner notes to Aboriginal Music Society, *Father of Origin*, Eremite Records MTE-54/55/56, 2011, 2 LPs, 1 compact disc.

33. Ali Abuwi, interview with author, September 24, 2009, digital recording, Brooklyn, NY.

34. Todd Gitlin, *The Sixties: Years of Hope, Days of Rage* (Toronto: Bantam Books, 1987), 344. The internal quotes in the passage are from a Berkeley Liberation Program, written by counterculturalists Stew Albert, Judy Clavir, and Tom Hayden in 1969.

35. Warren Smith, interview with author, September 25, 2009, digital recording, New York, NY.

36. A particularly unique manifestation of such openness came during my interview with James DuBoise, who remains focused on ways of bringing musicians together. As we spoke, DuBoise mentioned a more recent dream of setting up a nursing and hospice care facility for aging musicians, calling it, "A place where we can die together." DuBoise, interview with author.

37. Sam Stephenson, *The Jazz Loft Project: Photographs and Tapes of W. Eugene Smith from 821 Sixth Avenue, 1957–1965* (New York: Knopf, 2009); Jason Stanyek, "Brazil in the Lofts: Brazilian Jazz(mania) in New York City, ca. 1980," paper presented at the annual meeting of the American Musicological Society, New Orleans, Louisiana, November 3, 2012.

38. Stanley Crouch, interview with author, November 14, 2009, digital recording, Brooklyn, NY.

39. Flyer for Studio We concert "Pianists in Focus," 1975, Juma Sultan Archive, F0007.23, Kerhonkson, NY; Travis A. Jackson, "'Always New and Centuries Old': Jazz, Poetry and Tradition as Creative Adaptation," in *Uptown Conversation: The New Jazz Studies*, ed. Robert G. O'Meally, Brent Hayes Edwards, and Farah Jasmine Griffin (New York: Columbia University Press, 2004).

40. Race and class were often conflated in such description. For example, see Scott Saul, *Freedom Is, Freedom Ain't: Jazz and the Making of the Sixties* (Cambridge, MA: Harvard University Press, 2003), 271–336.

41. Prior to 1968, the department had been called the Office of Cultural Affairs (OCA). "DCLA History: 1965–80," accessed February 12, 2012, www.nyc.gov/html/dcla/html/about/history_65–80.shtml.

42. Many of the group's events took place at Forest Park in Queens.

43. Steve Tintweiss, interview with author, September 24, 2009, digital recording, New York, NY.

44. Described in chapter 3.

45. DuBoise, interview with author.

46. William Parker, interview with author, April 2004, analog tape recording, New York, NY.

47. Various documents relating to Studio We School, 1972, Juma Sultan Archive, folders F0017 and F0233, Kerhonkson, NY.

48. John S. Wilson, "Newport in New York—Harmony in Black and White," *New York Times*, June 24, 1973.

49. Press release for language and dance classes at Studio We, 1974, Juma Sultan Archive, F0167.11, Kerhonkson, NY.

50. Parker, interview with author.

51. Robert Palmer, "A Jazz Festival in the Lofts," *New York Times*, June 3, 1977.

52. Jazz Forum Flyer, 1980, Irving Stone Collection, Rutgers Institute of Jazz Studies, Newark, NJ; Ed Hazell, liner notes to Ensemble Muntu, *Muntu Recordings*, recorded 1975–79, NoBusiness NBCD7-8-9, 2010, 3 compact discs; T-shirt from WKCR-FM Lofts Festival, 1994, image provided by Ben Young; Palmer, "A Jazz Festival in the Lofts"; Various Artists, *Wildflowers: The New York Loft Jazz Sessions,* recorded May 14–23, 1976, Knitting Factory Works KCR 3037 / 39, 2000, 3 compact discs.

53. Patrick Burke, *Come On In and Hear the Truth: Jazz and Race on 52nd Street* (Chicago: University of Chicago Press, 2008), 1–3.

54. NYMO press release titled "George Wein Announces Joint Effort," February 6, 1973, Juma Sultan Archive, F0022.07, Kerhonkson, NY.

55. The statement is even more striking when we consider that the festival included a large number of white artists.

56. Laura Warren Hill and Julia Rabig, "Introduction" and "Toward a History of the Business of Black Power," in *The Business of Black Power: Community Development, Capitalism and Corporate Responsibility in Postwar America* (Rochester, NY: University of Rochester Press, 2012), 1–42.

57. My own identity as a white historian likely also had an effect on the way some of my subjects chose to frame these issues.

58. Smith, interview with author.

59. Ingrid T. Monson, *Freedom Sounds: Civil Rights Call Out to Jazz and Africa* (Oxford: Oxford University Press, 2007), 280.

60. Fischer, interview with author.

61. Ibid.

62. The problematic aspects of color-blind and / or power-evasive narratives in jazz are critiqued in Benjamin Piekut, "Race Community and Conflict in the Jazz Composers Guild," *Jazz Perspectives* 3, no. 3 (2009).

63. See also Benjamin Looker, *BAG: "Point from Which Creation Begins"—The Black Artists' Group of St. Louis* (St. Louis: University of Missouri Press, 2004), 67; Steven Louis Isoardi, *The Dark Tree: Jazz and the Community Arts in Los Angeles* (Berkeley: University of California Press, 2006), 96; George Lewis, *A Power Stronger Than Itself: The AACM and American Experimental Music* (Chicago: University of Chicago Press, 2008), 197–99; Robert Mike Mahaffay, *Free Life Loft Jazz (Snapshot of a Movement), Vol. 1* (Portland, OR: Mahaffay's Musical Archives [no catalog number], 2010), MP3 album download; Dave Liebman, *What It Is: The Life of a Jazz Artist*, in conversation with Lewis Porter (Lanham, MD: Scarecrow Press, 2012), 83–89.

64. Sultan, interview with author, September 11, 2009.

65. DuBoise, interview with author.

66. A few exceptions to this rule can be noted, such as the conflict between Rivbea and the Ladies' Fort detailed in chapter 3.

67. Organizers who reported variants of the organizer's dilemma included DuBoise, Cooper-Moore, Ahmed Abdullah, Mark Morganelli, and Patricia Nicholson-Parker. It is also referenced in Rashied Ali, interview with Mika Pohjola, August 5, 2009, digital recording in possession of author.

68. Cooper-Moore's patron was a banker from his hometown named Huntington Harris. Cooper-Moore, interview with author.

69. Jami, interview with author.
70. Smith, interview with author.
71. Cooper-Moore, interview with author.
72. Such as the social network analysis models developed by Georg Simmel, as well as by psychologists and ethnographers. David Frisby, *Simmel and Since: Essays on Simmel's Social Theory* (London: Routledge, 1992).
73. Certain writers substitute the word "actant" in order to avoid the association with human intentionality implied by "actor."
74. Bruno Latour, *Reassembling the Social: An Introduction to Actor-Network-Theory* (Oxford: Oxford University Press, 2005).
75. Edwin Sayes, "Actor–Network Theory and Methodology: Just What Does It Mean to Say That Nonhumans Have Agency?," *Social Studies of Science* 44, no. 1 (2014): 134–49; Richard Taruskin, "Agents and Causes and Ends, Oh My," *Journal of Musicology* 31, no. 2 (2014): 272–93.

In an African American context, the nation's fraught history of objectifying black bodies makes it especially imperative to respond to such critiques, especially considering the long-standing blind spot among many ANT scholars regarding issues of race, gender, and class. I follow the example of Benjamin Piekut in bemoaning this gap, while also maintaining that the fault lies more with the authors than with the theory itself, which does carry the potential for more nuanced analysis of systems of oppression. Benjamin Piekut, "Actor-Networks in Music History: Clarifications and Critiques," *Twentieth-Century Music* 11, no. 2 (2014): 209–12.

76. Michel Callon, "Some Elements of a Sociology of Translation: Domestication of the Scallops and the Fishermen of St. Brieuc Bay," *Sociological Review* 32 (1984): 197.
77. Piekut, "Actor-Networks in Music History," 195.
78. Ibid., 34–37.
79. John Field, *Social Capital*, 2nd ed. (London: Routledge, 2008), 43.
80. The best-known versions of social capital theory were advanced by Pierre Bourdieu, James Coleman, and Robert Putnam. Pierre Bourdieu's approach focuses on how social capital is wielded by dominant classes to maintain exclusive networks and structures of inequality. James Coleman argues that social capital is available to all regardless of class, and helps individuals develop networks of resources through the expectation of reciprocity. Lastly, Robert Putnam sees social capital as a resource held not by individuals, but in groups, arguing that collectivities with higher amounts of social capital have distinct benefits over those with less. Field, *Social Capital*, 13–47.

While drawing connections with social capital theory is not common within ANT, I take inspiration from a similar approach employed by Eric Drott in his study of musical genre. Eric Drott, "The End(s) of Genre," *Journal of Music Theory* 57, no. 1 (2013): 1–45.

81. For instance, paying fees for a social club might appear to be a loss of financial capital with no hope of recouping such losses. However, the club may offer forms of social support that are repaid at a later time.
82. Studio WIS did stage public concerts as well, but with less frequency than more publicly oriented spaces like Rivbea or the Ladies' Fort.
83. Smith's loft was funded through his dual income as a Broadway performer and college professor. The fact that he did not live in the space facilitated his efforts to encourage continuous musical activity there without disrupting Smith's family life.

84. Smith, interview with author.
85. Bennett, "Consolidating the Music Scenes Perspective."
86. Straw, "Systems of Articulation," 373.
87. Eric Porter, *What Is This Thing Called Jazz?: African American Musicians as Artists, Critics, and Activists* (Berkeley: University of California Press, 2002), 287–334.

CHAPTER 6

1. Constance Rosenblum, "The 3,200-Square-Foot Adventure," *New York Times*, September 26, 2010.
2. Ibid.
3. "Given Him by His Wife," *New York Times,* March 15, 1887; "Charged with Forgery: Nicholas A. M'Cool [sic] Arrested at the Instance [sic] of His Father's Counsel," *New York Times,* January 28, 1886; *1860 U.S. Census* [database online], New York Ward 20 District 1, New York, New York, Roll M653_817, Page: 505, Image: 507, accessed May 29, 2015, www.ancestry.com.
4. "Gossip of the Week: South of 59th Street," *Real Estate Record and Builders' Guide* 51, no. 1304, March 11, 1893, 367.
5. "Buildings Projected: South of 14th Street," *Real Estate Record and Builders' Guide* 51, no. 1307, April 1, 1893, 506.
6. "Bondsman Charged with Perjury," *New York Times,* September 21, 1897.
7. "Charged with Forgery," *New York Times.*
8. The new owner, who retained the building into the twentieth century, was Hattie Clark (née Rauth). "Mechanics Liens," *Real Estate Record and Builders' Guide* 53, no. 1349, January 20, 1894, 105.
9. New York City Directories for 1899, 1902–3, 1906, 1908, 1910, *U.S. City Directories, 1821–1989* [database online], accessed May 29, 2015, www.ancestry.com.
10. Moses Rischin, *The Promised City: New York's Jews, 1870–1914* (Cambridge, MA: Harvard University Press, 1962), 76–78.
11. "Leases: Borough of Manhattan," *Real Estate Record and Builders' Guide* 66, no. 1701, October 20, 1900, 502.
12. 1905 New York State Census, *New York State Censuses, 1880, 1892, 1905* [database online], accessed May 29, 2015, www.ancestry.com.
13. Ibid.
14. In the orphan application, Guloff listed next to his address "C/O Fieman" [sic]. City business directories show a tailor named Joseph Fienman listed at the address in 1902. New York City Hebrew Orphan Asylum Records, 1860–1934 [database online], Archive Collection I-42, Roll 9, accessed July 1, 2015, www.ancestry.com; New York City Directories for 1902, U.S. City Directories, 1821–1989 [database online], accessed July 1, 2015, www.ancestry.com.
15. Ibid.; New York City Hebrew Orphan Asylum Records, 1860–1934 [database online], Archive Collection I-42, Roll 14, accessed May 29, 2015, www.ancestry.com.
16. See chapter 2.
17. Daniel Carter, interview with author, October 29, 2009, digital recording, New York, NY.

18. Christopher Mele, *Selling the Lower East Side: Culture, Real Estate, and Resistance in New York City* (Minneapolis: University of Minnesota Press, 2000), 145. Sharon Zukin also observes that many Latino residents of the Lower East Side long opposed creating subsidies for artist housing, for fear that their arrival would threaten the presence of affordable housing. Sharon Zukin, *Loft Living: Culture and Capital in Urban Change* (London: Radius, 1988), 199.

19. Wendy Schuman, "SoHo a 'Victim of Its Own Success,'" *New York Times*, November 24, 1974.

20. Ingrid Bengis, "A SoHo Pioneer, But Disenchanted: The Disenchantment of a Pioneer in SoHo," *New York Times*, June 29, 1978.

21. Richard Skinulis and Peter Christopher, *Architectural Inspiration: Styles, Details & Sources* (Erin, ON: Boston Mills Press, 2007), 103.

22. It can be instructive to read this rebranding of lofts alongside the evolving deployment of "jazz" itself (as sound, as discourse, as romanticized lifestyle) by advertisers since the mid-twentieth century. As Mark Laver argues, "Advertisers have recognized [jazz] as an extraordinarily flexible signifier: it can lend a patina of luster, sexuality, and sophistication to an aspirant luxury car; it can link a diet soft drink to ideas of agency, cultural diversity, youth, and sensual indulgence; and it can allow a leviathan, international bank to demonstrate its community engagement, appreciation for cultural diversity, and environmental activism" (229). At the same time, such uses can entail problematic erasures: "By fracturing the idea of jazz from its history, advertisements threaten to mask—if not erase—this all-important surplus of cultural and historical meanings, and thereby its practical resonance" (230). Laver has also noted (personal correspondence) that such uses of "jazz" have also extended into the realm of real estate, particularly in the frequent appearance of "jazz-themed" condo complexes in North America during the early twenty-first century (see, for just one example, http://jazzcondos.com). Mark Laver, *Jazz Sells: Music, Marketing, and Meaning*, Transnational Studies in Jazz (New York: Routledge, 2015).

23. Zukin, *Loft Living*, 59.

24. Daniel Bell, *The Coming of Post-Industrial Society: A Venture in Social Forecasting*, Special Anniversary Ed. (New York: Basic Books, 1999).

25. Bell, "The Axial Age of Technology, Foreword: 1999," in *Coming of Post-Industrial Society*, ix–lxxxiv.

26. More broadly, visual artists from the SoHo loft movement have conveyed decidedly mixed feelings about industrial nostalgia. While some have dismissed it as shallow romanticism, others embraced the challenge of developing new work in dialogue with their surroundings. An insightful exploration of the topic is offered in Marcus Field and Mark Irving, *Lofts* (Corte Madera, CA: Gingko Press, 1999), 40–47.

27. Zukin, *Loft Living*, 59.

28. Richard Kostelanetz, *SoHo: The Rise and Fall of an Artists' Colony* (New York: Routledge, 2003), 37–38.

29. John Fischer, interview with author, November 12, 2009, digital recording, New York, NY.

30. Dave Sewelson, interview with author, June 8, 2011, digital video recording, New York, NY.

31. Hakim Jami, interview with author, October 1, 2009, digital recording, Brooklyn, NY.

32. John A. Agnew, "Space and Place," in *The SAGE Handbook of Geographical Knowledge*, ed. John A. Agnew and David N. Livingstone (Los Angeles: SAGE, 2011), 316–30.

33. Yi-Fu Tuan, *Space and Place: The Perspective of Experience* (Minneapolis: University of Minnesota Press, 2001), 3, 6.

34. Ibid., 6.

35. Perry Robinson, interview with author, July 30, 2010, digital recording, Jersey City, NJ.

36. The distinction between spatial and place-oriented modes of thinking has led to a series of recent debates in the field of cultural geography. The issues rarely hinge on the terms' basic definitions, but rather on which perception should be foregrounded in a particular philosophical or political context. Edward Agnew has traced several streams of these debates throughout the twentieth century. A few examples: (1) In the aftermath of World War II, a wave of geographers moved strongly away from paradigms emphasizing place, exemplified in the work of Martin Heidegger and in light of the philosopher's associations with the Nazi party. Here, "place" (specifically an essentialized idea of Germany) was framed as regressive, while open conceptions of space (i.e., thinking about ways of building new types of lived environments) were seen as progressive and democratic. (2) Several decades later, a group of neo-Marxist scholars began critiquing spatial thinking as giving rise to a bland sameness throughout the lived environment (strip malls, for example), and thereby losing the uniqueness of individual cultural practices. Spatial thinking therefore becomes a tool for a capitalistic colonialism while places become sites for the repressed to speak back. (3) Feminist and post-humanist scholars have sought to break down the distinction entirely, opposing grand narratives by arguing that position is always relational and constantly in flux based on the bodies, objects, and associations interacting in a particular location. Agnew, "Space and Place."

37. Michel de Certeau, *The Practice of Everyday Life* (Berkeley: University of California Press, 1984), 117.

38. Field and Irving, *Lofts*, 42.

39. James DuBoise, interview with author, September 21, 2009, digital recording, Staten Island, NY; Cooper-Moore, interview with author, October 16, 2009, digital recording, Harlem, NY; Jami, interview with author.

40. This observation is not intended to discount the work of other figures who have worked to protect loft spaces for reasons of architectural history and preservation. This includes not only historic preservationists, but also architects like Richard Gluckman and artists like Dan Flavin. It is stated only to point out that these priorities were not paramount among the musicians with whom I worked.

41. Flyer for "Sun Station, Black Light" by Karma Stanley at Studio Rivbea, June 14–22, 1975, Juma Sultan Archive, F0115.01, Kerhonkson, NY.

42. Fischer, interview with author.

43. Dave Burrell, interview with author, July 29, 2010, digital recording, Philadelphia, PA.

44. Cooper-Moore, interview with author.

45. Steve Dalachinsky, interview with author, June 8, 2011, digital video recording, New York, NY.

46. William Weber, "Concert (ii)," *Grove Music Online, Oxford Music Online*, accessed July 1, 2015.

47. Christopher Small, "A Place for Hearing," in *Musicking: The Meanings of Performing and Listening* (Hanover, NH: University Press of New England, 1998), 19–29.

48. Howard Thompson, "Going Out Guide: Home Sweet Jazz," *New York Times*, February 23, 1978.

49. Pianist Dave Burrell told of one loft that only started charging admission after too many guests began eating all of the food at the owner's weekly potluck dinners. Burrell, interview with author.

50. Rocco John Iacovone, interview with author, June 11, 2011, digital video recording, New York, NY.

51. Zukin, *Loft Living*, 69.

52. William Parker, interview with author, July 17, 2014, digital recording, New York, NY. These quotes refer, respectively, to 501 Canal, a private loft owned by Roger Baird, Studio We, and Rivbea.

53. Ibid.

54. David Kreuter, interview with author, June 8, 2011, digital video recording, New York, NY.

55. Madeleine Kamber, interview with author, June 11, 2011, digital video recording, New York, NY.

56. Ben Ratliff, "Irving Stone, Ardent Fan of the Downtown Music Scene, Dies at 80," *New York Times*, June 21, 2003, web edition, accessed July 1, 2015, www.nytimes.com/2003/06/21/obituaries/21STON.html.

57. Steve Koenig, interview with author, June 11, 2011, digital video recording, New York, NY.

58. Ras Moshe, interview with author, June 11, 2011, digital video recording, New York, NY.

59. Rashied Ali, interview with author, September 26, 2007, digital recording via telephone, New York, NY.

60. Elina Hytönen-Ng, *Experiencing "Flow" in Jazz Performance* (Farnham, UK; Burlington, VT: Ashgate, 2013), 116.

61. Les Ledbetter, "Jazzmen Sound Off on State and Status of Their Art," *New York Times*, July 7, 1972, 20.

62. Lest this sound too utopian, Moshe was also careful to note that his father tended to take him along to some lofts but not others, noting that certain spaces had reputations for being more (or less) kid-friendly.

63. Valerie Wilmer, *As Serious as Your Life: The Story of the New Jazz* (Westport, CT: L. Hill, 1980).

64. Ibid., 209.

65. Patricia Hill Collins notes similar critiques regarding sexism offered by major figures like Elaine Brown and Angela Davis in reference to the Black Panther Party and Maulana Karenga's US Organization. Patricia Hill Collins, *From Black Power to Hip Hop: Racism, Nationalism, and Feminism* (Philadelphia: Temple University Press, 2006), 107.

66. Imamu Amiri Baraka, "Black Woman," *Black World*, July 1970, 7–8.

67. Collins, *From Black Power to Hip Hop*, 111.

68. bell hooks, *Ain't I a Woman: Black Women and Feminism* (Boston: South End Press, 1981), 95.

69. Despite the invaluable critiques cited in this section, one should not infer that black nationalism was uniformly misogynistic throughout its history. An important counterpoint is offered by James Smethurst, who points out that not only did many nationalist leaders (including Baraka and Karenga) significantly revise their views on gender in later years, but that numerous women in the movement became influential figures in the women's liberation struggle. As Smethurst writes, "This is not to say that sexism and masculinism disappeared from the Black Arts and Black Power movements; far from it.... Rather, it is to claim that caricatured versions of those movements as fundamentally and unusually sexist distort them and the legacy of black women (and some men) in those movements as well as their contributions to the rise of second-wave feminism." James Smethurst, *The Black Arts Movement: Literary Nationalism in the 1960s and 1970s* (Chapel Hill: University of North Carolina Press, 2005), 87.

70. Wilmer, "It Takes Two People to Confirm the Truth," in *As Serious as Your Life,* 191–203.

71. For a more detailed analysis of the role of gender in distinguishing between public and private spheres, see Nancy Fraser, "Rethinking the Public Sphere: A Contribution to the Critique of Actually Existing Democracy," *Social Text,* nos. 25–26 (1990): 56–80.

72. Wilmer, *As Serious as Your Life,* 195.

73. Ibid., 201.

74. Ibid., 206.

75. Susan Mannheimer, "Jazz Lofts," *SoHo Weekly News,* April 18, 1974.

76. Other members of Presearch at various times included bassist Kim Clarke, pianists Renee Botofasina and Jackie Bonneau, drummers Marionette Monette and Sheila Grant, trumpeter Jean Davis, and cellist Akua Dixon.

77. Hetty Fox, interview with author, September 4, 2009, digital recording, Bronx, NY.

78. "BSU Leader Appointed to Black Studies Post," *Los Angeles Times,* March 5, 1969.

79. Fox, interview with author.

80. Jill Jonnes, *South Bronx Rising: The Rise, Fall, and Resurrection of an American City,* 2nd ed. (New York: Fordham University Press, 2002), 117–26.

81. Jeff Chang, *Can't Stop Won't Stop: A History of the Hip-Hop Culture* (New York: St. Martin's Press, 2005), 14–5.

82. David Gonzalez, "Summer Rituals: Play Street Becomes a Sanctuary," *New York Times,* August 2, 2009.

83. Fox, interview with author.

84. Ibid.

85. See, for instance, Hamiett Bluiett deriding the loft moniker as reducing musicians' work to a form of "building jazz" in Robert Palmer, "The Pop Life," *New York Times,* July 22, 1977.

CHAPTER 7

1. Arlette Farge, *The Allure of the Archives,* trans. Thomas Scott-Railton (New Haven, CT: Yale University Press, 2013), 94–101; Michel-Rolph Trouillot, *Silencing the Past: Power and the Production of History* (Boston: Beacon Press, 1995), 25.

2. Major figures associated with the archival turn in the humanities include Antoinette Burton, Jacques Derrida, Nicholas Dirks, Arlette Farge, Michel Foucault, Carolyn Steedman,

and Ann Stoler. For a summary of major themes in the discipline see Carolyn Steedman, *Dust: The Archive and Cultural History* (New Brunswick, NJ: Rutgers University Press, 2002), 1–16; Ann Laura Stoler, *Along the Archival Grain: Epistemic Anxieties and Colonial Common Sense* (Princeton, NJ: Princeton University Press, 2009), 44–46.

3. See, for instance, the Studio We mission statement discussed at the beginning of the introduction to this book.

4. Brent Hayes Edwards and Jed Rasula, "The Ear of the Behearer: A Conversation in Jazz," *New Ohio Review* 3 (Spring 2008): 42–64; Brent Hayes Edwards, "Black Radicalism and the Archive" (unpublished, W. E. B. Du Bois Lecture Series, Harvard University, March 24–26, 2015).

5. Ann Stoler, "Colonial Archives and the Arts of Governance: On the Content in the Form," in *Refiguring the Archive*, ed. Carolyn Hamilton et al. (Cape Town: David Philip, 2002), 83–100; Durba Ghosh, "National Narratives and the Politics of Miscegenation," in *Archive Stories: Facts, Fictions, and the Writing of History*, ed. Antoinette M. Burton (Durham, NC: Duke University Press, 2005), 27–44.

6. Nicholas B. Dirks, "Annals of the Archive: Ethnographic Notes on the Sources of History," in *Autobiography of an Archive: A Scholar's Passage to India* (New York: Columbia University Press, 2015).

7. Kate Eichhorn, *The Archival Turn in Feminism: Outrage in Order* (Philadelphia: Temple University Press, 2013), 7.

8. Stephen Farina, *Reel History: The Lost Archive of Juma Sultan and the Aboriginal Music Society (eBook)* (Middletown, CT: Wesleyan University Press, 2012), 269–74.

9. Stephen Farina and Johndan Johnson Eilola, *The Lost Archive of Juma Sultan*, unpublished short film, DVD.

10. Jonathan Sterne, *The Audible Past: Cultural Origins of Sound Reproduction* (Durham, NC: Duke University Press, 2003), 287–333.

11. Most of the equipment was loaned to us by Ben Young, then of WKCR-FM radio in New York. Ben also provided invaluable guidance and expertise in the early stages of the project.

12. Audio engineers might be baffled by the workflow described here: copying from tape to CD, and then to hard drive. A cleaner approach would be to go directly from the tape to the hard drive. Depending on software being used, this allows one to transfer at the higher fidelities favored by modern sound archives (our transfers were limited to CD quality: 16 bit, 44.1kHz). Our choice in the matter again resulted from a lack of available equipment. At the time, Sultan's only computer was a rather old home desktop that lacked the processing power needed to reliably run audio software. As we worried about system crashes in the middle of transferring fragile tapes (we tried to play each reel only once), the CD recorder seemed to be a more robust option.

13. For current standards strived for by major archives, see Mike Casey and Bruce Gordon, *Sound Directions: Best Practices for Audio Preservation* (Bloomington; Cambridge, MA: Indiana University; Harvard University, 2007).

14. Juma Sultan, interview with author, August 27, 2009, Kerhonkson, NY.

15. One example of the traces of older material occurs on tape T0160, which features a rehearsal by Sonny Simmons. The tape is recorded over what appears to be a radio or television interview with an unknown speaker. The interview becomes noticeably audible several

times when the music breaks. At one particularly humorous moment, just as the band finishes a take, the voice of the interviewee cuts through clearly, saying, "I can't do anything about it so I might as well make a buck with it!" Tape T0160, Juma Sultan Archive, Kerhonkson, NY.

16. Trouillot, *Silencing the Past*, 49.

17. David Morton, *Off the Record: The Technology and Culture of Sound Recording in America* (New Brunswick, NJ: Rutgers University Press, 2000), 150–62.

18. Sterne, *Audible Past*, 7–8.

19. Juma Sultan, interview with author, August 21, 2009, digital recording, Kerhonkson, NY.

20. George Lewis, *A Power Stronger Than Itself: The AACM and American Experimental Music* (Chicago: University of Chicago Press, 2008), 17–22.

21. Tapes T0157, T0158, and T0175, Juma Sultan Archive, Kerhonkson, NY.

22. Letter from unknown sender to Ali Abuwi requesting tapes, February 1, 1973, Juma Sultan Archive, F0206.02, Kerhonkson, NY.

23. Sultan, interview with author, August 21, 2009.

24. Documents pertaining to documentary *The New Music Scene in New York*, 1973, Juma Sultan Archive, F0044.03–06, Kerhonkson, NY. Clips from several of the films are online at Sultan's website, www.jumasarchive.org.

25. Benjamin Piekut, *Experimentalism Otherwise: The New York Avant-Garde and Its Limits* (Berkeley: University of California Press, 2011), 5. Piekut goes on to expand upon Nyman's conception in the following pages, but this basic characterization is sufficient for my purposes here.

26. Tape T0163, Juma Sultan Archive, Kerhonkson, NY.

27. Sven Spieker, *The Big Archive: Art from Bureaucracy* (Cambridge, MA: MIT Press, 2008), 21.

28. Ibid., 8.

29. Ted Daniel's Ujamaa Records and Alan Glover's Omolade Music are just two examples of such an approach.

30. Sultan's 2011 release of archival material by the group would be issued as Aboriginal Music Society, *Father of Origin*, Eremite Records MTE-54/55/56, 2011, 2 LPs, 1 compact disc.

31. Elvin Jones/Jimmy Garrison Sextet, *Illumination*, Impulse Records IMPD-250, 1998 [1963], compact disc.

32. Michael Heller, liner notes to Aboriginal Music Society, *Father of Origin*, Eremite Records MTE-54/55/56, 2011, 2 LPs, 1 compact disc.

33. Sonny Simmons, *Manhattan Egos*, Arhoolie Records CD-483, 2000 (1969), compact disc.

34. Sultan, interview with author, August 21, 2009.

35. Sonny Simmons, *Music from the Spheres*, ESP-Disk 1043, 1968, compact disc.

36. Tapes T0160, T0168 and T0179, Juma Sultan Archive, Kerhonkson, NY.

37. Lydia Goehr, *The Imaginary Museum of Musical Works: An Essay in the Philosophy of Music* (Oxford: Clarendon Press, 1992).

38. Georgina Born, "On Musical Mediation: Ontology, Technology and Creativity," *Twentieth-Century Music* 2, no. 1 (2005): 7–36.

39. Tony Whyton, *Jazz Icons: Heroes, Myths and the Jazz Tradition* (Cambridge: Cambridge University Press, 2010), 85–87.

40. Simmons, *Manhattan Egos*.

41. Sultan, interview with author, August 21, 2009.

42. Ibid.; Tapes T0120, T0157, T0161, T0231, T0403, and T0429, Juma Sultan Archive, Kerhonkson, NY. As the archive still contains other Simmons material that has not been transferred, other recordings of both pieces may be present as well.

43. Jed Rasula, "The Media of Memory: The Seductive Menace of Records in Jazz History," in *Jazz among the Discourses*, ed. Krin Gabbard (Durham, NC: Duke University Press, 1995), 140.

44. This organization should not be confused with the Woodstock-based Group 212 Intermedia Workshop, nor with choreographer Elaine Summers's Experimental Intermedia Foundation.

45. Intramedia, Inc. Funding Proposal, 1975, Juma Sultan Archive, F0196.02, Kerhonkson, NY.

46. Intramedia, Inc. Constitution and Bylaws (multiple versions), 1975, Juma Sultan Archive, F0146.02–3, Kerhonkson, NY.

47. Schedule for Intramedia, Inc. multimedia presentations, 1975, Juma Sultan Archive, F0012.01–4, Kerhonkson, NY.

48. Intramedia, Inc. proposals for multimedia archive and information center, 1975, Juma Sultan Archive, F0204.01, F0024.01, Kerhonkson, NY.

49. Completed acceptance forms for Intramedia, Inc. Advisory Council, 1975, Juma Sultan Archive, F0081.04, Kerhonkson, NY.

50. Juma Sultan, interview with author, September 11, 2009, digital recording, Kerhonkson, NY.

51. Steedman, *Dust*, 11, 70–71; Antoinette Burton, *Dwelling in the Archive: Women Writing House, Home, and History in Late Colonial India* (Oxford; New York: Oxford University Press, 2003), 23.

52. After moving to Orlando in 1991, Rivers founded a big band devoted to playing a massive library of compositions dating back to 1958, including many written in the loft years. He continued prolifically writing new compositions up until his death in 2011. Joseph Hayes, "Rivers' Edge," *Orlando Magazine*, July 2009, accessed July 1, 2015, www.orlandomagazine.com/Orlando-Magazine/July-2009/Rivers-Edge.

53. Although similar arguments permeate a great deal of (old and new) media studies, I draw the terminology of the mechanism from Matthew G. Kirschenbaum, *Mechanisms: New Media and the Forensic Imagination* (Cambridge, MA: MIT Press, 2008).

54. The ever-changing role of paper in the office has been a major topic in the growing field of paper studies, and includes contributions from scholars such as Joanne Yates, Cornelia Vismann, Bruno Latour, Lisa Gitelman, and Ben Kafka. For an overview of the field, see Ben Kafka, "Paperwork: The State of the Discipline," *Book History* 12, no. 1 (2009): 340–53.

55. Sultan, interview with author, September 11, 2009.

56. Letter from Juma Sultan to the National Endowment for the Arts, April 29, 1975, Juma Sultan Archive, F0220.09, Kerhonkson, NY.

57. Handwritten list of "People that can deal with the press," 1973, Juma Sultan Archive, F0232.02, Kerhonkson, NY.

58. Hetty Fox, interview with author, September 4, 2009, digital recording, Bronx, NY.

59. Robin D. G. Kelley, "The Jazz Wife: Muse and Manager," *New York Times,* July 21, 2002.

60. "About Cobi Narita," *Cobi Narita Homepage,* accessed July 1, 2015, www.cobinarita.com/aboutcobi.html.

61. Sylvia Levine Leitch, "Cobi Narita: A Special Place for Jazz," *JazzTimes,* November 8, 2011, accessed July 1, 2015, http://jazztimes.com/articles/28897-cobi-narita-a-special-place-for-jazz.

62. Leitch, "Cobi Narita."

63. Quoted in Peter J. Ling and Sharon Monteith, *Gender and the Civil Rights Movement* (New Brunswick, NJ: Rutgers University Press, 2004), 7.

64. Eric Porter's history of the CBA cites Narita's departure as a significant blow to the group's fundraising capabilities, contributing to their decline in the late 1970s. Eric Porter, "'Out of the Blue': Black Creative Musicians and the Challenge of Jazz, 1940–1995" (PhD dissertation, University of Michigan, 1997), 205.

65. The most complete paper archive of CBA activities does not rest with Sultan, but in the CBA collection at the Rutgers Institute of Jazz Studies. Collective Black Artists / Reggie Workman Papers, 1969–1987, Institute of Jazz Studies, Rutgers University, Newark, NJ.

66. Packet of materials relating to "Nation Time Productions," 1971, Juma Sultan Archive, F0143.04, Kerhonkson, NY.

67. Ibid.

68. "Classified Advertisements for Business Services," *New York Times,* March 20, 1977, sec. Business & Finance.

69. Jason Kao Hwang, interview with author, June 10, 2011, digital video recording, New York, NY.

70. Rick Lopez, "The William Parker Sessionography (website)," accessed July 1, 2015, www.bb10k.com/PARKER.disc.html.

71. Rick Lopez, *The William Parker Sessionography,* 1st print edition (New York: Centering Music, 2014).

72. Jim Eigo, interview with author, June 11, 2011, digital video recording, New York, NY; Irving and Stephanie Stone Collection of NYC Avant Garde Ephemera, ca. 1976–1992, Institute of Jazz Studies, Rutgers University, Newark, NJ.

73. Spieker, *Big Archive,* 21.

74. Ibid.

75. John Ridener, *From Polders to Postmodernism: A Concise History of Archival Theory* (Duluth, MN: Litwin Books, 2009).

76. Jacques Derrida, *Archive Fever: A Freudian Impression* (Chicago: University of Chicago Press, 1996). Derrida's most radical example of this possibility comes in his reading of the act of circumcision as an archive of Jewishness (or perhaps, the cultural memory of Jewishness) as a physical mark etched upon on the exterior surface of the infant's body.

77. Spieker, *Big Archive,* 20–22. Spieker also notes that these two locations—circulation and the archive—are connected in various ways. One is through *respect des fonds,* through which archived objects retain the connections amassed during the course of their circulation.

78. Antoinette Burton, "Introduction: Archive Fever, Archive Stories," in Burton, ed., *Archive Stories,* 2.

79. David Scott, "Introduction: On the Archaeologies of Black Memory," *Small Axe*, no. 26 (2008): vi.

80. The space was a loft located at 315 Broadway, which Sultan recalled as we listened to Tape T0271, Juma Sultan Archive, Kerhonkson, NY.

81. Later in our work together, Sultan chose to temper this policy somewhat. When we unexpectedly came across a cassette of Hendrix overdubs late in my fieldwork, I asked Sultan if he still wished to remove it. To my surprise, he instructed me to leave it in its sequence in the archive. Another tape contained a commercially available radio interview with Hendrix, which Sultan also said to leave in. I believe this shift was the result of two things: (1) by this time we had developed a higher degree of trust, and (2) our progress in the archive meant that our materials were among the best-organized parts of Sultan's collection, making it a more optimal place for storing such artifacts.

82. Michel Foucault, *Archaeology of Knowledge* (London; New York: Routledge, 2002), 146.

83. In a recent talk, Brent Edwards enacted a similar interrogation of *respect des fonds* in a discussion of archivist Robert Hill's work with the papers of Marcus Garvey's Universal Negro Improvement Association (UNIA). Brent Hayes Edwards, "The Politics of Scraps (Black Radicalism and the Archive, Part 1)" (unpublished lecture, W. E. B. Du Bois Lecture Series, Harvard University, March 24, 2015).

84. Annie Kuebler, interview with author, October 2, 2009, digital recording, Newark, NJ.

CHAPTER 8

Epigraph: Robert Palmer, "Loft Jazz Shifts to a Different Scene," *New York Times*, January 26, 1979.

1. Robert Palmer, "Jazz: Rivbea Festival," *New York Times*, June 25, 1979.

2. Of the four, Experimental Intermedia and Roulette were the only two located inside artists' homes.

3. Robert Palmer, "Cuban Jazz Finds Home in 52nd St. Loft," *New York Times*, June 12, 1981; Robert Palmer, "Anthony Davis—Beyond Jazz," *New York Times*, November 15, 1981; Edward Rothstein, "Jazz Trio: 'Some Music,'" *New York Times*, September 23, 1982; Tim Page, "Offbeat Music Thrives in Loft Settings," *New York Times*, October 10, 1982.

4. Palmer, "Loft Jazz Shifts to a Different Scene"; Robert Palmer, "Jazz at Entermedia Puts Soloists in Spotlight," *New York Times*, March 2, 1979; Robert Palmer, "Jazz at the Public Has a New Name and Variations on Its Theme," *New York Times*, September 12, 1980; Jon Pareles, "Volatility Fuels the Advance of Jazz," *New York Times*, September 11, 1983.

5. One important difference, however, was that Morganelli generally offered guaranteed payment amounts to his featured weekend artists. Performers on slower nights tended to be paid from the door profits. Mark Morganelli, interview with author, November 11, 2009, digital recording, Dobbs Ferry, NY.

6. Morganelli, interview with author.

7. One space that did continue in a very similar model to earlier lofts was Studio Henry. The space was run by Wayne Horvitz, Robin Holcomb, Dave Sewelson, and a number of other musicians who lived there in the early 1980s. Dave Sewelson, interview with author, June 10, 2011, video recording, New York, NY.

8. Palmer, "Jazz at Entermedia Puts Soloists in Spotlight."
9. Pareles, "Volatility Fuels the Advance of Jazz."
10. George Lewis, "Experimental Music in Black and White: The AACM in New York, 1970–1985," in *Uptown Conversation: The New Jazz Studies,* ed. Robert G. O'Meally, Brent Hayes Edwards, and Farah Jasmine Griffin (New York: Columbia University Press, 2004).
11. Ibid., 69.
12. Ibid., 70.
13. Neil Tesser, "Von and Chico Freeman: Tenor Dynasty," *Down Beat,* July 1980.
14. Robert Palmer, "Leaders to Debut at Sweet Basil," *New York Times,* May 30, 1986.
15. David Murray, radio interview with Paula Rich, January 6, 1994, WKCR-FM, New York, NY.
16. Ibid.
17. Ibid.
18. Ben Young, interview with author, March 16, 2012, digital recording via telephone, New York, NY.
19. The concerts featured performances by Ahmed Abdullah's Solomonic Quintet (with Carlos Ward, Mashujaa, Charles Moffett, and Billy Bang), a trio of Hamiet Bluiett, Reggie Nicholson, and Kevin O'Neal, a duo of Tom Bruno and Rick Dellaratta, and an expanded lineup of the band Other Dimensions in Music (adding Sabir Mateen and Andrew Lamb to the group's usual personnel of Roy Campbell, Daniel Carter, William Parker, and Charles Downs).
20. Tapes of WKCR Lofts Festival, 1993–94, WKCR-FM Archives, New York, NY.
21. Ibid.
22. Willard Jenkins, "Lost Jazz Shrines (page 9)," accessed February 15, 2011, www.jazzhouse.org/lost/.
23. Jim Eigo, interview with author, June 11, 2011, video recording, New York, NY.
24. Various Artists, *David X. Young's Jazz Loft,* Jazz Magnet Records #2002, 2000, 2 compact discs; Jim Eigo, interview with author, March 16, 2012, digital recording via telephone, New York, NY.
25. Jimmy Lyons, *The Box Set,* Ayler Records aylCD-036–40, 2003, 5 compact discs.
26. Ensemble Muntu, *Muntu Recordings,* NoBusiness Records NBCD7–9, 2010, 3 compact discs. William Parker, *Centering,* NoBusiness Records NBCD42–7, 2012, 6 compact discs.
27. Alan Glover, *The Juice Quartet Archives (Vols. 1–3),* Omolade Music, 2010, 3 compact discs; Ted Daniel, *Ted Daniel Sextet,* Ujamaa Records U-1001-A, (1970) 2006, compact disc; Ted Daniel, *The Loft Years: Volume 1,* Ujamaa Records 1002, 2009, compact disc; Cooper-Moore, *Outtakes 1978,* Hopscotch Records HOP-16, 2005, compact disc.
28. Sam Stephenson, *The Jazz Loft Project: Photographs and Tapes of W. Eugene Smith from 821 Sixth Avenue, 1957–1965* (New York: Knopf, 2009).
29. For a more extended treatment of the Duke archive, including a critique that the project's title courts a degree of risk in regard to historical understandings of the term "jazz loft," see Michael C. Heller, "Reconstructing Loft Legacies," in "Reconstructing We: History, Memory and Politics in a Loft Jazz Archive" (PhD dissertation, Harvard University, 2012), 221–60.
30. James DuBoise, interview with author, September 21, 2009, digital recording, Staten Island, NY.

31. Ted Daniel, interview with author, July 30, 2010, digital recording, Ossining, NY.

32. Ali Abuwi, interview with author, September 24, 2009, digital recording, Brooklyn, NY.

33. Steve Tintweiss, interview with author, September 24, 2009, digital recording, New York, NY.

34. Ahmed Abdullah, interview with author, November 11, 2009, digital recording, Brooklyn, NY.

35. More recently, Parker has been a prolific author and chronicler of the loft period. His output includes two books of interviews of musicians, most of whom are associated with the loft period. William Parker, *Conversations* (Paris: RogueArt, 2011); William Parker, *Conversations II: Dialogues and Monologues* (Paris: RogueArt, 2015).

36. Ebba Jahn, *Rising Tones Cross* (New York: FilmPals, 1985), DVD; A. Scott Currie, "The Vision Festival," in *Vision Festival: Peace*, ed. Patricia Nicholson (New York: Arts for Art, 2005).

37. The group included more than fifty artists over the course of its three-year lifespan. The personnel at a WKCR performance in 1994 presents a representative sample: Bill Cole, Will Connell, Jr., Cooper-Moore, Marco Eneidi, Rob Brown, Jemeel Moondoc, Daniel Carter, Lee Gongwer, Blaise Siwula, Richard Keene, Zusaan Kali Fasteau, Richard Keene, Rozanne Levine, Sabir Mateen, Perry Robinson, Jason Zappa, Karen Borca, Roy Campbell, Alex Lodico, Masahiko Kono, Vincent Chancey, Steve Dalachinsky, Steve Cannon, Yuko Otomo, Jeff Schlanger, Ellen Christi, Patricia Nicholson Parker, Mariko Tanabe, Ujaku, Akim, Paul Alix, Elaine Shipman, Christine Coppola, Bea Licata, John Blum, Matthew Shipp, Burton Greene, William Parker, Wilber Morris, Hideji Taninaka, Jason Hwang, Mark Whitecage, Jackson Krall, Denis Charles, Warren Smith, and Jerome Cooper. Personnel from Rick Lopez, *William Parker Sessionography,* accessed August 17, 2016, www.bb10k.com/PARKER.disc.html.

38. Patricia Nicholson, telephone interview with author, February 23, 2012, New York, NY.

39. Numerous accounts mistakenly name William Parker as the founder and organizer of the Vision Festival. In my three years of working for the festival, I discussed this frequently with both Parker and Nicholson. Both confirm that Nicholson has been the primary organizer since the festival's inception (though Parker does serve on the festival's board of directors).

40. Indeed, it was as a member of this community that I myself first became interested in the loft era itself. As an employee of the Vision Festival between 2003 and 2006, I repeatedly heard stories from older musicians about the city in the 1970s, when one could travel on foot to hear adventurous music played at any hour of the day.

41. Edwards was particularly aware of my work with Sultan, as he also served as a member of my dissertation committee and had read early drafts of my research.

42. William Parker, interview with author, July 17, 2014, digital recording, New York, NY.

43. Juma Sultan, interview with author, August 21, 2009, digital recording, Kerhonkson, NY.

BIBLIOGRAPHY

WORKS CITED

Abur-Rahman, Aliyyah I. "'Simply a Menaced Boy': Analogizing Color, Undoing Dominance in James Baldwin's 'Giovanni's Room.'" *African American Review* 41, no. 2 (2007): 477–86.

Agnew, John A. "Space and Place." In *The SAGE Handbook of Geographical Knowledge*, edited by John A. Agnew and David N. Livingstone, 316–30. Los Angeles: SAGE, 2011.

Ali, Rashied. "Exploitation among NYC Musicians." Personal Collection of Rashied Ali (copy in possession of author). New York, 1973.

Anderson, Alexandra, and Robert Christgau. "Bebop to Anarchy." *Village Voice*, September 1, 1975, 52, 93.

Austerlitz, Paul. *Jazz Consciousness: Music, Race, and Humanity*. Middletown, CT: Wesleyan University Press, 2005.

Backriges, Christopher. "African American Musical Avant-Gardism." PhD dissertation, York University, 2001.

Backus, Rob. *Fire Music: A Political History of Jazz*. Chicago: Vanguard Books, 1976.

Baldwin, James. *Giovanni's Room*. New York: Delta Trade Paperbacks, (1956) 2000.

Baraka, Imamu Amiri. *The Autobiography of LeRoi Jones / Amiri Baraka*. New York: Freundlich Books, 1984.

———. *Black Music*. New York: Akashic, (1967) 2010.

———. "Black Woman." *Black World*, July 1970.

Baskerville, John D. *The Impact of Black Nationalist Ideology on American Jazz Music of the 1960s and 1970s*. Lewiston, NY: E. Mellen Press, 2003.

Becker, Howard Saul. *Art Worlds*. Berkeley: University of California Press, 1982.

Bell, Daniel. *The Coming of Post-Industrial Society: A Venture in Social Forecasting*. Special Anniversary Ed. New York: Basic Books, 1999.

Bengis, Ingrid. "A SoHo Pioneer, But Disenchanted: The Disenchantment of a Pioneer in SoHo." *New York Times.* June 29, 1978.

Bennett, Andy. "Consolidating the Music Scenes Perspective." *Poetics: Journal of Empirical Research on Culture, the Media and the Arts* 32 (2004): 223–34.

Benston, Kimberly W. "'I Yam What I Am': Naming and Unnaming in Afro-American Literature." *Black American Literature Forum* 16, no. 1 (Spring 1982): 2–11.

Berendt, Joachim-Ernst, and Günther Huesmann. *The Jazz Book: From Ragtime to the 21st Century.* 7th ed. Chicago: Lawrence Hill Books, 2009.

Berlin, Isaiah. *Two Concepts of Liberty.* Oxford, Clarendon Press, 1958.

"Bondsman Charged with Perjury." *New York Times.* September 21, 1897.

Born, Georgina. "On Musical Mediation: Ontology, Technology and Creativity." *Twentieth-Century Music* 2, no. 1 (2005): 7–36.

Brothers, Thomas David. *Louis Armstrong's New Orleans.* New York: W. W. Norton, 2006.

Brown, Scot. *Fighting for US: Maulana Karenga, the US Organization, and Black Cultural Nationalism.* New York: New York University Press, 2003.

Brown, Scott E., and Robert Hilbert. *James P. Johnson: A Case of Mistaken Identity.* Metuchen, NJ: Scarecrow Press, 1986.

"BSU Leader Appointed to Black Studies Post." *Los Angeles Times,* March 5, 1969, SF8.

Burke, Patrick. *Come On In and Hear the Truth: Jazz and Race on 52nd Street.* Chicago: University of Chicago Press, 2008.

Burton, Antoinette M. *Archive Stories: Facts, Fictions, and the Writing of History.* Durham, NC: Duke University Press, 2005.

———. *Dwelling in the Archive: Women Writing House, Home, and History in Late Colonial India.* New York: Oxford University Press, 2003.

Buttenwieser, Ann L., Paul Willen, and James S. Rossant, eds. *The Lower Manhattan Plan: Visions for Downtown New York.* New York: Princeton Architectural Press, 1966 (2002).

Callon, Michel. "Some Elements of a Sociology of Translation: Domestication of the Scallops and the Fishermen of St. Brieuc Bay." *Sociological Review* 32 (1984): 196–233.

Carles, Philippe, and Jean-Louis Comolli. *Free Jazz—Black Power.* Paris: Galilée, 1979.

Caro, Robert. *The Power Broker: Robert Moses and the Fall of New York.* New York: Knopf, 1974.

Casey, Mike, and Bruce Gordon. *Sound Directions: Best Practices for Audio Preservation.* Bloomington; Cambridge, MA: Indiana University; Harvard University, 2007.

Chang, Jeff. *Can't Stop Won't Stop: A History of the Hip-Hop Culture.* New York: St. Martin's Press, 2005.

"Charged with Forgery: Nicholas A. M'Cool [sic] Arrested at the Instance [sic] of His Father's Counsel." *New York Times.* January 28, 1886.

Cohen, Anthony P. *The Symbolic Construction of Community.* London: Tavistock, 1985.

Collins, Patricia Hill. *From Black Power to Hip Hop: Racism, Nationalism, and Feminism.* Philadelphia: Temple University Press, 2006.

Crouch, Stanley. "Jazz Lofts: A Walk through the Wild Sounds." *New York Times Magazine,* April 17, 1977, 40–2, 46.

———. "Telescoping the Tradition." *SoHo Weekly News,* January 8, 1976.

Crow, Bill. *Jazz Anecdotes.* New York: Oxford University Press, 1990.

Csikszentmihalyi, Mihaly. *Flow: The Psychology of Optimal Experience.* New York: Harper & Row, 1990.

Currie, A. Scott. "'The Revolution Never Ended': Improvisation, Interdisciplinarity, and Social Action on the Lower East Side." Paper presented at the Annual Conference of the Society for Ethnomusicology, Philadelphia, November 17, 2011.

———. "Sound Visions: An Ethnographic Study of Avant-Garde Jazz in New York City." PhD dissertation, New York University, 2009.

———. "The Vision Festival." In *Vision Festival: Peace,* edited by Patricia Nicholson. New York: Arts for Art, 2005.

Dahl, Linda. *Morning Glory: A Biography of Mary Lou Williams.* New York: Pantheon Books, 1999.

Davenport, Lisa E. *Jazz Diplomacy: Promoting America in the Cold War Era.* Jackson: University Press of Mississippi, 2009.

"DCLA History: 1965–80." www.nyc.gov/html/dcla/html/about/history_65–80.shtml. Accessed February 12, 2012.

De Certeau, Michel. *The Practice of Everyday Life.* Berkeley: University of California Press, 1984.

Derrida, Jacques. *Archive Fever: A Freudian Impression.* Chicago: University of Chicago Press, 1996.

DeVeaux, Scott. "Constructing the Jazz Tradition." *Black American Literature Forum* 25, no. 3 (Fall 1991): 525–60.

———. *The Birth of Bebop: A Social and Musical History.* Berkeley: University of California Press, 1997.

Diamond, Edwin. *Behind the Times: Inside the "New" New York Times.* New York: Villard Books, 1994.

Dirks, Nicholas B. *Autobiography of an Archive: A Scholar's Passage to India.* New York: Columbia University Press, 2015.

Drott, Eric. "The End(s) of Genre." *Journal of Music Theory* 57, no. 1 (2013): 1–45.

Du Bois, W. E. B. *The Souls of Black Folk.* Mineola, NY: Dover, (1903) 1994.

Edison, Matt. "History of the Pittsburgh Musicians' Union Local No. 471." Pittsburgh: University of Pittsburgh Libraries Website, Digital Collections, www.library.pitt.edu/labor_legacy/MusiciansHistory471.htm. Accessed December 15, 2011.

Edwards, Brent Hayes. "Black Radicalism and the Archive." Lectures presented at the W. E. B. Du Bois Lecture Series, Harvard University, March 24, 2015 (unpublished).

——— and Jed Rasula. "The Ear of the Behearer: A Conversation in Jazz." *New Ohio Review* 3 (Spring 2008): 42–64.

——— and Katherine Whatley. "'Ornette at Prince Street': A Glimpse from the Archives." *Point of Departure,* www.pointofdeparture.org/PoD53/PoD53Ornette.html. Accessed March 9, 2016.

Eichhorn, Kate. *The Archival Turn in Feminism: Outrage in Order.* Philadelphia: Temple University Press, 2013.

Ellison, Ralph. *Invisible Man.* 2nd Vintage International ed. New York: Vintage, 1995.

Farge, Arlette. *The Allure of the Archives.* Translated by Thomas Scott-Railton. New Haven, CT: Yale University Press, 2013.

Farina, Stephen. *Reel History: The Lost Archive of Juma Sultan and the Aboriginal Music Society (eBook)*. Middletown, CT: Wesleyan University Press, 2012.

Field, John. *Social Capital*. 2nd ed. London: Routledge, 2008.

Field, Marcus, and Mark Irving. *Lofts*. Corte Madera, CA: Gingko Press, 1999.

Finnegan, Ruth H. *The Hidden Musicians: Music-Making in an English Town*. Cambridge: Cambridge University Press, 1989.

Flicker, Chris, and Thierry Trombert. "Newport Jazz Festival À New York." *Jazz Hot*, September 1972.

Foucault, Michel. *Archaeology of Knowledge*. London; New York: Routledge, 2002.

Fraser, Nancy. "Rethinking the Public Sphere: A Contribution to the Critique of Actually Existing Democracy." *Social Text*, nos. 25–26 (1990): 56–80.

Frazier, George. "Newport: (1954—?)." *Boston Globe*, July 7, 1971.

Frisby, David. *Simmel and Since: Essays on Simmel's Social Theory*. London: Routledge, 1992.

Gabbard, Krin. "The Jazz Canon and Its Consequences." In *Jazz among the Discourses*, edited by Krin Gabbard, 1–28. Durham, NC: Duke University Press, 1995.

Gates, Henry Louis. *The Signifying Monkey: A Theory of Afro-American Literary Criticism*. New York: Oxford University Press, 1988.

Ghosh, Durba. "National Narratives and the Politics of Miscegenation." In *Archive Stories: Facts, Fictions, and the Writing of History*, edited by Antoinette M. Burton, 27–44. Durham, NC: Duke University Press, 2005.

Giddins, Gary. "Blythe and Murray Tower over the Loft Underground." *Village Voice*, June 20, 1977.

———. "Taking Chances at 501 Canal." *Village Voice*, June 13, 1974, 68.

———. "Up from the Saloon: Lofts Celebrate Alternate Jazz." *Village Voice*, June 7, 1976.

Gilmore, Mikal S. "Jazz Sizzles into the 70s." *Music Journal*, May 1971, 18–21.

Gitlin, Todd. *The Sixties: Years of Hope, Days of Rage*. Toronto: Bantam Books, 1987.

"Given Him by His Wife." *New York Times*, March 15, 1887.

Goehr, Lydia. *The Imaginary Museum of Musical Works: An Essay in the Philosophy of Music*. Oxford: Clarendon Press, 1992.

Goldblatt, Burt. *Newport Jazz Festival: The Illustrated History*. New York: Dial Press, 1977.

"Golden Age / Time Future." *Esquire* 51, no. 1 (January 1959): 112–18.

Gonzalez, David. "Summer Rituals: Play Street Becomes a Sanctuary." *New York Times*, August 2, 2009.

Gridley, Mark. "Misconceptions in Linking Free Jazz with the Civil Rights Movement." *College Music Symposium* 41 (2007): 139–55.

Grof, Stanislav. *Realms of the Human Unconscious: Observations from LSD Research*. New York: E. P. Dutton, 1976.

Haley, Alex. *The Autobiography of Malcolm X*. 2nd Ballantine Books ed. New York: Ballantine Books, 1999.

Hayes, Joseph. "Rivers' Edge." *Orlando Magazine*, July 2009.

Hazell, Ed. Liner notes to Ensemble Muntu, *Muntu Recordings*. Recorded 1975–79. NoBusiness NBCD7-8-9, 2010. 3 compact discs.

Hebdige, Dick. *Subculture: The Meaning of Style*. London: Methuen, 1979.

Heffley, Mike. *Northern Sun, Southern Moon: Europe's Reinvention of Jazz*. New Haven, CT: Yale University Press, 2005.

Heller, Michael. Liner notes to Aboriginal Music Society, *Father of Origin*. Eremite Records MTE-54/55/56, 2011. 2 LPs, 1 compact disc.

———. "Reconstructing We: History, Memory and Politics in a Loft Jazz Archive." PhD dissertation, Harvard University, 2012.

———. "So We Did It Ourselves: A Social and Musical History of Musician-Organized Jazz Festivals from 1960 to 1973." MA thesis, Rutgers University, 2005.

Hill, Laura Warren, and Julia Rabig, eds. *The Business of Black Power: Community Development, Capitalism and Corporate Responsibility in Postwar America*. Rochester, NY: University of Rochester Press, 2012.

Hoffman, Abbie. *Steal This Book*. New York: Pirate Editions, distributed by Grove Press, 1971.

hooks, bell. *Ain't I a Woman: Black Women and Feminism*. Boston: South End Press, 1981.

Hytönen-Ng, Elina. *Experiencing "Flow" in Jazz Performance*. Farnham, UK; Burlington, VT: Ashgate, 2013.

Isoardi, Steven Louis. *The Dark Tree: Jazz and the Community Arts in Los Angeles*. Berkeley: University of California Press, 2006.

Jackson, Travis A. "'Always New and Centuries Old': Jazz, Poetry and Tradition as Creative Adaptation." In *Uptown Conversation: The New Jazz Studies*, edited by Robert G. O'Meally, Brent Hayes Edwards, and Farah Jasmine Griffin, 357–73. New York: Columbia University Press, 2004.

Jenkins, Willard. "Lost Jazz Shrines (page 9)." www.jazzhouse.org/lost/. Accessed February 15, 2011.

Johnson, James Weldon. *The Autobiography of an Ex-Colored Man*. New York: Penguin Books, 1990.

Johnson, Tom. "Free Jazz: A Scrawly Texture." *Village Voice*, September 14, 1972, 41.

Jonnes, Jill. *South Bronx Rising: The Rise, Fall, and Resurrection of an American City*. 2nd ed. New York: Fordham University Press, 2002.

Josephson, Barney, and Terry Trilling-Josephson. *Cafe Society: The Wrong Place for the Right People*. Urbana: University of Illinois Press, 2009.

Jost, Ekkehard. *Free Jazz*. New York: Da Capo Press, 1981.

Kafka, Ben. "Paperwork: The State of the Discipline." *Book History* 12, no. 1 (2009): 340–53.

Karenga, Maulana (Ron). "Black Cultural Nationalism." In *The Black Aesthetic*, edited by Addison Gayle, Jr. New York: Doubleday, 1971.

Kelley, Robin D. G. *Freedom Dreams: The Black Radical Imagination*. Boston: Beacon Press, 2002.

———. "The Jazz Wife: Muse and Manager." *New York Times*, July 21, 2002.

Kenney, William Howland. *Chicago Jazz: A Cultural History, 1904–1930*. New York: Oxford University Press, 1993.

Kernfeld, Barry Dean. "The Bop Revival." In *The Blackwell Guide to Recorded Jazz*, 414–42. Cambridge, MA: Blackwell, 1995.

———, ed. "Loft Jazz." In *The New Grove Dictionary of Jazz*, 2nd ed., Oxford Music Online, www.oxfordmusiconline.com/subscriber/article/grove/music/J273300. Accessed February 13, 2012.

Kirschenbaum, Matthew G. *Mechanisms: New Media and the Forensic Imagination*. Cambridge, MA: MIT Press, 2008.

Kodat, Catherine Gunther. "Conversing with Ourselves: Canon, Freedom, Jazz." *American Quarterly* 55, no. 1 (March 2003): 1–28.
Kofsky, Frank. *Black Nationalism and the Revolution in Music.* New York: Pathfinder Press, 1970.
Kostelanetz, Richard. *SoHo: The Rise and Fall of an Artists' Colony.* New York: Routledge, 2003.
Koyama, Kiyoshi. "Ornette at Prince Street." *Swing Journal,* October 1969.
Latour, Bruno. *Reassembling the Social: An Introduction to Actor-Network-Theory.* Oxford: Oxford University Press, 2005.
Laver, Mark. *Jazz Sells: Music, Marketing, and Meaning.* Transnational Studies in Jazz. New York: Routledge, 2015.
Ledbetter, Les. "29 Jazzmen in Rousing Jam Session on Mall." *New York Times,* July 11, 1972.
———. "500 Jazz Artists Form New Group." *New York Times,* September 2, 1972, 15.
———. "Dissonants Hear Another Jazz." *New York Times,* July 6, 1972.
———. "Jazzmen Sound Off on State and Status of Their Art." *New York Times,* July 7, 1972.
———. "Street Fair's Wares and Music Attract Thousands in Harlem." *New York Times,* July 3, 1972.
Lees, Gene. "Newport: The Trouble." *Down Beat,* August 18, 1960.
Leitch, Sylvia Levine. "Cobi Narita: A Special Place for Jazz." *JazzTimes,* November 8, 2011. http://jazztimes.com/articles/28897-cobi-narita-a-special-place-for-jazz.
Levi-Fasteau, Susan. "Music: The Religion of Ecstasy." MA thesis, Wesleyan University, 1970.
Lewis, George. "Experimental Music in Black and White: The AACM in New York, 1970–1985." In *Uptown Conversation: The New Jazz Studies,* edited by Robert G. O'Meally, Brent Hayes Edwards, and Farah Jasmine Griffin, 50–101. New York: Columbia University Press, 2004.
———. *A Power Stronger Than Itself: The AACM and American Experimental Music.* Chicago: University of Chicago Press, 2008.
Liebman, Dave. *What It Is: The Life of a Jazz Artist.* In conversation with Lewis Porter. Lanham, MD: Scarecrow Press, 2012.
Ling, Peter J., and Sharon Monteith. *Gender and the Civil Rights Movement.* New Brunswick, NJ: Rutgers University Press, 2004.
Litweiler, John. *Ornette Coleman: The Harmolodic Life.* London: Quartet Books, 1992.
———. *The Freedom Principle: Jazz after 1958.* New York: W. Morrow, 1984.
Looker, Benjamin. *BAG: "Point from Which Creation Begins": The Black Artists' Group of St. Louis.* St. Louis: University of Missouri Press, 2004.
Lopez, Rick. *The William Parker Sessionography.* 1st print edition. New York: Centering Music, 2014.
Lord, Tom. *The Jazz Discography—TJD Online.* www.lordisco.com. Accessed July 30, 2013.
Mannheimer, Susan. "Jazz Lofts." *SoHo Weekly News,* April 18, 1974, 16–17.
Martin, Henry, and Keith Waters. *Jazz: The First 100 Years.* 3rd ed. Boston: Cengage Learning, 2010.
Mele, Christopher. *Selling the Lower East Side: Culture, Real Estate, and Resistance in New York City.* Minneapolis: University of Minnesota Press, 2000.
Monson, Ingrid T. *Freedom Sounds: Civil Rights Call Out to Jazz and Africa.* Oxford: Oxford University Press, 2007.

Morton, David. *Off the Record: The Technology and Culture of Sound Recording in America.* New Brunswick, NJ: Rutgers University Press, 2000.
Munslow, Alun. *Deconstructing History.* 2nd ed. New York: Routledge, 2006.
"Newport Jazz Festival Moves to NY." *New York Amsterdam News,* January 22, 1972.
O'Meally, Robert G. *The Jazz Cadence of American Culture.* New York: Columbia University Press, 1998.
Page, Tim. "Offbeat Music Thrives in Loft Settings." *New York Times,* October 10, 1982, H19.
Palmer, Robert. "Anthony Davis—Beyond Jazz." *New York Times,* November 15, 1981, D27.
———. "Cuban Jazz Finds Home in 52nd St. Loft." *New York Times,* June 12, 1981, C12.
———. "Jazz at Entermedia Puts Soloists in Spotlight." *New York Times,* March 2, 1979, C9.
———. "Jazz at the Public Has a New Name and Variations on Its Theme." *New York Times,* September 12, 1980, C12.
———. "A Jazz Festival in the Lofts." *New York Times,* June 3, 1977, C18.
———. "Jazz in New York's Lofts: New Music in a New Setting." *New York Times,* October 10, 1976, D25, D30.
———. "Jazz: Rivbea Festival." *New York Times,* June 25, 1979, C14.
———. "Leaders to Debut at Sweet Basil." *New York Times,* May 30, 1986, C23.
———. "Loft Jazz Shifts to a Different Scene." *New York Times,* January 26, 1979, C19.
———. "The Pop Life." *New York Times,* July 22, 1977, C19.
———. "The Pop Life: Alice Cooper Returns Snakes and All." *New York Times,* July 15, 1977.
Pareles, Jon. "Volatility Fuels the Advance of Jazz." *New York Times,* September 11, 1983, H18.
Parker, William. *Conversations.* Paris: RogueArt, 2011.
———. *Conversations II: Dialogues and Monologues.* Paris: RogueArt, 2015.
Pfeiffer, Kathleen. "Individualism, Success, and American Identity in *The Autobiography of an Ex-Colored Man.*" *African American Review* 30, no. 33 (1996): 403–19.
Piekut, Benjamin. "Actor-Networks in Music History: Clarifications and Critiques." *Twentieth-Century Music* 11, no. 2 (2014): 191–215.
———. *Experimentalism Otherwise: The New York Avant-Garde and Its Limits.* Berkeley: University of California Press, 2011.
———. "Race Community and Conflict in the Jazz Composers Guild." *Jazz Perspectives* 3, no. 3 (2009): 191–231.
"Point of Contact: A Discussion." *Downbeat Music '66 (11th Yearbook),* 1966, 19–21, 24–26, 28–31, 110–11.
Porter, Eric. "'Out of the Blue': Black Creative Musicians and the Challenge of Jazz, 1940–1995." PhD dissertation, University of Michigan, 1997.
———. *What Is This Thing Called Jazz?: African American Musicians as Artists, Critics, and Activists.* Berkeley: University of California Press, 2002.
Priestley, Brian. *Mingus: A Critical Biography.* London: Quartet Books, 1982.
Provine, Doris Marie. *Unequal under Law: Race in the War on Drugs.* Chicago: University of Chicago Press, 2007.
Rasula, Jed. "The Media of Memory: The Seductive Menace of Records in Jazz History." In *Jazz among the Discourses,* edited by Krin Gabbard, 134–62. Durham, NC: Duke University Press, 1995.
Ratliff, Ben. "Irving Stone, Ardent Fan of the Downtown Music Scene, Dies at 80." *New York Times,* June 21, 2003, web ed. www.nytimes.com/2003/06/21/obituaries/21STON.html.

———. *The Jazz Ear: Conversations over Music.* New York: Times Books, 2008.
Reich, Howard. *Let Freedom Swing: Collected Writings on Jazz, Blues, and Gospel.* Evanston, IL: Northwestern University Press, 2010.
Ridener, John. *From Polders to Postmodernism: A Concise History of Archival Theory.* Duluth, MN: Litwin Books, 2009.
Rischin, Moses. *The Promised City: New York's Jews, 1870–1914.* Cambridge, MA: Harvard University Press, 1962.
Rosenblum, Constance. "The 3,200-Square-Foot Adventure." *New York Times,* September 26, 2010.
Rothstein, Edward. "Jazz Trio: 'Some Music.'" *New York Times,* September 23, 1982, C14.
Saal, Hubert, and Abigail Kuflik. "Jazz Comes Back!" *Newsweek,* August 8, 1977, 51.
Santosuosso, Ernie, and Nathan Cobb. "Riot Threatens Early End to Jazz Festival." *Boston Globe,* July 4, 1971, 17.
Saul, Scott. *Freedom Is, Freedom Ain't: Jazz and the Making of the Sixties.* Cambridge, MA: Harvard University Press, 2003.
Sayes, Edwin. "Actor–Network Theory and Methodology: Just What Does It Mean to Say That Nonhumans Have Agency?" *Social Studies of Science* 44, no. 1 (2014): 134–49.
Schramm, Adelaida Reyes. "Explorations in Urban Ethnomusicology: Hard Lessons from the Spectacularly Ordinary." *Yearbook for Traditional Music* 14, no. 2 (1982): 1–14.
Schuman, Wendy. "SoHo a 'Victim of Its Own Success.'" *New York Times,* November 24, 1974, R1, R10.
Scott, David. "Introduction: On the Archaeologies of Black Memory." *Small Axe,* no. 26 (2008): v–xvi.
Shank, Barry. "Transgressing the Boundaries of a Rock 'n' Roll Community." Paper presented at the First Joint Conference of IASPM [International Association for the Study of Popular Music]-Canada and IASPM-USA, Yale University, October 1, 1988.
Shelemay, Kay Kaufman. "Musical Communities: Rethinking the Collective in Music." *Journal of the American Musicological Society* 64, no. 2 (Summer 2011): 349–90.
Shepp, Archie. "A View from the Inside." *Downbeat Music '66 (11th Yearbook),* 1966, 39–44.
Simmel, Georg. "The Web of Group Affiliations." Translated by Reinhard Bendix. In *Conflict: The Web of Group Affiliations.* New York: Free Press, (1955) 1964.
Skinulis, Richard, and Peter Christopher. *Architectural Inspiration: Styles, Details & Sources.* Erin, ON: Boston Mills Press, 2007.
Slobin, Mark. *Subcultural Sounds: Micromusics of the West.* Hanover, NH: Wesleyan University Press, 1993.
Small, Christopher. *Musicking: The Meanings of Performing and Listening.* Hanover, NH: University Press of New England, 1998.
Smethurst, James. *The Black Arts Movement: Literary Nationalism in the 1960s and 1970s.* Chapel Hill: University of North Carolina Press, 2005.
Smith, Robert Charles. *We Have No Leaders: African-Americans in the Post–Civil Rights Era.* Albany: State University of New York Press, 1996.
"SoHo Wins Landmark Fight." *SoHo Weekly News,* October 11, 1973, 1.
Solis, Gabriel. *Monk's Music: Thelonious Monk and Jazz History in the Making.* Berkeley: University of California Press, 2008.

Spellman, A. B. Liner notes to John Coltrane, *Ascension*. Recorded June 28, 1965. Impulse A95, LP.
Spieker, Sven. *The Big Archive: Art from Bureaucracy.* Cambridge, MA: MIT Press, 2008.
Stanyek, Jason. "Brazil in the Lofts: Brazilian Jazz(mania) in New York City, ca. 1980." Paper presented at the annual meeting of the American Musicological Society, New Orleans, Louisiana, November 3, 2012.
Steedman, Carolyn. *Dust: The Archive and Cultural History.* New Brunswick, NJ: Rutgers University Press, 2002.
Stein Crease, Stephanie. *Gil Evans: Out of the Cool: His Life and Music.* Chicago: A cappella, 2002.
Stephenson, Sam. *The Jazz Loft Project: Photographs and Tapes of W. Eugene Smith from 821 Sixth Avenue, 1957–1965.* New York: Knopf, 2009.
Sterne, Jonathan. *The Audible Past: Cultural Origins of Sound Reproduction.* Durham, NC: Duke University Press, 2003.
Stoler, Ann Laura. *Along the Archival Grain: Epistemic Anxieties and Colonial Common Sense.* Princeton, NJ: Princeton University Press, 2009.
———. "Colonial Archives and the Arts of Governance: On the Content in the Form." In *Refiguring the Archive,* edited by Carolyn Hamilton, Verne Harris, Jane Taylor, Michele Pickover, Graeme Reid, and Razia Saleh, 83–100. Cape Town: David Philip, 2002.
Straw, Will. "Systems of Articulation, Logics of Change: Communities and Scenes in Popular Music." *Cultural Studies* 5 (1991): 368–88.
Tapscott, Horace, and Steven Louis Isoardi. *Songs of the Unsung: The Musical and Social Journey of Horace Taspcott.* Durham, NC: Duke University Press, 2001.
Taruskin, Richard. "Agents and Causes and Ends, Oh My." *Journal of Musicology* 31, no. 2 (2014): 272–93.
Taylor, J. R. "In The Lofts: Bond Street Breakdown." *Village Voice,* July 18, 1977, 50–51.
Tesser, Neil. "Von and Chico Freeman: Tenor Dynasty." *Down Beat,* July 1980, 24–28.
Thompson, Howard. "Going Out Guide: Home Sweet Jazz." *New York Times,* February 23, 1978.
Tirro, Frank. *Jazz: A History.* 2nd ed. New York: Norton, 1993.
Toomer, Jean. *Cane.* Norton Critical ed. New York: Norton, 1988.
Trouillot, Michel-Rolph. *Silencing the Past: Power and the Production of History.* Boston: Beacon Press, 1995.
Tuan, Yi-Fu. *Space and Place: The Perspective of Experience.* Minneapolis: University of Minnesota Press, 2001.
Tucker, Mark, ed. *The Duke Ellington Reader.* New York: Oxford University Press, 1993.
Turner, Victor. *The Ritual Process: Structure and Anti-structure.* New York: Aldine de Gruyter, (1969) 1995.
Von Eschen, Penny M. *Satchmo Blows Up the World: Jazz Ambassadors Play the Cold War.* Cambridge, MA: Harvard University Press, 2004.
Watts, Jerry Gafio. *Amiri Baraka: The Politics and Art of a Black Intellectual.* New York: New York University Press, 2001.
Webb, Jeff. "Literature and Lynching: Identity in Jean Toomer's 'Cane.'" *English Literary History* 67, no. 1 (Spring 2000): 205–28.
Wein, George, and Nate Chinen. *Myself among Others.* Cambridge, MA: Da Capo Press, 2004.

West, Hollie. "From Newport to New York." *Washington Post,* January 5, 1972.
Whyton, Tony. *Jazz Icons: Heroes, Myths and the Jazz Tradition.* Cambridge: Cambridge University Press, 2010.
Wilmer, Valerie. *As Serious as Your Life: The Story of the New Jazz.* 1st U.S. Revised Edition. Westport, CT: L. Hill, 1980.
Wilson, John S. "3-Day Loft Jazz Festival Veers to the Avant-Garde." *New York Times,* June 6, 1976, 61.
———. "Newport In New York—Harmony in Black and White." *New York Times,* June 24, 1973, D17, 25.
Yablonsky, Lewis. *The Hippie Trip.* New York: Pegasus, 1968.
Young, Ben. *Dixonia: A Bio-Discography of Bill Dixon.* Westport, CT: Greenwood Press, 1998.
Zukin, Sharon. *Loft Living: Culture and Capital in Urban Change.* London: Radius, 1988.
Zwerin, Michael. *Swing under the Nazis: Jazz as a Metaphor for Freedom.* New York: Cooper Square Press, 2000.

LIST OF INTERVIEWS

Abdullah, Ahmed. 2009. Interview with author. Brooklyn, NY (11 November).
Abuwi, Ali. 2009. Interview with author. Brooklyn, NY (24 September).
Ali, Rashied. 2007. Telephone interview with author. New York, NY (26 September).
———. 2009. Interview with Mika Pohjola. Digital copy in possession of author. New York, NY (5 August).
Bang, Billy. 2010. Interview with author. New York, NY (27 July).
Borca, Karen. 2011. Interview with author. New York, NY (10 June).
Brennen, Patrick. 2011. Interview with author. New York, NY (10 June).
Burrell, Dave. 2010. Interview with author. Philadelphia, PA (29 July).
Campbell, Roy. 2009. Interview with author. New York, NY (2 October).
Capp, Todd. 2011. Interview with author. New York, NY (11 June).
Carter, Daniel. 2009. Interview with author. New York, NY (29 October).
Cohen, Jeffrey. 2011. Interview with author. New York, NY (8 June).
Coleman, Ornette. 2009. Interview with author. New York, NY (22 October).
Cooper-Moore (Gene Ashton). 2009. Interview with author. New York, NY (16 October).
Crouch, Stanley. 2009. Interview with author. Brooklyn, NY (14 November).
Dalachinsky, Steve. 2011. Interview with author. New York, NY (8 June).
Daniel, Ted. 2010. Interview with author. Ossining, NY (30 July).
Davis, Anthony. 1994. Radio interview. WKCR-FM. New York, NY (14 January).
Downs, Charles (Rashid Bakr). 2009. Interview with author. Brooklyn, NY (3 October).
DuBoise, James. 1993. Radio interview with Ben Young. WKCR-FM. New York, NY (6 December).
———. 2009. Interview with author. Staten Island, NY (21 September).
Ehrlich, Marty. 2010. Interview with author. New York, NY (25 June).
Eigo, Jim. 2011. Interview with author. New York, NY (11 June).
———. 2012. Telephone interview with author. New York, NY (16 March).
Ellington, Duke. 1964. Television interview with Byng Whittaker. CBC-TV. Toronto, CA (2 September).

Fischer, John. 2009. Interview with author. New York, NY (12 November).
Fox, Hetty. 2009. Interview with author. Bronx, NY (4 September).
Galanter, Bruce. 2010. Interview with author. New York, NY (29 June).
Glover, Alan. 2009. Interview with author. Poughkeepsie, NY (29 September)
Greene, Burton. 2010. Interview with author. Cambridge, MA (27 February).
Howard, Noah. 2007. Telephone interview with author. Tervuren, Belgium (9 July).
Hwang, Jason Kao. 2011. Interview with author. New York, NY (10 June).
Iacovone, Rocco John. 2011. Interview with author. New York, NY (11 June).
Jami, Hakim. 2009. Interview with author. Brooklyn, NY (1 October).
Kamber, Madeleine. 2011. Interview with author. New York, NY (11 June).
Keepnews, James. 2011. Interview with author. New York, NY (8 June).
Koening, Steven. 2011. Interview with author. New York, NY (11 June).
Kopp, Johanna. 2011. Interview with author. New York, NY (11 June).
Kuebler, Annie. 2009. Interview with author. Newark, NJ (2 October).
Kreuter, David. 2011. Interview with author. New York, NY (8 June).
Levine, Rozanne (with Mark Whitecage). 2010. Interview with author. Montville, NJ (28 July).
McIntyre, Kalaparusha Maurice. 2010. Interview with author. New York, NY (28 June).
Moshe, Ras. 2011. Interview with author. New York, NY (11 June).Morganelli, Mark. 2009. Interview with author. Dobbs Ferry, NY (11 November).
Murray, David. 1994. Radio interview with Paula Rich. WKCR-FM. New York, NY (6 January).
Nicholson Parker, Patricia. 2012. Telephone interview with author. New York, NY (23 February).
Parker, William. 2004. Interview with author. New York, NY (April).
———. 2014. Interview with author. New York, NY (17 July).
Parran, J. D. 2010. Interview with author. New York, NY (25 June).
Quiñonez, Juan. 2011. Interview with author. New York, NY (11 June).
Rigby, Joe. 2011. Interview with author. New York, NY (10 June).
Rivers, Sam and Bea. 1994. Radio interview with Ben Young, Jennifer McNeely, and Sarah Schmidt. WKCR-FM. New York, NY (9 January).
Robinson, Perry. 2010. Interview with author. Hoboken, New Jersey (30 July).
Schlanger, Jeff. 2014. Interview with author. New Rochelle, NY (13 August).
Serro, Dan. 2010. Interview with author. New York, NY (28 June).
Sewelson, Dave. 2011. Interview with author. New York, NY (8 June).
Smith, Warren. 2009. Interview with author. New York, NY (25 September).
Stanley, McClinton Karma. 2010. Interview with author. Brooklyn, NY (13 March).
Sultan, Juma. 2004. Telephone interview with author. Kerhonkson, NY (16 November).
———. 2009a. Interview with author. Kerhonkson, NY (21 August).
———. 2009b. Interview with author. Kerhonkson, NY (27 August).
———. 2009c. Interview with author. Kerhonkson, NY (2 September).
———. 2009d. Interview with author. Kerhonkson, NY (11 September).
———. 2009e. Interview with author. Kerhonkson, NY (5 December).
———. 2009f. Interview with author. Kerhonkson, NY (11 December).
———. 2009g. Interview with author. Kerhonkson, NY (14 December).

———. 2009h. Interview with author. Kerhonkson, NY (15 December).
———. 2009i. Interview with author. Kerhonkson, NY (17 December).
———. 2009j. Interview with author. Kerhonkson, NY (18 December).
———. 2010. Interview with author. Kerhonkson, NY (26 July).
Tintweiss, Steve. 2009. Interview with author. New York, NY (24 September).
Whitecage, Mark (with Rozanne Levine). 2010. Interview with author. Montville, NJ (28 July).
Young, Ben. 2012. Telephone interview with author. New York, NY (16 March).

DISCOGRAPHY AND VIDEOGRAPHY

Note: Unpublished sound recordings from the Juma Sultan Archive are not listed here. They are instead noted in the archival reference list below.

Aboriginal Music Society. *Father of Origin*. Eremite Records MTE-54/55/56, 2011. 2 LPs, 1 compact disc.
———. *Whispers from the Archive*. Porter Records PRCD4070/PRLP027. LP and compact disc.
Ayler, Albert. *Spiritual Unity*. Recorded July 10, 1964. ESP-Disk 1002, LP.
Blythe, Arthur. *In the Tradition*. Recorded October 1978. Columbia Records JC36300, LP.
———. *Lenox Avenue Breakdown*. Recorded 1978. Columbia Records JC35638, LP.
Burns, Ken, Lynn Novick, and Geoffrey C. Ward. *Jazz*. Washington, DC: PBS DVD, 2000. DVD.
Campbell, Joseph, Bill D. Moyers, George Lucas, and Catherine Tatge. *Joseph Campbell and the Power of Myth*. New York: Mystic Fire Video, 2001. DVD.
Coleman, Ornette. *Free Jazz*. Recorded December 21, 1960. Atlantic SD-1364, LP.
———. *Friends and Neighbors: Ornette Live at Prince Street*. Flying Dutchman FDS-123, 1970. LP.
Coltrane, John. *Ascension*. Recorded June 28, 1965. Impulse A95, LP.
———. *Live at the Village Vanguard Again*. Recorded May 28, 1966. Impulse AS-9124, 1966. LP.
Cooper-Moore. *Outtakes 1978*. Hopscotch Records HOP-16, 2005. Compact disc.
Daniel, Ted. *In the Beginning*. Recorded April–May 1975. Altura Records ALT 1, 1997. Compact disc.
———. *The Loft Years: Volume 1*. Ujamaa Records 1002, 2009. Compact disc.
———. *Ted Daniel Sextet*. Ujamaa Records U-1001-A, (1970) 2006. Compact disc.
Ensemble Muntu. *Muntu Recordings*. NoBusiness Records NBCD7-8-9, 2010. 3 compact discs.
Farina, Stephen, and Johndan Johnson Eilola. *The Lost Archive of Juma Sultan*. Unpublished short film (copy in possession of author). DVD.
Glover, Alan. *The Juice Quartet Archives (Vols. 1–3)*. Omolade Music 2010. 3 compact discs.
Jahn, Ebba. *Rising Tones Cross*. New York: FilmPals, 1984. DVD.
Jones, Elvin, and Jimmy Garrison Sextet. *Illumination*. Impulse Records IMPD-250, 1998 [1963]. Compact disc.
Lyons, Jimmy. *The Box Set*. Ayler Records aylCD-036-40, 2003. 5 compact discs.

Mahaffay, Robert Mike. *Free Life Loft Jazz (Snapshot of a Movement), Vol. 1.* Portland, OR: Mahaffay's Musical Archives [no catalog number], 2010. MP3 album download.
Parker, William. *Centering.* NoBusiness Records NBCD42–7, 2012. 6 compact discs.
Reid, Steve. *Nova.* Mustevic MS-2001, 1976. LP.
Simmons, Sonny. *Manhattan Egos.* Arhoolie Records CD-483, 2000 (1969). Compact disc.
———. *Music from the Spheres.* ESP-Disk 1043, 1968. Compact disc.
Umezu, Kappo. *Seikatsu Kōjyō Iinkai.* Recorded August 11, 1975. Self-released, 1975. LP.
Various Artists. *David X. Young's Jazz Loft.* Jazz Magnet Records #2002, 2000. 2 compact discs.
———. *Wildflowers: The New York Loft Jazz Sessions.* Recorded May 14–23, 1976. Knitting Factory Works KCR 3037/39, 2000. 3 compact discs.

ARCHIVAL REFERENCES FROM THE JUMA SULTAN ARCHIVE

Note: All materials remain in the possession of Juma Sultan in Kerhonkson, NY. References are organized by catalog (JSA) number. A number beginning with "F" refers to a paper document, with the numbers before the period indicating a folder number and after the period indicating an item number. "T" refers to audio recordings. "V" and "P" (none present here) refer to visual materials and photographs, respectively.

Documents

F0007.07	Menu from Ali's Alley. Date unknown, possibly 1976.
F0007.15	Flyer for "Loft Music" at Studio WIS. Monday series beginning January 3. Year unknown, likely 1972 or 1977.
F0007.17	Flyer for African Street Carnival at "The East." June 18–July 4, 1974.
F0007.23	Flyer for Studio We concert "Pianists in Focus." October 31, 1975.
F0012.01–4	Schedules for Intramedia, Inc. multimedia presentations. 1975.
F0016.07	Flyer for play "The Pygmies and the Pyramid" at Olatunji Center of African Culture. April 11, 1976.
F0016.10	Announcement and call for participants for the New York Musicians' Jazz Festival. Spring 1972.
F0017.02	Registration forms and informational materials relating to the Studio We School. Fall 1972.
F0020.04	Press packet on the 1973 New York Musicians' Jazz Festival.
F0020.08	Letter to Juma Sultan from Ralph Lamberti, Deputy Borough President of Staten Island. Letter commends NYMO on the park concerts of 1974, and offers to write in support of future programs. June 18, 1974.
F0022.07	Press release written by the New York Musicians Organization titled "George Wein Announces Joint Effort." February 6, 1973.
F0022.49	Letter from the Board of Directors of the New York Musicians Organization to Sam Rivers. Written in response to his request to resign from the board. March 26, 1973.
F0024.01	Intramedia, Inc. long-form proposal and budget projection for multimedia archive and information center. 1975.
F0044.03–7	Planning documents for documentary titled "The New Music Scene in New York City." Circa 1973–74.

F0054.11	Program for a performance by the Sam Wooding Orchestra at Cami Hall. June 13, 1973.
F0054.12	Press release for performance by Ted Daniel's Third World Energy Ensemble. Performance date: May 28, 1975.
F0054.19	Flyer for "Three Days of Peace between the Ears." Festival in July 1970.
F0068.19	DuBoise, James. Letter to All States Management Corporation, requesting a ten-foot-tall statue of Uncle Sam for the stage of the Bicentennial Jazz Festival. February 19, 1975.
F0070.14	Financial report and final budget of the 1972 New York Musicians' Jazz Festival. January 22, 1973.
F0075.09	Press information sheet about the ensemble Kuntu. Date unknown.
F0075.12	Performer contracts for New York Musicians Jazz Festival. Summer 1972.
F0081.04	Completed acceptance forms for Intramedia, Inc. Advisory Council.
F0096.02	Letter from unknown sender (likely Juma Sultan) to Volunteer Lawyers for the Arts. Incomplete. November 19, 1975.
F0097.01	Susan Levi-Fasteau (Zusaan Kali Fasteau). "Music: The Religion of Ecstacy" (incomplete copy). MA thesis, Wesleyan University, Anthropology Department (not officially approved). 1970.
F0108.22	Internal memo circulated by organizers of the New York Musicians' Jazz Festival. 1972.
F0113.08	Flyer for a performance by William Parker and the Aumic Orchestra at Third World Cultural Center. March 25, 1973.
F0113.24	Studio Rivbea brochure and schedule. April 1973.
F0114.12	Flyer advertising a schedule of "Live Loft Jazz" at the Ladies' Fort. September 1975.
F0115.01	Flyer for "Sun Station, Black Light" by Karma Stanley at Studio Rivbea. June 14–22, 1975.
F0137.01	Schedule for "Summer Loft Jazz Festival" at the Ladies' Fort. June 14–July 6, 1975.
F0143.04	Packet of materials relating to "Nation Time Productions." 1971.
F0146.02-3	Intramedia, Inc. Constitution and Bylaws (multiple versions). 1975.
F0150.02	Jazz Composers Orchestra of America Brochure. Circa 1971–73.
F0156.21	Flyer for concert by Andrew Cyrille's Maono at the Countee Cullen Public Library. March 19, 1975.
F0167.11	Press release for language and dance classes at Studio We. 1974.
F0169.14	History and funding proposal for Studio We. Author unknown. Incomplete. 1974.
F0196.02	Funding proposal for Intramedia, Inc. 1975.
F0204.01	Intramedia, Inc. proposals for multimedia archive and information center. 1975.
F0206.02	Letter from unknown sender to Ali Abuwi requesting tapes. February 1, 1973.
F0215.03	Poster and schedule of "Live Loft Jazz" Festival at the Ladies' Fort. April 1977.
F0220.09	Letter from Juma Sultan to the National Endowment for the Arts. April 29, 1975.

F0232.02	Handwritten list of "People that can deal with the press." 1973.
F0233.03–6	Various documents relating to Studio We music school. Fall 1972.
F0245.03	Programs from Berliner Jazztage. 1976.
F0248.03	Fiscal year-end report for the New York Musicians Organization. Includes list of demands sent to George Wein of the Newport Jazz Festival. Circa late 1972.
F0248.09	Rivers, Sam. Letter of Resignation from the New York Musicians Organization. March 19, 1973. (Date absent on JSA copy, but present on another copy of the same letter from the collection of Rashied Ali.)

Sound Recordings

T0114	Sam Wooding and Rae Harrison, radio interview with Lewis K. McMillan. Conducted for syndicated radio program "Swinging with Lewis K. McMillan." June 9, 1975.
T0120	Private sessions featuring Sonny Simmons, Juma Sultan, and the Depth Probers. December 1, 1967.
T0128	Sam Wooding Orchestra at Cami Hall. June 13, 1973.
T0157	Aboriginal Music Society sampler tape. Includes performances of "Dance of the Seven Cities," "Ode to a Gypsy Sun," "Sun Dance and Hand Clapping," and "Dinwiddie's Dance." Circa 1970.
T0158	Aboriginal Music Society sampler tape. Includes performances of "The Dance" and "Sun Dance and Hand Clapping." Circa 1970.
T0160	Private sessions featuring Sonny Simmons and the Depth Probers. N.d. Circa late 1960s.
T0161	Private sessions featuring Sonny Simmons, Juma Sultan, and the Depth Probers. April 1968.
T0163	Juma Sultan and others improvising near a lake filled with frogs. Late 1960s.
T0168	Private sessions featuring Sonny Simmons and the Depth Probers. N.d. Circa late 1960s.
T0175	Sampler tape. Contains excerpts by the groups Aboriginal Music Society, Nkanyezi Zi Afrika, Charles Tyler Big Band and We Music House (according to ear identifications by Juma Sultan). Circa 1972.
T0179	Private sessions featuring Sonny Simmons and the Depth Probers. February 24, 1968.
T0231	Private sessions featuring Sonny Simmons, Paul Smith, and Juma Sultan. N.d. Circa late 1960s.
T0271	Aboriginal Music Society / Poetry Recitation by Charles Gordone. January 25, 1972.
T0403	Sonny Simmons and the Depth Probers, 1966 / Aboriginal Music Society, 1969.
T0429	Sonny Simmons and Juma Sultan duo.

INDEX

Page numbers in italic refer to figures.

AACM (Association for the Advancement of Creative Musicians), 2, 6, 118, 196n13, 197n20; as central node for Chicago avant garde, 123; control over actions of individuals, 93; decline of lofts and, 59; disdain for phrase "loft jazz," 182; "energy music" and, 91; Free Life Communication modeled after, 45, 202n42; goals and mission of, 22–23; influx of artists into New York, 55, 205n86; interdisciplinary collaboration in, 23; naming practices and, 74, 75; white artists excluded from, 24–25, 119; work with outside musicians, 24, 199n17

Abdullah, Ahmed (né Leroy Bland), 15, 73, 79, 187, 215n67, 227n19

Abdullah (band), 75

Aboriginal Music Society, 42, 75, 103–104, 153

"Aborigine Dance in Scotland" (Simmons), 155

Abrams, Muhal Richard, 24, 55, 74, 75, 198n16, 205n86

Abuwi, Ali (né Oliver Anderson), 8, 42, 73, 74, 153; Aboriginal Music Society and, 103–104; on private tapes in archives, 186–87; spiritual practices of, 78–79; at Woodstock, 213n30

acoustics, 3, 4, 32, 180

actor-network theory (ANT), 97, 122–23, 126, 215n75, 216n80

advertising, 3, 34, 87; for alternative venue concerts, 109, *110–13*; jazz as signifier in, 218n22

AFM (American Federation of Musicians), 20, 36

African American music/musicians, 24, 36, 48, 115, 117; artist-run initiatives, 20; perceived ghettoization in lofts/nightclubs, 59

African Americans, 15, 20, 66, 70–71

African identities, 81

African Street Carnival (The East cultural center), *112*

Afrikan Carnival Association, 166

Afrocentrism, 68, 77

Agnew, Edward, 219n36

Akim, 228n37

alcohol, venues' sale of, 135, 136, 138, 180

Ali, Rashied, 35, 38, 50, 73, 138; on exploitation of musicians, 101; NYJMF and, 45; NYMO and, 48; organizer's dilemma and, 215n67

Ali's Alley (nightclub), 35, 49, 109, 180; avant garde musicians at, 52; domesticity in, 138; "Lost Jazz Shrines" concert series and, 185; on maps, *116*, *117*; renamed "Alley's Bars," 54; soul food menu, 50, *53*

Alix, Paul, 228n37

Allen, Marshall, 89

245

INDEX

Allman Brothers Band, 40
Altamont Free Concert (1969), 40
Altsax record label, 42
Altshul, Barry, 213n30
Altshul, Dave, 204n69
Amburger, Chris, 94, 120
Anderson, Fred, 24
Andrew Cyrille and Maono, *111*
Apogee, 90, 94, 120, 124
Arabic names, black identity and, 71–74
archives, 1, 2, 146–49, 177–78; "archival turn" in humanities, 13, 221n2; digitization of, 10; ethnography of, 148; gaps and omissions in, 162; human actors and, 170; musician-curated, 7; *respect des fonds* approach, 170, 171, 175, 225n77, 226n83. *See also* Juma Sultan Archive
Armstrong, Louis, 196n15
Art Blakey and the Jazz Messengers, 180
Art Ensemble of Chicago, 75, 87, 88, 196n15, 205n86
art galleries, 3, 49
Artist House, 34–35, 40, 45, 54, 102
Artists Tenants Association (ATA), 29
arts funding, politics of, 162
As Serious as Your Life (Wilmer, 1977), 138–39
Ascension (Coltrane), 89
Atlanta International Pop Festival (1970), 40
audiences/listeners, 3, 32, 91, 103; cover charges and, 101; festivals and, 59; listener experience, 12–13, 141; loft environment and experience of, 19; modes of listening, 155; promotion of music to, 34; socializing between performers and listeners, 137–38, 180, 188; straight-ahead versus avant-garde, 104–105
Aumic Orchestra, 113
avant garde, 50, 52, 60, 90, 185; communities of play and, 103; economic groundwork to support, 102; end of loft scene and, 179; "energy music" and, 88, 89; loft venues' legacy and, 61; musical mainstream and, 181; straight-ahead style versus, 104–105, 125–26; Vision Festival and, 188
Ayler, Albert, 89, 90, 212n108
Ayler Records, 185–86

BAG (Black Artists Group), 2, 6, 93, 196n13, 197n20; all-black membership policy, 25, 119; interdisciplinary collaboration in, 23; work with outside musicians, 24
Baker, Chet, 181
Bakr, Rashid (Charles Downs), 73, 102, 208n33

Baldwin, James, 98
Bang, Billy, 16, 85–86, 227n19
Baraka, Amiri (Leroi Jones), 31–32, 89, 202n40; gender politics of, 139, 140, 221n69; name change, 72, 208n29
Baraka, Kimako, 42, 167, 202n36
beatniks, 29
bebop, 4, 5, 30, 41
Becker, Harold, 99
Beirach, Richie, 204n64
Bell, Daniel, 132
Bennett, Andy, 99, 124
Benston, Kimberly, 70, 71, 76
Berendt, Joachim-Ernst, 5
Berger, Karl, 186, 213n30
Berliner, Paul, 195n8
Berliner Jazztage, 205n92
"Bicentennial Jazz Festival," 49
Birnbach, Steve, 81
Black Artists for Community Action, 110–13
"Black Arts Imperative," 44, 168
Black Arts Movement, 25, 221n69
Black Arts Repertory Theater, 32
black identity, 23, 25, 45, 71–74, 119
black nationalism, 23, 24, 67, 118; gender politics and, 221n69; "hippie" counterculture and, 77; promotion of black-owned business practices, 115. *See also* cultural nationalism
Black Panthers, 8, 220n65
black power, 24, 68, 69, 221n69
Black Theater Alliance, 166
Blakey, Art, 66, 180
Blanton, Jimmy, 74
Blondie (new wave band), 107
Bluiett, Hamiet, 59, 227n19
Blum, John, 228n37
Blythe, Arthur, 55–56, 105, 205n86
Bonneau, Jackie, 221n76
Booth, Juney, 36, 156
Borca, Karen, 228n37
Boston, 26
Botofasina, Renee, 221n76
boundary discourses, 12, 96, 112, 125
Bourdieu, Pierre, 216n80
Bowie, Joseph, 55, 205n86
Bowie, Lester, 88, 205n86
Brackeen, Charles, 74
Braufman, Alan, 94, 120
Braxton, Anthony, 35, 74, 90, 92, 202n42
Bronx River Neighborhood Center, 109
Brook, The, *116, 117*, 133
Brooklyn Academy of Music, 87, 182

Brooklyn Musicians Registry, 166
Brooks, Roy, 31
Brothers, Thomas, 197n17
Brown, Elaine, 220n65
Brown, Marion, 33, 90
Brown, Rob, 228n37
Brubeck, Darius, Danny, and Chris, 164
Brubeck, Dave, 20
Bruno, Tom, 120, 227n19
Buddhism, 73, 79
Buddy Rich Orchestra, 120
Burnett, Jacob, 138
Burns, Ken, 196n15
Burrell, Dave, 33, 77, 109, 134, 181, 203n57
Burrell, Kenny, 66
Burton, Antoinette, 14, 171–72, 221n2
Byrd, Donald, 66

Café Society (late 1930s), 30
Callon, Michel, 122
Cami Hall, 87
Campbell, Joseph, 76
Campbell, Roy, 87, 227n19, 228n37
Cannon, Steve, 228n37
canon/canonical model, 4, 7, 14, 66, 158
capitalism, 80, 159, 219n36
Carmichael, Stokely (Kwame Ture), 72
Carnegie Hall, 20, 41, 46, 182
Caroll, Baikida, 205n86
Carter, Daniel, 38, 227n19, 228n37
Cary, Dick, 31
CBA (Collective Black Artists), 50, 93, 109, 197n20, 225n64; all-black membership policy, 119; archives of, 186, 225n65; CBA Ensemble, 165
Cellar Café, 32
Center for New Music, 50
Center for the Exploration of Consciousness, 81
Chadbourne, Eugene, 126
Chambers, Joe, 109, 203n57
Chancey, Vincent, 228n37
Chapman, Emmett, 107
Charles, Denis, 228n37
Cherry, Moki, 139
Chicago, 2, 6, 22, 54, 123, 197n17
children, 138, 141
Children's Workshop, at La Mama Theater, 55
Christi, Ellen, 120, 228n37
Christian, Charlie, 74
churches, 49, 60, 109
city parks, jazz in, 45, *46*, 49, 105–107, *106*

civil rights movement, 11, 34, 42, 44, 69, 115
Clark, Robin, 203n57
Clarke, Kenny, 71
Clarke, Kim, 221n76
Clarkson University, 9, 151, 176
class, 15, 80, 124, 210n63, 215n75
classical music, Western, 158
Clef Club, 20
Cleveland, 89
Cleveland Cultural Center, 36
Cobi's Place, 166
coffee shops, 8, 31
Cohen, Anthony, 100
Cohen, Michael, 156
Cold War, 67
Cole, Bill, 228n37
Coleman, Anthony, 74
Coleman, James, 216n80
Coleman, Ornette, 74, 102, 141, 201n24; Artist House and, 34–35; "energy music" and, 89–90; *Free Jazz*, 89
collective bargaining, 22
collectivism, 69, 70, 77
Collins, Patricia Hill, 139–140, 220n65
Colson, Adegoke, 205n86
Colson, Iqua, 205n86
Coltrane, John, 21–22, 74, 89, 198n11
Columbia Records, 55–56
Columbia University, 9, 183, 184, 186, 188–89
Coming of Post-Industrial Society, The (Bell, 1973), 132
Commitment, 187
communalism, 69, 70, 77, 83, 103, 104
communitas, 79–80, 91, 92
community, 13, 16, 95–96, 100, 124, 126, 187; "community" abandoned as term by music scholars, 98–99; community ownership, 47; community-based studies, 4, 5, 6; intergenerational, 188; "loft community," 15; memories and, 172; parables of uncommunity, 120–21; of pay, 100–103; of place, 105–107, *108*, 109, *110–12*, 112; of play, 103–105; of race, 112, 115, 118–19; social fragmentation and, 97–98
Community Crossroads, 166
concert halls, 181, 182
"Confusion and Fusion" (Tirro), 196n14
Connell, Will, 205n86, 228n37
Connor, Robert T., office of, *108*
Consortium of Jazz Organizations, 166
Cook, Will Marion, 20
cool jazz, 4

Cooper, Jerome, 228n37
Cooper-Moore (né Gene Ashton), 15, 75–76, 91, 134, 186, 209n42; on community, 94–96; "energy music" and, 90, 212n107; ideals of loft movement and, 120; Improvisors Collective and, 228n37; loft renovation and, 134; loft scene as isolating experience, 120–21, 124; organizer's dilemma and, 215n67
Coppola, Christine, 228n37
Countee Cullen Library, concert at (1975), *111*
counterculture, 12, 77, 79, 82, 103
cover charges, 101
Cranshaw, Emanuel (formerly Gordon Emanuel), 24, 25
Creative Music Foundation, 50
Creative Music Studio (Woodstock, N.Y.), 186, 189, 213n30
Crosby, Bing, 66
Cross, Earl, 203n57, 213n30
Cross-Bronx Expressway, construction of, 142
Crouch, Stanley, 54–55, 205n86; critique of "energy music," 88; feud with Rivers, 58–59, 204n69, 206n102; on jazz audiences, 104–105; on transcendent spirituality among musicians, 78
Cruz, Emilio, 205n86
Cruz, Patricia, 205n86
Csikszentmihalyi, Mihaly, 80
cultural capital, 124
cultural nationalism, 44, 68, 202n40; African aesthetics and, 81; African names and, 72; community-ownership strategies and, 47; gender discourses and, 139. *See also* black nationalism
Currie, A. Scott, 80–81

Dalachinsky, Steve, 135, 228n37
Dance of Magic, 75
Daniel, Ted, *37*, 88–89, 90, 186
Dankworth, Johnny, 66
Danola record label, 31
Davis, Angela, 165–66, 220n65
Davis, Anthony, 74, 87–88
Davis, Jean, 221n76
Davis, Miles, 196n15, 205n90
De Certeau, Michel, 134
De Veaux, Scott, 195n8
Debut record label, 20
deconstruction, 7
Dee Gee record label, 20
Deep River Boys, The, 207n4
DeFade, Ray, 66
Dellaratta, Rick, 227n19

democracy, 65, 67
Depth Probers, The, 155, 156
Derrida, Jacques, 171, 221n2, 225n76
Detroit, 26, 89
Diggers (counterculture group), 84
Dirks, Nicholas, 148, 221n2
discography, 178
discourses, 4, 6, 11
Dixon, Akua, 221n76
Dixon, Bill, 21, 22, 24, 32, 42, 46
DIY aesthetics/practices, 135, 168, 169, 188
DLMA (Downtown Lower Manhattan Association), 27, 28
Dolphy, Eric, 155
Donald, Barbara, 139, 155, 213n30
Donaldson, Sonny, 203n57
"door gigs," 50, 206n102
"double consciousness," 97
Douglas Records, 204n74
Down Beat magazine, 31, 89
Downs, Charles, 227n19
Downtown Music Gallery, 137
Doyle, Arthur, 203n57
drug use, 69, 81–83, 86, 138
Du Bois, W.E.B., 97
DuBoise, Andrea, 164
DuBoise, James, 36–38, 40, 42, 74, 92; on community among musicians, 101–102, 214n36; in front of Studio We, *37*; on Newport Jazz Festival, 41; NYJMF and, 45; NYMO and, 48, 160; organizer's dilemma and, 120, 121; on park series, 107; on record companies and contracts, 186; Studio We and, *38, 131*, 134, 203n57; at Woodstock, 213n30
Duke University archives, 186, 227n29

Earth Wind and Fire, 161
economics, 4, 7, 91, 129
education, 22
Edwards, Brent Hayes, 148, 188, 195n8, 226n83, 228n41
Edwards, Marc, 94, 102, 120
Eichhorn, Kate, 148
Eigo, Jim, 169, 185
electric instruments, 5
Ellington, Duke, 65, 98, 196n15
Elliott, Malinke, 25
Ellison, Ralph, 71, 98
Elvin Jones/Jimmy Garrison Sextet, 155
empowerment narratives, 2, 19, 32, 73, 77, 95; black racial, 23; freedom and, 68, 69; self-empowerment, 7, 34, 60

Eneidi, Marco, 228n37
"energy music," 12, 55, 69, 89–92, 156, 212n108; move away from work-oriented ideals, 159; roots outside of New York, 88–89. *See also* free jazz
Ensemble Muntu, 186, 187
Environ, 133, 134, 205n93
ESP Records, 90, 156, 212n108
ethnography, 84, 149, 177, 178; collaborative, 170; community and, 14; Juma Sultan Archive and, 13, 148, 174; participant observation, 148
Europe, James Reese, 20
European music, 6, 22
Evans, Gil, 30, 33
Experimental Intermedia Foundation, 180, 226n2
"Exploitation Among NYC Musicians" (Ali), 48

Farge, Arlette, 221n2
Farina, Stephen, 151
Fasteau, Kali Z. (née Susan Lévi-Fasteau), 80, 139, 209n61, 210n63, 228n37
Father of Origin (Juma's Archive Project), 10
feminism, 139, 140, 221n69
Few, Bobby, 37, 89
Finnegan, Ruth, 99
Firehouse Theater, 49, 204n64
Fischer, Francis, 164
Fischer, John, 55, 101, 118–19, 133, 213n25; interest in multisensory experiences, 134; organizing activities of, 164; as self-archivist, 147
Five Boroughs Jazz Festival, 49
501 Canal Street, 54, 124, 134, 204n81
Flanagan, Tommy, 180
Flavin, Dan, 219n40
"flow states," 80, 91, 92
flyers, historicity of, 168–69
Foster, Frank, 109, 203n57
Foucault, Michel, 221n2
Fox, Hetty, 141–44, 164, 210n81
France, 46
free jazz, 4, 5, 6, 93, 174, 196n14; multi-genre diversity and, 87–88; at Studio We, 38; Sultan and, 8. *See also* "energy music"
Free Jazz (Coleman), 89
Free Jazz (Jost), 87–88
Free Life Communication, 45, 204n64
freedom, jazz and ideal of, 65–68, 92–93, 95, 103, 188; "freedom" in titles of jazz works, 65–67, 66, 207n4; "freedom to" versus "freedom from," 69

freedom dreams, 12, 68; self-creation, 70–77; of sonic energy, 86–92; of transgression and transcendence, 77–86
Freedom Is, Freedom Ain't (Saul, 2003), 65
"Freedom Jazz Dance" (Harris), 66
Freedom Principle, The (Litweiler, 1984), 65
Freedom Sounds (Monson, 2008), 11, 65
Freedom Suite (Rollins), 66
Freeman, Chico, 183, 184, 205n86
Friends and Neighbors (Coleman, recorded 1970), 35
fusion (jazz-rock), 5, 196n15

Gabbard, Krin, 195n8
Galaxy Dream Band, 81
Gale, Mugo Eddie, 74, *110*
Gallanter, Bruce, 137
Garrison, Jimmy, 109, 203n57
gender, 14, 80, 166, 196n9; actor-network theory (ANT) and, 215n75; lofts as gendered spaces, 138–141; male domination, 138
gentrification, 15, 123, 126
geography, cultural, 133, 219n36
Giddins, Gary, 54, 55, 88, 205n93
Gillespie, Dizzy, 20, 71
Gitlin, Todd, 77, 104
Glover, Alan "Juice" (Akinjorin Omolade), 74, 109, 186, 204n64
Gluckman, Richard, 219n40
Goehr, Lydia, 158
Golson, Benny, 20
Gongwer, Lee, 228n37
Goodman, Benny, 66
Gordon, Dexter, 196n15
gospel music, 115, 174
graffiti, 143–44
Grant, Sheila, 221n76
grants/grant applications, 162
Graves, Milford, 37, 42, 45, 48
"Great Black Music" motto, 22, 24
great figures and works, 4, 14
Green, Grant, 66
Greene, Narada Burton, 35–36, 37, 74, 129, 228n37; "Borders are boring" statement, 77; on "energy music," 90–91; on spiritual aspect of music, 78; at Woodstock, 213n30
Grimes, Henry, 32
Grof, Stanley, 81–82
Group 212 Intermedia Workshop, 103, 224n44
Gryce, Gigi, 20
Guloff, Alter, 128, 217n14
Gushee, Lawrence, 177

Hall, Pat, 137
Hamilton, Chico, 66
Hancock, Larry, 89
Handy, W. C., 207n4
hard bop, 4, 88
Harlem Cultural Council, 50, 109
Harris, Barry, 180
Harris, Beaver, 203n57
Harris, Eddie, 66
Harris, Huntington, 215n68
Harrison, Rae, 87
Heath, Eddie, 42, 213n30
Heath, Jimmy, 74
Hebdige, Dick, 99
Heidegger, Martin, 219n36
Hemphill, Julius, 205n86
Hendrix, Jimi, 8, 145, 174, 175, 226n81
Henry Street Settlement, 109
Hentoff, Nat, 21
Herman, Woody, 20
Hicks, Rod, 213n30
Higgins, Billy, 78
Hill, Andrew, 109
Hippie Trip, The (Yablonsky), 84
hippies, 29
Hoffman, Abbie, 82, 86
Holcomb, Robin, 226n7
Holland, Dave, 204n69
hooks, bell, 140
Hopkins, Fred, 205n86
Hopps, Jimmy, 76, 94
Horvitz, Wayne, 226n7
Howard, Noah, *37*, 42, 45, 48
Huesmann, Günther, 5
Hwang, Jason Kao, 168, 228n37

Iacovone, Rocco John, 136
identity politics, 12
idiophones, 76
improvisation, 4, 80, 133–34, 154, 160; "energy music" and, 69, 88, 156; free jazz and, 87; jazz tradition and, 105; long-form, 3; "Mohammedan" scales and, 158; rehearsals and, 156
Improvisors Collective, 187, 228n37
Impulse record label, 205n90
In the Beginning (Daniel, recorded 1975), 197n23
In the Tradition (Blythe, recorded 1978), 56, 105, 205n90
individualism, 65
influence, progression of, 4
integrationism, liberal, 68
Interface, 75

Interpreters, The, 66
interracial projects, 24
Intramedia, Inc., 160–61, 173
Invisible Man (Ellison), 71, 98
Irving Stone collection, 186
Islam, 72–73
Isle of Wight Pop Festival (1970), 40
Isoardi, Steven, 6
Izenson, David, 90

Jackson, Eugene, *38*
JAG (Jazz Artists' Guild), 20–22
jam sessions, 3, 8, 31, 86, 135; drug use and, 82; intimacy of, 34; at Minton's Playhouse, 30; at Studio Rivbea, 50
Jami, Hakim, 72–73, 84–85, 121, 134; on appeal of Ladies' Fort, 133; as self-archivist, 146–47; at Studio We, *131*
Japan, 46, 184
Jarman, Joseph (Shaku Gyo), 74
jazz: framed as product of African American communities, 44; freedom associated with, 65; improvisatory nature of, 158; individual-collective duality of, 80; re/constructed narratives of the 1970s, 4–7; role in civil rights era, 11
Jazz (Burns documentary), 196n15
jazz collectives, 5–6, 12, 20, 166; lofts' differences from, 100; paper documents and, 162; race relations within, 25; rhetoric of self-employment and, 34
Jazz Crusaders, The, 66
Jazz Forum, 114, 125, 137, 180–81
Jazz Hot (French journal), 46, 203n50
Jazz Interactions, Inc., 165
Jazz Loft Celebration (1977), 109
Jazz Loft Project (Duke University), 186
"Jazz Lofts: A Walk through the Wild Sounds" (Crouch), 54
Jazz: The First 100 Years (Martin and Waters), 196n13
Jazz Workshop–Ruhr Festival, 66
Jazzmania, 116, *117*, 135–36, 205n93
Jazzmobile, 109
JCG (Jazz Composers' Guild), 21, 56, 102, 197n20
JCOA (Jazz Composers Orchestra of America), 102
Jefferson, Eddie, 42
Jenkins, Leroy, 35, 202n42
Jethro Tull, 40
Jim Crow era, 20
Johnson, James P., 30

Johnson, James Weldon, 98
Jones, Elvin, 31, 33
Jost, Ekkehard, 87–88
Ju-Ju, 75
Juma Sultan Archive, 7–10, 11, 13, 146–49; amateur recordings, 151–55; incompleteness of, 13–14; NYJMF documents in, 45; paper holdings, 160–69; Sonny Simmons's presence in, 155–56, *157*, 158–160, 222–23n15; tapes transferred to hard drive, 149–151, 222n12

Kamber, Madeleine, 137
Kapp, Bobby, 33
Karenga, Maulana (né Ron Everett), 72, 139, 202n40, 220n65, 221n69
Kawaida, 72
Keene, Richard, 228n37
Kelley, Robin D.G., 12, 68, 165, 195n8
Kenney, William Howland, 197n17
Kharma record label, 31
King, Martin Luther, Jr., 26, 44
Kirby, John, 66
Kitchen, The, 59, *116*, *117*, 180, 181
Koch, Edward, 57
Koenig, Steven, 137
Kono, Masahiko, 228n37
Kostelanetz, Richard, 132–33
Kowald, Peter, 187
Krall, Jackson, 228n37
Kreuter, David, 137
Kuebler, Annie, 176–77
Kuntu, 90
Kuza, Vera, 73
Kwanzaa, 167

La Mama Theater, 55
Ladies' Fort, 49, 58, 84, 109, 204n64, 205n93; annual summer festival, 211n92; appeal to musicians, 133; "Lost Jazz Shrines" concert series and, 185; on maps, *116*, *117*; public concerts at, 216n82; renovation of, 134
Lake, Oliver, 205n86
Lamb, Andrew, 227n19
Lancaster, Byard, 33
land use, 15, 57
landlords, New York, 28–29, 31, 35, 56, 57, 142
Landmarks Preservation Committee (New York), 28
Lasha, Prince, 31
Lasley, Phil, 203n57
Lateef, Yusuf, 21–22
Latin jazz, 104

Latino artists, 199n18
Latour, Bruno, 122, 123
Laver, Mark, 218n22
Law, John, 122
Leary, Timothy, 82
Led Zeppelin, 40
Lee, Gene, 198n7
Lenox Avenue Breakdown (Blythe, recorded 1978), 56, 205n90
Leslie, Charles, 57
Let Freedom Swing (Reich, 2010), 65
Levine, Rozanne, 80, 228n37
Lewis, George, 6, 14, 20, 74, 183, 205n86; on AACM exclusion of whites, 24–25; on informal nature of lofts, 59; on the "loft generation," 182
liberation narratives, 65–66
Licata, Bea, 228n37
Liebman, Dave, 45, 204n64
Lincoln Center, Philharmonic Hall, 41, 46
Lindsay, John, 41
Live at the Village Vanguard Again (Coltrane), 89
Lodico, Alex, 228n37
loft jazz, 3–4, 13, 16, 60, 182; as contentious term, 15, 59, 130, 182, 183; defined, 198n1; as designation for specific musical genre, 86–87; diverse modalities of, 11; end of, 179; multiple definitions of community and, 100; published accounts of, 31, 54; re-creation of, 184
loft movement, 6, 7, 45, 60, 128, 142, 190; community and, 96, 100; freedom dreams and, 68; ideals of, 120; pleasures of improvisation and, 159; political focus of, 135; self-determination and, 15; space and, 133, 144; of visual artists, 58, 218n26
"loft scene," 2, 6, 34, 97, 174; decline and end of, 126, 179, 195n6; early post-loft years, 179–184; fragmentation of, 7; maps of, *115–17*; New York Musicians' Jazz Festival (1972) and, 19–20; scenes perspective and, 125
lofts, 12, 49; community impeded by, 120; converted to residential use, 127; decline of, 57–61; domestic imagery in, 135–38; early scene in 1950s and '60s, 30–33; events besides music concerts in, 134; in former industrial buildings, 3; as gendered spaces, 138–141; historical legacies since 1990s, 184–87; industrial nostalgia and, 130–34, 218n26; in mid-1970s, 49–56; press coverage of concerts, 54; stages of loft conversion, 129–130
Logan, Giuseppe, 89, 212n108

252 INDEX

LOMEX (Lower Manhattan Expressway), 27, 199n31
Looker, Benjamin, 6, 25
Los Angeles, 2, 6, 23, 165, 205n86
Lost Archive of Juma Sultan, The (fundraising video, 2007), 149
"Lost Jazz Shrines" concert series (1998–99), 185
Lowe, Carmen, 139
Lowe, Frank, 37, 109
Lower East Side, 8, 32, 33, 58, 95, 142; changing landscape of, 26–30; discourse of place and, 105; drug use in, 83; Jewish community of, 128; Latino residents' opposition to artist housing subsidies, 218n18; punk rock and new wave in, 107. *See also* Manhattan, lower
Lower Manhattan Loft Tenants (LMLT), 29
Lower Manhattan Plan, The (DLMA document), 27
Lyons, Jimmy, 186

Mahaffey, Mike, 109, 204n64
Makgoba, Paul, 109
Malcolm X, 44, 71, 208n24
Manhattan, lower, 26, 28, 42, 102, 168, 189; avant garde cultural movements in, 29; deindustrialization after World War II, 27; destructive urban policies in, 85; downturn in real estate market, 6; experimental music communities in, 14; former industrial buildings, 3; rent increases in, 57; SoHo, 29–30, 199n38. *See also* Lower East Side
Manhattan Egos (Simmons, recorded 1969), 156, 158
Mannheimer, Susan, 141
Marcus Garvey collection, at UCLA, 172, 226n83
Maria, Mary, 139
Marsalis, Wynton, 125
Martin, Henry, 196n13
Mashujaa, 227n19
Mateen, Sabir, 227n19
McCall, Steve, 205n86
McCool, Nicholas, 128
McIntyre, Kalaparusha Maurice, 74, 205n86, 205n92
McIntyre, Makanda Ken, 74
McNeeley, Jennifer, 184
Mele, Christopher, 29
Melodic Art-Tet, 75
Melotone publishing company, 20
memories, 4, 10, 12–14, 146, 177, 185; archives and, 171, 174; of camaraderie, 104; "counter-memory," 172; of a "golden period," 184;

history and, 171; industrial nostalgia and, 132; Sultan Archive and, 149, 170; tradition and, 11
Memory Lane nightclub (Los Angeles), 165
Menwem Writers Workshop, 166
Mid/Western collectives, 23–24, 26, 55, 91–92
Mingus, Charles, 24, 31, 46, 66; "energy music" and, 88; JAG (Jazz Artists' Guild) and, 20, 21; naming practices and, 74
Minton's Playhouse, 30
modernism, 1, 5
Moffett, Charles, 227n19
"moldy figs," 5
Moncur, Grachan, III, 33
Monette, Marionette, 221n76
Monk, Thelonious, 31, 65
Monson, Ingrid, 14, 195n8, 208n26; on role of jazz in civil rights era, 11; on structural inequality, 42, 44, 202n38
Moody, James, 42, 202n36
Moondoc, Jemeel, 228n37
Morganelli, Mark, 180–81, 215n67, 226n5
Morris, Butch, 205n86
Morris, Wilber, 228n37
Morton, David, 152
Moses, Bob, 45
Moses, J. C., 37
Moses, Rakalam Bob, 74
Moses, Robert, 27, 28, 142
Moshe, Ras, 138, 220n62
Moye, Famoudou Don, 74
multiculturalism, 6
Muntu, 75, 117
Murray, David, 55, 183–84, 205n86
Murray, Sunny, 213n30
Music Ensemble, The, 75, 86, 187
Music from the Spheres (Simmons, recorded 1968), 156
Musical Directions Ensemble, 75
musicians, 13, 119; female, 139–141; income, 3, 21, 226n5; loft environment and experience of, 19; models for empowerment of, 20–26; musician-ownership, 54; organizing activities of, 164; press attention and professional opportunities, 55; reconstruction of jazz history and, 7; wives of, 140–41, 164–65
Musicians' Club (Pittsburgh), 36, 37
musicking, 4, 196n10
My People (Ellington), 98
Myers, Amina Claudine, 74, 205n86

names/naming practices, 70–77, 208n33
Narita, Cobi, 165–66, 225n64

Nation of Islam (NOI), 72
Nation Time Productions, 167
National Black Political Convention (Gary, Ind., 1972), 44, 68, 202n40
National Endowment for the Arts, 9, 150, 163, 176
Nelson, Oliver, 66
neoclassical movement, 196n15
New Haven, 26
"new jazz studies," 4, 177
New Muse Community Museum, 109
New Music America festival, 182
"New Music Scene in New York City, The" (unfinished film about NYJMF), 45, 153, 203n47
New Orleans, 54, 197n17
new wave music, 107
New York, upstate, 21
New York City, 2, 54, 80; Clef Club, 20; Department of Cultural Affairs (DCLA), 106, 107; downtown new music scene, 180; "energy music" in, 88–92; graffiti in, 143–44; Harlem rent parties (1920s), 30; housing codes, 29; influx of artists from Mid/Western collectives, 55, 89, 91–92; intergenerational community of improvisers in, 188; "loft jazz era," 3; urban ecology in 1970s, 12; urban ecology in late 1960s, 19. *See also* Lower East Side; Manhattan, lower
New York Jazz Repertory Company, 5
"New York Loft and Coffee Shop Jazz" (Baraka), 31–32
New York Loft Jazz Celebration (1976), 205n93
New York Musicians' Jazz Festival (1972), 8, 12, 40–42, 44–49, 50, 59; Central Park jam session, 45, 46; city park performances after, 105; demands sent by organizers to Wein, 42, 43; dissolution of, 107; dues paid by performing groups, 45, 2903n46; as germinal moment for loft scene, 19–20; positive press coverage of, 46–47, 203n50; press release on jazz and black culture, 115; Sultan's recordings of, 153
New York Women's Jazz Festival, 166
Newport Jazz Festival, 20, 40, 41, 48, 59, 201n22; events staged in Manhattan, 46; NYJMF designed as corrective to shortcomings of, 44–45
Newton, James, 74, 205n86
Nicholson, Patricia, 187, 228n37, 228n39
Nicholson, Reggie, 227n19
Nicholson-Parker, Patricia, 215n67
nightclubs, 12, 59, 60, 135, 159, 179; children prohibited from, 138; JAG-organized strike against, 22; loft venues' move in direction of, 180; pay discourses and, 100–101
Nkrumah, Kwame, 72
NoBusiness Records, 186
NoHo, 58
Nova (Reid, recorded 1976), 197n23
NYFMC (New York Free Music Committee), 106–107
Nyman, Michael, 153
NYMO (New York Musicians Organization), 1–2, 8, 160, 197n20, 202n35, 203n53; formation of, 47–48; paper documents generated by, 162, 163–64; promotion of events, 153; racial politics and, 119; splintering of, 48; Studio We summer park series and, 107
NYSCA (New York State Council on the Arts), 40, 45, 50, 164

Occhigrosso, Peter, 54
October Revolution in Jazz, 21, 32, 42
"off-the-grid" living strategies, 69, 77, 83–86, 92, 211n91
Olatunji, Babatunde, 21–22
Olatunji Center, 109
O'Meally, Robert, 65
O'Neal, Kevin, 227n19
open-studios movement, 209n40
oral histories, 147, 161, 170, 177, 178, 189
organizer's dilemma, 120, 215n67
Other Dimensions in Music, 75, 187, 227n19
Otomo, Yuko, 228n37
Overton, Hall, 31
Owens, Jimmy, 165

Pakistan League of America, 129
Palmer, Robert, 54, 179
Pan Africanism, 44, 72
Pan Afrikan Peoples Arkestra, 23, 24, 199n18, 207n16
Papp, Joseph, 59, 179
Parker, Charlie, 74
Parker, William, 85–86, 102, 168–69, 186, 190, 227n19; on domesticity in loft spaces, 136–37; Improvisors Collective and, 187, 228n37; multidisciplinary collaborations and, 187; on music as local outreach, 107; as self-archivist and historian, 147, 187, 228n35; Vision Festival and, 228n39
Parran, J. D., 205n86
patriarchy, 139, 140
performance, 3, 11, 19, 86, 123; domesticity in loft spaces and, 136; everyday life and, 70;

performance *(continued)*
  identity creation and, 75–76; nightclub, 12; pay discourses and, 100–101, 213n25; racial politics and, 119; sexuality and, 140–41; socializing between performers and listeners, 137, 180, 188; at Studio We, 38, 39
Peterson, Oscar, 66
"Pianists in Focus" concert, at Studio We, 105
Piekut, Benjamin, 122, 153, 215n75
Poettential Unlimited, 166
Pollock, Jackson, 90
Porter, Eric, 44, 195n8, 225n64
Porter, Lewis, 177
"post-industrialism," 132
postmodernism/postmodern practices, 4, 7, 71, 76
Presearch, 142, 221n76
preservation, historic, 1, 28, 219n40
Priestley, Brian, 20
private sphere, 10
protest marches, 70
Public Theater, 59, 126, 179
punk rock, 14, 29, 107
Putnam, Robert, 216n80

queer subculture, 29

race, 7, 12, 15, 80, 96, 196n9, 210n63; actor-network theory (ANT) and, 215n75; communities of, 112, 115, 118–19, 124; nationalist discourse about, 24; utopian image of color-blindness, 119
race and gender theory, 4
Radano, Ronald, 195n8
Radio City Music Hall, 41
Ramsey, Guthrie, 195n8
Rasula, Jed, 4, 8, 160, 196n9
Reagan, Ronald, 57
re/construction, 4–7, 10–11, 77, 172
Reconstruction Era, 7
records and recordings, 1, 4, 8, 177
rehearsals, 3, 33, 86, 104, 124, 190; rehearsal halls/spaces, 32–33, 36; rehearsal/recording binary, 159; "work-centric" concept of musical production and, 158
Reich, Murray, 127
respectability, social/cultural, 4, 32, 86
"Revolutionary Concepts in the Arts" (Shepp lecture), 109
Revolutionary Ensemble, 75
Richmond, Danny, 66

ritual theater, 81, 87
Rivers, Bea, 49, 50, 164, 179, 204n65
Rivers, Sam, 31, 42, 109, 179, 205n90; feud with Crouch, 58–59, 204n69, 206n102; NYJMF and, 45, 49, 204n65; NYMO and, 48, 49, 203nn59–60; on rent increases, 57; on role of white jazz artists, 204n69; sheet music archives of, 162, 224n52; Studio Rivbea and, 49; Studio We and, 37, 120, 203n57; at "Three Days of Peace between the Ears" festival, 38, 39
Roach, Max, 20, 21, 66
Robinson, Perry, 133, 228n37
rock 'n' roll, 5, 36, 196n14
Rockefeller, David, 27
Rogers, Kenny, 165
Rogers, Shorty, 66
Rollins, Sonny, 65, 66, 94, 196n14
Ross, Brian ("Nairb"), 155, 156
Roulette, 180, 226n2
Rouse, Charlie, 74
"rump festival" (Newport counterfestival), 20–21, 198n7
Rusten, Shelly, *131*
Rutgers Institute of Jazz Studies, 176, 225n65

St. Louis, 2, 6, 23, 205n86
St. Mark's on the Bowery church, 109
Sanders, Pharoah, 102, *106*, 201n24, 212n108
Saul, Scott, 198n7
scenes perspective, 97, 124, 125
Schaap, Phil, 185
Schlanger, Jeff, 147, 228n37
Schmidt, Sarah, 184
Schramm, Adelaida Reyes, 97
Schuller, Gunther, 177
Scott, David, 11, 172
Scott, Shirley, 66
Scott, Tony, 74
Scully tape recorder, 31
Seikatsu Kōjyō Iinkai (Kappo Umezu, recorded 1975), 197n23
self-creation, freedom dreams of, 70–77
self-determination, 42, 95, 144, 159, 181, 186; ideal of freedom and, 188; progressive politics of, 15; self-creation and, 70; space–place distinction and, 134
Serro, Dan, 31, 33, 200n48
Sertso, Ingrid, 213n30
"Seven Dances of Salome" (Simmons, 1969), 158
Sewelson, Dave, 133, 226n7

Shaki, Bembe, 158
Shank, Barry, 99, 124
Sharrock, Lynda, 139
Shaw, Charles Bobo, 55, 205n86
Shaw, Woody, 180
sheet music, 1, 162
Shelemay, Kay, 99
Shepp, Archie, 32, 41, 102, 109, 201n24; as critic of jazz industry, 103; "energy music" and, 88, 89–90; on ghettoization of jazz in bars, 138; musical mainstream and, 181; NYJMF and, 202n45; Studio We music school and, 203n57
Shipman, Elaine, 228n37
Shipp, Matthew, 228n37
Shirley, Don, 66
Simmons, Sonny, 153, 155–160, 190, 213n30, 222n15
Sinan, Rashied, 109
Sirone, 137
Siwula, Blaise, 228n37
Skies of America (Coleman), 201n24
Slobin, Mark, 99
Slugs (jazz club), 45
Sly and the Family Stone, 40
Small, Christopher, 196n10
Smethurst, James, 140
Smith, Harold, 37
Smith, Jimmy, 74
Smith, Paul, 155, 156
Smith, Sonelius, 38
Smith, W. Eugene, 31, 33, 186
Smith, Wadada Leo, 74
Smith, Warren, 104, 118, 124, 137, 204n64; Improvisors Collective and, 228n37; as self-archivist, 147
Smith, Willie "The Lion," 30
Smith-Miller, Henry, 134
social capital, 124, 216n80
social networks, 4, 96, 99, 182
SoHo, 58, 127, 206n99; first wave of visual artists' lofts in, 130, 218n26; rent increases in, 57, 129
SoHo Artists' Association (SAA), 29, 57
SoHo Weekly News, 54
Solis, Gabriel, 11, 14
Solomonic Quintet, 227n19
SOUCA (Society of Universal Cultural Arts), 36, 37, 40, 42; NYMO and, 49; Studio Rivbea and, 50
Sound Out festivals (1968), 103
Sound Unity Festivals, 61, 187
Soundscape, 180

Space for Innovative Development, 45, 54
space–place distinction, 133–34, 141, 219n36
Spieker, Sven, 154, 155, 169, 171, 175, 225n77
Spirit House, 32
Spiritual Unity (Ayler), 89
spirituality, 78, 79, 86, 89, 104, 211n101
spirituals, 115
Stanley, McClinton Karma, 45, 81, 134
"star system," 80
Steal This Book (Hoffman, 1971), 86
Steedman, Carolyn, 221n2
stereotypes, 98
Sterne, Jonathan, 152
Stoler, Ann, 222n2
Stone, Irving, 137, 169, 188
Stone, Stephanie, 137, 188
Stone, The, 188
Storefront Museum, 109, 166
Straw, Will, 99, 124
"stride" piano, 30
Studio Henry, 209n40, 226n7
Studio Infinity, 55
Studio Museum in Harlem, 109
Studio Rivbea, 42, 48, 49, 54, 58, 209n40; brochure and schedule from, 50, *51*; closing of, 195n6; domesticity in, 136; events besides music concerts, 134; listener experience at, 141; "Lost Jazz Shrines" concert series and, 185; on map, *116*; NYJMF and, 45; organizational tasks at, 164; public concerts at, 216n82; rent increases and, 57; Summer Music Festival, 50, *52*, 185
Studio 77, 50, 53, 209n40
Studio We, 42, 85, 87, 101, 142, 209n40; as archetypal early loft, 35; black leadership at, 119; on map, *116*; music school plans for, 48, 203n57; NYJMF and, 45; NYMO and, 49; office work of, 164; performance at, *131*; "Pianists in Focus" concert, 105; prehistory of 193 Eldridge Street, 128–29; recordings made at, 8, 103–104, 197n23; Sultan and, 1, 8, 9, 119; summer park series, 107, *108*; "Three Days of Peace between the Ears," 38, *39*; We Music House rehearsal at, *38*; "wild and woolly" reputation of, 129
Studio We Park Concert Series, 49
Studio WIS, 49, 121, 137, 147, 204n64, 209n40; "Loft Jazz Celebration," 211n92; on map, *116*; public concerts at, 216n82; social capital fostered by, 124
stylistic diversity, 4–5

subcultures, 99
Sudler, Monette, 139
Sultan, Juma (né Edward Lewis), 1, 25–26, 42, 92, 102, 148; Aboriginal Music Society and, 103–104, 153; on building instruments, 76; criticism of Newport Jazz Festival, 41; name change, 74; NYJMF and, 45; NYMO and, 47–49, 119, 153, 160, 161; as presence in his own archive, 170–77; preservation assistance from WKCR, 188–89; on racial politics, 119; recording technology used by, 152; spiritual practices of, 79; Studio We and, 1, 8, 9, 37, 119, 203n61; at Woodstock, 213n30. *See also* Juma Sultan Archive
Sultan, Maria, 145–46, 174
Sun Ra, 75, 88
"Sun Station, Black Light" (Stanley, multimedia exhibit), 134
Sunrise Studios, 49, 109, *116, 117,* 204n64, 205n93, 209n40
Swahili names, 72
Sweet Basil, 52, 78, 184
swing, 4, 5, 41, 115
Swing Journal (Japanese publication), 46
Swing under the Nazis: Jazz as a Metaphor for Freedom (Zwerin, 2000), 65

Tanabe, Mariko, 228n37
Taninaka, Hideji, 228n37
Tapscott, Horace, 23, 198n16, 207n16
Taylor, Billy, 66
Taylor, Cecil, 74, 88, 187, 196n15, 201n24; as critic of jazz industry, 103; recruitment of loft players into bands of, 102, 120
Taylor, J. R., 54
Tchicai, John, 32
teleological perspective, 182
Third World Cultural Center, 109, *113*
Third World Energy Ensemble, 75, 90
third world solidarity, 68
Thomas, Leon, 52
Thompson, Malachi, 205n86
Threadgill, Henry, 205n86
"Three Days of Peace between the Ears" festival, 38, *39*
ticket sales, 3, 45, 50, 56
Tin Palace, *116, 117*
Tintweiss, Steve, 33, 106–107, 187
Tirro, Frank, 196n14
Tolliver, Charles, 74
Toomer, Jean, 98
Totem Music publishing company, 20

Touré, Sékou, 72
trickster spirits, 209n42
Tristano, Lennie, 20, 66
Triumvirate, 22
Trouillot, Michel-Rolph, 151
True Creation from Vibrations (art gallery), 155
Truth and Reconciliation Commission (South Africa), 171
Tuan, Yi-Fu, 133
Tucker, Sherrie, 195n8
Turner, Victor, 79
Two Generations of Brubeck, 164
Tyler, Charles, 74, 89, 185
Tyner, McCoy, 161

UGMAA (Union of God's Musicians and Artists Ascension), 2, 6, 23, 24, 93
Ujaku, 228n37
Ujamaa label, 186
Umezu, Kappo, 109
Universal Jazz Coalition, 166
universities, jazz curricula at, 5
urban ecology, 11, 12, 91
Urban League, 42, 44
US Organization, 72, 220n65

Vass, Jimmy, 38
vegetarianism, 84, 85
"View from the Inside, A" (Shepp), 89
Village Gate, 52
Village Vanguard, 52, 94, 184
Village Voice, 54, 205n93
Vision Festival, 61, 80, 186, 187–88, 228nn39–40
volumes, extreme, 89
Volunteer Lawyers for the Arts, 1
Voodoo Bembe, 158

Wagner, Robert, 41
Walton, Cedar, 78
Ward, Carlos, 89, 227n19
Ware, David S., 94, 102, 120
Ware, Wilbur, 109
Warhol, Andy, 132
Warren, Peter, 213n30
Warwick, Dionne, 40, 201n20
Washington, Kenny, 78
Washington Square Methodist Church, 109
Waters, Keith, 196n13
Watts riots (1965), 23
We Insist! Freedom Now Suite (Roach), 66
We Music House, 38, *38*
Weatherford, Elizabeth, 127

Wein, George, 40–42, 44, 48, 201n20, 201n22; civil rights causes supported by, 42; demands sent by NYMJF organizers to, 42, 43
Whispers from the Archive (Juma's Archive Project), 10
White, Josh, 66
white jazz artists, 20, 24–25, 45, 118, 199n18
Whitecage, Mark, 33, 92, *131*, 211n91, 213n30, 228n37
Whyton, Tony, 158
Wildflowers: The New York Loft Jazz Sessions (five-LP set, recorded 1976), 50, 204n74
Williams, David, 78
Williams, Mary Lou, 30
Williams, Tony, 74
Wilmer, Valerie, 33, 138–39, 141
Wilson, Joe Lee, 84, 109, 204n64, 211n92
Wilson, Nancy, 161
Wilson, Philip, 205n86, 213n30
Winding, Kai, 66
WKCR-FM radio station, 59, 112, 186, 222n11; historic preservation and, 188–89; Improvisors Collective and, 228n37; loft radio festival (1994), 183, 184–85
Wonder, Stevie, 161

Wooding, Sam, 87
Woodstock, New York, as counterculture mecca, 103, 104, 186, 213n30
Woodstock festival (1969), 8, 77, 86, 103, 174
Woody Herman Orchestra, 120
Workman, Reggie, 165
workshops, 3, 8
world music, 5
Wright, Rev. Frank, 89, 212n108

Yablonsky, Lewis, 84, 210n81
Yoruba names, 74
Yoruba religion, 72, 79
Young, Ben, 184, 188, 222n11
Young, David X., 31, 185
Youth International Party (Yippies), 82

Zappa, Jason, 228n37
"Zarak's Symphony" (Simmons, 1968), 156, *157*, 158, 159
Zawadi, Kiane, 73
Zitro, Jim, 156
Zodiac (Rivers), 48
zoning/rezoning, 28, 29, 57
Zorn, John, 126, 188
Zukin, Sharon, 26–27, 57, 131–32, 136, 218n18

Delia's Story

Cassie B

Delia's Story

Written by Cassie B

Published with the services of TamaRe House, UK, 2009

www.tamarehouse.com – info@tamarehouse.com - +44 (0)844 357 2592

Cover by Third-I-Design

Printed by Lightning Source, UK, 2009

Copyright © Cassie B, 2009

All rights are reserved. No part of this book is to be reprinted, copied or stored in retrieval systems of any type, except by written permission from the Author. Parts of this book may however be used only in reference to support related children books or subjects.

ISBN: 978-1-906169-64-0

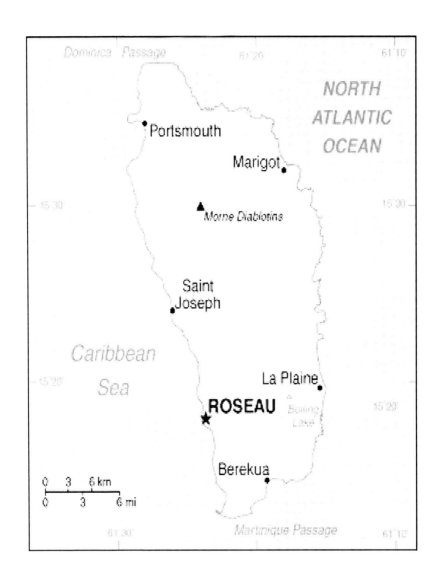

Commonwealth of Dominica

Delia's Story

Thoughts of you
By S.G.Harry 15/03/03

I sit alone and think of you,
Thinking what is it you do
To make me have you in my thoughts,
What magic makes me think of you so much?
Occupying myself, what the hell,
I am only fooling myself.

When first I saw you, your face it was grand
Vast oceans of water, children playing in the sand
The smell of salt in the air
Boatman, busmen, folks moving without a care
Taking their own time
Walking in rhythm and rhyme,
I felt the sun on my face
As I stood near the market place
Listening to the yelling and the dealings going on
Listening to the different types of market sounds
I stood there with glee, whilst scratching
My knee, the mosquito bite I got the night before,
On arrival, just stepping in, the front door.

Whilst folks going past, turned round as I cursed
The stupid look on my face
Faces turning round in haste
I laughed to myself as I started to walk
Thinking Dominica, you are much, much, too much.
I sit with friends and think of you

Thoughts of You

Thinking why it is you do
What you do, to have you in my thoughts.
The magic that makes me miss you so much
I now write down my thoughts, thoughts of you
Dominica.
Beautiful isle of love.

Delia's Story

"I was caught in a mix of fantasy and reality. The story took me back to the Caribbean once again. Oh what an addictive read!"

Sherry-Ann Dixon
Women on the Crossroads

Contents

Chapter One	9
Chapter Two	29
Chapter Three	48
Chapter Four	88
Chapter Five	121
Chapter Six	159
Chapter Seven	168
Chapter Eight	183
Chapter Nine	205
Chapter Ten	213

Delia's Story

Chapter One

It was another one of those days in the beautiful, lush green isle of Dominica. The heat from the sun's rays beat down upon the people's backs as they went about their business. There was hardly any breeze at all, and although the people liked the weather, they wouldn't have it any other way. There were always the few who complained, Delia was one of them, a beautiful, brown skin woman. People always stopped and complimented her, asking her how is it that she is not a model, or on television since she is so warm in nature and so beautiful. Today she did not feel beautiful at all, today her body ached, her long legs were tired from all that walking in the burning Dominican heat.

   Delia born of original Dominican parents on Dominican soil, she had been sent to England at a young age, but she remembered that time as if it were yesterday; running around with no shoes on her feet, forever, in trouble with the neighbour. She would never forget Theo. He was her very best friend, the twinkle in her eye, but Theo was not always allowed out. His father, a teacher from school was a very strict man and did not like his children unoccupied, but when Theo got the chance to go out, they would wander on the Savannah playing silly games and eat all sorts of berries. Their hands and mouths stained by them, even

Delia's Story

their clothes and they would end up in the sea to try get rid of the evidence. Sometimes they would take bits and pieces of food from their homes, kill some birds and cook it in an old tin or whatever suitable item they could find, or just roast them on an open fire.

Those were the days, but now she was older. Sometimes she had to go work in the fields, the few acres of land left to her by her grandmother who had passed on a few years ago God bless her; a very strong woman, she was the man and woman of the house since grandpa had gone to the other islands to find work, she was her gran's favourite grandchild, and had spent most of her childhood following gran about the place, learning about herbs and their uses, now here she was digging the red soil and planting herbs for the kitchen and natural medicine. This was very different from working as a secretary or the various other jobs she was accustomed to doing in England. There were lilies of different colours and shape and her roses, to keep her in business. It was hard, very hard indeed. It was not so bad in the early hours of the day when she would leave the house in her truck and head for the garden. Everything would be cool and dandy until it got to midday, which is when the heat started to get unbearable and she would prefer to sit down and relax under a mango tree with a tall glass of ice-cold lime juice.

However, the work had to be done. She had given her workers the day off since there was not really much to be do, just some watering for the roses and a little pruning, and the only other help she had kept on for the day had let her down at the last minute; something about picking up an aunt from the airport, who

Chapter One

was coming to pay a visit to the family after being in England for the last forty years of her life. Oh well "ces't la vie," said Delia to herself, "What will be, will be, I just have to get on with it," as she used her short sleeve to wipe the sweat from running to her eyes.

    By four o'clock Delia was totally shattered and what with the sweat pouring down her face and running into her eyes, she decided it was time to call it a day, and make her way home to a warm, long shower to ease her aching and sweating body. As she got closer, she could see the view of her white house gleaming in the sun. The other surrounding houses were not quite the same. Some of them were wooden with galvanized roofs and there were the few made with cement, but hailing her from the centre of it all, her beautiful modernised stone house. It had a flat concrete roof and on top of the concrete was galvanized steel, on which she would bake cacao in the sun for making chocolate.

There was lavender plants and designer pepper plants just on the inside of her low stone wall, and a few steps leading to the main entrance; a place she could finally call her own. She did not have to pay rent, no gas bill, just the electricity. No husband to run home to, no children, been there, done that, just herself and Christine, that is unless Christine decided to up and leave, and find her own nest. But she would live each day as it comes and tend to her business; it was enough to keep her occupied.

    The smell of well-seasoned fish being fried in olive oil, met Delia as she approached her gate. The smell slowly trekked its way up her nostrils, she could taste it; there was a hint of baked sweet potato mixed with the fish and her stomach started speaking to her.

She made her way to the back of the house and entered through the back door, which led directly to the kitchen where her cousin Christine was standing by the sink, cleaning up lettuce and other ingredients for a salad. The counter that was between the cooker and the sink was adorned with different plates of fried fish, the sweet potato she had tasted outside, boiled yam and bananas. The gravy was almost ready. Delia gave her cousin a friendly slap on her buxom bottom. Christine was bare foot in the kitchen, her bow legs had a few red marks where she had been bitten by sand flies. She stood there dressed up in her black shorts that was like a second skin and boob top that could hardly be seen under the flowered apron she was wearing, she cried out as if the slap hurt.

"Mmmm, smells delicious" said Delia, as she hugged her cousin and planted a kiss on both cheeks, then turning round, she lifted the lid of the pot sitting next to the gravy and smiled at the gongo peas, stewing in its juice, the smell was making her mouth water, Delia absolutely loved gongo peas. Her cousin replied with a smile and said " I was hoping this would be ready by the time you got home, but never mind, it's going to be another ten minutes ok?" "No problem," replied Delia, who was now pouring herself a glass of orange juice from the fridge. "I need to have a shower anyway! That will take me another half an hour or so, so no rush," and she made her way down the narrow corridor with her drink, to her cool and spacious bedroom, leaving her cousin to

Chapter One

continue doing what she was doing.

Delia came out her room, and entered the round, cream walled dining room. It was not too cluttered, just a few relics from her former life she had brought with her when she left England; her ornaments, a few family pictures, and a three-piece mahogany edged settee. The brown mahogany dinner table which sat in the middle of it was already laid, cutlery and plates waiting to be of service and Christine was waiting patiently to serve. The choice was too much, Delia was not sure if she should have the fish with just salad and gongo peas, or if she should have it with the sweet potato and salad, so she let her cousin decide for her. Christine gave her a taste of everything and took the same for herself. Delia complimented her cousin and told her how much she would make a man happy with her culinary skills. The fish was boneless, it melted in her mouth, mingled with the peas and ground provisions, it was to die for, and to finish it off, a tall glass of crushed iced lime juice with a hint of white rum.

Once dinner was over, they sat down to, watch television and talk about their respective day. Christine told Delia about a hold up in the Co-op Bank in Massacre. She laughed, and wiped the tear that sat at the corner of her eyes because, she said, she couldn't understand how, in such a small village where everybody was always gathered outside, even when rain was falling, that the bank could get robbed and no one had a story to tell the police. They even had hostages and the bank clerk was shot. The thieves got away, but still no one saw anything. Delia was in stitches by the time her cousin had finished telling the story, she laughed so

Delia's Story

much there were tears in her eyes.

"That's village intelligence for you, anyway, the police soon catch up with them you know that; I mean where they can go and D.A is not such a big place."

Delia got up from the table and stretched, belching as she did so, she laughed at the expression on her cousin's face. "Wow, that was a big one, the food is really doing its job," said Christine to her cousin who was now bending down in front of the television changing the channels.

"The news is over now, so how about something a little more cheerful?" said Delia to her cousin, who was still sitting at the table watching as Delia switched from channel to channel, searching to find something cheerful to watch.

As she clicked over to channel 29, there was music playing and talks about the up and coming carnival month. Everybody was talking about carnival, people coming from near and far for the carnival. Yes she was really looking forward to the occasion, even if she did not join the melee and jump up like a kangaroo, she still enjoyed the festive vibes. The people dressed really colourful in all the different costumes representing the Islands. They will be having the Calypso king show, the carnival queen, the prince and princess; oh those little children in their costumes doing their little thing, for real she was really looking forward to it. As she was coming out of her little day dream, Delia heard the presenter of the show saying the magician would be in town, and they were showing his previous victory in the calypso king events. Unfortunately he would not be singing since he lost the crown to

Chapter One

someone else last year, but he would be helping at this occasion. She stopped listening, she started looking hard at the person on the television, she knew the face but she did not remember the name as magician. She was absolutely sure she knew him.

He was about thirteen the last time she saw him and she was eleven, playing under the mango tree next to the little church the family attended every Sunday and most nights of the week. Something was always going on. There were prayer meetings, baptisms for both babies and adults, plus other celebrations that were a bit too difficult to understand His family were a God fearing people, and although he didn't always go to church, outside the church is where you would find him playing most times.

Delia thought, I know him and it has been 20 years and some since I last saw him. She wondered if she was being stupid wondering if he would remember her, it had been such a long time.

Delia's cousin who had been sitting watching her from the armchair shook her head and laughed. She asked her, "What's up cousin? "You look like you're hungry. Why are you staring at Theodore like that? I know he is the sweetest and most perfect looking man I have ever seen, so tall and manly mmm, but babe, you look like you're in love."

"No, no, no," Delia said, "It's nothing like that, but I have got to meet with him, does he live in the country Cuz? Is he in the phone book? I know him, I knew him as a child. You know when we were children, we went to the same school and we played

Delia's Story

together sometimes, when I was allowed to play out, because you know how strict mum was in those days, and then when my little brother came she got soft, oh well! Never mind that", her eyes glaze over with tears as she tried not to remember those days long ago before she lost her mum and brother in an accident, and Theo had helped her unknowingly to ease the pain, it was something she never spoke about, not even to him; she brushed them away, but still it seemed like it was just yesterday. "Yes I know him, Theodore Samson that's his name and I would really like to meet him again." "Ok!" Christine said, who would do almost anything for her cousin without question, anyway she could understand her cousin wanting to see her childhood friend, catch up on old times and such. "I can help you with that, but not tonight. I have an appointment with this man about a dog, you know. We'll talk some more tomorrow, good night my cousin," and with that she was gone, straight down the hall to Delia's little brother's no longer used bedroom which she was using as a studio flat and closed the door behind her, smiling as she did so.

Delia sat down as she continued staring at the image of Theodore, looking so 'finger licking good' Her kind of man, tall, fair and good looking, especially with his glasses on, he looked so flipping edible looking back at her from the TV screen. She wondered what was he like. What was he doing with himself apart from his music, singing or whatever? Did he have a wife or a girlfriend? Because the longer she stared at him, some strange thoughts were going through her head and they were not all good. Please God forgive her, she's not so well at all! It depended on

Chapter One

how you looked at it. It could be fun, oh yes! Real enjoyable fun, getting to know him again, swimming naked with him again, hmm interesting she said to herself, as she told herself off for the third or was it fourth time, she laughed at the idea and decided it was best she went to bed.

Delia got up off her knees from praying. She says that praying is very important, God in all things. She folded over the bedcovers; otherwise she would get no sleep from being too hot. She thought about Theo, as she preferred to call him and really wished that she could see him again, he was the last thing on her mind as she fell asleep.

The alarm went off at 6.00am; Delia reached to it and turned it off. She was not quite ready to get up yet, her bed was so comfortable; it had cost her quite a bundle but had been worth every penny for the comfort she got from it. No backache in the mornings, no kind of discomfort whatsoever and also, she was in the focal point of a dream and boy, the dream was good. She smiled, her eyes sparkled as she hugged herself closer, and she did not want to lose it, not just yet anyway. The dream felt real; it was about her meeting with Theo.

She met him at the same little church where he played as a boy. In the dream he was a man and when they met, he looked at her, and smiled. "Hi sugar. I didn't think I would remember you, but you haven't changed, you've only gotten older," and while saying those words he was drawing her closer to him, and she let him, not fighting the feeling, as if she was in shock. It was a bit confusing but the feeling was good, it was comfortable and then

Delia's Story

he kissed her. Not a lingering kiss but it made her feel something she could not put a name to, and not knowing quite what to do she laughed as he smiled down at her, looking straight in her eyes, he said, "This is strange. I feel as if we have been missing out of each other's life for some years, but it sure feels good, how do you feel?" Yes thought Delia, how do I feel? She looked at him trying to look composed and said, "Strangely enough so do I, and I don't quite understand it." "Never mind," he said as he took her by the hand, "it's probably a spiritual connection thing, because I'm at one with you, yeah the feeling is good. So, where's the family, introduce me to them." Delia said "Ok. Come on then" and took him to the house to meet everyone. How they got to the house? She did not have a clue. They were just one moment by the church, next, they were standing on the top stair in front of her door, and she introduced him to the family who were sitting in the porch. Then they were sitting alone, talking about foolish days and the way as children, how they used to behave; the beatings they got for the things they were accused of, whether they did it or not oh yes! They laughed at the memories. They continued to talk and as they talked, he began to slowly, slowly, make tiny circles on her upper arm, up the base of her neck, and he kept talking to her as he did this; she could hear the words, but yet she could not understand what he was saying. The sensation was making her a little dizzy, she turned and looked straight up into his eye and saw magic in them. She gasped, a feeling caught her tight in her chest as he drew her closer to him, and just as his lips touched hers the alarm went off, and now she could not get back into the dream.

Chapter One

Feeling a little upset, she forced herself out of the bed and headed for the bathroom to get ready for the day. She turned on the shower, took off the little she had on, she did not sleep in pyjamas and she did the occasional nightdress; but most of the time; it was just her panties and bedding. She liked to be cool between the sheets, and if she was going to be dreaming about Theo, then chances is she would really need to be cool between the sheets or on top of it as it were. She got under the shower, feeling the water beating softly against her flesh, touching her places she would never forget; water can get so personal; stroking and washing away sleep's sweat, dream's fatigue, making you feel nice and fresh, lighter in your step. Oh yes! Being under the shower was always a good thing, she thought. Not like sitting in the bath, as the water gets dirty around you and you there, sitting in your grime and rinsing off in the same grimy water. No thank you, and in the shower you can have a pee without worrying about it. Being in the shower is the all time best; laughing at herself, she wondered if Theo likes having showers.

Delia got out of the shower she felt good, refreshed. She started singing to the glory of God; she liked singing, but other things get in the way sometimes and she does not sing as much as she used to. She came from a musical family, everyone could sing. Some were players of instruments traveling about as session musicians and trying to earn from it. For a while, after the accident things went on fine, but things pass and some styles do not last, people get old and move on. Occasionally, the family would get together and have a little music session, Aunty gene

Delia's Story

leading with her guitar, oh well; it's not the way it was, but music was still her joy. Finally, she was dressed and ready to face the world, and her little piece of land awaiting her attention.

Christine loved her cousin very much, and would do almost anything in the world for her. So when Delia, asked her for help in finding out about Theodore, she made up her mind to help. Fortunately for her cousin, Christine, moved around with a group of musicians, so she was sure to find out about Theodore from them if nothing else worked. Carnival was in a few weeks' time; she was certain that by the end of the month he would be in the neighbourhood. She went over to the calendar and checked the date. Today was Tuesday, yes she was certain by next week Friday he would be in town; but just to make sure, she picked up the phone sitting on the dressing table in her bedroom and dialled Jackson. Jackson was her one time teenage lover and also the town tabloid. If there were anything you wanted to know about anything, then, just call Jackson. The relationship had only lasted six months, and then some years later he just took off and went to St Thomas on some wild goose chase, at least, that is what she had called it when he rang her three days after disappearing, to explain the situation to her. He stayed in St Thomas for three years, and then went on to America where he spent a few years then s got married to a Canadian woman who unfortunately died of cancer after their fourth wedding anniversary. He then made his way back home to Dominica and has been here ever since.

Chapter One

Jackson answered the phone. Christine said their usual greeting then got the chitchat out of the way, wanting to know the latest gossip, who did what with whom and where? She then asked him if he knew when Theodore was coming down to the village She listened attentively while he told her the information she wanted then she thanked him, said they would link up later and hung up the phone.

Christine then had a shower and put on her glad rags for her appointment with the man about the dog. She laughed, if only Delia knew who the man was that she was going to see, she would have a fit, but never mind, she would not tell her. If she was careful enough, and so far she has been doing this for a couple of months, and no one knew. Her cousin would never know until she was supposed to know, if ever. Christine made her way to the cab parked at the end of the road, which was waiting for her. While walking to the cab, Christine started thinking about her appointment with Greg. Greg used to be Delia's love, but like most things, the relationship ended and left her cousin being wary of men. Greg was tall well toned and he had the sweetest smile. It was often said, that his smile could melt butter, and that probably was true. His hair was jet black and curly; Christine liked playing with his hair, she did not understand why the feel of it through her fingers, really turned her on, and he did not seem to mind.

They had started seeing each other whilst Christine was working for C and W one of the main Cable Company's in town

Delia's Story

He was an engineer for the company and had been working outside Princess Margarette Street the morning she started the job. She always liked the way he looked, and after the break up with her cousin she had not seen him for a while, a very long while. Even after meeting him, she had tried her best to avoid being anywhere close to him, which was really difficult, because he was always there, wherever she turn there he was, and he always seemed to be staring at her each time she looked in his direction. He would turn away, and so it carried on for a while until one day, she went up to him and said, "I have had enough of this, why do you stare at me and when I look you always turn away? And please, before you even try to start to deny it, don't". She had enjoyed the look of shock on his face, standing there with his mouth open, then he started laughing, and she also finding it funny joined him in the laughter. When eventually the laughing was over, he turned round to her and said" Ok, you've caught me red handed, why don't we do lunch and I will explain it to you." She said "No thanks" and he asked why? "Is it because of your cousin? Come on, that was a long time ago, I am sure she must have moved on by now?" to which Christine replied, "How little you know". However, he was insistent, very persistent and those eyes of his, that smile trying to lure her into him. She agreed, and so it was they had been going out every now and then, but now it was every now more than then. Her cousin must never know. She went into the waiting cab. Anyway she thought, after the way I saw her looking at Theodore, all things are possible, and with that as her comfort, she went to her appointment with a smile on her

Chapter One

face "Yes all things are possible."

    She met Greg at the top of Princess Margarette Street where he lived on his own, not too far from work in a beautiful bungalow. She liked the way the sun reflected the colours of his stain glass windows giving the place a feeling of being somewhere else, out of this world, so calm and peaceful, but what she liked most of all? Apart from walking into the house and the way it smelt of lavender, was the way he made her feel as if she was mistress of the house.

    She remembered the first time not so long ago, when he had brought her home after raving the night away at one of his friend's birthday bash. She had been feeling a little tipsy after smoking an ital spliff and drinking Southern Comfort. She had had one too many and asked him to take her home before she fell over and made a fool of herself in front of all those people. Taking her by the hand and guiding her to the room where she'd left her shawl, "this is Dominica, I don't need a jacket" she had replied to him when he'd asked her why she wasn't wearing one. He found the shawl and they made their way home. She'd dozed off whilst he drove them home and when she woke up it had taken her a while before she realized he had not driven to her place but his. "What's up" she asked him panic in her voice. "Where am I?"

    "Hey why are you fretting? What kind of man do you think I am? I thought you trusted me. Look!" he was saying, and frowning at her, "I know it's a little early in the relationship but you are a little drunk, so instead of driving to your house and having your cousin see you in such a state, plus I'm about a couple years too late, I don't think she wants to see me, do you? She'd heard him and realized she was being a little foolish. She'd realized he was right and told him so. He then got out of the car, came over to her side opening the door for her, the perfect gentleman she'd thought He helped her out of the car saying he's not taking the chance of her falling over. "Man I was only tipsy," she mumbled, but anyway she let him. He locked the car and before she knew what was happening, he had lifted her off the ground and carried her into the house laughing away her protesting sounds.

Yes, she said to herself, "I will always remember that, and since then whenever I come over to his place I always feel so at home."

Greg was still in his work uniform. Christine was a little surprised and asked, "What! Aren't we going out tonight?" as he pulled her close for a squeeze and kissed her on her forehead.

Christine did not resist, she liked the smell of him, so manly; the smell of his Wild Stallion after-shave mingled with his natural body odour made her high, a natural high she called it. "Nope, not tonight baby," he said still holding her to him. "Tonight I thought we could stay in and chill, we're always burning the candles at both ends and I am feeling a little tired, anyway! It's time we spent time with each other without the company of others, you know what I mean?" as he slowly, without seeming to move led her over to the settee to wallow in each other's company.

Chapter One

It was Thursday, and Delia, after having done half a day's work in the fields, was on her way home to freshen up and then head up to town. She had not heard from her cousin since before she went to bed last night and she was wondering why her cousin was taking so long to get in touch? Especially as she wanted to know, had she made contact with Theo, or any news of when he would be in Dominica?

"Man, where was she and why is she taking so long? I mean, it's not every day I ask her to do me that kind of favor and she knows I haven't got any patience," Delia was actually talking to herself. Kicking the gate shut, she went inside to find out whether her cousin had left a message for her, only to find none. She fumed a little more and made her way to her room to freshen up. As she approached her room, about to push the door open the telephone started to ring, She nearly fell over herself in her rush to answer the phone. As she answered she heard her cousin's voice calling her name, but, she could hear another voice in the background and she thought it sounded familiar. She thought it sounded like Greg, but that couldn't be possible. Why would her cousin be in Greg's company?

"Hi Cuz" she said, before Christine could say another word, "What's up? Any news? Where are you? I haven't spoken to you since before bed last night and I was wondering if you had forgotten about me and my problem" "Boy!" replied her cousin; "You really want this bad isn't it? So many questions and not a breath in between, you must really want this bad. Anyhow, in regards to your problem, I have spoken to a friend and he informs

25

me that, your friend should be landing at Canefield Airport sometime next Thursday evening. He will be staying at the family home in town and if you like, there is going to be a get together at the farm the same night. Perhaps you might want to go along? Oh, and it's a sure thing that Theo is going to be there and who knows?"

"Cuz stop, you know I don't like the farm, you know it's not my kind of enjoyment, plus it gives me the creeps, I'm sure it's haunted; why don't you just give your friend my telephone number and ask him to give it to Theo, tell him my name and that I would like to link up with him if possible eh? That would be easier wouldn't it?" "Oh, ok then," Christine said, "We'll talk later," and hung up the phone leaving Delia on the other end, receiver in hand, and a big grin on her face. She did not know why she suddenly felt so elated, but she was. Still grinning, she replaced the receiver and floated on down to her bedroom, all thoughts of going to town gone out of her head.

She found herself wanting to write, she found her notepad and a pen, she wrote.

"Curiosity is, curiously been.
Curiously, curiosity is overshadowing me.
Curiosity frightening, curiously wanting
Tell me why am I so curious about he?
He being so tall and so manly,
I wonder if he could ever get curious about me.
But curiosity is what curiosity is."

Chapter One

She put down the pen and went to the kitchen to eat and finish doing her accounts.

It would have been a peaceful night in Goodwill that night, a glowing, full moon surrounded by an array of beautiful sparkling bright stars. The neighbours were sitting outside enjoying the night as they always did, chatting to one another as neighbours do. Instead, the quiet night was shattered by the sudden uproar emerging from the top of the street; three men were quarrelling. One had a bottle in his hand and the other two were egging him on to use it. It seemed that the one with the bottle was always creating problems with one of the other men and he apparently had had enough, and was going to do something about it when his friend came along and offered his help. Now it seemed the man with the bottle was losing his grip on the situation. He turned tail, and started to run in the opposite direction from where they had started, the other two started chasing after him, picking up stones on the way and throwing them after him. One of the stones made contact; the man fell to the ground. You could hear the sound of his body hitting the ground as it echoed through the street.

The two men who were doing the chasing, were satisfied with the result. They could hear the people laughing as they made their way back to whence they came, and joining in the laughter, as they imitated the sound of the stone hitting the man, and him falling to the ground. They were almost positive the stone had made contact, conking him on the head, was the term used. Still laughing they went about their business, leaving the people to get

Delia's Story

back to whatever it was they were doing before the interruption and so the night went on.

Chapter two

Theo had woken up late this morning. He wasn't in any rush to do anything, no work, just relax, relax, relax, he told himself. "After a busy week like the one that I had, I am just going to take my time and relax."

Theo did not like having to work for someone else. He'd always wanted to be his own boss, but things had not worked out in his favour. He was a very intelligent person and he had a knack for grasping things quickly. The only thing that kept him going was his love of music. It was his getaway, but the music business was not so easy to get into, and money mattered. Money was very much needed to get things started, and in order to get money you have to work.

Theo hated his job; he worked for Hollins & Hollins, solicitors extraordinaire, one of the largest and best companies of solicitors in the country. But when looking at the brown stone manor house from outside, you would never think so. The windows looked as if they could do with a fresh coat of paint, the once black window sills, were covered in bird's mess, the paint on the walls outside were crying for attention and the gate at the front of the building squeaked. The firm had been there for quite a while. Inside the building was quite a different story, he liked inside the building, he did not like his job, but it paid the bills.

Delia's Story

Monday mornings at the office was always the same, you drag yourself reluctantly out of your bed to get ready for what is going to be a day of total disaster, it was something that never changed. As you get in the car to drive down the long motorway, bustling with Monday morning psychotics all in a rush, you find yourself in a near collision with some crazy parent, taking their child to school. You end up stuck in traffic for the longest time, and then to find your boss waiting for you as you enter the office, wanting information from you instantly. Even though you know deep down, that it is still going to take you another twenty-four hours to re-assemble yourself, get your brain in some order- what? Did he think people were machines or what? Talking about machines, those crazy computers are always breaking down, and making your workload heavier.

Monday is not a good day at all, not like Tuesday or Wednesday when your brain has had time to click in and weekend is only a couple of days away. But today was the best; today was Wednesday and tomorrow I will be flying home to the island. Today no work, just chilling in the billing, no crazy bosses making demands on me. Tomorrow I will be leaving this chocked up city behind me, and going to fill my lungs with some fresh country air and find me some nice countrywomen to take care of my every need. The one I have is tasteless and I need new blood.

Theo was in a no win situation with a girl named Wanda. She was a dancer at the Ritzy in Brooklyn Boulevard, a nice girl with ambitions. She wanted to be a Children's doctor and needed money to buy her books. She studied nights when she wasn't

Chapter Two

working and days, when she'd had some sleep. She had approached Theo at a function being held by some friend of his, and she was there looking stunning in a one piece, black lace dress, with splits at the sides from the top of the thigh all the way down. Black thin strapped, high-heeled sandals, the dress hugged her shape, she looked naked and he wasn't sure if she was wearing anything underneath, but the dress worked. She had introduced herself to him, and made some silly remark about casting a spell, you know! Her name being Wanda, and he being the magician.

They chatted on for a while and he warmed to her. When it was time to go, they left together, he dropped her home and she'd invited him up for coffee. He had accepted because he knew where the coffee would lead to and he was in the mood for some distraction.

Wanda opened the door to her apartment and invited him in; "Make yourself comfortable," she told him. So he made himself as comfortable as he thought right. He took off his jacket, and laid it over the arm of the settee where he was sitting. Wanda had wandered off to her bedroom to make herself comfortable, returning in a red-laced negligee and matching slippers. Theo could see the shape of her body through the negligee, the firmness of her breast and the way her nipples pushed against the material as if they were trying to escape from their prison.

He took her in as she approached, from her head to her feet; her island was covered by a small piece of material, just big enough and transparent enough to make the blood rush. He felt a stirring in his trousers; she approached him, and asked him if he would like a drink, coffee or otherwise. he chose the otherwise. She handed him a white rum chased with coconut water on the rocks, then she went over to the stereo and turned it on, asking if he wanted to dance, He'd said no problem. She put on a Marvin Gaye CD that was sitting in the unit. They danced, then they drank some more, they talked a little, and after a while Wanda got up and went to the fridge. She asked Theo if he liked chocolate ice cream. He said "Yes," she took the tub of ice cream out of the fridge, and shut it, and then she got herself a scoop, saying a spoon was too small for what she wanted it for.

She made Theo take of his shirt and lay back on the floor; he obeyed, enjoying the occasion. She started feeding him little bits of ice cream and then while he was busy eating ice cream she, would smear some on his body, making him jump from the sudden coldness on his hot body, bringing him out in goose pimples. She put ice cream on his nipples, the coldness making them firm and she licked it with off with tender strokes of her tongue, moving downwards, she sucked the ice cream off his stomach. The feeling was great, and his 'boy' was getting hard. Theo was enjoying himself, he laid back and relaxed, enjoying the moment, not for once since leaving home to party had he thought his day would have ended like this.

Wanda undid the belt of his trousers, pulled down the zip and last of all the button, she went down to the bottom of his legs and pulled off his trousers and then his briefs. He did not say a word, just merely lifting his ass off the floor so that she could strip him naked. She took his boy in her hand and stroked it, liking the

Chapter Two

way it felt in her hands, so muscular, so strong, pulsating as she cupped it between her palms. She complimented him on the size and firmness of it, as she wiped it with her hand gently, and then placed it to her mouth. Theo gasped, and he was loving it. She sucked on it like a lollipop. She took it out of her mouth and played a game with her tongue, and when he thought she was finished, she took some of the melted ice cream and covered his boy with it. She started eating, she went down on him and he could not hold back any longer, spurting forth his white stuff, in her hands and on her face. She looked at him and laughed saying, "Mmmm, chocolate and vanilla". Both of them laughed at her joke. She got up, wiping her face with the negligee, as she took it of and let it fall to the floor and stood there in her thong. She took Theo by the hand, helping him to get up and then led the way into her bedroom and did some dirty dancing of their own.

  At the time Theo had thought Wanda to be wicked in the bedroom. She was loud and crass between the sheets but she had given him the best blow job he had ever had and he told her so, complimenting her on her skills as a temptress, she liked the compliment so much, she blushed and so he'd decided to keep her around for a while, but after six months of much the same thing, he had had enough. Her time was up, he needed more than what he was getting, Wanda was ok for what they had but something was missing, he had told her so once or twice but she would not get the message. She kept talking as if she wanted to be the next Mrs. Theodore Samson or something, with children to go along with it; he just could not understand where she was coming from.

33

Delia's Story

He had given her no reason to believe that there was anything serious going on between them. He liked her yes, but she was not the woman he felt he needed to spend the rest of his life with. He had deleted her phone number from his cell phone and promised only to remember her address on special days like Christmas, Easter and possibly her birthday, like friends do, so what was her problem? Perhaps this time spent away from the US of A, and away from her would make her see reason, and see how serious he was.

Theodore landed at Canefield airport Thursday, at five thirty in the afternoon. He had an incredible physique, tall, strong; thanks to the gym he attended twice a week and one hundred percent masculine. He was clean-shaven, but very annoyed, in fact he looked thunderous, he was thinking about his last meeting with Wanda. Dressed in his khaki shorts, white stringed vest, sandaled feet, and his bag in hand, he made his way to the waiting area after the hustle and bustle of getting through security check. You would think that after all these years; he wouldn't have to undergo the same old boring questions, what is in the bags? Did he pack them himself? Was he carrying any large amounts of money? And the rest of the bullshit that went with it.

As he approached the waiting area, he saw his school friend waiting for him. He smiled, he was glad to see Michael, they had been very close at school, especially after Delia was no longer in the country, they were always watching each other's

Chapter Two

back, and they were always getting into trouble for something or another. The headmaster's office was their least favorite place, but they were always there. The headmaster was a friend of Michael's dad and so Theo supposed that's why they never got excluded, but they always got punished, punished by the teachers and when they got home, punished by their parents; those were the days, my friend those were the days.

As he reached Michael, he dropped his bag and the friends hugged each other like long lost brothers, both talking at the same time and laughing at themselves; "Ok!" said Theo, "You go first."

"No" said Michael, "What I got to say can wait. Why you don't start by telling me what you've been up to since the last time we spoke, which was when? Carnival last year?" he said, answering the question for himself and Theo laughed. "Well brethren, speak to me," said Michael.

Theo started telling him about his business ventures, the work he was doing with the other musicians in the States, and he was hoping to release a new album in the near future; thanking Michael for the name Magician. It had been one of those days, they had been throwing stones at birds close to the schoolyard, one of the stones that Theo threw went further than anticipated and broke the school window missing some children in the classroom, as soon as they heard the smashing of the glass, Theo went off like lightning, nowhere to be seen. When Michael finally found him about half a mile away sitting under a mango tree by the river. He called out, "Hey mister magician, how you just disappear like that" the both of them had broken into laughter at

Delia's Story

the Name but Theo kept it and used it as his stage name and was glad he did, it seemed to open doors. And so they chatted as they made their way to the chauffer driven car parked outside waiting to take them home.

Michael was a very wealthy man. He owned a lot of property in town and part of the countryside left to him by his father a few years ago while he was still linked to the force, Dominica was his paradise. His father, Hesford Shillingford, had been a strict man, but had loved his son dearly and being his only son after four daughters, plus, thinking he was cursed in never having a boy to carry on the family name, was very thankful for his blessing. Michael knew it and his sisters knew it, but they did not mind since they loved their brother very much.

Hesford Shillingford, had worked himself from a one net fisherman to being the owner of half of Dominica, and when he died his children were not for wanting especially Michael, who, as his only son and heir to the family fortune, had his fortune made. Although he was one of the richest men on the island, it did not prevent him from being nice to people. Even after joining the Police force he had not changed and he was very charitable to strangers. His town people loved him and spoke very highly of him.

Michael loved Theo as a brother and his best friend. They had known each other for the longest time even, if they did not keep in touch, as they should anymore. However, that was not a

Chapter Two

problem because whenever Theo was home, they would link up and paint the town whatever colour they choose and checking the babes together, they had fun.

They had always had fun especially when they were young, boy! The mischief they got up to, locking their English teacher in the toilet, had been his favourite. He would never forget how after the teacher had embarrassed him in front of the classroom, because he had forgotten the names of three ships Christopher Columbus had used to travel to the Caribbean and claimed that he discovered it. How can a man be so foolish? How can a man who got lost in his travels, find a place full of people living there, eat and drink with them turn round and claim he discovered the place. What happened to the Arawaks and The Caribs? Just to mention a few. It seems to me the place was discovered already.

Anyway, after the teacher started calling him stupid in front of everyone he'd decided to get his revenge with the help of his accomplice Theo. They followed the teacher at lunchtime and got their chance When they saw him go into the teacher's toilet, they waited a while. Being the kind of children they were, you would not be surprised at the kind of things they carried around in their school bag. Super glue, happened to be one of these things. Michael pushed the toilet door open slightly, checking to see if there was anyone else in there and saw no one. He told Theo to wait outside and play lookout for him, he will not be long. He then disappeared behind closed doors to re appear almost immediately, and put some distance between themselves and the teacher's toilet still laughing at what they had done. Today was a good day. It was good to have his friend home again.

Michael had entered the toilet and found that except for the locked cubicle his English teacher was occupying, it was empty. He found a piece of wire by the sink, used it to jam the lock on the cubicle; then emptied half of the tube of superglue to the jammed lock. Then, just to be on the safe side, he emptied the rest of the glue on the inside of the entrance door to the toilet and in the groove where the door catches. He remembered it took the other teachers about an hour, before they realized teacher was in the toilet. In addition, when they'd found him, his hand was stuck to the cubicle door latch. It appears the glue, had somehow leaked through the gap in the latch, and when teacher tried to open the door, he found he couldn't let go of the latch and on releasing his hands free he had left some skin behind.

Yes! Thought Michael those were the days, and he looked over at his friend and smiled to himself. Finally, they were at their destination.

The journey to Theo' family home was not a long one, but it was long enough and the friends were glad to be able to sit down with a cold bottle of Kubili and make plans for the coming days that Theo would be in Dominica.

Theo's parents, were still alive and living in Dominica, but were not home when the two friends got there. Theo loved his parents very much, especially his father, Cedric Samson, who had been a very strict man when Theo was in his teenage years, even before that. He tried not to remember how hard he thought his father was back then, always handing out the punishment, taking people's word over his especially when he told the truth. Therefore, it came to be that he did not say anything he just took the blame. Now that he was a man he could understand, after all; he was not an easy person himself, he had taken after his father in ways he could not believe and he hoped if ever he had children he would try to be more understanding. His mother, Andra Jones was a gentle Carib woman, who never once raised her voice, but had a tone that caught your attention. She was his father's best friend and they went everywhere together. They discussed their problems and there was never a time that he could remember hearing his parents argue, and so he had told himself, if ever he had a relationship with anyone, he would like it to be like his parents.

The phone was ringing. Theo let it ring, "Let it go to the answering machine" he said, as Michael looked at him inquiringly. "Not in the mood for any calls at the moment," Theo explained. "I'll just put my bag away and we can relax, I need to relax, planes and flying, you know the stress?" Michael nodded in agreement, as his friend went to dispose of his travel bag, and went into the kitchen. He liked the kitchen; it was tiled, all the way round in white and blue ceramic, with little birds from around the world printed into them. The kitchen unit matched the décor glass table, on one side surrounded by chairs with little birds carving looking inviting, with a vase of different coloured roses, sitting in the centre of the table. Michael went to the fridge, took out two bottles of Kubuli beer, one for himself and the other for his friend. He took them over to the table and sat down, opened the bottle with his teeth, he had strong teeth; and as he flipped the lid of the bottle he remembered his dad telling him what a bad habit it was opening bottles with his teeth. Michael smiled, he missed his dad sometimes. It was worse before, picking up the phone to talk to his dad and remembering that he wasn't there anymore, and when he thought he would lose his sanity, it was Theo who was there for him. Yes Theo, god bless him, if ever a man was blessed to have a true friend, then he was blessed because he had such a friend, and there was nothing he would not do for him.

"Hey man! What you thinking about so hard"? Asked Theo, entering the kitchen, "I suppose that drink is for me right?" Michael nodded, "Cool", said Theo, walking over to the table, picked up the Kubuli and opened it with the bottle opener, lying by the vase sitting in the middle of the table. He held the drink towards his friend and said, "To brothers," and emptied half the bottle before taking it away from his mouth. "I needed that, wow, it's so hot, but it's also real good to be home". "Well bro' it's good to have you home" answered Michael. "So what time are we stepping out this evening, 'because the local radio station is expecting you at the farm tonight in case you had forgotten."

"No! I haven't forgotten," said Theo. I was thinking we would go there about eleven this evening, after we go check a few brethrens. I have some distributions to make; you know how it is with the people, when you come from foreign, you, have to have something to give. Otherwise, they will be calling my name for

Chapter Two

the next millennium, or even write about it in one of their calypso songs and I cannot have that! A man have a reputation to keep, one has to be seen, to be doing the right things. You of all people should know about that!" Michael laughed at his friend's words, and said, "Come on bro' the people aren't that bad?" "If you say so," replied Theo. "Anyway I better go have a fresh, won't be long." "Cool," answered Michael.

"Oh and make yourself at home", said Theo, laughing at the expression on his friend's face. They both knew that Michael was at home here, at the family's home; it was what you would call, home away from home. It had been his home as long as they could remember. When they were younger, they were always at each other's place, they grew up in each other's house, and it had always been that way with the two of them.

Eleven pm. found them still making their way to the Farm. The friends were having fun and joking about a friend, they had just met on the way to visit a few calypsonians living in Goodwill. Jackman was a clown or so everyone said. He looked funny the way he walked down the street, walking with the perception of a woman. His hips, swinging to and fro, from left to right, but he claimed to be all man. Even the way he spoke, trying to be speaky, spokey, with his stammer; yes he was funny. "It seems", Michael was saying "Jackman got in a fight with a policeman some time gone, over a goat he had tied up by the road. The goat got loose, went over into a neighbour's yard, and started eating everything in his path. The neighbour, it seemed at the time, was doing some washing and had left the clothes to go answer the

Delia's Story

phone. Anyway, the goat was eating the woman's washing, and when she came back, the goat was still there with the woman's panty in its mouth. Well, you can imagine Dominican women right? The woman picked up the first thing she could lay her hands on, which happened to be a cutlass. She picked up the cutlass and she flung it after the goat; the cutlass flew straight at the goat's head and 'bodduff,' the goat fell down dead. Apparently blood was squirting everywhere, ruining the woman's clean clothes". Theo was in stitches, "How do you know all this man?"

"Well!" said Michael, it just so happened I was in the police officer's house when the call came through. We went to the station together, and there they were, this woman, a dead goat and Jackman, making a wail of a noise. They were trying to fight each other when this young policeman came, and tried to stop them, but they wouldn't stop. The policeman tried to grab Jackman, Jackman hit the policeman so hard, that the policeman hit the wall and he fell down to the floor unconscious. Three days later, he died in hospital and so they threw Jackman in jail. And when he was released, what you saw of him just then, is what you get".

"Wow," said Theo. "It was funny at the beginning but the jokes gone sour. Come, let us go to the farm and have some fun tonight, yeh man, let us go paint the town pink, we have plenty time to paint it red later."

It seemed everyone who was anyone, was at the farm tonight and the place was buzzing with activity. The music coming from the speakers round the room was vibrant. It seemed to want to take a person off their feet, and make them dance whether they wanted to or not, everybody's body was rocking. Theo was feeling blessed, nice; he and Michael had linked up with some friends and were enjoying the long time no see vibe, and it was a good one.

Christine, arrived sometime after midnight with Greg walking behind her like the bodyguard, and they looked good together. They looked like they had been tailor-made together, and eyes watched as they approached. Christine noticed Jackson standing with a group of friends, and made her way in their direction, Greg still following behind her. Jackson had noticed Christine and was beckoning her to come over: "Boy is he late I was going over there anyway," and she smiled at Jackson. When eventually they made it to the other side of the hall, Jackson introduced Christine to his friends. It seems Greg and most of them had gone to school together so no introduction was necessary. After the introduction was over, Christine asked Jackson if he'd managed to give the message to Theo, looking at Theo as she did this and he said, "Everything was cool, done, did and delivered, no problem; your cousin should be getting a call anytime from tomorrow ok?"

"Thank you Jackson" she replied, kissed him on the cheek, and left him to return to Greg. "I'm all yours now baby" she whispered in Greg's ears while her hands teasingly pinched his behind, "Well at least for the time being" and they both laughed as Greg moved her body to his and started to dance.

Delia's Story

Delia decided that she would stay home and read a book; she got out a classic by Raymond Chandler, and started to read; it was about a detective, Phillip Marlowe who had been hired to find a beautiful woman. While reading her mind started to stray, she was seeing herself as the woman and Theo was the detective. She shook her head, what is the matter with me? She asked herself, thinking all these things about someone I have not seen for most of my life.

Delia is generally a cautious person. She had decided after her relationship with Greg, she would not wear her heart on her sleeve, and she had no intention of feeling that way about anybody again. So what was up with her constantly thinking about Theodore? It must be curiosity, she told herself again as she saw him in her mind's eye, tall, fair and good looking, broad shouldered. She imagined him drawing her close to his naked muscular body, looking as finger licking as can be. Foolish woman, what is your problem? She asked herself again. I need to see this man so that I can put myself out of this misery.

She put the book down. It really was not capturing her attention, so she decided to go for a drive, and she needed to do something. She drove down towards Portsmouth, one of the towns in Dominica, housed with its vast university complex and inundated with foreign students. Even the Dominicans who wanted to attend the university, had to be foreign exchange students to get in there. Strange, she thought, as she drove past the countryside where mango trees, coconut trees, banana trees and different kinds of fruit trees waved her on, as she drove by doing

Chapter Two

50 miles per hour on a 30 mile per hour road. She needed to clear her head and this was helping, the breeze in her face, and whispering sweet nothings in her ears. She turned on the radio and joined in with the midnight groovers, singing at her from the four tiny speakers in the car door.

Delia pulled up at a bar called Cabrits, meaning Goats, in Portsmouth, a place once inhabited by the British in the slavery days, and some parts of it were still owned by them. She should not be drinking, but! She told herself, if it comes to the worst, I would take a taxi home. She had just ordered herself white rum with coconut water and ice, when she noticed a jukebox in the corner, standing waiting for the next heartbroken soul to find some comfort from the old songs that it played. Delia feeling in the mood, dropped four coins in the jukebox and decided to let the bar person choose the song that would be played, which he obliged. The first song that played was by Elvis Presley. Are you Lonesome Tonight? Oh boy! Thought Delia, here we go; and so it went on from Elvis to the blues by Fats Domino, and the final one, the one, the straw that broke the camel's back, was Rocking With You by the one and only Theodore Samson. Delia started to laugh; she thought it was so funny, the way things happened.

There she was all alone and contented, getting on with her life in Dominica after leaving England, where she had spent the first quarter of her life. She had met and married Greg Beau Pierre in England; he was from Roseau, one of the capitals in Dominica like herself. She was glad at the time, about both of them being Dominican. That, was the way she had dreamed her life would be, raising her family in Dominica.

When she met Greg, she thought she had her wish. Thing had not worked out the way she thought at all. After they had been married for two years, she got pregnant with a set of twins, they were premature and the image of Greg. Beautiful babies they were, a boy and a girl, and they were identical. However, nothing ever lasts. Tragically, the twins died of cot death and after that, Greg changed. She hardly saw him, and when she did, it was unbearable. She herself was no good to anyone, including herself. She stopped paying attention to her appearance, she stopped cooking, and she would just get up each day and mope around the house and crying for her dead children.

Then one day, she decided to go out of the house for some fresh air, and try to get herself in order. She had woken up that day and realized what a mess she was, her husband was nowhere to be found. In fact, he had not been around since after the funeral, but at the time, she hadn't noticed. Now she had and she wondered where he could be, where has he been all this time? She wondered if she would ever see him again some years later Delia was making her way across Central Park Road when she saw Greg. He was with another woman, holding hands and teasing each other on the street. She did not approach him nor he her, she simply went back to home to her house called up her solicitor and put in a claim for divorce.

She got the divorce quicker than she thought she would. Greg did not fight against it, so when it came through she decided to pack up her bags, leaving behind what memories she could,

Chapter Two

especially her ex husband and migrate to her birth land, Dominica. This was not going to happen to her again she told herself, she would not make the mistake of falling in, nor out of love again, "No way daddy, not for all the nutmeg in Grenada." Not if she could help it, she swallowed her drink, paid the bar person and left to make her way home, she needed to sleep off tonight and her joy, would come in the morning.

Delia's Story

Chapter Three

The dream was so real it was a nightmare she was trapped in a metal cage, hanging from the ceiling of her bedroom. There was people in the room, two men, and they were playing chess, and she was the prize, but both were as good as each other and they always came to a stalemate. Then she was in a large arena in the Botanical garden, surrounded by a circular pit, filled with a raging fire and she, still in the cage, sweat pouring off her, feeling like the Sunday roast; could see the two men quarrelling, who was the one for her? And try as she might she could not see their faces and beyond the two men, she could see a woman crying, crying and trying to get the attention of one of the men, but they paid her no mind. Delia woke up in a start, sweat pouring off her; that woman, that woman in the dream; she looked like her cousin Christine, but who were the two men? Who were they? What does it mean? She got out of bed and had a shower, dried herself and went back to bed, taking up her bible to read, until she fell asleep again.

The phone ringing woke Delia up, she reached out to get it but it stopped, and just as she was about to take her hands away it started to ring again, she answered it. "Hello, how can I help

Chapter Three

you?"

"Well, you can help me by letting me speak to Delia please", said the voice on the phone, it had an American accent and the tone so vibrant, not so deep but deep enough to stir something in her.

"This is Delia speaking, Theo is that you?" "Yep, it's me and I got a message from someone that you wanted me to give you a call."

"Yes, that's right. I saw you on the television the other day and realized I knew you from childhood and figured it would be nice to see you again, you know for childhood sake". Yeah!" He replied, "I hear you girl, I hear you; ok, is it all right then if I come over and see you tomorrow about midday. I already have your address." "No problem, ok" said Delia, "midday it is then."

Saturday morning found Delia in very high spirit, she'd woken up and after having her shower, went to fry some plantain for breakfast, plantain and salt fish; yes, she thought and then season some of that fish in the fridge for lunch. When Delia was finished, she turned on the radio to listen to some music and wait for Theo to turn up.

At quarter to twelve, just as she was making her way from the shop across the road, she noticed a jeep driving slowly down the road and the driver looking left and right, as if he was looking for something or someone. Delia smiled to herself, telling herself it was Theodore, and walking now in the direction of the oncoming vehicle, the driver noticed her in the road. He smiled and stopped the jeep, as she approached the open window of the jeep; she heard him say, "Delia, sugah, my word, girl is that you? You haven't changed except for getting older." She could not believe her ears. "Come on! Get in, which is your house"?

Delia pointed straight with her finger towards a white bungalow and he started to drive, stopping when she told him; all that time she was sitting in the car, she had not spoken a word, and her mind was racing.

The words he had spoken, she had heard them before in her dream, and the first night she had seen him on the television. He opened the door for her and helped her out of the vehicle. She thanked him and invited him inside. No one was home, and her cousin had not been home for a couple of days, although they had spoken over the phone.

"Come on in; have a seat, would you like a drink? She asked him "Ok," he answered, "What kind of poison do you have?" She gave him a short list, and he settled for some coconut water and a little rum. "So tell me" he was saying, how is it after all these years you still remember me?" "I have no idea," she said, just one of those strange things in life I suppose, and I must say; you look like your father, how is he? "Oh, he's ok, still full of life and we're still politically indifferent, but yeah! He's cool. What about you? How you doing? What's been happening in your life?" he asked. "Not a lot, she replied, "a little bit of this and that and now I am here in DA trying to run my own business. And so they chatted on, filling in most of the gaps of the years gone by and three hours later Delia looked at the clock on the wall and said "Gee! Is that the time already, I was going to fry some fish for

Chapter Three

lunch, but it looks like I am going to have to make that supper. Are you hungry Theo? Would you like something to eat?" He declined the offer of food and settled for another drink, this time omitting the alcohol. "Hey, can I ask you something? I have a couple of spots and I wondered if you don't mind squeezing them out for me, are your hands clean?" "Yes," Delia answered. "No! I don't mind squeezing them out for you, but tell me who squeezes them out for you normally?"

"Normally, I do that myself, especially there, look you cannot miss them" he said to Delia, as he bent back his head and pointed to the base of his chin. Delia went to the bathroom to wash her hands, came back and sat down on the chair in front of the television, "Ready when you are, she told him" and he came and sat down between her legs, casually commenting on the beauty of them, as she tried to keep her cool squeezing out his spots.

Theo's finger's were stroking her legs and it was causing her a strange sensation, then he said, "Do you know this feels really comfortable and you smell heavenly," still stroking her legs, at which point she brushed his hands away as she replied trying to keep her voice steady,

"I know what you mean". When Delia was finished with Theo's spots, he got up, faced her, and said, "You have the strangest effect on me." He was saying, "Do you know, last night I had the strangest dream and I swear you were in it" "Really?" she said, "Tell me more. "Ok," he continued, "from what I remember, there is a woman in a metal cage, swinging from the

51

ceiling in someone's bedroom. Probably hers. Anyway, there she is, in this cage and I and someone else, a man, were duelling over this woman in the cage. We had to do tests of sorts to find out who was the one for her. Strange dream it was; but then I woke up." She was quiet the whole of the time it took for him to tell her his dream, her mind was racing, what was happening? How is it they were having the same dream? What is going on? Theo was still talking, but this time he was saying he had to go, had to meet up with some family, but could he give her a call the next day and she said "No problem." "And oh", he said, "Before I go, can I show you something?" "What's that?" she asked. He took her hand, placed it against his penis, it was firm and throbbing she felt the stirring in his trousers, "Oh my gosh, but man you bright," she cried as she pulled her hands away, "That is what" he said, "You do to me". Delia, trying her best to keep control, replied, "I bet you say that to all the girls" he laughed, said goodnight, promised to call her again and left Delia standing at the door as he drove off, not realizing the fire he had ignited down there in her loins.

Christine came home later that afternoon, not long after Theo had taken his leave, she wanted to know all there was to tell, but Delia was still trying to figure it out for herself.

"What do you mean you trying to figure it out for yourself? Asked Christine. "If you don't want to tell me then say so. Tell me to mind my own damn business and I will understand." "No, no no", replied Delia, angry at her cousin for accusing her of such a thing. "Honestly, this is how it is," she went on to explain the situation to Christine. Telling her about the

Chapter Three

dreams, she has been having, and the dream Theo had. Then she asked her cousin if she understood what all of it meant and if she could understand her dilemma.

"Sorry cousin, said Christine, you really got me there, perhaps you need to speak to uncle, uncle knows all about dreams and the meaning of them, perhaps he can help you with this."
"Hmm yes, perhaps you are right" said Delia, and headed for the phone to give uncle a call.

Uncle Joseph lived in town, about two and a half miles away from Delia, but being the busy man that he was, it was always best to inform him when deciding to pay him a visit. He lived alone because he liked it like that, but had been married as long as Delia could remember. His wife lived in another house with the children, where uncle would eat sometimes, but having to spend so much time doing whatever it was he did, he needed thinking space, which was why he chose to live separately from his family, but everybody was happy, everyone knew who was who.

He was not home when Delia phoned, but she left him a message on the answering machine, for him to contact her when he got her message. She placed the receiver back on its cradle and went over to speak with her cousin, wanting to know what she had been up to for the past couple of days? Was there a new love in her life? Christine looked at Delia and smiled. "Yes there was a new man in her life but as for love? That she was not sure of yet. "We are still learning about each other, there's nothing to tell as

Delia's Story

yet, but when there is; you will be the third to know. Since we will be the first and second," and with that she laughed and changed the subject. She did feel a little uncomfortable about the situation and was sad that she could not tell her cousin about how things were with Greg, she knew how Delia felt about him, at least she think she knew how her cousin felt, but time had passed, her feelings might have changed, but for now she would just watch and see, She told herself as she scratched her head.

The phone rang, Christine answered it and gave it to Delia "I think this one is for you" she said. "Thanks Cuz," she replied taking the receiver from her cousin's hand; placing the phone to her ear she said, "Hello?" The voice replied "Hi, just making sure you haven't forgotten me." "I don't think that's possible," she answered. "I have never been so caught up like this before, and I have only known you for a few hours." He laughed and said, "That's good, since I'm in dilemma of my own. Think of me while you sleep, and I will see you tomorrow, goodnight." And with that he hung up the phone, leaving a puzzled face Delia looking at the receiver in her hand as if she wasn't sure what to do with it.

"Delia" called out Christine; "I just had a thought, if Greg was to walk in through this door now, what would you do?" Delia came alert at the mention of Greg's name, "What are you saying, have you seen Greg? Why bring him up now? "Sorry "said Christine, "I was just thinking, that's all" "Well please don't, not right now, I don't need to talk about Greg, ok." "Ok, don't bite my head off" said her cousin.

Chapter Three

The phone rang again, this time, Delia answered it. It was her uncle on the other end. "Hello uncle, how you doing?" she asked and they spoke for a while. Then she told him about her problem, and her uncle told her; it was best she came over to his place, as such matters should not be discussed over the telephone. They arranged a time when it would be convenient for the both of them, said their goodbyes and she hung up the phone.

Theodore was in a state of confusion; he was not so sure, what the reason was that made him behave the way he did at Delia's place, and he had been very comfortable, sitting between her legs having his spots squeezed out, but even before that. When the fellow at the farm had given him the message, he thought it might have been an old flame, or even one of his many fans, who might have wanted to get it on with him. He had gone out of curiosity, and because it would have been rude after the people went to all the trouble of finding him.

Delia sounded cool on the phone, so polite and all that. He told himself that he needed to see her; he liked the sound of her voice calling him Theo. Still not sure what he was going to find, he woke up that morning, with nothing else on his mind but his strange dream he had last night; and if he remembered correctly, he'd had the dream before or one very similar to it, and that woman in the dream, who was she?

He made a call to Michael, wanting to know what was on the agenda for the evening. Michael told him they were going to meet up in Massach, at the sports bar later on about eight pm. Theo said Ok and hung up, and then he got himself ready, looking casual in his T-shirt, shorts and sandals. It was going to be hot today, he was sweating already and it was only eleven in the morning.

He got to Bowers Lane, which was the address that had been given to him and started his search for the house where she lived, this person who said they'd known him from childhood. As he was driving and looking at the door numbers as he passed by, he noticed someone walking up towards his jeep, and the person was looking familiar, but from where? He smiled, she looked like she was smiling too, he said to himself, so he stopped his vehicle and she approached the jeep, stopped at the opposite window to where he sat and smiled at him. Theo could not believe his eyes, the person standing before him was someone, he never thought he would see again, not since she'd disappeared as a child, one minute she was there, next she was gone. And look! There she was, twenty how many years later standing before his very eyes; his heart seemed excited by the way it was beating, and there was a stirring in his loins. Wow, ain't nobody ever made me feel this way yet and I have met a few, thought Theo as he greeted her. He could not believe how she had not changed much at all, and he told her so except for getting older, which we all have to do; he invited her into the jeep and drove them to her home. Her place was comfortable, he liked the colour scheme, although outside was sweltering with the heat, inside her place was cool like when you stepped into Mac Donald's and she was cool; she was disturbing his thought flow. She offered him a drink, he accepted coconut water with rum with ice, then they sat down to catch up

Chapter Three

on old times, wanting to fill in the gap for most of the years gone by. After an hour of talking, she had offered him food, but he had declined the offer of food for another drink. Theo started playing with his hair and asked Delia, if her hands were clean. She laughed at the question, but she had said yes, and she had even accepted when he asked her to squeeze out his spots for him. But sitting between her legs, became the hardest thing he ever had to do with composure.

It was warm there and she smelt clean, mingled with the hint of her female scent, the feel of her skin against his skin, and sent the blood rushing to his head. His fingers with a mind of their own started stroking her legs to satisfy their curiosity and he felt her move to slap his hands away, he smiled to himself; the feeling was good and he was enjoying himself too much, his little coal had blossomed into a Diamond. He wondered why Delia was still single, she did not look sick or nothing, somebody did not know how to treat this jewel, or God must have a plan for them, hmm that would be just ideal, he thought to himself with a smile. Theo decided to take his leave after a while, promising to call her again the following day, and before going out of the door, he had taken her hands and placed it against the bulge that he was sure she could see in his trousers. She had pulled her hands away as if she had been electrocuted, but that was all good, then she said goodnight to him. He could not wait to see her again. That night when Theo went to sleep, there she was waiting for him and he was happy.

Delia got up on Sunday morning, got ready for church and

Delia's Story

left the house about eight thirty in the morning. She walked it to the church. The walk would do her good, help to clear her head enough for her to take in the service she was about to attend. After church was over, she would be meeting with her uncle. She knew she had to met with Theo today but, that was much later on in the afternoon when he would find out that they were going out for dinner; or even just to pass the time away in each other's company, anywhere but her house. The service finished at twelve, midday, after starting at nine am. There was always a lot to discuss in church; the pastor doing his best for god and the people, ensuring us great rewards if we follow the right path, and so he went on until someone else came up to speak. They sang songs and had a great time giving god the glory.

When service was over, Delia stepped out of the church and found her uncle waiting for her. "I thought I would save you the walk to my place," he said, kissing her on her forehead. She hugged him, and thanked him for being so thoughtful. "Come, let's go for a drive and you can tell me all your problems," uncle said to her. Delia got in uncle's pickup and off they went, heading for the coast.

The scenery was breathtaking. Delia loved Dominica more than any other place on earth. Not that she had done too much travelling in her time. The sun was shining bright and heating up the place with his rays. The different shaded of blue and green of the sea in the distance, and the vast arrangement of flowers coating the ravines and colouring the edges of the roads; she always felt enchanted by it. She took in a breath and savouring the

Chapter Three

taste floating in the gentle breeze passing by, she sighed.

"So, what is it that's troubling you Sugah" asked uncle as they drove. Sugah was Delia's pet name from childhood and some people still called her by that name; she did not mind at all, she quite liked it. She started telling her uncle her story, starting from seeing Theo on the telly to the stirring in her loins, and her uncle laughed. "But Sugah, I thought you had the gift of dreams interpretation?" "Yes uncle", she replied, "but only other people's dreams it seems, which is why I came to you, when Christine suggested it." "Hmm", said her uncle, hmm, I see. Christine, how is she by the way?" "Oh she's getting on with her life," Delia told him. "Well you give her my love and tell her I'm still alive" said Uncle Joseph. "No problem uncle, I will tell her," answered Delia. "Know what were you about to tell me about my dream?" "Well." He went on to say that her dream was quite simple really. It means you have a feeling for this Theo and you still have feelings for Greg. "But no uncle," protested Delia, "I don't love Greg anymore, I don't think about him, haven't done so for some time now, and how can I have feelings for a man I just met? It's probably just lust, I've been too long without a man in my life and the attention is causing my system to malfunction." "Well I don't know" said her uncle, but that is how the cookie crumbles, you'll have to figure it out for yourself, I was just showing you the picture that's all." They finally got to where uncle had to be, so uncle asked Delia to excuse him while he went to see a colleague. Delia waited in the pickup with these crazy thoughts running through her brain.

Delia's Story

She had not got any feelings left for Greg, apart from contempt for forsaking her when she most needed him that is all. She was over him without the shadow of a doubt, but Theo, well! He was a different matter altogether. A very different kettle of fish, yes, he stirred her curiosity, she found him very attractive and yes, he seemed to be upfront in her thoughts these days, not forgetting that tone of his. However, if she was to be completely honest with herself, then yes, Theo turned her on. "Oh well", she said to herself. "I will just have to play this thing out with Theo and see where it leads." Her uncle returned from his meeting and drove her home, wishing her well with her problem, and that is exactly what it was, a problem.

Theo turned up at five thirty later on that afternoon, looking as ravishing as ever, and Delia let him in, she was the only person home; Christine had done another one of her disappearing acts again. Theo kissed her on her cheek and smiled at her.

"So what happening Sugah?" he asked, "Oh not much, I was just getting prepared for you to take me out to dinner, that's all," she replied with a teasing smile, "Oh! Ok then," he said, smiling back; "I can go for that, so what you fancy eating then?" Lord knows I wouldn't mind having you for dinner, thought Delia, but to him, she said she was not sure what she fancied to eat. "That's not a problem" he replied, "My plan was to take you home to my place and feed you there, is that alright with you?" Delia felt elated at his suggestion, that is a start she told herself, "Yes that is fine with me" she answered him.

Chapter Three

Delia came out of her room, looking like a million dollars in a plain, open front white dress, with gold buttons, matching sandals, bag, and her long hair, in a ponytail. Theo liked the way she looked in her simple but well cut open front dress that accented her shape to a T. She was wearing gold earrings with cross and chain to match, She wore light make up, and was looking delicious, the light dancing in her brown eyes. He was going to have to behave himself, but it would not be an easy task. "Well? Asked Delia, "How do I look?" "You looking fine" Theo replied, "Real fine, shall we make a move then?" Theo needed to leave the house, Delia looked truly delicious and boy! He was feeling hungry and it was not for the food he had prepared at home, waiting for them to eat. He needed to behave himself, but he felt he needed to be holding on to Delia; no, no, no, he was telling himself, I need to behave.

"Come on, let us go," he said to Delia taking her by the hand, and leading her outside to his jeep, not paying any attention to the curious smiles of the neighbours and passersby.

When they got to Theo's home, Delia's heart was in her mouth. She felt like a schoolgirl on her first date. Theo introduced her to his parents, and left her to speak with them while he went to set the table for them to eat. His parents had already eaten so it was just going to be the two of them; he placed a bottle of wine in a pail of ice and placed it on the table. Then he got the candles out of the draw, lit them and placed them on the table. Theo had no idea why he was making such a fuss, but he seemed to be in that kind of mood, so why not, a beautiful atmosphere for a very

Delia's Story

beautiful woman, he told himself.

Theo excused Delia from his parents, and led her to the dining area. Delia could not believe her eyes. The lights were turned down low and when she looked at the table, it was well set with a bottle of wine and the candles. She wondered if this is how he truly was, or if it was just one way of getting into her good books; on his way down to her panties, anyway! She liked the way things were looking.

The dinner was wonderful, a traditional Sunday dinner with salad and roast potatoes. The chicken was delicious, it melted on Delia's tongue. "This is better than any restaurant in town," Delia said to Theo, "Who did the cooking?" she asked, "I did," Theo replied, "but I never imagined that I, would have had the honour of having you eat my cooking." For dessert they had vanilla ice cream with strawberries, "Mother made the ice cream," Theo told Delia, who was enjoying the ice cream and strawberries so much, she hadn't said a word until the last spoonful. "It happens to be my favourite, said Theo." "My favourite ice cream happens to be chocolate first and vanilla second," she answered.

After dinner was over, they cleared up the dirty dishes and went in to join Theo's parent, but they were on their way up to bed, so they bade Delia and Theo good night and to Delia, they said they hoped they would see her again. Theo and Delia sat down to watch television, Rambo the Movie was just about to start. Theo went into the kitchen and came back with their unfinished wine and two glasses half-filled, handed one to Delia, then sat down next to her making himself comfortable but not too

Chapter Three

familiar. They proceeded to watch the movie, laughing and making comments, when it was called for. Delia was enjoying herself, she found herself thinking how at ease she felt in Theo's company. When it was over, Delia asked Theo if he would be kind enough to take her home, she had to be up early the next morning for work. Theo obliged.

They spoke little on the way home; both engrossed in their own thoughts, but broke it when they approached her house. "I had a very lovely time this evening, the meal was superb and the company delightful", said Delia to Theo. He responded by saying "the pleasure was all mine, mine lady, all mine," as he drew her close to him, gently placing a kiss on both her cheeks. Delia could feel his body heat and the fire in her burnt a little harder. She drew herself from him, the heat between them was a little too much She not really wanting to let things part this way, but it was much too soon, very much too soon, and they were not children anymore.

That night Delia could not sleep. Her body was aflame with desire. Every time she tried to close her eyes, all she would see was Theo, naked as the day he was born, stepping out of the shower and, she dressed in nothing, her passion raging, she could already feel his finger teasing, playing along her hot flesh, gentle butterfly kisses making a trail, caressing down slowly down her nape, she stirred on Satin sheets waiting for him to have his own loving way with her permission.

She got up and had a shower, as she stepped out of the shower. The phone started to ring. She looked at the clock next to the phone, it said three am. She wondered who could be calling her at that time of the morning, she went to the phone and picked it up and said, "Hello?" The voice at the other end said "Hi Sugah, I can't seem to get to sleep, something on my mind, so I thought I'd give you a call, see if you are still awake". "Well as you can see I am still awake," she replied. "I was feeling a little hot, so I went and had a shower."

"Perhaps you should have invited me to wash your back for you, and perhaps massage you to sleep," he replied. "Hmm, perhaps," answered Delia. "So what's keeping you awake?"

"Oh just this dream I keep having, about me being naked in the shower, and a lady waiting for me on the bed, and for the life of me, I can't seem to get to the bed. I don't understand it, I was hoping the lady wanted me as much as much as I was dying to have her".

"Yes," interrupted Delia, knowing exactly what he was referring to, but not taking the bait, "Dreams have a way of being disappointing sometimes, promising but not fulfilling the promise," she told him. "Well I was just wondering if, the lady is playing hard to get or do I really have to win the duel with the other fella, to get her for myself and will it be worth it. Anyway goodnight, sleep tight."

"Good night Theo" replied Delia, placing the receiver in its cradle, then went to her bed with her Bible, and fell straight asleep.

Chapter Three

Christine had booked herself into the Layou River Hotel, her eyes swollen and red from crying. She took the keys from the patron and went to her room, she was not ready to go home as yet. She was not able to face her cousin looking the way she did and that would be the first place Greg would look. Instead, she sat down on the bed and cried some more, at the same time talking to herself asking, "Why life was so unfair, and why were men so fucking disgusting?"

She was upset, very upset. She had woken up after Delia went off to church. She cleaned the house then had a shower, after which she got dressed. She decided to do some writing. She loved to write. She wrote poetry to express herself and of life experiences, but she could not find her book. "Damn," she cursed, "that means I will have to go back to Greg's." She phoned for a taxi because the walk would take much too long and the buses even longer. Within minutes the taxi was at the top of the road. She went out to meet the taxi, got in and went to Greg's place.

Christine turned the door knob and the door opened. Since Dominicans don't like locking their doors while they are at home, she was not surprised to find it so. As she entered, she heard what sounded like a woman's voice. She listened. It was begging Greg for more. More? Thought Christine, more of what? She headed for the spare bedroom, because that's where the sound was coming from. As she pushed the door open, she could not believe her eyes, no! She would not dare believe her eyes; they had to be lying, what she was seeing? Greg was in bed with another

Delia's Story

woman? No! but yes, Greg's was ass up in the air, ready to launch his attack on the naked body, whose hands were reaching out to grab his behind and help him find his target; to god, she could not believe it. No, not Greg, that couldn't be Greg fucking with another woman.

Christine walked out of the room saying to the couple, who had by now noticed her standing there, "Excuse me, she said, "wrong address." She picked up her book which was lying on the coffee table and left the house. She walked to the top of the road, got on the first bus that came along going to Portsmouth. She got off the bus outside the Layou River Hotel and booked herself in. She had been there for a few hours before she decided to call her cousin, to let her know that she was all right and would be home in a few days; she had some business to sort out.

Delia was not home when Christine called. She was glad. It made the lie easier, so Christine left the message on the answering machine.

The more Christine tried to understand what she had witnessed, the angrier she got, and she took out her little book, found a pen and wrote these words to remind her of this day.

Life can bring us disappointment, with its every little turn
Life can bring some disappointment
And the lessons they teach, we learn
Never take all things for granted
Live for the moment that is all that is granted
Never love anyone too much

Chapter Three

Treat them like salt, just one touch
And when your day with them is done
Send them back to where they came from
Each and every single one.

After she had finished writing, she still wasn't feeling any better. In fact she was feeling worse and the words she had in her head for Greg, could not be put down on paper, they might burn the page; Christine never knew she could get that angry over a man. She never had before, "Perhaps," she told herself, "it's because I liked him a lot more than anyone she had played with in the past, and a little bit more".

The man was a dirty, filthy disappointment, stinking cur, vermin she cursed. I should go back to his house and ask him what that was all about, no, I should go there and kick him like the dog he wants to be, but no, I won't give him the satisfaction. Instead, she cleaned up her face, trying to look presentable, the make up almost worked and a pair of shades to hide her red, swollen eyes.

She decided to go to the bar to drown her sorrows with some Rye and Nephew white rum on the rocks; boy was she drowning her sorrows. After she had drunk three quarters of the bottle, she wanted to dance with Greg, but stupid Greg was the reason she was here in the hotel getting drunk. The slime, she thought, I should give him some of his own medicine. Perhaps I should find some man and fuck with him. After all, what is good for the goose, is supposed to be just as good for the gander.

Delia's Story

Christine was now on a mission. She did not care about anything but getting even with Greg.

She did not have to wait very long before a young man approached her. He was saying something about having seen her at the farm Thursday night gone, but she had been too busy to notice him. His name was Kenroy; what was her name? "My name is Christine, and you don't have to worry. Tonight I won't be too busy for you ok?" He smiled and she said, "Good, what about the drink you said you were buying me? Make it Rye and Nephew on the rocks, because that is where I am heading, on the rocks." Kenroy smiled, and said, "Ok, back soon." Kenroy came back to find Christine dancing on her own, in the middle of the dance floor and went to join her. She danced without passion, sipping on the drink Kenroy placed in her hands. She even found herself comparing the way he danced in comparison to Greg.

Greg, that stupid, stupid man. She had only gone and fallen for him and she thought he felt the same way. What a fool she was. She should have listened to her cousin Delia, she ought to know. She was married to him once, and look at how he had treated her. Christine decided that she'd had enough of dancing for the night and invited Kenroy to her room to continue the drinking, to which he agreed. And up they went together. Christine found out to her amazement that she could not go through with sleeping or having sex with another man. She found out that it was one thing to talk about it, but quite another to actually go through with it. She was starting to feel sick, her stomach was in a mess and it was not just the alcohol she was

Chapter Three

drinking, she told Kenrick, she was sorry but he would have to go, she wasn't feeling up to it, she needed to find her bed.

Kenroy on the other hand had different intentions. He had wanted to have a piece of Christine from the first moment he had laid eyes on her at the farm, but she had been busy with someone else. However, tonight, it looked like the someone was out of the picture, from the way he saw her crying. Look, he figured, she and the man had gone their separate ways.

Tonight he was not taking no for an answer, and he did not. When Christine refused him, he pushed her down in the settee, and held her down with one arm, while with the other he tore at her clothes, tore her panty to one side, pulled open his trousers and took out his penis, roughly he jammed it into her vagina, making her cringe, he forced her legs apart, the tears were rolling down the side of her face, he didn't care, he simply took it. He used her as if he was using the piss pot in the men's toilet. She was under the influence of the alcohol, she been drinking, not caring whether she was alive or dead. When he was finished, he got up from her, straightened himself up and left, pulling up his zipper as he shut the door behind him. Christine crawled into the shower turned it on and just sat under it. She noticed her blood flowing along with the water, and she cried; she cried until she had no tears left. She threw off the wet, stained, clothes and went to bed, laying there alone and heartbroken until sleep claimed her.

Greg was sitting on his bed, the bed he shared most nights with Christine, from the time he had carried her home tipsy from a friend's birthday party. This bed, his home, he shared with no one else but her. It has been almost a week. Today was Thursday and the last time he'd seen Christine was Sunday when she'd returned to the house and found him ass up in the air, giving it to another woman. She had not said much, she had simply left the house, leaving him to his business and he had not seen her since. Greg was ashamed of himself, but who could he tell that to, no one. He wanted to speak to Christine, but she seemed to have disappeared. She had not been to work all week. He wanted to call her home, but that was a different matter altogether.

When Christine had gone home on Saturday evening, after they had spent a very satisfying weekend in each other's company, he had gotten a call from a friend of his, inviting him to a boy's night out. Since he was home alone, he accepted the invitation and went to link with the boys. There was a lot of alcohol afloat, and he found himself drinking. He drank until he was so drunk, he wasn't able to drive. One of his friends offered to drive him home, but this friend happened to be a woman, a long time fling looking to come back into his life again, but Greg was too drunk to take heed. He accepted the offer of a lift home.

Olivia was the woman's name. She had driven him home and helped him to bed, and then made herself comfortable in the spare room. She had woken up the Sunday morning and made breakfast for him, saying it was just to thank him for letting her stay the night in the spare room. They had spent the rest of the day talking about old times. One thing led to another. The next he knew he was doing the horizontal Lambada with her, until Christine walked in the room and caught him at it. Now, he did

Chapter Three

not know what to do with himself. He had thrown himself off Olivia and grabbed his shorts to put on, to run after Christine, but by the time he got to the door, she was nowhere in sight. Olivia had the sense to get dressed and get out; she did not even say goodbye, just in case. Smart woman thought Greg, as he watched her go through the front door and shutting it behind her as she left.

Bright and early Monday, Greg went to work but found he could not concentrate, so he left early. Tuesday was the same thing, plus he had not slept well last night worrying about Christine. Every time his phone rang, he thought it might be her, and when he answered, only to find out it was not, he became more anxious. He decided to take the rest of the week off from work, he could not concentrate.

Christine left the Layou River Hotel on Friday morning to go home. When she got there no one was home. She was happy about that. It would give her more time to compose herself. The phone started to ring; she didn't answer it just in case it was Greg. Half an hour after that, the phone rang again, this time she answered it "Hello, who is it?"

"Chris, it's me Greg, can we talk?" He asked in a sorry voice, his soft voice even softer now. Christine looked at the receiver in her hand and replaced it back on its cradle. The phone rang again, and again until eventually it stopped. Just as it stopped ringing Delia came through the door. She found her cousin sitting down watching the television. "Hello stranger,' she greeted her cousin. "To what do I owe the pleasure of your company, or is it that you remembered where you live?" Christine started to cry;

Delia's Story

Delia ran over to her cousin and cradled her to her bosom, asking her what the matter was. "Come on tell me, maybe I can help."

"Nope not this time, you cannot help with this one at all," said Christine, wiping the tears from her eyes. And continued to tell her cousin what had happened, everything from top to bottom. About finding her man in bed with another woman and needing space to think, happenings at the Layou River Hotel with Kenroy, and even a basic description of him, but not once did she mention Greg's name. Delia listened in silence, and by the time her cousin had finished, Delia was crying. She could feel her cousin's pain, she cuddled her cousin closer. "Never mind baby, never mind," she said. Delia's thoughts were blazing, "something will work out, God is good, just believe and you will receive, something will definitely work out," and she continued to comfort her cousin. Have you been to the hospital to get a checkup? You can never be too careful you know; if you haven't I can take you." Delia continued talking and comforting her cousin until she nodded off.

Later that evening after Christine had gone to bed, Delia made a few phone calls. She was trying to find Kenroy and when she found him, she was going to break his legs. How dare he take liberties with her cousin? She had been drunk for God's sake, and to make matters worse, she had said no; once you change your mind, that must mean no. Imagine the gall of the man, but not to worry, when she found him he would pay.

Delia had no joy on the phone, so she put on her shoes and

Chapter Three

went out for a drive down to the Layou River Hotel. When she got to the hotel, she went to the receptionist and made inquiries. She was told the only person who would know anything about her cousin would be the patron, since he was the one on duty the night her cousin had checked herself into the hotel. Unfortunately, he was not in that night, so she would have to call back. Delia thanked the receptionist and went home.

When she got home she phoned Theo; he was on his way to visit a friend in town. He had taken the car instead of the jeep. He thought it would be best, since he wasn't sure where his friend would end up taking him, plus he was tired of driving the jeep. However, when he got Delia's call he changed his direction and went to her place instead.

Theo was very glad to go to Delia. He would phone her every chance he got to talk to her, since it was not always possible to visit; she was a busy woman. A woman with responsibilities, who kept her priorities in order and he liked that, because he thought if she ever got interested in him and made him a priority, he would be the happiest man in the world. They had been out together and had enjoyed themselves. Friends and family had told Theo that Delia suited him, and he believed them, since he was of the same opinion. In fact, he thinks he had fallen for her.

She was nothing like Wanda, his last affair. Wanda's beauty was more outward than in, whereas Delia was beautiful from inside. Her oval face, beautified by the hazel brown coloured eyes, to have them behold him as he made love to her. She was the woman he would like to have his children. His parents would love her those lips always inviting him to kiss them. Oh how he longed to bite them, just to taste them, have them whisper sweet secrets to him. However, he had to control himself; her body was perfect. The goddess Venus had nothing on her. When God had made this woman; he had thrown away the mould. He could not wait to hold her properly against his naked body, skin to skin working the rhythm, flesh to flesh, as their two bodies made one. Thinking about Delia always turned him on, and right now, his heart was beating faster and he could feel his body rising, coming to life in his trousers, but he just had to control himself. Who knows? One day he might get lucky. One day his wish might come true.

Delia was sitting on the porch when he pulled up; she waited for him to get out of the car and come to her. He kissed her on the cheeks, took her by the hand and led her to the sedan on the porch where they could sit and be comfortable, and then she could tell him what was troubling her, regarding Christine. When she had finished relating the story to him, he asked what he could do to help. She asked him if he could go to the hotel, pretend that Kenroy was a long lost friend and see where it leads them to. He agreed.

Theo left Delia and went to the Layou River hotel. He entered and headed straight for the bar, ordered a drink and sat down to drink it. The bar was not very busy that night, so Theo decided to ask the bartender if he knew Kenroy, giving him a basic description as had been given to him by Delia, who had got it from Christine. Saying he was a friend of a friend, and that he

Chapter Three

had an important message to give to Kenroy seemed to ease the bartender. Also, the fact that Theo was a well-known Calypsonian singer in Dominica and certain parts of overseas helped. Theo did not have much problem obtaining the information the bartender was able to give him. The bartender said he knew Kenroy. He was a bus driver who frequented the hotel on weekends and so if he wanted to speak with him, it would have to be then. Theo thanked the bartender and asked him not to mention anything to Kenroy if he should see him first, because he wanted to surprise him. He tipped the bartender and left.

He went back to Delia and told her what he'd found out, and that he would have to return to the hotel on the weekend. Delia said ok, not a problem, but would he be available to assist her on the weekend since he had his other commitments to attend. He said he would be available if she needed him to be.

Greg had gotten tired of waiting for Christine to call. Today was Saturday, almost a few days since he had seen her and now he was giving up hope of ever hearing from her again. He made up his mind to do the inevitable. He would have to go to her home, even if it meant having to meet with his one-time wife, and this had to be done. He got himself prepared and headed for Delia's. The drive was exhausting. It was a very hot day and there was no breeze to cool the hot air. Traffic was moving slow, drivers blaring their horn at other drivers to move on, but nothing changed. A drive that would have normally taken Greg half an hour at the most, took him an hour that morning. When he got to Delia's house, the top he had on was soaked from the sweat he was sweating from the heat and the thought of meeting his ex wife

He got out of the car, not paying a mind to his appearance, went to the door and tapped on the glass with his keys. He got no response. He tapped harder the second time, the door opened. Delia stood there looking at him. She had heard the tapping the first time and had left what she was doing to go answer the door. As she got closer to the door, her eyes flew open wide, the breathe she was about to take got stuck in her throat and she froze on the spot. For a little while she stood there, not believing what she was seeing, or rather who, Greg in the living flesh standing on her doorstep, tapping her glass with his keys.

There was a knocker on the door, but oh no, he had to be different. Why couldn't he knock the door like everybody else? Delia managed to gain some composure by the time he tapped again went to the door and opened it.

"Well good morning Greg, what brings you to my door this bright Saturday morning?" she asked him "Good morning to you too and how are you?" replied Greg. "Since my health stopped being important to you some time ago, then it's of no importance to you how I am.

"So what brings you to my door? What do you want?" she answered. "I'm looking for Christine," he answered, "I need to speak with her," he continued. Delia looked at him hard, turned her back on him and went to let Christine know that she had a visitor.

Christine was in her room doing some writing, she looked up at her cousin who had entered without knocking, "You have a

Chapter Three

visitor," said Delia to her. "Who is it asked Christine?" Delia looked at her for a while, then said, "my ex husband".
"Oh!" said her cousin, "I had better go see what he wants." "Whatever" replied Delia, "whatever".

By the time Christine opened the door to Greg, her whole body language had changed. Her face was now very serious, and she looked at him as if he was a stranger. Greg felt the cold and he accepted it. Greg had told himself that he was prepared for whatever she threw at him, but he was not as prepared as he thought he was. His mouth went dry, he coughed. He could not begin to find the words to say to the woman standing in front of him, looking at him with such coldness, her whole attitude towards him was cold, Ok then, he thought, how do I begin?

When he finally managed to speak, he said to her, "Chris, I am really sorry. I realize what I have done and I am really very sorry." And with that, he turned around and left. He could see that she was not ready to deal with him yet.

Christine watched as he drove away and when he had disappeared in the distance, she shut the door. "Well, that was a quick visit," said Delia emerging from the kitchen. "He didn't have that much to say," answered Christine. "Anyway, what are you doing, are you baking cake?" continued Christine, trying to change the subject.

Delia would not have it. "Stop trying to change the subject, what did he want?" asked Delia, pointing with a finger in the direction of the front door. "If you must know, he was passing and thought he would stop and inquire of my health, that's all,"

Delia's Story

"Hmm, if you say so" replied Delia. "Anyway I will leave you to whatever it was that you were doing," Christine said to her cousin, "I am going to my room, excuse me. Things to do, carnival will be here soon," and with that she was gone.

Delia did not believe her cousin's excuse for Greg's visit, something was not quite right, but she would not beat herself up about it right now, time will tell, and what's done in the dark always comes to light. She assured herself with that thought as her cousin disappeared out of her sight. Christine went to her room threw herself down on her bed. Turning on to her back, she stared at the ceiling, trying her best not to think about Greg. How she missed him, how she wanted to pick up the phone and curse him, she was still hurting. She could still see him on top of the woman. She needed to get over the disappointment before she could speak to Greg again. He looked so tired and had lost weight. Oh well she sighed; she just was not ready yet.

Carnival month was passing by fast and almost everyone had some preparation to be getting on with for the day when carnival would be in town. With the king and queen of carnival parades, bands would be playing their music loud and clear for all to hear, all in competition with each other, because somebody had to wear the crown. It had always been that way and even better in the days gone by.

Theo had to attend a couple of rehearsals, since he would be acting as conductor for the band. The rehearsal was taking long to get started; he had somewhere to be later and did not want to be late. TWO weeks of this, he was not sure he could take it if this

Chapter Three

was how it was going to be. He had made a promise and he intended to keep it. Finally, rehearsal started and it turned out to be a beautiful session.

When it was over Theo wasted no time, it was six o'clock. He would get to Delia about six twenty, plenty of time left to sit and relax, feel her vibes before they left to go to the Layou River Hotel.

Delia fed Theo when he got to her place. After all, it was the least she could do and it was not the first time he had eaten from her. After eating, they relaxed and talked about each other's day and the preparations for the carnival. Delia asked Theo, "What it felt like to be playing conductor for the band, instead of singing or even playing an instrument?" "Well it's fun, it's different, and I enjoy fun and different," he answered. "For instance," he continued, "look at you; you are different from other women I have ever had close encounters with." "I think you should have studied philosophy," answered Delia, laughing at his comment. "Why are you laughing at me?" he asked. "I'm trying to pay you a compliment and you're making a man feel foolish." "Ahh, you poor baby," answered Delia teasingly. "Anyway we should be making a move now," she said, looking at the clock. "I will just go put on my shoes." Delia returned with her shoes on ready to make that move down to the Layou River Hotel to find Kenroy.

They got to the hotel, with its bright neon sign half lighting the car park. Delia looked around, checking out the cars to determine the business of the bar. The car park was half empty.

Delia's Story

They entered the hotel and headed straight for the bar behaving as if they were strangers to each other, to give anyone looking the desired impression, and it was working.

Delia felt herself being watched as she stepped into the bar and the feeling continued as she sat down, calling to the bartender and ordered her drink and proceeded to sip it. Theo was walking around, mingling with other people in the place, but keeping a watchful eye on Delia. Kenroy left the corner seat where he was sitting observing Delia, sipping on her Southern comfort on the rocks. He slowly made his way to the bar. He ordered a drink for himself and told the bartender to ask the woman, referring to Delia, if she would like a drink and what was her pleasure? The bartender relayed the message to Delia and she accepted the offer, asking for the same again.

Kenroy drew himself closer to Delia and introduced himself, asking what was a beautiful woman like her doing all on her own. Was she waiting for someone? And could he keep her company until the person turned up? Delia looked at him, smiling at him as she said, "My, you do ask a lot of questions don't you Kenroy? I did not come here to talk about myself; I came here to forget my problems with a couple of drinks. So what about you, what is your story?" "Well as you see me," he answered, "I'm trying to drown my sorrows in your beautiful eyes." Delia wanted to kick him, but she had to keep her cool and carried on talking to Kenroy, all the time wondering what Theo was up to and hoped he was keeping an eye on things.

Chapter Three

After a couple of drinks, Delia said that she was going outside and Kenroy suggested they go sit in his bus, to take the weight of her feet. The night air was fresh and a cool breeze was blowing, stars twinkling in the sky, Just as she looked up she saw a star shooting across the sky. Delia held her breath; that was one of the most beautiful sights she had ever seen. That was one of the reasons she loved the island, you could always expect to see the unexpected. The bus was parked three cars away from where they were standing. Delia looked around before she answered, she saw Theo lurking at the entrance of the hotel; then turned back to Kenroy and said, "Ok then, let's go sit in your bus."

Once in the bus, Kenroy proceeded to make her comfortable, He turned the radio on asking her preference in music; she settled for KAIRI FM, they were playing some calypso by the legendary Sparrow. Delia loved Sparrow's music. The lyrical contents of his songs were witty, making her laugh with his double meanings; he truly was funny. Kenroy placed his arm on the back of her seat and shifted his position closer to her. She pretended not to notice, she let him; and then he took his hands off the back of her seat and placed them on her shoulder, making small circular motions with his fingers. Delia brushed them off asking him what he was playing at. "Easy baby, relax," he said. I thought you were up to having some fun, you know?" "No I do not know," answered Delia "You said you wanted to drown your sorrows in my eyes and I don't remember my eyes being where those hands are going," slapping his hands away at the same time from off her lap.

Delia's Story

Just as Kenroy attempted to force himself on Delia, the door of the bus flew open. Theo grabbed Kenroy by the scruff of his neck and threw him off the bus. Kenroy fell against a car parked close by. He tried to get up and he fell. He tried again with success that time. He charged at Theo, who was waiting for him to get closer, and when he did, Theo punched him in the face, so hard he flew backward landing against the same car and fell to the ground, and passed out stone cold with blood running from his nose. Theo picked Kenroy up and put him in his car. He shut the door of the bus, and got in his car sitting next to the unconscious Kenroy. Delia got in the driver's seat and they drove away from the Hotel. They drove down to the savannah where Delia's old house was situated. It was still fully furnished because she rented it out sometimes and used it as a getaway other times.

Christine was already at the house and she came running out when she heard the car stopping outside. She had been told the situation by Delia earlier on that day, so she had made her way down from town by bus, and was now identifying the body in the car as the person who had taken liberties with her. "Yes" she said, "that him, that's the scum who abused me."

Theo dragged Kenroy out of the car and carried him into the house; they tied him to a chair and then Delia, phoned the police.

When the police arrived, Christine told them she wanted to report a rape. The police asked who the rape victim was. Christine replied she was, and the man tied to the chair, (pointing to Kenroy) was the assailant. Then Delia also stated she wanted to

Chapter Three

press charges against Kenroy for molestation and harassment. The policeman shook his head, spoke in his walkie-talkie, then wrote down what he had been told on his notepad. He then handed a note to Christine and told her she would need go to the police station, herself and Delia, then she would need to go down to the hospital for tests; after they got the results they would let her know further about court dates and so forth.

Through all this, Theo had not said a word; he was just sitting watching Kenroy with hatred written all over his face. The police officer then untied Kenroy, handcuffed him, and led him to his car and drove off with him down to the local police station.

After the police officer had taken his leave, Christine hugged her cousin and Theo, she thanked them, and then she said, "That's one less thing to deal with, one more to go." "What do you mean one more to go?" asked Delia, holding her cousin at arm's length, "what are you up to Chris?" "Nothing," answered Christine, "just a little something I have to deal with on my own, don't worry; I can manage. No disrespect to you Cuz, or to you Theo, but I really can manage this one without your help." Seeing the pleading look in her cousin's eyes, Delia said, "Ok, but if you should need help, just holler in my direction alright?" saying that as she kissed her cousin on the forehead. Christine smiled back at her and said "Ok."

Before heading back to town, Theo dropped them of at the station to fill out a statement and assists the police with any further inquiries they might have while they were there. Christine was told because she had taken so long to come forward with her case, and the fact that she had not even been to the hospital was totally stupid and the chances of finding any concrete evidence was not very good.

The drive back to town was quiet; everyone to their own thought. Delia was listening to the radio. Theo was thinking about the situation he had just left behind and Christine, who had been a lot quieter lately, since the Sunday when she had found Greg in bed with another woman and the aftermath at the hotel, was thinking how she was going to deal with Greg.

When they finally got to Delia's, Theo parked the car by the steps. Christine got out of the car and made her way upstairs. As she was going in Delia stopped her and told her she was just going out for a while, she would be back soon. Theo drove down to the seaside and parked the car next to a tamarind tree. He turned off the engine and turned to Delia saying, "Thank god it was all over, if I had to go through another minute with that man (referring to Kenroy) putting his hands all over you, I would have killed him." He had felt that way at the time, It was all he could do to control himself. He never liked it one bit, and she, sitting there with Kenroy, smiling and looking like she was enjoying the whole thing. "Ahh come on," replied Delia "when that man came over and started talking to me, smiling was all I could do to stop myself from throwing up all over him I had to do it to prevent him from seeing how much he repulsed me. I mean, we came here for that purpose, and I had every intention of seeing it through to the end. However, on the bus when he tried to put his hands where he should not have, I was wondering why you were taking so long,

Chapter Three

where were you?" "What do you mean where was I? I wasn't taking my time," he said shouting, "the stupid door was stuck, it would not open, anyway I don't want to talk about this anymore; it's upsetting my vibes." "Ok" said Delia "let's not."

Theo turned the radio on, tuning in to KAIRI FM, he liked listening to that radio station, and they were playing some mellow songs, Mowtown's greatest hits. He reached across to Delia, drawing her closer to him he said, "When are you going to let me have my wicked way with you hmm D? Can't you tell how much I want you, hmm?" as he nibbled on her earlobe and making his way down to her pulse spot on her neck, sending different sensations pulsating through her body; she felt good, and she wanted him. But she did not know if she was ready and if he just wanted a holiday affair Delia wanted Theo much more that she would admit to him, but said nothing, she just smiled. While he on the other hand, tried his best to let her know how much he wanted her, to feel the heat of her body against his. "Are you wearing any panties? He asked, "Could I see for myself?" His hands were making their way up under her skirt to find out for himself. Placing her hands on his, Delia stopped him from obtaining his objective, but didn't remove the hand. She liked the feel of it against the bare skin of her thighs. He found her lips, kissing them gently, nibbling on them, and then showering them with butterfly kisses. "I just don't know what happening to me, I only know you make me crazy, I can't seem to behave when you are near me" he confessed as he continued kissing her neck.

Delia's Story

Delia was feeling horny, and she did not want him to stop; she felt like parting her legs and inviting him in. She remembered how firm he had felt beneath her fingers and how much she would like to feel it again, in her hands gently caressing and listen to him whisper her name. Oh man!! She was feeling that feeling her temperature was rising, but she had to stop. She reached out her hands to put him away from her and instead found her hand against his bare chest and the little hairs that were growing there, twisting them round her fingers, and playing with them. Theo groaned; she felt the groan beneath her fingers his heart was beating fast. She had to stop this; she could not do this out here, no not like this. She had to stop it now before she could not stop it at all.

"Theo," called Delia softly. "Mmmm?" he answered. "Theo," she repeated. "Ok, I'll stop," he replied. He stopped but he did not relinquish his hold on her, and she did not mind. They stayed there for a while wrapped up in each other, enjoying the feeling. The winds changed, it started to get cold so they decided to call it a night and head home.

The next morning, Delia went with Christine to her doctor for a check up, telling him what had happened as she handed him a note from the police. The doctor was to check her for any kind of venereal disease she might have received from her abuser.

It was five days later, before Christine received a letter from her doctor since her visit, and she was curious to know the state of her health, even though she was feeling fine. In her rush to open the envelope she managed to cut her finger on the edge of it

Chapter Three

and, all the letter told her was that the relevant information had been sent to the police station and if she wanted any other information she was to make an appointment with the nurse at the surgery.

Chapter Four

The day for the Calypso King competition had finally arrived, and the place was bustling with activities, noise coming from everywhere. Theo had already left his house and was standing in the venue, a large fenced off area opposite the Dominican Bank of Agriculture, where the event was to be held. The stage was up already; all the electricians and their equipment in disarray all over the place. Theo was looking forward to this day; after all the work put in by the performers, both singers and players of instruments. He felt in his bones that at the end of the day, everything was going to be fine. The people would enjoy the show; he knew that because he had seen the rehearsals. He walked around, telling the engineers where things go and how the microphones were to be placed, how many were needed, and whatever else they needed to know.

About four o'clock, Theo was finished, everything was set up, the actual show would start at seven o'clock, so he could leave and be back for six thirty. He decided to go home and relax, he wondered what Delia was doing, after the dream he had last night he thought it best to go home.

Theo had gone straight to bed when he got home last night after dropping Delia off. He dreamt the same dream he had been having since coming down to Dominica. He'd stepped out of the

Chapter Four

shower, water glistening on his naked body; the lady laying on the bed made up of white satin sheets in her blood red negligee, waiting with arms outstretched, inviting him to come to her. And for the first time since he'd began having these dreams, he saw the face of the woman on the bed, and realised it was none other than Delia. It was Delia who had been tormenting his dreams, he should have known. It was so obvious, now that he thought about it. She tormented his thoughts in the daytime, so why should the night be any different? He remembered the other dream he had with the woman in the cage; that must have been Delia as well, but who was the other man and what had happened to him? Anyway, he thought, that is good; it must mean there is a chance for me after all with this other character out of the way. He was just going to have to be patient.

The calypso king competition started on time. There were thirteen competitors for the crown and all thirteen were brilliant, with their different interpretations of politics and dazzling performances. The crowd was going crazy; everyone was having a good time. It would be difficult to pick a winner. The showcase had been tight. Then came the time for a king to be crowned. The people made a mad rush for the stage shouting, 'Animal talk! Animal talk!' and there was talk of stoning the judges if the crown was not given to the Ice Ray.

    Ice Ray was one of the performers. His stage performance was astounding along with his song, titled the farm yard. His act

Delia's Story

included using animals to show the behaviour of politicians and their argument for power and position, the way people were manipulated and oppressed, and wanting to be rich by whatever means necessary. In addition, when you looked up on the stage, you could see real live animals, and people dressed up as animals in the House of Commons doing their thing, but the funniest part was when two goats started mating on stage, it sent the people wild. The crowd of people were rocking to the beat, whilst laughing at the lyrics and commotion on stage, the song was funny, yet serious and educating.

Contender number two was the Obsessor. He also sang songs of oppression and love for the common people; it was a difficult choice for the judges to make and finally, after what seemed like ages, a choice was made and the Ice Ray got the crown. The people were happy, they were ecstatic. You could tell by the way they were jumping up and singing Animal talk, calling out for an encore. Yes! It had been a happy and fulfilling day for Theo. Now that the show was over; it was time to head for home, tired, happy, and alone.

Delia had gone to the show to enjoy the artists and to see Theo play at being conductor. Christine had gone to the show to get out of the house and "hopefully" see Greg. They enjoyed themselves, and when it was over, they went home. Delia was happy but wanting, and Christine, missing her man. She had seen him at the evening. She had caught him staring at her. She tried to ignore him by turning away, making him feel unimportant, like she did not care for him anymore. Greg could not stand being

Chapter Four

without Christine, she was his mate. It had been a couple of weeks since he had touched her, smelt that familiar smell of her body; how he longed to hold her. He watched her for a while as she pretended not to notice him.

Monday was 'jump up day.' People playing mass bacchanal style, when the street sounds and the street bands would be doing their thing, entertaining the crowd, who could make them jump up and who was best at it. At the end of it on the second and final day, a winner would have to be chosen, this happened every year. Christine woke up that morning feeling light and cheerful; it felt like a good day, something good was going to happen. She bathed and got dressed, went to the kitchen for breakfast. Delia had already made breakfast for the two of them, but she had eaten already and was on her way out when she stepped out of her room, smiling at her cousin. "Morning Cuz, beautiful day isn't it?" "I can see you are back to your old self," said Delia. "That's good. I am just popping down to uncles. Oh by the way, your breakfast is ready when you are; I will see you when I get back, if you are still here." "Ok, see you later then," said Christine.

After breakfast, Christine tidied what needed to be tidied around the house, and then turned the radio on to compliment the way she was feeling, calypso blaring from the speakers. She got tired of being in the house, she needed some fresh air. She grabbed her purse and keys and made her way to town, to see what was happening. Music was playing everywhere, from every nook and cranny, calypso playing loud. You could not mistake the day for what it was at all, people all about; everyone feeling the spirit and she felt good. She stopped at a bar called Hibiscus, she needed a cold drink, and she was feeling the heat, because boy, it was hot out there, but then it is always hot in Dominica, even when it is raining.

Christine got her drink and went to sit at a corner table, just to chill and take in the activity around her. After what seemed like an hour later, her bottom began feeling numb; She got up and made her way to the flagstone patio. The feeling was coming back to her backside. She stood by the door watching the people as they went by, jumping up, throwing themselves on each other and shouting, laughing and enjoying themselves. "You look so beautiful standing there in the shadows." Christine jumped, she knew that voice from anywhere; it was none other than Greg Beau Pierre. She turned towards the sound of the voice, her hands covering her beating heart. "Hello Greg," she said. "Where did you spring from?" "I was just passing and I thought I saw you standing there, so I came over to see if you were ready to talk?" he replied stepping a little closer to her; she stepped back. He was wearing a sleeveless t-shirt, khaki shorts, and loafers and she could smell the faint scent of his aftershave and it reminded her of when they were lovers. She really missed him and today seemed like a day for good things so she agreed to listen to what he had to say. Greg asked her if she would like a drink, she accepted, then made her way back to the table in the corner, where she had been sitting previously and he followed. "So what is it you want to talk

Chapter Four

about?" she asked, "I'm not quite sure where to begin," he answered softly. "Well, the top is a good place to start, but if it's a story you're going to tell, then you begin at the beginning," she said with a touch of sarcasm, which didn't escape his attention.

"This is much harder than I thought," he said. "Ok, look baby." "Baby? I'm not your baby. If I were your baby, you would not be giving away my milk," she snapped back at him. "Ouch," said Greg, screwing up his face, "that's cold, but I guess I asked for that; what I am trying to say is, do you think you can find it in your heart to forgive me for what you saw. It was something that should never have happened. She was an old friend of mine, we were talking about old times, and things went a little too far." "You can say that again," said Christine, as he continued to speak; "I have nothing else to say in my defence, except that I miss you, the way you feel in my arms, I miss holding you. I can still smell you in my bed, your scent in the place and you not there, is just not good. I really need you to consider this, and yes I know you might need some more time to think, but if you feel anything for what we had, please Christine, I need you to consider this."

"I'll tell you what," said Christine, "if you're not busy why don't we go to your house and talk about this some more. I'm tired of sitting in this place." Greg not quite sure how to answer got up from his chair and said, "Ok, let's go to my house." When they got to the house which was not too far from the bar, Christine felt the old familiar feeling come back to her, how much she liked being there, tidy as usual. The door to the spare bedroom was shut. She looked at it, trying her best not to remember what she had seen that Sunday morning.

Everything was in its place, Greg was a tidy man, She figured it must have been a discipline he had learned in the force and she liked that about him. She went and sat down on the chair closest to the window. She asked Greg for a drink, he came back with a cold Kubuli. Then she asked him if he was still in contact with his lady friend, he said no. She got up from where she was sitting, went, and sat opposite Greg, but facing him. She looked him in the eye and said, "So you want me to forgive you?" Greg sat studying her face, trying to find something in her expression. "Well! Will you?" he asked "Will you, can you forgive me? Christine did not reply, as she sat there looking at him, she then got up off the chair, knelt in front of him, looked him straight in the eyes and said, "Kiss me Greg." "Does that mean I am forgiven?" he asked. "I am thinking about it," she said, "but kiss me anyway."

Greg drew Christine closer to him and started kissing her and she was kissing him back, then he stopped, looked at her with such longing in his eyes, and continued kissing her. This time he did not stop, he held her with one hand and with the other, he undressed her, first taking of the tiny top she had on, then her bra. She did not stop him, she was in heaven, she had missed him so much; she was on fire.

Taking off his top, kissing his chest, making little circles with her tongue round his nipples, he gasped, and squeezed her tight. He took one of her nipples in his mouth and nibbled on it,

Chapter Four

his hands roving and touching her where she liked best. She moaned, calling his name. Greg picked her up from the floor where she was still kneeling, carried her to the bedroom, and gently laid her on the bed. The bed where until some days ago she was the mistress of, where he had made love to her so many times before, oh how he missed her. Greg got in the bed next to Christine. She turned to him and looked at him, her eyes dazed with emotion. "Take me Greg," she said softly, do it to me like you used to." He did not need to be told a second time, take her, he did, and she could feel him inside of her and she called out his name. He felt it; he was all fired up like a stallion ready to win the gold cup, working up a sweat, heading for the finishing line. When they were done, he collapsed next to her. Christine laid there with her eyes closed, thinking about what had just happened, how much she had enjoyed him. She had missed him so much. That's what had taken possession of her, seeing him in the shop, sitting and talking with him. It had been good, but all the time she sat there listening to him talk, she kept thinking how much she would love to make love to him, oh how she longed to undress him, how she missed him holding her while she slept, his smell after they had made love. She had decided there and then to take him home and have him fulfil her desires, and she knew he would not deny her the pleasure. She knew he liked her a lot, she also knew that because of that same feeling and the fact that he wanted her back in his life, anything she asked of him that was in his power to give, he would give. She knew she loved Greg, she could not lie to herself about that, yes, she loved him, but she was not going to let him off that easy. Greg was the last man she had slept with willingly, so there was nothing wrong with sleeping with him again, while she considered how long before she let him off the hook, and whether she should tell him about Kenroy. While Greg lying next to her, his arm across her stomach had fallen asleep praying she had forgiven him; he needed to have her in his life. Later that evening Christine left Greg and went home, promising as she left to keep in touch.

On Monday night driving home from Delia's, Theo noticed that he was being followed. He carried on driving, but kept his eyes on the vehicle behind him, and took the turning before the one leading to his home. The car following him carried on driving straight, but Theo noticed it stopping further on down the road and he waited to see what would happen next. The car took off again, continuing to go straight he turned his car around and headed home. He wondered what that was all about, who would be following him and why? He decided to phone Michael and tell him about it, he had not spoken to him in a couple of days; anyway, he was due a call. Michael was not available, so he left a message for Michael to call him when he was able to, then he wondered if he should mention it to Delia, but thought better of it and went to bed.

The next morning Theo got a call from Michael and Theo told him about being followed. Michael thought it insane, and why would anyone be following Theo? He wondered, "Who did you upset bro?" he asked Theo, "I do not quite know for sure," Theo answered. "You haven't been interfering with nobody's wife

Chapter Four

have you?" Michael asked again. "Not that I know of" Theo answered. "Ok, I'll tell you what, later on tonight I will meet up with you and we can try to find out what exactly is occurring, cool?" said Michael. "Cool," replied Theo then he hung up the phone.

The phone rang again. T, this time it was the airport reminding him of flight his in two days time; Theo had forgotten, he would be flying back to the States so soon. He will have to think of something, he could not leave Delia now that he had found her; she's not going to like that one bit.

Theo did not go anywhere that day, he stayed home and did some work on his computer. Six o'clock came and found him still engrossed in whatever he was creating on the computer and that was how Michael found him when he came round to visit. "Hey man," he said to Theo, "turn that thing off and talk to me. I did not come here to watch you work, and we have things to go take care of."

"I hear you man, I hear you," said Theo as he turned off the computer. They went out for a drive and to discuss matters. Theo did not want his parents overhearing the conversation; he did not want them fretting over him. So he drove to the sea front, stopped the car close to a dimly lit bar and Theo told Michael what he had been up to since he'd been in Dominica for the last few days. Michael listened, not saying a word until Theo had finished telling his story. "So do you think this Kenroy might be the one following you?" asked Michael. "I couldn't think of anybody else," said Theo.

Delia's Story

"What about this Delia, does she have anyone who might want you out of the way? You might be stepping on his turf you know what I mean?" Michael asked. "Bro", said Theo, "it's like I told you before I really don't know. I've not seen her with anyone who was of that kind of importance. She wants me man and I want her very badly in fact." Michael looked at him with that knowing smile "So what's taking you so long bro, normally you have the female species eating out of your hands. Oh, and don't forget you're going back to the States in a couple of days," "Boy, this woman is something special, she's not like the other women I've dealt with and as for going back to the States, well, we'll see," said Theo. "In the meantime let's concentrate on matters at hand. What are we going to do?" "I suggest," said Michael, "you go visit your lady friend and leave the rest to me. I'll call you in a couple of hours to let you know if I've found any clues. Oh and Theo, please tell your lady about this, just in case ok." Theo nodded yes. Michael dropped him off in Goodwill, outside Delia's house and drove off to play detective. Theo went up the stairs, knocked the door, and went in to find Delia, who was on her way from the kitchen to see who was knocking the front door?

Michael decided he would go enlist the help of a friend, who had been in the force with him, although his friend had been ranked a station higher than him. So he drove up to Princess Margarette Street and stopped outside a little bungalow. He got out of his car and went to the door. As he got to the door, it opened and Greg stood there looking at him. "Well old friend, long time no see," saying this as he hugged his friend. "Yea, it

Chapter Four

been a long enough,., Listen I have a problem and I thought you might want to help me solve it," said Michael not beating round corners. "Bring it on," said Greg, inviting Michael into the house and shutting the door behind them. They went in and Michael told Greg his problem over a couple of drinks.

Greg listened, and as he listened, he realised he did not like what he was hearing, because it sounded like Michael was talking about his ex wife, the mother of his dead children, and he hoped the cousin mentioned was not Christine, because if it was, then somebody was going to pay dearly. Michael was still talking; he suggested they go to town, check out a few friends, and then head down to Layou, for further investigations.

Michael noted that Greg was looking vex, but not knowing the real situation, he thought it was because the story had left a bad taste in his mouth. Both of them had sisters and if any man disrespected their sister in that way, then there would be hell to pay. Greg was crying on the inside. Delia was a very special woman to him; she might think he doesn't care, but far from it. She was the first woman to ever make him feel complete, the first woman to bear his children, and after the babies died, he had lost his way and his wife. He knew that Delia had not forgiven him and he had carried on living his life, doing his thing until he met Christine; she reminded him of Delia in a way, but she was still her own person and he loved her for that and for other reasons he wouldn't mention. If this Kenroy had messed in any way with his woman, he was going to make him pay. Delia had done her best, now it seems I have to do the rest. "Ok," said Greg, noticing

Michael staring at him, "let us get moving." Greg said to Michael. He was keen to get going.

They drove around for a while, talking to a few friends on the way and finding nothing, they decided to go down to Layou. They went to the Hotel; there was no one in the bar, and so they left and went for a walk to see what they could find. Greg spotted Kenroy's bus parked outside a restaurant/Bar and he told Michael. They then went to the restaurant, ordered some food and sat down to eat, waiting to see if Kenroy would show. He did not show. However, Greg was listening to a conversation being held by two men sitting at the table behind him; they were talking about fixing a fella tonight. Someone had beaten up their brother at the Layou River Hotel some nights ago, and then had him arrested on the say so of a woman who offered him sex and then changed her mind. "How can a woman treat a man like that?" they were saying. Well anyhow, it seems their brother had not taken no for an answer and had taken advantage of some woman, whom he said was drunk at the time, they laughed. Greg listened, as they continued talking. Now they were planning to kidnap the Magician and give him a beating. "And that woman of his better not get in the way, otherwise she will get what she was asking for." Greg turned and looked at his friend and said, "Let us go." He paid for their meal and left. "Why the hurry Greg?" asked Michael, picking up his step to catch up to Greg, whom it seemed all of a sudden, was in a hurry. "Well friend," Greg said, "if you had been listening to them fellas sitting behind us, you would have wanted to leave the place. Now all we have to do is wait for them to come out and see where

Chapter Four

they lead us. The friends waited, and while waiting, Greg repeated what he had heard, and Michael understood why he, would have left the restaurant.

They did not have long to wait, out came the two men from the restaurant, got into Kenroy's bus and drove off. Michael and Greg followed. The men drove down to Mero and stopped the bus outside an off licence. The younger of the two men, got out of the bus, and got in a car parked on the other side of the road, started up the engine then headed for town, with the other man in the bus following behind. Greg and Michael still following to see what exactly they were up to. They drove to Wall House and stopped at a house in Ann Marie Street. Both men got out of their vehicles went into the house shutting the door behind them. Michael and Greg waited, and waited, and after two hours when it seemed the men would not be coming back out for the night, they went back to Greg's house and made plans for the next day. Michael went home. He phoned Theo, who was still with Delia, to let him know the situation, telling him what Greg had overheard in the restaurant and following the men back to Wall house. He told Theo he had not seen Kenroy, but had reason to believe that the two men in the restaurant were his brothers. He also warned him to be careful and keep close to his woman. Theo understood and agreed with his friend, saying goodnight, and Michael hung up the phone and got ready for his bed.

Knowing now what was in the air Theo told Delia. She surprisingly took it well that is except for the look that was now in her eyes. Theo also told Delia about his leaving in a couple of days, explaining to her how it was, especially not knowing of her when he came to DA, and now that he did, he didn't know what to do. Though there was no one special to go back to, he had his job and other commitments, but he really would like some more time to get to know her; he did not know what to do.

Delia listened, then said to him that he must do what he thinks best, she would understand whatever the outcome. Delia was hurting inside, she wanted to cry. Why she of all people had to fall for a man who was only here on holiday; why was she so unlucky, but she was not going to cry in front of him. She just sat there and looked at him. Suddenly Theo jumped up from where he was sitting, grabbed hold of Delia, looking her straight in her eyes he said, "D! Let me make love to you?" "And what would be the point of that she cried," returning his look. "The point is you want me to and I want to, so what else is there?" he replied. "Well," said Delia, "there is the fact that you will be going away in a couple of days, and when you go what about me? Isn't it best left like this?" "I don't know," said Theo. "Look I'm tired, and do you mind if I crash on your sofa?" "No, she replied, "I don't mind. Your right, it is late, I'll just get you a couple of blankets," and off she went. Returning with the blankets and a pillow, "Good night Theo, sleep well." "You too," he answered. Delia turned and made for her bedroom, leaving Theo to his thoughts and she, to the nightmare she was already having and she had not even gone to bed as yet.

So he was going away in a couple of days. How dare he come into her life and want to leave after a couple of days, what

Chapter Four

was she going to do? Knowing how much she would miss him, she started to cry. Theo sat on the sofa listening to the quiet and to Delia crying in the bedroom. He wanted to go to her, but she wouldn't want that, she needed her privacy. Delia cried, thinking about the man out there sleeping on her sofa and how much she ached for him. She went to bed, she did not bother to shower, and she just threw off her clothes and lay on top of the bed, begging sleep to claim her.

   Theo could not sleep. He was feeling very frustrated, his boy was standing firm in his shorts, ready for action. He got up and went to Delia's bedroom door and stood there, suddenly unsure of himself. Delia could hear him pacing outside, and then she heard him stop outside her bedroom door. She got out of the bed, went to the door, sat down on the floor and listened, wondering to herself if he was man enough to come into her bedroom and give her what it was they both needed so very much, but he didn't. Theo went back to the sofa, and waited for the night to end. Delia fell asleep behind the door where she had sat listening to Theo during the night.

On recollection, Delia should have figured something had to come out of the situation with Kenroy, one way or another, but the way she thought was nothing compared to what his brother's were trying to achieve. They wanted to hurt Theo and herself most likely. She would not tell Christine about it, she would ride it out and see. The post arrived while Theo was in the kitchen making breakfast for the two of them. There were two envelopes the same, one addressed to her and the other to Christine. She opened her letter, it was from the police, saying that due to the lack of evidence, they had been obliged to release Kenroy Masters, from their custody. The letter was dated two days ago, so that meant Kenroy was already on the streets, so it really was him wanting revenge. He had better be careful what he wishes for; he might surely get it she thought.

She took both letters and hid them in her bedroom. Then she went back to breakfast with Theo, she told him about the letter and what she thought, he agreed and asked her if it best her stay with her another day, she said yes, that would be nice even if the situation was not. She would take the time off work and enjoy his company since he would be travelling the next day. When breakfast was over, they went for a drive around the island, sharing the moments and taking in some sights.

Delia thought she had never enjoyed herself so much, Theo was laughing his head off at some silly comment made by a passer-by; he was really enjoying himself, the feeling was good almost like their childhood except they were now adults, like a Part two of Delia and Theo hmm interesting. . They went to the Cabrits in Portsmouth, and Delia told Theo about the time when she came to the place to get away from her thoughts, only to find they were there drinking with her at the bar. Especially when she had asked the bartender to select some songs for her and what happened when he did. Theo laughed. "Well did you get over whatever thoughts you were running from? He asked. "No," she

Chapter Four

replied. "Instead it manifested right before my eyes." And she laughed, he looked at her and the strange expression on her face, like she was wishful thinking, her eyes were sparkling. Delia truly was a sight for his sore eyes. What was he going to be like without her? Who would have guessed that in a matter of weeks, I could meet and love someone like her. They left the Cabrits, drove up to the Carib reserve, the sulphur lake, and wished they brought their swimming outfits. They visited the nature park and then went to sign the night out with a movie; it was a classic love story with Humphrey Bogart and Katherine Hepburn, African Queen.

They cuddled up close together at the back of the Theatre being used as a cinema, and watched the movie in silence. When the movie was over, they left the theatre holding hands and went to the car parked out in front ready to go home. They drove home in silence, enjoying each other's company.

Theo took Delia home and spent a little time with her then made his way home. As he drove past the Dominican Bank of Agriculture he noticed he was being followed. He continued driving, still keeping an eye on the car following him, he failed to notice a car parked by the way side. Suddenly the parked car pulled up and drew brakes in front of him, causing him to swerve to avoid hitting the other car, he stopped and turned off his engine, got out of the car to find out what the problem was, only to find himself in the company of Kenroy and his brothers. Theo was in a predicament, he did not know what to do, or where to turn, cursing himself and asking himself why he hadn't stayed in his car.

Kenroy, approached him, he had a knife in his hands, he started pointing the knife at Theo, and shouting abuse at him, "So you think you can beat me up, have me locked up in a cell and get away with it hmm? You must be thinking I am a nice person, well brother you are very wrong, as you will find out soon enough."

Kenroy called to his brothers, telling them to tie up Theo. They tied him up, threw him into one of the cars, and drove up to the hill, where Kenroy had his garden and in the middle of the garden a little house where he stayed during harvest. They took Theo to the house and threw him none too gently in a corner. Kenroy went over looked at him and kicked him in his stomach. Theo cursed Kenroy, and so Kenroy laughed and kicked him again. "Oh, so you want to play tough?" Kenroy called his brothers told them to pick up Theo and hang him on a nail. The brothers found a nail, hammered it into the wall and hung Theo up on it. They then took turns in torturing him; slapping him with the flat side of a cutlass across his face, punching him in his stomach and one of the brothers got a wet towel, folded it, tore Theo shirt from off his body and started beating across his back. Theo's nose was bleeding; his face and one of his eyes swollen and bruised, his body now aching from the beating he just received from the brothers. The two brothers were enjoying themselves so much; they wanted a piece of Theo's flesh as a memento. They took hold of Theo's right hand and the brother with the cutlass was just about to relieve Theo of one of his fingers, when Kenroy shouted

Chapter Four

at him, telling him not to be so stupid. He does not want anybody to cut nothing from Theo. It was not like that, and instead he told them to leave Theo hanging where he was. Then they went home leaving Theo hanging.

Theo was in agony, the stretching of his arm muscles was much more than he could bear, but there was nothing he could do. He hung there thinking about the day he had spent having fun with Delia before he went back to the States tomorrow, never once thinking that the day would end like this. Still he was glad that he had taken Delia home, she had been spared all this. Kenroy and his brothers were capable of anything. They did not behave like rational people, but he would get out of this and when he did, God help them. And they had better make sure that they do not go interfering with Delia or her cousin, because even if he died he would be back with a terrible vengeance, and then he passed out.

Kenroy Masters was not a nice person. Most people who knew him had little to do with him. Even as a child people avoided him, and at school, he did not have many friends and the ones he had never lasted long. He was the eldest of three sons. His mother had tried her best with them, but being a single parent, earning next to nothing working in the field, they had to make do. His father was living in America. He has been living there as long as he could remember, married to another woman with three children of her own and two for him.

Delia's Story

His father was not a supportive parent. He did not give a damn about them; so he started stealing to feed himself, got into trouble with the police at the age of fourteen and that was the way he had grown up. He has had to fend for himself all his life, and as a result of that he was a very hard and cold person, taking what he wanted when he wanted it, he would not take no for an answer.

That night at the hotel when he had seen Christine, he was feeling in a good mood, restless, and needed something to do with himself; he had been working all day driving his bus, which was how he made his living these days, and now that work was over, he wanted to have some fun.

He remembered her from the farm. She was a beautiful woman. He would like to have a woman like that by his side and in his bed, but she had been with another man, who kept her occupied all night. Even if he wanted to approach her, she would not have noticed him. He had stood watching her all night, so when he saw her walk into the bar he thought he would try his luck. He went over and introduced himself and she was polite enough to answer him, it made him feel good. She was drinking already so he offered her a top up and she accepted; they drank for a while, chatting, she was a little drunk and he noticed that she seemed a little upset, but he paid no mind to that, that was not his problem. They drank some more, then she invited him up to her room she said to do some more drinking, but she seem to be inviting him for more than a drink, she did not seem to care and he was game. They went to her room.

Chapter Four

After some time sitting there talking about nothing in particular, he moved in on her, but she did not seem interested anymore, she started talking about being tired and not being in the mood. While he was in the mood and was not going anywhere until getting what he came there for, imagine he had even bought her drinks. Kenroy was getting angrier by the seconds, angrier because she thought he could be played like that, the bitch, well we will see, he was telling himself as he pushed her from sitting position to lying on her back. She started to struggle, but he being stronger than she is, it was to no avail. Holding her down with one hand while with the other he tore at her clothes, ripping her panties, then pulled down the zip of his trousers took out his hungry dripping penis and lying on top of her, he jammed his member into her, he remembering her cringing. So roughly he forced her legs apart to get comfortable, she laid there with tears falling down the side of her face, but behaved as though he did not notice, not caring at all, much too busy, cursing and calling her names as he banged away, accusing her of asking for it, playing hard to get..Bitch. Christine could do nothing but lie there trying to put herself in another place, another world, where this was not really happening, it was just a bad, bad dream and she needed to wake up. Five minutes later when he was ended, he got up pulled his zip up and went about his business, leaving her in the same place, same position and not even looking back to see if she was aware.

Kenroy did not think that she would have told anyone about it, but after having got what he wanted, she no longer existed to him, he had already moved on. It was a great shock finding himself being beaten up by Theo. He liked The Magician, he enjoyed his music, but he felt insulted that the Magician would dirty his hands in something that, as far as he was concerned, had nothing to do with him. However, on the say so of that same bitch and her friend; her friend who had been playing games with him at the Layou River Hotel, and then the Magician threw him out of his own bus and knocked him flat out. Had him locked up in a stinking police cell for a whole week. The woman had offered herself to him; she had no right to change her mind; it was too late, he had to have what she had offered. Theo should learn to mind his own flipping business, he was thinking; let us hope this night's event will teach him that. He had enlisted the help of his brothers to aid him in his vendetta; they were only too happy to oblige. Kenroy was their older brother. He had always been there for them, and so if he needed help, they would help him. Kenroy told them what happened and being as ignorant as their brother was, they were of the same mind that the woman had no right, to hold back on what she had offered their brother, so it was right for Kenroy to help himself to it.

They planned to kidnap Theo and hold him for ransom, but Kenroy thought better of it. He decided he would kidnap Theo, but hold him for a few days, tie him up somewhere and torture him for a while. He did not want him dead. He just wanted revenge and to teach him to mind his own damn business, so the brothers agreed.

Chapter Four

They followed Theo around for a while. At first he had not noticed he was being followed. But one night after following him from Goodwill, they realised he had seen them and was now aware that he was being followed, so they'd laid low for a couple of days and it was only by accident they had managed to catch him. One of the brothers had gone to the theatre and saw Theo enter with Delia, Delia; he had telephoned Kenroy and told him this.

When the movie was over they watched as Theo got into his car and drive off. They followed at a distance behind, they waited when he dropped Delia home and went in with her, they waited a little more till he came back out, got in his car ready to drive home. They waited for the right opportunity to present itself, and enough distance between Delia's house and Canefield, where Theo was heading before they made their move.

Now he had him strung up in the hills, and he was going to keep him there for a couple of days; by then he'll be out of Dominica. He had bought himself a ticket to England the day after he had been released by the police. He had planned this, and was praying it would work out; kidnap the magician, give him a terrible beating and leave the country before they find him, because if they did then he would be going to jail and he did not intend to go there ever. When he got to Antigua, he planned to make an anonymous call to the police or his parents and tell them where Theo is. As for those brothers of his, they will have to leave the island as well; but they are not going with him.

Delia's Story

After his brothers had gotten rid of Theo's car and had taken their leave, Kenroy went back into the house, took the unconscious Theo off the nail and left him tied up on the floor. He locked the door behind him and went home to prepare himself for his departure, and he had to speak to his brothers.

Michael had already left his house at cockcrow, which is around six am, in the morning. He was going to Theodore's home to see his friend off. He was glad that nothing had happened to his friend since knowing of his troubles he and Greg had spoken of, since the time they had followed the two men back to Ann Marie Street. They had made plans to pursue the brothers when Theo was safely off the island. Michael drove to Theo's house, parked his car in front of the yard and went to knock the door, noticing on his way that Theo's car was not in the driveway. Theo's dad opened the door and let Michael in, asking him if he had seen his son. Michael said no, the last time he had spoken to Theo was last night and he was fine at the time. Perhaps he slept over at friends and has forgotten what day it was.

"Perhaps you are right," replied Theo's dad. Michael decided to give Theo a call on his cell phone. The phone rang then went to voicemail. He tried again and it did the same thing. Michael decided to drive up to Goodwill, to see if Theodore was at Delia's, he made his excuses to Theo's dad and off he went, praying to god that Theo was at Delia's and he was safe. When he got to where Delia lived he did not see any sign of his friend's car, he got out of his and went to knock the door. Christine opened the door after a while "Yes, can I help you?" she asked, Michael said

Chapter Four

yes, he was looking for Theodore or Delia. Christine answered and said, "I don't think Theo is here but if you wait I'll get my cousin for you, she might be able to help; by the way what's your name?" "Michael, my name is Michael and Theo is my brother" he replied, "ok, wait there" said Christine as she went to get her cousin for him.

Delia's heart started to beat fast when Christine told her that Michael was here looking for Theodore, if anyone is supposed to know where Theo was, it should be him, as Theo had mentioned to her he and Michael were like brothers, she was worried. She went to the door and invited Michael into the house, "The last time I saw Theo was a couple of nights ago, when I dropped him off here at your house" Michael was saying to Delia, and I spoke to him after that," he continued; "but now he seems to have disappeared into thin air." "I saw him last night, he dropped me off after the movie and headed home to do some packing," Delia was saying to Michael as she paced the floor. She knew something was wrong, she had not slept very well last night and Theo had not called, and when she had tried, there was no reply, but she just figured he was tired from having so much fun that day, he had fallen straight asleep; and this morning she had been waiting for him to call and say goodbye. But he hasn't, "and now you are here asking for him, oh god, I hope he is all right" 'Hey, Hey, don't play him out for dead now, he might be ok, I'll just phone his cell and see what happens" said Michael. The cell phone did not ring, the worried look on Michael's face caused Delia to burst into tears, she was trying to speak, but the words

Delia's Story

would not come out. Christine heard her cousin crying and came to see what the problem was, she went to her cousin, held her in her arms and comforted her, then when Delia seemed to have calmed down she asked, "What's up D? Why are you crying?" Paying no attention to Michael standing there looking as if someone had died, "Delia what is wrong?" She asked, with no nonsense tone this time. "Theo has disappeared, we cannot find him, he's supposed to be flying off today back to the states and, and, she said stuttering, his phone is off or perhaps the batteries are dead, but I know something is wrong," "Ok, ok, ok, I see; said Christine, "when was the last time any of you saw Theo or spoke to him? The other night, "Last night" replied Michael and Delia in unison. "And what makes you say that he has disappeared? Asked Christine, "come on Christine said Delia, is it not obvious, the man left here to go home last night to get ready for his voyage back to America. He is not at his house, he hasn't arrived at his house, and his phone is not happening, you don't need to be Sherlock Holmes to see where this is going do you?" "No I guess not," replied Christine, "so what are we going to do about it?" she asked, "first things first, we need to report this to the police, but most important of all, I have to go tell his parents I cannot find their son", said Michael.

"Ok, said Christine, give me your cell number, and here's our numbers; give us a call when you have spoken to Theo's parents please," "no problem" said Michael as he went out the door and made his way back to Canefield. On his way down, he phoned Greg, who at this time of day was on his way to work.

Chapter Four

On receiving the call from Michael, Greg telephoned his workplace, telling them he would not be in for a few days, he had just received an emergency call from a member of his family, and he had to attend. The Secretary told him he could only have two days off and he Greg would have to give notice for them or else there might be repercussions. Greg said to her that they could do as they choose to do, he had an emergency and he was going to deal with it, and with that; he hung up the phone and headed towards Canefield to link up with Michael.

Theo's parents were upset, but they handled their emotions well. Life in Dominica had made them that way, learning to hold one's emotion in check. Andra, Theo's mother couldn't take it, she was worried for her son, her first and only son, born after losing two other sons in miscarriage, she went to her room and cried, leaving the men to deal with phoning the police and other matters.

Greg arrived at The Samson's house and sounded his car horn to let Michael know he was waiting outside. Michael heard the sounding of the car horn, made his excuses to Theo's dad, who had already phoned the police, and was told that he should wait at least twenty-four hours before they could report Theo as missing, but they would keep an eye open as a favour to the magician.

Michael joined Greg in his car and they drove off heading towards the last place they had seen Kenroy's brothers, when they got there however, no one was home. The place was in darkness, no transport outside; all windows were shut, so they drove down to Layou, first visiting the hotel, then the restaurant where Greg had overheard the men in conversation. Still no joy, they waited for a while then just as they were about to give up, they saw the bus pull up outside the same restaurant.

The brothers went into the restaurant, sat down to discuss their newly made plans over a cold beer. Greg and Michael entered the restaurant, ordered some food, and sat at a table not to close to the brothers, but close enough to overhear the whispers of their conversation. Greg was good at that, he'd always said he had musicians ears, he could hear a pin drop, so it was not a problem for him to listen in on the conversation going on between the two brothers. He learnt that the brothers were planning to travel in a couple of days time, but they would not be flying from Dominican airport, he also learned that Kenroy would be travelling first thing tomorrow morning, heading for England after his revenge beating of Theo. They had beaten the boy so bad; it was not good things for them to hang around anymore; they were planning to abandon Theo wherever they had him tied up and run.

Greg had an idea, he whispered to Michael and Michael, nodded in agreement, "I heard that boy Theodore has gone missing" said Greg to Michael, loud enough for the brother who in their own conversation to hear. "Yeah man, the magician missing, and I heard them say his mother is one Wicked Obeah lady, so I sorry for the body who had anything to do with that boy disappearing". Said Michael holding back a smile "and I for one, know for sure that the Carib magic is really powerful" he continued, looking at Greg for help. "Yeah man it's true, I heard she was responsible for that boy, you know that boy you always

Chapter Four

see walking up and down Mero, naked as the day he was born wearing his pants on his head? Said Greg, in response to Michael's plea, the plan was working; the brothers had stopped talking and instead were listening to what was being said at the table not far from them, they were listening to Michael and Greg. They looked at each other, both of them now worried, very worried, they had heard about Carib magic and they had seen the boy walking down Mero with his pants on his head, so they believed and now they were worried for themselves. They got up and left the restaurant, Michael and Greg were in stitches, but they had to keep it down, after five minutes they also left the restaurant, just in time to see the brothers get into their transport and started up the engine ready to move. They got into Greg's car and took off before the brothers could move off, but waited at the top of the road for them to go past.

They followed the brothers back to Wall house, waited for them to go into the house, and made their move, parking the car in front of the brother's transport, Michael and Greg got out of the car. Greg went to the boot of the car and took out his machete and Michael followed with a baseball bat. Locking the boot, they headed for the front door of the brothers house and Michael knocked the door with the top of the bat.

The door opened and the brother was surprised to see the two men from the restaurant on the doorstep, Michael pushed past him, Greg pushed through him, shutting the door behind him as he stepped on the brother. Taking in his surroundings all at once, Michael was making his way through to another room, searching

Delia's Story

for the other brother; who it seemed was busy packing. Greg picked up the brother he had stepped on and started interrogating him, but he refused to talk; Greg punched him in his mouth and said to him "it would be best for you my friend, if you just told me what I need to know" but the brother refused to say anything. "Ok", said Greg since you have nothing to say, we will keep it that way" and on saying that he took the brothers head in his hand, saying "oh Well", and he snapped the brothers neck, letting the body go as it slumped to the floor.

Michael came out of the bedroom with the other brother, who at this time had been more fortunate than his now dead brother, who he could see slumped on the floor and Greg standing over him as though he had been of no importance. "So has he told you anything as yet Mike?" Greg asked. "Not a Diddly squat said Michael, "methinks he needs a little more oiling to loosen his tongue," "if you need any help, you only have to call, I will be only too happy to oblige" said Greg. Michael put the brother to sit down on a chair and asked him where was Theo, and what had they done to him? The brother refused to talk, "oh so you like it rough?" said Michael, as he brought the baseball bat crashing down on the brothers knees, both at once, and he repeated the action, you could hear the crack of the knee bones as they broke under the pressure of the second lick. The brother cried out, that time, he really felt the pain, so he told them Theo was at his brother Kenroy's place, that was all he knew, and the place was up in the garden. "Where is this garden?" asked Michael, "I don't know" said the brother, "I've only ever been there after dark and it

Chapter Four

was just the once, under the influence of alcohol and a bit of smoke." Wrong answer said Michael, as he brought the bat crashing onto the brother's knees, the brother slumped, sweat was pouring off him, and blood was staining his trousers from his upper thigh down to the bottom of his foot. But Michael did not give it a second thought, these brothers had hurt his brother, had him tied up somewhere and they would not say, on the say so of their perverted brother Kenroy. Well they would see, they would find out exactly whom they were playing with. Michael looked over at Greg, "nothing much here" he said to him, "then clean up and let us get going" said Greg.

    Greg, bent down over the bleeding man slumped on the floor in a sort of semi conscious state, he took the head in his hand looked at him hard, then dropped the head to the floor and it landed with a thud. The friends did not have to worry too much about fingerprints, since they were wearing gloves and setting fire to the place as they left, no one around to see them leave the house, and no one noticed the fire till it was to late, the friends were already on their to find Kenroy.

    Michael's phone rang, it was Delia, she wanted to know if he had found out anything, and what could she do to help. Michael told her the only thing she could do at this time is to be patient, he was following up on a lead and she would be the second to know. In the meantime, if she could phone the two airports and check up on Kenroy, he was planning to fly out to England via Antigua and they needed the time of the flight. Delia said "ok" and hung up the phone, straight away phoning the airports for the information, she on one phone and her cousin on the other. Getting through to the airport's switchboard could take a while. Meanwhile the two friends were already driving down to Canefield airport to see what they could find out for themselves.

Greg was sitting quietly listening to Michael speak to his ex wife, and for an instant he wanted to talk to her and tell her it would be ok, he would find her friend for her, but he held his ground and did not say a word. They got to the airport and went to the desk, pretending to be a friend of Kenroy's. They told the clerk they were supposed to be seeing him off but they could not remember which airport, they had had too much to drink last night at Kenroy's leaving party. The clerk believed them and told them that Kenroy was not booked at the Canefield airport for anytime that day and all seats were taken. So anyone wanting to leave the island from here would have to wait another day, maybe they should make their way to Melville hall airport there was a flight leaving from there in a few hours, which would make that about six this evening and the time is already two thirty in the afternoon. It would take them about two hours and a half to drive to Melville hall, so they thanked the clerk and headed for the Melville hall airport.

Chapter Five

Michael's phone rang, it was Delia with the information he had requested. He thanked her and said he would call her back later. Delia did not like sitting doing nothing so she decided to go for a drive, Christine went with her. They drove around town, then, they headed for country asking people as they went if they had seen the magician around the place, saying that someone had mentioned seeing him drive down from town and they would like to get his autograph. No one could help. After driving up and down, the cousins ended up at Melville airport, and stopped there to see if Kenroy might be there. They did not see him so they left the airport and headed home. Delia had a terrible headache, and as the night was approaching, it was getting worse. They drove home in silence, Christine did not know how to console her cousin, she tried comforting words, telling her not to worry, Theo would turn up, but that did not seem to help. Delia did not say a word, she just looked at her cousin, nodded her head yes and carried on driving, not even when they got back to the house. Delia went straight to her room, shutting the door behind her, leaving Christine, still standing by the front door, watching as she disappeared into her room. Christine shut the door and went to switch on the television, to see if any news of Theo's disappearance might be mentioned, but it was not; so she went to her bed wishing there was more she could do to help her cousin. She knew at this time it was best to leave Delia to herself, when she was ready to talk, she Christine would be there to listen.

After leaving Canefield airport, Michael and Greg heading for Melville hall airport, they picked up an old man on the way heading for the savannah, who started telling them a story about a haunted house in the hills, but the friends were not paying attention to the ramblings of an old man. They were thinking about Kenroy, and what they were going to do to him when they caught up with him. The old man was saying he was passing a house up in the gardens and he could hear moaning coming from in there, only it wasn't really moaning but someone calling out a name, like Lydia or Delia, he wasn't sure.

The house belonged to a bus driver, who only stayed there sometimes, but it had been abandoned lately, he had not seen the owner for a while, just as he finished speaking, Greg was stopping the car for him to disembark, he had reached his destination. The old man got off, thanked them, turned right heading to his destination, while Greg kicked into gear, and continued driving without stopping to pick up any other passengers until he got to Portsmouth.

He stopped at the only gas station around for miles to refuel his car; he parked next to a bus. He recognised the bus. He signalled to Michael and told him to occupy the driver of the bus while he filled up the tank, the bus driver could be the person they were looking for.

Chapter Five

Michael was leaning on the bus when Kenroy came out of the station; he looked at Michael inquiringly and approached him. "Hi said Michael, I wondered if you were heading towards the airport, I am heading that way myself and the brethren I am with is only going as far as the next turning on the right to the Carib reserve."

Kenroy looked at him, then he looked at Greg who was making his way towards them, Michael turned to him and said, "Yes Brethren, I was just asking this bus driver if he was heading towards the airport, since you can't drive me all the way, but he hasn't said yes or no as yet." "Well it would be great if he could, it would save you a journey" replied Greg, Kenroy noting the exchange between the two men thought to himself it would be ok, if he dropped the fella to the airport, since he was going that way himself. "Ok" said Kenroy, introducing himself, and putting his hands out for Michael to shake, Michael introduced himself, but did not shake Kenroy's hand, making an excuse about his hand not being clean. Kenroy did not seem to mind, Greg excused himself from their company, said goodbye to Michael and got in his car with the intention of driving off. Kenroy and Michael got on to the bus, and made their way to the airport. Michael was making small talk with Kenroy, asking him why was he running from Dominica and where was he going that can possible be as beautiful as this place. Kenroy told him that it was said, "A change is as good as a rest", and he needed to visit some family across the sky. "Oh I see," said Michael, "and you, what about you? Kenroy asked, "Where are you running to?" "Me? I'm not running to anywhere, I am on my way to settle some business," said Michael, "So are you going to England or America to settle this business? Asked Kenroy, keen to know more, this man could be a possible contact if he was going to England, he was thinking. "No! Said Michael, I don't think you quite understand. You see I have to find a friend of mine, and in order for me to find him, I have to find the person who knows where he is.

Kenroy started to sweat. He opened the window a little wider. Michael was now standing a little closer to Kenroy and looking outside the bus. "You see that car just in front of you?" Michael was saying, "My brethren from the gas station is driving it. He will stop any moment now and when he does, you must also stop your vehicle. I don't want you to try and be a hero. I just want you to stop the bus, so that we can have a little talk." Kenroy was pouring with sweat. He knew it was he they were after, and he remembered where he had seen the man driving the car before. Kenroy wanted to pee; his bladder was suddenly full, and if he did not go soon, he would piss himself, and the way things were looking he did not think he would get to relieve himself. The man driving the car was the other half, of the woman in the Layou River hotel; he was the one with her at the farm, the night of the dance. And if he was correct, the fella on the bus with him was the brother of the Magician. Kenroy knew he was going to meet his maker that day, this very day. He had not slept at all last night. He had visited Theo, to see if he was still alive, had left a bucket of water in the place, in case he got thirsty. He was still tied up and the door was locked. He did not think they would have caught up

Chapter Five

with him so soon. He thought he had ample time to at least get to Antigua before they noticed anything.

"Theo is a man," Kenroy was saying to himself "he supposed to have dirty habits, like plenty women, staying out late or even for a few days, it seems Theo was not the man he supposed him to be," Kenroy had not given thought to Theo's friends and relatives, and how far they would go for him. Michael interrupted his thoughts and told him to pull over, turn of the engine, and hand over the keys for the bus, since he would not be using it no more. Kenroy noticed Greg had stepped out of the parked car and was coming towards the bus; Greg opened the door to the driver's side and roughly helped Kenroy out of his seat. Michael laughed; Greg dragged Kenroy to the back of the bus and tied him to the spare tyre attached to the back of the bus, using rope he had in his car for work. He then got into the bus started up the engine and headed for the Carib reserve.

The roads leading up to the reserve was very quiet and very wet, the red clay soil with its bounty of Banana, orange, Breadfruit trees and other variety of plants, all heavy and laden with fruits of their nature, stone houses hiding in the midst of it all, plus you could smell the sulphur and the richness of it all due to the rain falling on that spot more often than anywhere else, and being so close to the more natural, part of the island, it was also very rugged and steep, the mountains surrounding the background were covered with unspoilt deep green forest, hiding all the sulphur springs and waterfalls. Kenroy was going to feel the bumps and he was going to be sorry, so sorry that he would want to tell them what it was they needed to know.

It seemed to Michael his friend has lost the rational part of himself for the moment, but he Michael was of the same mind and if it helped them obtain the objective they were seeking, it was all for a good cause. However, if that stupid pervert did not speak soon, Michael could think of other ways to make him see the light. There were people at home worried and fretting over Theo, and he wanted to bring him back home to them, it was not time for him to lose his best friend and brother.

Michael was driving Greg's car, and Greg was leading with Kenroy's bus, it was not long before Kenroy had had enough of his ordeal; plus it had been raining and the air was chilly. He started begging to be untied, he would tell them where Theo was, if only they untie him, Michael heard him, and so he sounded the car horn to let Greg know to stop the bus.

Theo was in serious pain when he came back to consciousness. He was afraid to stretch his limbs for fear of the pain, but he knew he could not stay curled up as he was. He could smell the dry blood on his body. He could barely open his eyes, they were so swollen. It was dark, there was no light to guide him, and he could hear the scuttle of cockroaches running across the floor. He had no choice, so he stayed where he was for the time being. He thought of Delia and her sweet smell, her smile, her delicate nature and the fact that he wanted her so much and hadn't the opportunity to hold her in

Chapter Five

his arms and make sweet passionate love, all the things they haven't had the chance to do. All this he was thinking to make himself feel better, he wished he was with her rather than the predicament he was in at the moment, and he wondered what she was doing? Then he fell asleep.

A noise outside woke him. He listened, but he did not hear it again. He started to think about Michael and if he had found any clues to who might have been following him, even if he Theo, already knew who the culprits were. Also, how long before they would find him shut away in the middle of nowhere. He prayed for his parents, and he cursed Kenroy and his brothers for having him like this, he cursed the day they were born. He tried again to stretch his legs. He managed it with difficulty. The pain, oh god the pain. As the pain shot through his body as he tried to stand, Theo dropped back to the floor and stayed there for a while. He could hear his stomach churning; it had been a while since he had eaten anything and he was also very thirsty. He could smell water. He wondered if it was safe to drink, and though it was not far from his reach, but the pain he would have to endure it in order to quench his thirst..

Delia had fallen asleep without even realising. One minute she was staring at the ceiling with tears running down the side of her face, the next she was dreaming. The dream was confusing, and it was a nightmare. She tossed and turned, she could see men running, four men; three of them were chasing the other. Then it changed, some strange things were happening and the people looked dead. They were reaching out to her. The bony fingers stretching, trying to grab the hem of her skirt She pulled away, but there was one hand, belonging to a newly dead man and he was pointing towards a cottage in the distance. Delia tried to keep the detail in her brain, she started walking towards the cottage, but the more she walked the further away it seemed. Along the way she met an old man who warned her not to go to the house.

"The place is haunted. The spirits are having a party in there, keep away," but he just kept walking fast, as he kept on talking fast. Delia looked at him walking away, shook her head, and carried on her way towards the house in the distance. As she got closer to the house, she thought she could hear someone calling her name, or was it calling for Lydia. She started running, running towards the house. Delia was tossing and turning in her bed; she was sweating in the dream and in reality. She could hear Theo. She was running, running fast and just as she got to the door of the house, she stopped dead in her tracks. Kenroy was standing there with a smile on his face and blood running down the side of it, he looked a mess. Delia jumped. As she jumped, she fell out of her bed and woke up. She went to the bathroom and washed her face. She was feeling hot, she was sweating like a pig, but the night air was cool. She blamed the nightmare for how she was feeling, she would not talk about the dream to anyone, she needed to find out the meaning for herself, but she would need to meditate and fast. So Delia went back to her bed, praying before she laid down again, but sleep would not come, and she laid there thinking about the dream and if it meant what she thought. But where was

Chapter Five

he? Where was the house? That house it belonged to Kenroy, and he looked dead, but where in Dominica was it?

Greg had stopped the bus on hearing Michael sounding his horns; he got off the bus and went to find out what the problem was. Kenroy was ranting, and raving at the back of the bus saying. "Please man, I will tell you where your friend is if you just let me go, me and my brothers won't go near him again I swear." "You are so right about that one," said Greg, as he went and stood in front of Kenroy; because your brothers are dead and when I am finished with you, you can join them in hell." Kenroy started sweating, "What do you mean dead, my brothers cannot be dead?" he was saying, and "who killed them eh? You, You killed my brothers?" "Yes that's right and when I am finished with you, its bye, bye rapist. Tell me something Kenroy, did you enjoy playing with my woman eh, did you enjoy fucking her? When she told you she had changed her mind, did you pay any attention to that? Or did you just take that dirty, dirty, stinking country dick of yours and disrespect my lady, Brethren before this day is over, your life, will be over; I am making you that promise." All this Greg said to Kenroy, who was still tied to the bus sweating, and had now pissed his pants, Michael was half standing, one foot in the car and the other outside of the car, caught in that position when he heard the words that Greg had just spoken to Kenroy.

    He did not say a word; he only stood there and listened, he could see the steam rising from Greg, he would have to talk to

Delia's Story

Kenroy quickly before he was not allowed the opportunity. Michael was learning new things about Greg; he was a sly one. All the while, they had been chasing after these people, Greg had never once mentioned the fact that he was related to the girl who had been raped, not even when he had first told him about it in his home. He remembered the way Greg had reacted that night; he had put that down to other reasons, now he could see; now he understood Greg a little bit more.

Michael went over to Kenroy and asked him to tell him where Theo was. Kenroy refused to give up the information. Michael asked him again, but still he refused. Michael respected the brothers their stubbornness, but thought them stupid nonetheless. He went over to the car and came back with the baseball bat; he thought it might encourage Kenroy to speak. Kenroy would not speak, he figured he was going to die. He knew that for sure, he had seen the look in Greg's eyes. Yes, he knew more than anything that look, it had finality about it and if he was going to die, there was no reason why he should tell them anything. If he told them they would kill him, if he did not tell them, he was going to die anyway, so what the heck, he thought, if he went so would Theo. Michael whacked Kenroy across his stomach with the bat, knocking the wind out of him; Kenroy coughed up blood, couple of his ribs broken after that assault. Michael asked him to tell him where he had Theo tied up, but still he remained like a nun doing penance, quiet. Michael knew he was wasting his time asking Kenroy questions. The man was more stubborn than a mule. He looked at him and said, "Well my

Chapter Five

friend, your time has come" and with that he beckoned to Greg who was waiting for his turn. This man was his, this man who had made his woman's life a nightmare, he tried not to see the picture he was painting in his mind, the tears falling from his eyes.

Greg walked over to where Kenroy was still tied to the bus took Kenroy's face in his hands. Kenroy looked at Greg and said "Ok, ok, I'll tell you where your friend is" he said Michael smiled at Kenroy's sudden change of heart, "Then speak now or forever be silent" said Greg holding the head firmly. Kenroy told them that Theo was tied up in a house situated in the middle of no man's land, which was also the name of the house; he said, "If you were to drive to the top of the reserve, take a left turn by the guava tree. It will lead you to a roundabout, when you get to the roundabout do a sharp right and you will be there on no man's land." "Are you sure you telling us the truth boy? Because your spirit won't rest easy if I find out you lying to us" said Michael, looking past Greg at Kenroy, who looked like he did not give a damn any more. Michael was a bit dubious about the piece of information, for all they know this man could be sending them to their graves. Kenroy nodded yes in reply to Michael's answer. "Are you sure there is nothing else you would like to say, like sorry for all the trouble you have caused these people?" asked Greg. Kenroy did not say a word, he looked up at Greg and spat in his face, "that, is all I have to say to you." Michael gasped, Greg took a flannel out of his pocket, and wiped the spit of his face, then he looked around for a wet leaf, found one with water on it; he levelled his face to the leaf, the spot where the spit had landed and washed the area. He did not use the flannel again; he put it back in his pocket and went back to where Kenroy was, still tied to the back of the bus. Michael went and sat back in the car, he knew what was going to happen next, Greg got on the bus and started the engine; he drove the bus to the edge of the road.

Dominica was an island with some very dangerous places, especially when driving, some very long drops into very steep ravines, if you took the turning wrong on one of those mountainous roads. This place was just like that; chances are you would not survive, and nobody would know about it until it was too late or they were driving the same road at the time.

Greg got off the bus, went to where Michael was sitting in the car, and indicated for Michael to move over and he did. Then Greg got in the driving seat, strapped himself in and started the engine. He drove up to where the bus was parked on the edge of the road and started to nudge the back of the bus with the car, with Kenroy still tied to it. There were tears in Kenroy's eyes; the friends paid him no mind. "He had brought this upon himself," thought Michael "tit for tat and all of that. The bus started to move forward, then it started to rock like a see saw and Greg sat back to watch the bus slowly but surely move forward as it kept rocking, then suddenly the rocking stopped as the bus toppled over the edge of the cliff and disappeared out of sight. Greg changed gear and started to drive off as the sound of the bus exploding reached their ears. Greg smiled and Michael shook his head, "so are you feeling better now?" he asked Greg, "Yes, much better" replied Greg still smiling, "now it's only a matter of

Chapter Five

finding Theo, if what Kenroy told us was the truth that is," and off he drove in search of no man's land.

They drove through the Carib reserve, not paying much attention to the people waving to them, or the beautiful baskets and wares laid out on display for passer-bys or tourist to feast their eyes on and hopefully buy them.

Today the friends had other things on their minds; they were on a mission and it was getting late. They drove following the course given to them by Kenroy. They were now at the roundabout but they could not see the sharp turn, there was no sharp turn. Greg stopped the car and they got out to go in search of the house, but there was no house, no sharp turn, just the edge of a ravine and nothing else but the banana trees and other greenery growing there. No flipping house, no Theo, he kicked at the nearby bush and cursed the now dead Kenroy and his brothers, got back in the car and they continued searching.

They drove up and down, this time asking people whom they met if they knew Kenroy, or where he had his house in the gardens, but no one could help. They made their way home to Greg house to have something to eat and freshen up themselves to go back on the road.

The phone rang while Delia was in the shower, she had asked Christine to go shopping for her, saying she needed to be in the house in case Michael or anyone called about Theo, and Christine had agreed. With her hair still wet and water dripping

Delia's Story

from her Delia went to answer the phone. "Good morning, how can I help you?" It was a Detective Hunter, from the police station "May I speak with Ms Beau Pierre please, this is Detective Hunter from the Roseau Police station". "This is Delia Beau Pierre speaking, how can I help you Detective?" "Well I have been informed that you were probably the last person to see Mr Theodore Samson alive and so we would like you to come down to the police station to assist us with our enquiries" the Detective told her, "What time would you like me to meet with you then?" she asked him. Trying not to think of what he had just said about last person to see Theo alive, Theo was not dead, she knew that, she just needed to find him that's all and she did not need any Detective referring otherwise. "The time is now ten o'clock, would midday be fine with you?" he asked. "? Yes midday is fine with me, I will see you then, goodbye Detective," and with that she placed the phone back in its cradle and went back to finish in the shower.

Christine came home just as Delia was about to leave the house, "Where are you off to Cuz? Asked Christine stopping in the doorway with shopping in her hands. "Got to go see a Detective Hunter in town about Theo" Delia answered. "Well if you wait there I'll come with you, just let me put this shopping away." Delia waited; she did not have to wait long because Christine knew how important this was to her. They got to the police station

Chapter Five

and Delia parked in the first available space she found, and then went in to meet with Detective Hunter.

It was ten to twelve, she was early. As Delia and Christine entered the police station, Detective Hunter was standing at the counter talking to an elderly couple, who Delia took to be Theo's parents. She had met them once before at their house when Theo had taken her to dinner, she remembered the light in the house had been dimmed and it had been a while since that night. The man standing before her had Theo's looks and his build; the woman was of the same colouring as Theo. The Detective saw Delia as she entered, and excused himself from the couple. He approached her, inquiring if she was Ms Beau Pierre and she confirmed that she was, also introducing her cousin Christine. The Detective took them over to Theo's parents and introduced them to each other, not realising that they had met before. Delia told them how sorry she was about Theo's disappearance and her eyes started to burn from the tears that were threatening to fall.

Mrs Samson noticing Delia's pain, went to her and hugged her, telling her it would be alright, she said she felt her son was in a great deal of pain, but he was not yet dead and God willing they would find him soon. Delia hugged Mrs Samson and kissed her on the cheeks, thanking her for her comforting words and saying it should be she Delia comforting her after all. Delia was only his friend, and she was his mother, Mrs Samson smiled and said it was ok, and that Delia should give her a call later; the number is in the local Directory, Delia thanked her, hugged her. Then shook hands with Mr Samson again, just before they excused themselves from the Detective, and headed for the exit leaving Delia, to assist the police in any way that she could.

The Detective invited Delia and her cousin into his office, offering them a seat; in his mind, he began assessing Delia, her cousin he already knew from a time ago. He had tried to introduce himself to her at a party and she totally ignored him, treating him as though he was not some-bodies child, man, she was hot, but not as hot as her cousin Delia, the lady was firing. He wondered if they had anything to do with the magician's disappearance, perhaps they were conspiring with someone else, and had kidnapped him for a ransom, sometimes these things happened, and the Samson family were quite well off. Then he switched on a tape recorder sitting on the desk, informing them of protocol and began questioning Delia, "What is your relationship with Theodore Samson?" he asked, "we're just good friends" she replied, "How long have you known him?" He continued, "I have known him all my life" Delia replied, "when was the last time you saw him?" Delia replied, "I saw him two nights ago." "Where did you see him and what was he doing, did he give you any reason to believe that he was in any trouble, or was having problems of any kind? Asked the Detective "well," said Delia, When I saw him last, we had gone to the movies and then he dropped me of home, leaving me about one in the morning to go home to pack his bag, because he was travelling back to the states that following morning. And yes! I do believe he was in some problem with some people or a person." She continued to tell the Detective about Kenroy and her cousin Christine, the rape and how Theo

Chapter Five

had helped her have Kenroy arrested. She believes that Kenroy might have something to do with Theo's disappearance. In addition, Theo had mentioned to her before his disappearance that he believed someone had been following him and he thought it was Kenroy.

Christine listened to her cousin relating all this to the Detective and felt sorry for her, she watched the Detective making notes in addition to the tape machine he had switched on when they had started the enquiry. When Delia was finished telling the Detective what she knew, he asked her which police station was it that she had reported the rape charge to, and she told him.

He thanked her for the information; switched off the machine, looked over at Christine and told them he would be in touch once he had been in touch with the village police station they had mentioned, and then he escorted them out of his office and left them in the reception area to return to his duties.

"Wow, that was quite something" said Christine, "I'm not sure I like that Detective, he looked too smug, like he's gold and we are copper." "Never mind him, just as long as he uses the information I gave him to find my friend, that's all I care about," answered Delia, as she opened the door of the station to get out into the fresh air. She needed some fresh air, the police station was stuffy, and she was worried about Theo. She missed him.

Delia phoned Michael. After a while Michael answered the phone, he sounded tired. She told him she was just phoning to find out how he was and if he had found out anything. Michael related most of what had happened to him since he had spoken to her last, but did not mention Greg, or anyone being killed. He told Delia he had enlisted the help of a close friend and they were still searching the countryside to see if they could find him. Delia then told him of her meeting with the police and that she was waiting to see what they would come up with. Michael said ok and he would link up with her at some point that day. They exchanged goodbyes and Delia hung up her phone. She was thinking about the dream she had, she knew it would lead her to Theo, but she hadn't quite figured it out as yet. Dreams are the strangest of things she thought shaking her head.

Theo's parent's had gone straight home from the police station, Mrs Samson remarking what a sweet person she thought Delia was. She remembered her from the night when Theo had invited her over for dinner. Mr Samson agreed, but at the same time he was saying that you cannot trust everyone you meet, they did not know anything about Delia, except her name and the fact that their son liked her very much otherwise he would not have brought her over to the house. "That's my point exactly," said his wife, "our son would not have brought her to the house and introduced her to us. Did you not see the pain she was in poor child, I do believe she is in love with our son." Anyway, let us try to be positive, she has done nothing wrong, we will find him and find him alive," she said trying to reassure her husband and probably herself. She walked over to the television and turned it on; the news was on, there was a picture of her son on the news, "Look honey, look she

Chapter Five

said to her husband pointing to the TV. "Look they are talking about Theo's disappearance, listen."

The reporter was a beautiful brown-skinned Carib female wearing a T-shirt with The magician written across her chest and his picture beneath the inscription. She was standing in the foyer of the Theatre in town where Theo was, supposedly last seen. She was saying, "It seems that the last time Theo was seen, was a couple nights ago when he visited this theatre in town with a female friend. We are not at liberty now to bring you any comment from this friend. It seems she is suffering from stress brought on by Theo going missing, and is not able to talk to us now, the family naturally; being very worried for their son would like the co-operation of the Dominican community. If you have seen Theodore Samson, also known as the famous Calypsonian, the magician, or have any knowledge of his whereabouts, please we would like you to call this number with your information; the number is four, four, eight, zero, zero, zero, one or four, four, eight, zero, one, zero, two. Thank you for taking the time." Mrs Samson turned off the television and turned back to her husband, "well my dear" she said, all we can do now is pray. Her husband looked at her, shook his head and said, "if you say so dear, if you say so" and left her standing there looking at him, her head cocked to one side; as he headed upstairs to their bedroom to make a few more phone calls.

There had to be something more he could do, there just had to be. He was not going to sit down and let everybody else do the work. Theo is his son and he loved his son more than himself.

Delia's Story

He could understand his wife wanting to do what was best for her, she could pray and wait, but he would pray and try to do something. He reached over to some pictures of his son sitting on the dressing table. He picked up one of Theo as a youth and remembered how much trouble that boy had given him whilst growing up, the amount of trouble he and Michael were always getting themselves into, and running into his for refuge. He had punished the both of them on many occasions and in different ways but it never deterred them for the pranks and mischief they would get up to. Whenever he told them off, his wife would sneak them into the kitchen and comfort them with little goodies. How she would tell him off in jest, "Cedric, leave the boys alone, boys will be boys," and reminded him of how he himself used to be as a boy growing up in the village. Now his son was a man, he is supposed to outlive his father, not the other way round. Which sons of bitches was it, keeping his boy away from his family? He would like to get his hands on them. Putting the picture back in its place, Cedric Samson sat down on his bed and cried, it had been a long time since he had felt hot scalding tears falling down his cheeks, he cried for his son and the fact that he Cedric, felt so helpless. His wife found him crying, she cuddled her husband and cried with him, she knew the pain he was feeling; she was his wife and mother of his only son.

The police could not find any trace of Kenroy Masters or his brothers. They had put out an APB on the brothers, they checked

Chapter Five

both airports, and what available cars they had, was out on patrol. Everyone was to keep an eye open for the brothers and Theo. They believed there to be a connection between the Masters and Theodore Samson. The only information they had gathered was things they already knew, up to the point of him dropping Delia to her house the night of his disappearance. They wished someone would turn up with some new information, but it had not happened yet. No one wanted to think the worst of the situation but after the third day, they were worried.

    Michael was looking bad, he had not slept much that night worrying about his best friend, he was very tired and Greg was the same, they did not know where else to look, but they would keep on looking. Dominica was not that big an island, but she was good at keeping secrets with all her dense forests, mountains, hills, and valleys; it was not that easy to get around, but they would not give up trying.

Theo was sitting huddled against the wall, weak, hungry, thirsty, and dirty, the water in the container now tasted badly, so he refused to drink from it. He was still tied up, and in agony, wondering why no one had found him yet, what was happening and why he had not seen nor heard the brothers return since they had left him in this rotten place to die. He thought about his parents, wondering how they were dealing with him missing. "Oh Delia" he cried, "how I miss you, how I would love to see your face again." The pain his body was in was nothing compared to the pain he felt when he thought he might never see her again, and Michael his brother and best friend. Would they get another chance to paint the town red, why was he taking so long in finding him, had he gone to the police, he hoped he or his parents had contacted the police by now; and if so, why were they taking so long?

Delia had lost weight, she had trouble sleeping. Every time she closed her eyes, her nightmares would begin. She could hear Theo calling her name but she could not get to him, she could not see him; she could just hear him calling her name. Christine was getting worried for her cousin, so she had taken time off work to stay home with her, she did not know what to do. She wanted to call Uncle Joseph, but she did not think Delia would appreciate that, and Greg was out of the question.

Delia stayed in her room most of the time, not speaking to anyone if she could help it, could not even write, but keeping an eye on the news in case they had found him or any information that might lead her to him.

The Police had been in touch, but had not been very informative; they had phoned merely to inquire about Kenroy. Whether Delia had had any knowledge of him before the incident, she told them what she had told them before. However, when she had asked them if they had found any lead to Theo's whereabouts, they had been very quick to mumble thank you but if she wanted to know anything about the investigation, she would have to make an appointment with the Detective in charge of the case and hung up the phone. Delia was vex, she wanted to call them back and

Chapter Five

shout at them, tell them how rude they were, but that would not help at all; it would only make things worse for her, and any information she might want they would probably refuse to give it to her. However, in the morning, she would make an appointment to see the detective if Theo had not turned up by then.

An overcast sky veiled the morning sun; the Island Mountains covered in mist, making the light seem dull as it cloaked the springtime warmth. In Salisbury, a village in Dominica, an old man sitting down with his breakfast in his humble home, about to listen to the news on the television. Normally at this time of the day, he would have been on his way to his garden up in the hills, but today he had felt a little tired so he had decided to take the day off and relax at home. He had no wife, since his wife had gone to meet her maker three years ago, quietly one night in her sleep. She was one of the lucky ones, he had told himself, she had not suffered one little bit, she had kissed him goodnight and left him watching the news as he always did before he went to bed. Then when it was over he had gone to join her, she had been asleep, he could hear her breathing softly as she slept, he had got in the bed next to her, kissed her on her forehead and whispered goodnight to her. He remember her mumbling in her sleep as if answering him goodnight and then listening to her breathing, as he always did because it helped him to fall asleep.

Delia's Story

He had woken up before her in the morning and went to buy some fresh bread from the bakery, knowing she would be awake on his return, preparing their breakfast, before he left and went to the garden to do his day's work. But things did not work out that way for him that day, on his return, his wife was nowhere to be found, no smell of frying eggs or frying plantain, he'd called out to her, no answer.

He remembered how quiet the house seemed at the time; So he'd made his way cautiously to the bedroom, not being quite sure why he was being cautious, but cautious nonetheless. When he got to the bedroom, his wife was still in the bed, he called to her, but she did not answer, he went over to the bed to shake her, calling her name at the same time, still no response. He had taken the cover from round her and looked at her, he had checked her pulse, nothing was happening and she was getting a little cold. Therefore, he had gone to the phone and called the Doctor, who arrived at the house ten minutes later, only to tell him fifteen seconds later that his wife was dead. She had died sometime in the night; it seemed she had had a stroke. How could she have a stroke he had asked, she was so healthy, but the Doctor could only tell him sorry.

He did not like to think about his dead wife, he still had not gotten over her, and still missed her very badly; he sometimes thought he could hear her in the house. Oh well life has to go on he told himself as he turned his attention back to the television to hear the reporter talking about Theo's disappearance, and asking for any one with knowledge of his whereabouts or the

Chapter Five

whereabouts of the Masters brothers to call in with the information. The old man stopped eating and listened, he wondered if he knew anything. He knew Kenroy Masters had a house up in the hills by his garden, and he had been hearing strange noises coming from the house lately, making him a little uptight to go past late in the evening. He never made the sun go down before he went past the house. He wondered if Kenroy was locked up in the house, and what did Kenroy have to do with the magician's disappearance. He got up from his breakfast and went to speak to his neighbour. He related his story to the neighbour.

The neighbour told him it was best to phone the police and tell them what he knew, just in case it was of any help to them and the case, and he might get a reward. The old man listened and agreed with the neighbour, went back to his home and phoned the police in the village, "Hello this is the Salisbury village police station, how may we assist you?" said the voice on the other end of his phone. "Hello, the old man replied, my name is Mr Patrick Vidal," "Yes Mr Vidal, this is Pc. Collins, what can I do for you sir?" said the voice. "Well, I was watching the news just now, and I heard them say, if anyone had any news concerning Kenroy Masters or his brothers, they should call. But I didn't write down the number and I did not know who else to call, so I called you" said the old man "Well if you would just tell me what it is you know Mr Vidal, I am sure it will be of the utmost help to the case" said the voice.

"Alright then" said the old man and he proceeded to tell the police constable what he knew about Kenroy Masters, and the

Delia's Story

house in the Hills where he has his garden. He told them about the noises he keeps hearing coming from inside the house and how frightened he had become. The police officer asked him how long he had noticed the noise coming from the house in question and the old man scratched his head, he wasn't quite sure when it was he first started hearing the noise, but it seemed to have been forever; he told him about six days. The policeman thanked the old man for his help, told him they would be in touch again. He also asked if it was possible for him to give them the correct location of Kenroy's house, and if it was possible for them to pick him up to show them the place, if in case they needed him to. The old man told the police officer he would be very happy to help them in any way he could. The police officer thanked him again and hung up the phone. The old man was glad he had phoned the police, he hoped that it would help them find what they were looking for and with that he went back to finish his breakfast, and waited to see when the police would call him again. He had the strangest feeling they would be calling on him again real soon.

After speaking with the old man, the police officer from the village police station immediately got in touch with Detective Hunter from the Roseau Police station, informing him of the call he had received from the old man. Detective Hunter was very pleased, he was so pleased he called Theo's parents informing them of the latest news, and made arrangements to have them picked up after they had checked out the latest information they had received. Detective Hunter then got back in touch with the village police station to have them pick up the old man and bring

Chapter Five

up to town, so that they could check out the information he'd given, and to have him take them where the house was supposed to be located.

Once the old man arrived with the police from the village, they made their way to the house on the hill. They drove through town and headed towards Wall house, passing, Wall house and going straight as if they were going to Grand Bay. After Grand Bay they kept driving for what seemed a very long time and just when they were about to query the old man about the location, they found it.

Detective Hunter and the other police officers arrived at the house in the afternoon, it was about two o'clock. The house looked derelict, surrounded by bushes which made it almost impossible to find unless you knew where you were going and what you were looking for. The house was locked and all windows were barred. Detective Hunter got out of his car, followed by another two officers, and left the old man in the car, the officers went to the door and listened to see if he could hear any sound coming from inside, but they did not hear any sound at all. Detective Hunter got the other police officers who were with him to breach the lock and gain entry into the house.

It was dark in the house, the air was stale and dank, and insects scurrying across the floor in fear of being stamped on. The officers could hardly hear anything except for the slow, quiet breathing of someone or something to their right hand side, in the corner. Detective Hunter called out "Theodore Samson, are you in here?" the Detective did not get a response; he asked one of the other officers to get him a torch, so he could have some light in the place. The officer went to get the torch, while Detective Hunter continued calling to Theo, but also moving closer to where the huddled bundle laid in the corner. The stench was becoming too much for the Detective, the smell of stale blood and urine, he took a handkerchief out of his trousers pocket and covered his nose. The officer came back with the torch and handed it over to Detective Hunter, who took the light from the officer and pointed it over to where the bundle lay, recognising a body huddled in the corner, facing the wall.

He went over to get a closer look at the body, the Detective turned over the body to get a look at the face which was dirty, badly bruised and swollen, the blood caked on parts of his face, his eyes swollen shut. "My god! It's the magician" He exclaimed, "Quickly," he beckoned to the other officers, get this man into one of the vehicles quickly, he is alive thank god; he is not looking good at all, and his breathing is shallow. We have got to get him to the hospital as soon as possible." The two police officers did not have to be told twice; they moved quickly doing as they were told. One of them went out to the car, returning with a blanket, threw it around Theo's body; then he and his partner lifted him gently off the floor and carried him to the car outside. Detective Hunter pulled the house door shut behind him and rushed to the cars waiting on him to take Theo to the hospital. It was a long drive back to the hospital, but eventually they got there.

Chapter Five

Detective Hunter rushed inside the hospital and got the attention of a male nurse just on his way back from Theatre. Theo was now aware of his rescue and was very happy about it, he thanked God that he would be able to see Delia again, he believed that with all his heart, because that was all he prayed for. He thought at least whether he lived or died his parents would find some closure now that he had been found. He tried to open his eyes, but it was not possible so he stopped trying and just laid there listening to the fuss going on around him, he longed to hear Delia's voice, feel the touch of her hands on his face, "oh love that will not let me go". He drifted off to sleep writing love poems in his thoughts.

The sight of the magician really unnerved the nurse, he quickly called for a doctor and also making sure a bed and drip was made available and although it looked like his injuries were not going to kill him, to have him taken for x-ray to check the extent of damage that might have been done to him.

Delia waited anxiously all afternoon, waiting to hear the phone ring. She was certain that Michael or the police would be calling to tell her they had been making real progress with the case, but when the phone refused to ring she felt obligated to change her mind, but she would not give up hope.

Delia was going through some accounts and trying to make sense of it for perhaps the sixth time, it was doing her head in, trying to concentrate, focus on the figures that were swimming before her eyes when her phone started ringing, it was eleven in the evening. She did not need the disturbance of a telephone

Delia's Story

ringing, but she was glad for it especially since she was waiting on news of Theo, she would definitely answer it, for sure. She was surprised to hear Theo's mother on the other end of the line. "Hello, Mrs Samson, how are you, is something wrong, have they found Theo?" All these questions Delia asked, before realising she had not given Theo's mum a chance to say hello. Delia fingers were hurting and her knuckles a little white, when she realised how tightly she was holding the receiver, "are you ok, and are you alone? Mrs Samson asked her, "no my cousin is here with me, why you ask?" "I just wanted to let you know, the police have found Theo, he's been taken to the Roseau hospital, and we are waiting for more news from the Doctor. I just thought you would like to know," Delia was speechless, her heart started pounding in her chest, tears were pouring down her face, she could not speak. "Are you ok my child?" asked Mrs Samson again, "Yes Thank you Mrs Samson, I'm ok," said Delia gaining some control, " thank you, thank you!" Delia placed the receiver back in its cradle.

Delia spun around the room, grabbing her car keys and a jacket; she headed for Christine's room, calling for Christine as she approached the door. Christine opened the bedroom door and looked at her cousin, wondering what on earth could be the matter, why is Delia making such a din? Before Christine could interject with her cold voice queries, Delia grabbed her by the hand and said "Come on, we're going to the Hospital in town," "Why? Who are we visiting in the hospital at this time of night?" asked Christine. "The police have found Theo and he is in the

Chapter Five

hospital, come on Christine, why are you taking so long?" Asked Delia, who was trying her best, to pull Christine towards the front door, "hold on a minute, cut in Christine, pulling her cousin to a stop, "First, let me get my jacket, while you get your breath or take a hold on yourself, Ok," "ok," said Delia, just hurry up and get your jacket, I'll go start up the car, look she said to her cousin, I've calmed down, are you satisfied?" "Thank you," Christine said to her as she made her way to her bedroom for the jacket.

    The drive to the hospital was quick, Delia was driving and she was in a hurry, she drove the car as if she was in the Grand prix and heading for the winning line. The receptionist was painting her nails when they approached the desk, "Excuse me" said Delia. "Yes, what can I do for you? Asked the receptionist. "I am looking for Mr Theodore Samson please," said Delia. The nurse looked at her and said "Sorry, but we have no Theodore Samson in this hospital." Delia looked at her cousin and she shook her head, she looked back at the receptionist and said to her, "look, I am not in the best of moods, Theodore Samson, the magician was brought here this evening, I know that he's here because his mother told me so." "Well I am sorry, but you must be mistaken, said the receptionist, while I have been at this desk, no Theodore Samson or magician, has been registered here."

    Just as Delia was about to reach over the desk for the receptionist's register, a voice behind Christine said "Hello, yes, perhaps I can be of some assistance?" it was the staff nurse, she walked over to the desk and stood in front of Delia who was very upset and about to express it. Christine coming forward to her

Delia's Story

cousin's side looked at the staff nurse and explained the situation to her. Staff nurse smiled at Delia, took her by the arm and said "Come with me, I will take you to Theodore Samson. You see," she started to explain to them, whilst leading them to a section of the hospital that seemed to be very private and out of the way, "because the situation with Theodore was a little tense, the police felt it would be best if he was admitted to the hospital in secret. The less people who knew he was in the hospital, alive, the better for them and for him, which is why his name was not in the register and also why the receptionist could not help her." Delia said she understood and Christine merely nodded in agreement.

When they got to the room where Theo was being kept, his parents were there talking to Detective Hunter and a Doctor, they stopped talking when they saw Delia and her cousin approaching them, led by the Staff nurse. Delia shook hands with Theo's dad and hugged him, telling him how glad she was that Theo had been found at last, he agreed. She looked at him and could see the shadows around his eyes and the presence of the tears that once were, she let him go and went to greet Mrs Samson. Mrs Samson kissed her on her cheek and smiled at her, "He's okay my child," she said to Delia, "just a little dehydrated, tired and a mild infection, but he said he wants to see you as soon as you got here" Delia kissed Mrs Samson and said "Thank You mum, thank you very much."

Chapter Five

    Christine was glad that Theo was safe at last, she wasn't sure how much more of seeing her cousin go through sleepless nights she could take, and if Theo was on the mend then she could go back to work, and try to get some order back in her life, she still had to deal with her problem. Delia turned to her cousin and told her she would not be long, her cousin said "ok" and watched Delia disappear into a room. The curtains were shut, so you could not see what was happening in there, Christine found herself a seat next to Mrs Samson who at this time, had left Delia and had made herself as comfortable as she could while she waited for Delia to come out of the room where her son was resting.

    When Delia entered the room, Theo was lying down and she thought he was asleep, she crept to his bedside and looked at him, her heart beating hard in her chest, and the tears threatening to fall, tears of joy mingled with tears for the way he looked, so battered and bruised. His face was a little black and blue, one of his eyes a little swollen and his nose was bandaged, and a drip attached to his hands. Delia reached out to touch his face, at her touch Theo opened his eyes, he tried to smile at her but he was still in pain, "Hi lady he whispered, why didn't you come when I called you?" "Shhh" said Delia "don't try to talk if its painful," "didn't you hear me calling?" asked Theo, "yes I did said Delia as the tears started to fall, "I heard you, but I could not find you, I looked, but I did not know where to search, but don't worry you're safe now, and I am here ok." "Don't leave me ok, don't go" said Theo as he drifted off to sleep. Delia sat down and she cried, she was feeling ashamed, she knew she could not have done much, but Theo seemed to think that she could have done much more. She had dreamt about him, she had heard his call, but she did not know where to find him. She prayed and thanked God for his safe return and asked him to deal with Kenroy for the torment he had put them through. When she had finished, she kissed him on his forehead and went back to her cousin and Mrs Samson who were waiting for her return.

Michael woke up with a headache; it was almost as if the pain had been waiting for him to go to sleep last night to take hold of him. He felt as if he had been drinking and as a result had a terrible hangover, but he knew that was not the case, it was just lack of sleep and he had not been eating properly since Theo had gone missing.

He had put all his energy into finding his friend, so much so, that he had forgotten about everything else, including food and sleep.

Forcing his eyes open, he focused of the wall clock trying to figure what time of morning it was, it was later than he thought, it was just gone ten am. And he should have been up already. He wanted to go visit Theo's parents and then check on Delia to see how she was and if anything had come up. However, before he could do any of those things, he needed to freshen up and eat some breakfast, he was starving, and his stomach was starting to growl at him. Yawning he got out of bed, cursing his headache and telling his stomach to be silent. Some minutes later he headed

Chapter Five

for the kitchen, dressed in t-shirt and jeans. He was so intent on his breakfast that he did not answer the phone ringing its way off the coffee table; he fried himself some plantain and had them with a cup of hot chocolate. After breakfast was over he decided to phone Delia to find out if she had called, Delia was not at home so he called the Samson's. When Cedric Samson heard Michael on the phone he was glad, because he had been trying to call him but never got an answer. He told Michael Theo had been found, and he was at the hospital if he wanted to see him, but first he would have to see Detective Hunter to clear himself, because they thought that Theo needed protection from Kenroy and his brothers whom the police had not been able to locate as yet.

Michael listened and when Mr Samson had finished telling, him he smiled to himself, because he knew the police would never find the Masters brothers alive, if they found them at all, he had friends in high places, but he did not disclose that piece of information to Theo's Dad.

When they had finished speaking, Michael hung up the phone, picked up his car keys and was just on his way out of the door, when he remembered Greg. He decided to give him a call, letting him know that the police had found Theo. Greg was glad to hear the news, he was also tired from all the searching they had been doing, plus he had to get back to his commitments and his unfinished business with Christine. The friends said goodbye to each other and made an appointment to meet later.

Theodore was sleeping when Michael entered his room at the hospital, drugged, by the pain killers and other tablets he had

Delia's Story

been given, he'd fallen asleep while Delia was with him and had not woken up till now, he opened his eyes to find Michael sitting in a chair nearby watching him, there was no Delia in the room. Lying on his side, his face cushioned by the pillows, he greeted his brother; Michael got up from the chair and went closer to the bed. "Well" he said, "it's good to have you back with us, you gave us all one heck of a time," "brother you know me," said Theo, "always did like to be the centre of attention." "Well then I beg of you please, next time you want to be the centre of attention, try something else ok, you really had us worried man. And those women of yours, well bro, just don't do it again. "You say that as if I planned the whole thing," replied Theo, just wait till I get out of this place; I and those boys have some unfinished business." "Mmm I hear you bro, I hear you," said Michael smiling to himself, "Bro, You know I love you right, so there is no need for you to worry about Kenroy and his brothers, I will take care of them, don't fret. All you need to do is lie back here and get better, plenty people waiting for you out there and we all love you ok, so relax. Theo looked at his brother, he wonder what Michael was hinting at, and said, "Ok, I hear you," they talked for a while, discussing the weather, and what had been happening with the calypso king and the music business. Then Theo looked at Michael and asked him if he had seen Delia when he came by earlier, Michael said, "yes, she was here, but I told her to go home and sleep, she looked tired. I believe she was here all night with you while you slept, she did not want to leave, but I called her cousin, who came and took her home. Don't worry my brother,

Chapter Five

she will be back later," "You really think so?" asked Theo, "Man, I know so," said Michael, "I also know that you are one lucky brother, and if you don't do something about it quick, you are going to be one sorry brother."

Theo started coughing and he put a hand to his head, stroking his temple, "are you in pain?" asked his brother, "Yes, my head hurts, but those pills they make me feel sick. I don't like having to take them" answered Theo, "look if you don't like them and they are making you feel sick, then tell the nurse next time she comes in with your medication, I'm sure they could change it for you." "Yes, you're probably right, but bro, if you'll just excuse me I need to sleep, and with that Theo closed his eyes and went straight to sleep. Michael sat back down and waited for the nurse and for Delia.

The hospital was quiet; it was just after five in the afternoon. Delia entered Theo's room and found him asleep and sitting in the chair was Michael who was also fast asleep. She got a little annoyed at him for sleeping, he should be watching Theo. Suppose she had been Kenroy, what then? She turned and looked at Theo, she smiled, he looked so peaceful in his sleep, and his bruises were fading.

She went over to his bed and stroked his face, he felt Delia's hand, her tender hand stroking his face, he opened his eyes, and smiled at her, he licked his lips, "would you like a drink of water?" She asked him "yes please" he replied. She opened her bag and took out a bottle of cold water she had taken from the fridge at home, it was still icy. She rinsed the glass sitting on the

Delia's Story

little table next to his bed, then poured the water into it, helped him to sit up and gave him to drink. "I needed that," he said, "thank you," "no problem" she answered. Just then, Michael woke up, standing up and going over to where Delia was standing next to the bed, he smiled at his brother and kissed Delia on the cheek.

He said to Theo "I see that you are in good hands, I will leave you now, I have to meet a man about some business," and he left.

Chapter Six

Christine woke up that morning feeling sick. She rushed to the bathroom and threw up in the sink. She did not know what could be wrong with her, she had not eaten anything different yesterday than she normally ate. She wondered at the thought of being pregnant, she had started her period, although she was a week early, she was on her second day, and so what could be the matter with her. She would wait out the next couple of days and see how she felt. She was probably stressed, after that entire problem with Theo and her cousin, plus her own episode which started the ball rolling. If it continued she would have to go see her doctor. She did not mention any of this to Delia, Delia had her own problems to deal with and she, could not put a finger to her own problem so what was she going to say to her cousin. "Oh yeah, Cuz, "I think I might be pregnant, I'm not sure, because I am seeing my period at the moment, oh, and I threw up this morning," nope she would not say a word to anyone just as yet, Christine got herself ready and went to work.

Delia was not home, she had been spending time in the hospital, playing nurse to Theo, which was good because it kept her occupied and made her happy.

Delia's Story

Greg had just pulled up outside the Cable and Wireless building where they both worked. At the same time as Christine, he got out of his car and pretended to ignore her, walking toward the entrance of the building, then stopping and barring her way just as she approached the door, arms folded across his chest and leaning against the doorpost. "So are you going to put me out of my misery?" he asked, there was a hint of sarcasm in the way he asked the question, but serious enough for her to know he was wasn't joking, "Look, it's not that I mean to be difficult, I just..." "I know, I know," said Greg, "you just need time to make me suffer some more, making it quite clear that all my intention to have you back in my home, where I can have you to my mercy is fruitless" she felt embarrassed. "There's no need for you to try making me feel bad," she answered sharply. "Look all I am trying to do is get some sort of semblance in my life, I thought I had it with you, but you opened my eyes to another point of view, so." "I know what you're trying to say, so let's leave it at that for now shall we?" said Greg as he turned abruptly, pulling the door open and walking off, he was in the building before Christine had time to say anymore to him.

"Wonderful, she thought first, the vomiting and now Greg, I wonder what's next, and they say it happens in three's. Christine pulled the door open and entered the building making her way straight to her office, praying she did not meet with Greg again for the day. Although after that scene, she doubted if he would ever talk to her again, which was ok with her for the time being, exactly what she wanted in fact, but it didn't make her feel any

Chapter Six

better, when she thought about it, in fact she was starting to feel depressed.

Greg wasn't as angry as he was upset; he had promised himself to be good to Christine if he ever saw her again. Sure he missed her, he missed hearing her laughter, the way she frowned when she concentrated on something and he would wipe it away with a kiss, she would laugh and kiss him away. Her smooth and beautiful, brown skin. Yes! He missed her, but still, he had not expected her to keep him dangling like a puppet on a string. He was the one who usually set the rules, he had not been interested in a long-term relationship with anyone after Delia, and he guarded his space and his privacy. He should feel relieved that she wanted some space, but somehow Christine had gotten under his skin and he could not shake her off, he did not want to shake her off, he wanted her by his side.

That's an awfully looking glum expression on your face Greg, said the receptionist to him as he approached her desk for his worksheet. "What's the matter, turn you down did she?" Greg laughed, "I was just being friendly as any good neighbour should," "so you didn't score then, never mind." Greg could hear the laughter as he walked away from the desk and made up his mind to keep to himself in future. When Christine decided she wanted to communicate with him she would have to make the move.

On the way home from work, Christine debated whether she should stop at Greg's and apologise for this morning. If she saw his car then she would knock, she didn't want to be a nuisance or nothing. She felt a little embarrassed and she did not want him to get the wrong impression about what she wanted from him especially after what happened the last time she was at his house.

Her problem was solved for her, as she approached Greg's house she noticed his car was not there, so she made her way home.

Theo had been in the hospital for a week and healing nicely. The drip had been taken out of his arm and Delia had been spending most of her time with him, she had employed extra help to work in the garden. On the sixth day in the hospital, Theo's temperature has risen sky high and he had at terrible fever. The doctor said it was probably too much excitement, ever since Theo had been admitted to the hospital; his bedside has never been empty. His parents came in every day, and stayed for most of the twenty-four hours, with the privilege of coming and going as they pleased. Delia was classed as family so she was tarred with the same brush. It seemed that Theo was a much loved young man, although the police wanted his stay in the hospital to be kept as quiet as possible, it seemed the family was making sure he was never left unattended.

Theo had been given some medication to bring down his temperature and had fallen asleep. Everyone had gone home except Delia, who was always the last one to leave his bedside. The light in the room was not very bright, so she could not read

Chapter Six

the book she had brought along for company at times like these, it was very quiet in the room except for Theo's raspy breathing.

Somewhere in the middle of the night, Delia heard her name being called, she had fallen asleep in the chair and Theo was calling to her. She got up and went to him. He was sitting up in bed and pouring with sweat, she found his towel and dried him, and then she changed his pyjamas. While all this was happening to him, Theo just sat there looking at her, she propped up his pillows and as she finished, he took hold of her hands, looking at her he said, "Come and lay down next to me." She looked at him, shook her head and said "That's not a good idea, you know that, but I will sit with you for a while, or at least till you fall asleep, ok." "No, that's not ok, but lay down with me then till I fall asleep, it will help chase away the bad dream I keep having," Delia wondered if he was exaggerating a little but said "ok, but only till you fall asleep."

Delia stripped down to her knickers and bra, she knew that getting into bed with Theo was a bad idea, but if it helped him to sleep then here goes, she said to herself. Theo pulled her closer to him and wrapped his arms around her, making her his prisoner and burying his face in her hair. It wasn't long before she felt something nudging her thighs, she was getting hot and she was feeling horny. Theo was nibbling on her earlobe and making his way down her neck, showering her neck with kisses, his hands, one holding her ever so gently, cupping her left breast with the other. She wanted to turn and face him, but she thought better of it, if she did there would be no stopping him, she would be powerless to do so. As if reading her mind, Theo turned Delia around to face him, he was smiling at her She could not resist, she just wanted to have him make love to her, here and now. She did not care about nothing else at that moment, but the man in the bed next to her, she wanted to feel his passion.

He leaned forward and kissed her on the tip of her nose, he kissed her eyes, her cheeks and then he kissed her on the lips and she melted. She was under his control and she let him lead her where he would, his hands roving and searching, tantalising her senses, her body was screaming for him, then he found her pleasure place. His fingers they stroked, they searched and they teased, Delia leaned towards him, moaning, begging, kissing, wanting, and needing more her hands reached down and took matters into her own hand. Theo got the message, he turned her around, with her back facing him, drawing the lower half of her body closer to him, his fingers playing with her pleasure zone, she was wet, soaking wet. Delia wriggled and giggled her body in the bed, she was ready and wanting, she arched her back towards him. Theo felt her passion. Then with a gentle thrust he was in heaven, a place he had so longed to be; his hardness into her wetness, forever under her spell. Delia felt as if she had died and gone to heaven, the way she felt when she had first made love to Greg had been the greatest thing in her life, which was what she thought at the time. Now she knew better, this was it, this is the kind of thing that spoils it for others, after Theo there will be no other. This is totally correct, oh Theo, my sweet love, I did not realise until now how much I missed you, so long she'd wanted this, oh so long

Chapter Six

waiting, finally at last after all that time. Muscles acting like suction, clenching and unclenching, holding on then letting go, juices flooding her walls, he was not sure how much more of it he could take, he wanted her to enjoy herself as much as he was, he wanted this to be the best moment of their lives, he could hear her whispering his name, oh he wanted to come, to fill her up with his juice and give her his baby.

When eventually they were done, Theo stayed in the same position; the two of them joined as one and fell asleep. She had fallen asleep after him with a smile on her face.

Delia woke up and got dressed, just in time before the morning staff came in to administer Theo's his medication and check his temperature. It seemed his temperature had dropped and he was much better. Delia smiled to herself as she thought of what had gone on in the night; she wasn't really surprised to hear what the nurse had to say.

Two days later, the doctor said it was fine for Theo to go home, he was well enough, his condition was no longer critical, in fact he simply needed to eat some home cooked food and take things easy for the first couple of days, but if he had any problems he could see his doctor.

The streets were adorned with banners welcoming the Magician, wishing him love and blessings, his music was being played on

Delia's Story

every street corner, the television stations was broadcasting the return of the magician the radio's stations were celebrating the return of the magician, well wishers in and out of the family home. A party was held for him at the Young hotel in town, he was a little tired but he could not let down the people, they wanted to let him know how much he was loved, but there was always the questions, everybody wanted to know who did it, why they did it, what happen to them and everyone had their own answers. All his friends were there, his parents, they had fun and when finally he had had enough, he gave a little thank you speech and then departed.

Theo was glad; he could finally get back into some decent clothes and have a proper shower. No nurses watching over him, and he had things long overdue, to take care off. He needed to spend more time with Delia. He smiled and thought how pleasurable a woman she was, he wanted more of her. He might have been in a fever the night it happened but the memory of it played over and again in his head and his smile got broader.

Three days later Theo was on a plane to the states, he had not seen Delia since he had been discharged from the hospital but had spoken to her. Seems she was busy with work after spending so much of her time with him at the hospital. She had spent so much time away from her business so she had to make sure everything was in order, make sure the plants were growing properly and the weeds had to be sprayed, to prevent them from growing and becoming a nuisance.

Chapter Six

She had said to him on the last day that she was sorry he had to fly away so soon, but it was inevitable, he had another life to take care of and he must get back to it. They had discussed the matter, he had even asked her if she could fly over to the states to join him, but she had said, it was impossible, she had her own affair in Dominica to take care o;, she couldn't just up and leave. Neither of them could find a way to ease the situation and so he had gone and she would have to get on without him for a while.

Delia had accepted the fact that she would be alone again, she was not sure how long before she saw Theo again, but she knew she would eventually. The only thing that bothered Delia was the night of passion in the hospital, neither one of them had spoken about it; it was as if it had never happened, just a dream. She wondered if Theo had been so delirious that night, that he had no memory of it happening, but she just kept playing it over, and over in her head. They had not taken any precaution and Theo had been in his fever. Perhaps she ought to go check the Doctor just to make sure everything was all right with her.

Delia decided she would discuss it with her cousin when she got the opportunity; Christine had started work again and would often come home late especially since Delia herself had been otherwise occupied.

Delia's Story

Chapter Seven

Early in the morning of the second day of his arrival back in the states, there was a knock at Theo's door; he wondered whom it could be knocking so early, he had not reported his return to work or anyone else. It was Wanda, she was the last person he wanted to see right now. All smiles and questions, dressed for jogging, she brushed past him and entered the apartment. He dared not try guessing at what she wanted, but he would be polite. Theo shut the door behind her and smiled to himself, he knew she was here to find out if he had found someone new or if she still had a chance, but no chance, she did not have a leg to stand on. She was history. "So exactly what was it you wanted?" he asked her. "Oh nothing, just popped by to see how you were after your visit to the islands," she answered, as she continued to make herself comfortable. "Did you bring me back a mango or anything?" "No I did not bring you back anything," he said. "So what did you do out there then, how was the carnival?" "The carnival was fine." "So did you terrorise the women, meet anyone special?" "Not that it's any of your business, but yes, I met someone." "Special is she?" asked Wanda. "Like I told you before, it really is none of your business, in fact if you don't mind I am really very busy at this time, so do you mind if we do this another time, perhaps never?" "So that's the way it is, is it? You

Chapter Seven

want me to leave? I came by to see my friend, find out a little about his holiday and he throws me out," she said, looking at him with sadness in her eyes. "I get the message, but we're still friends right?" she asked. "Just as long as you remember that, anyway I really need some time alone so if you don't mind," he said all at once, and opened the front door for her. She did not question him anymore, she could see he was serious, so she left him to his space, wishing him well as she did so.

     Wanda was a little surprised at Theo, she thought his manner a bit abrupt, and she had hoped that on his return he might have reconsidered about her and the fun they used to have. However it seemed she had wasted her time, Theo was not interested in having any relationship with her and if she had not know it before, she knew it now.

Two weeks later Christine decided to get in touch with Greg. The morning sickness had continued and gotten worse so she'd made an arrangement to see her Doctor, who, after examining her, testing her urine and taking a sample of her blood for further tests, told her she was going to be a mum. Christine was a bit shocked; she did not know what to say to the Doctor, because he asked her, "Aren't you pleased with the news?" "I don't know" she answered, "I'm not sure if I want to be a Mum, you see, it's a bit complicated at the moment." "What, having trouble with the partner? Asked the Doctor. "Yes something like that" she answered. "Look why don't you just talk to him, babies are a blessing. He might like the idea of being a dad, and does he have any other children?" "No! He doesn't have any children," she told the doctor. "Anyway I will go and see him and take it from there." "Yes that's the best way to begin, the baby might bring you some good fortune, oh and make an appointment with the nurse at the desk as you go out. See you in a couple of weeks, bye for now." Christine said bye and left the Doctor's surgery, her mind full of questions and answers she already knew. She knew he would be happy about the baby, but she also knew that it would mean the end of her own independence. Greg would want her where he could see her, he would want to take charge and she did not want it that way, plus a lot of other stuff like her cousin Delia; yes, she had to speak to Greg.

She was about one month pregnant if she calculated properly, carnival was a month ago and that was the last time she had had sex with Greg. She had known about the pregnancy for a week now and had taken that long to decide after sleepless nights of tossing and turning. She'd even started having bad dreams about telling her cousin. She was sure her cousin knew about her being pregnant, she hadn't said anything and Christine hadn't told her anything; it was just the way her cousin kept looking at her especially when she thought she wasn't looking. How could she tell Delia she was pregnant with Greg's baby, Greg who was once married to Delia; she had to speak to him, she needed to know how he felt and then she would know what to say to Delia.

Chapter Seven

Greg was surprised to get the call from Christine. It was two weeks since they had last spoken and if truth be told, he thought it would have been a no win situation with her. He was even more baffled when she suggested he meet with her somewhere neutral, not at his home.

They met at the Fort Young Hotel, a Victorian building situated at the seafront in town, Christine was already settled at the bar when Greg arrived, she, was sipping on orange juice. Greg noticed the orange juice and thought it strange for Christine to be drinking orange juice, she must be ill or something that's why she asked to meet with him. Christine watched him as he got closer, her heart thumping at the sight of him, how she loved him, but she would never say those words to him. Greg sat down on the stool next to the bar where she was. "So to what do I owe the pleasure of your call?" he asked her. Without even giving thoughts to first saying hello, "I'm pregnant," she told him. She had decided to tell him straight, there wasn't going to be any beating around the bush, but she wasn't quite prepared for the way he flew out of his seat, not paying any attention to anyone in the place, as they stared at him and his sudden outburst in their quiet surroundings. He growled at her, "What do you mean you're pregnant?" "What do you mean, what do I mean, I said I am pregnant" she told him again. "So ok then, if you are pregnant and you wanted to tell me about it why choose this place, why the public setting, why choose this blasted place to tell? Why couldn't we do this at my house, we have done everything else there so why not this?" he asked, getting angrier by the minute, "Because I felt it would be better

Delia's Story

this way," she answered, but now she was thinking perhaps it was not such a good idea judging by his obvious displeasure.

People were staring at them, and Greg was staring at her as if trying to decide on his next move, "Come on," he said to her, grabbing at her wrist. "Come on to where, where are we going?" she asked him as he literally pulled her of her stool. "Where are we going to?" "Where we should have gone in the first place, we're going to my house" he told her, as he none too gently lead them to his car parked in the hotel's car park. It was the best news he had had for the longest time. He was going to be a father again after such a long time, but he wished Christine had chosen a different way and place to tell him about it.

When they got to his place he asked her if she would like a drink, she declined the offer so he got straight to the point, "Ok so how far gone are you with this pregnancy?" he asked, "About a month or so" she told him, "So how is it, that I'm only finding out about it now? He asked. "Because I wasn't sure how you would take the news, and I only just found out myself," she told him. "What do you mean you weren't sure how I would take it? Since when did I turn into such an animal Chris? You could not talk to me, you could not tell me about the baby before. I mean it is my baby right? He asked her. Christine was starting to feel guilty, he was sounding very hurt. She knew she had nothing to be guilty of; it was only common practice to accept the news before she could have told him, especially since things weren't the same as before.

Chapter Seven

But he was getting way off line with his anger. "Look," she said "if you're going to start talking rubbish to me about whose baby is it, then we should just forget we ever had this conversation and I will see you whenever."

Christine picked up her bag and headed for the door, Greg stopped her and apologised for his madness "You are the most infuriating woman I have ever had the pleasure of meeting since Delia," he told her. "You are not leaving this house until we have finished discussing my child." "No Greg, our child," she said correcting him.

She sat back down and Greg followed suit. There were tears in his eyes, she was not sure if they were tears of joy or what. "So what's the matter?" she asked him, "Why are you crying? He wiped the tears away, he could not tell her he was crying for his dead children, and how he missed them even now..

After they had buried the twins, he had promised himself never to impregnate another woman again, if he could help it. He had loved the twins more that his life, and when they died, his world had died along with them. Now he was going to have the opportunity again. God knew best, he was happy about being given a second chance. But how was Delia going to feel about it? He was worried because he knew how broken she was when the twins died. How was she going to cope with the fact that her cousin was going to be the mother of his child? He wasn't sure about that one; there was something he had to do. It was time to go and pay his ex wife a visit.

Delia's Story

Greg put Delia at the back of his mind and turned back to Christine, who was sitting there, looking worried about the tears. He told her he was crying because he was happy, but the only thing that was bothering him now was Christine herself. Ok, so she is pregnant with his child, but where did that leave them? "So what do you want from me Christine?" he asked her. "What do you mean?" she asked. "Well you are having my baby, so are we in a relationship or am I just the baby's daddy" he replied. "I don't know, I would like us to be in a relationship, but not just because we're having this child, but because we want to be in one and there's no chance of me coming here and finding another woman in the place, unless it's your mother and since there won't be no chance of that, you know where I stand. "Fine, said Greg, no other woman in the place, that one is too easy and just to prove it to you here, take this" he said, as he placed the keys for the house in her hands, "that way you won't have to worry too much, you can always let yourself in, this is also your home." Christine took the keys from him, and then making some excuse about the time, she left him and went home to her cousin.

After Christine had gone Greg sat down thinking about Delia, he still loved his ex wife, he would always love his ex wife. There was not a woman in this world who could move him like Delia, but he also knew that because of their past, there was never any chance of them getting back together again. The pain they shared was too much, so he had played around after the divorce, travelled to the islands, went back to England, never staying one place for too long, but he knew why that was. He had followed

Chapter Seven

Delia back to the island, but she never knew that, something in him needed to be close to her wherever she was. When he first met her cousin, it was just sex, but she seemed to possess some of Delia's qualities and it made the attraction much more sincere.

He was still in love with his ex wife, he still missed her sometimes in the cold of the night, how she felt in his arms, her body perfume, but he could never turn back the hand of time. He loved Christine, she made him laugh and she might not be Delia but she was enough and she loved him, he knew that. She might not say the words but he could see it in her eyes.

Greg knew he had to speak to Delia without Christine's knowledge, not that it mattered if she knew because eventually, she would find out, but he preferred if she found out later rather than sooner. He needed to speak to his ex wife alone so that they could bury the hatchet, if his relationship with Christine was going to work. "Man, why does life have to be so complicated?" said Greg to himself. He waited a few days before calling on Delia. He wanted to make sure that Christine was well out of the way.

One morning when he was sure that Christine was at work and Delia was alone he made his move. He didn't even bother to phone, he drove to Goodwill and just as he pulled up outside her house, she was about to leave the house for the garden dressed in her dungarees and an old pair of trainers. "If you're looking for Christine then I am sorry to tell you she is not here at the moment," she told him as he approached her on the stairs. Greg smiled at his ex wife, "I actually came here to see you." "Me? What could you possible want to see me about? I didn't think we had anything left to say to each other," she said to him." "Well, I came to see you because I thought it was time for us to learn to be civil to each other. We owe that to ourselves and the children we once shared." Delia did not answer; she tried to pretend she had no interest in what he was saying. "Delia please we were not always like this, we loved each other once very much, if I remember correctly, and if only for the sake of that love and the memory of what we had." "Cha man, who sent you to bother me so early in the day; if I knew today was going to start like this, I would have stayed in bed."

Greg laughed, it was one of the things he remembered about Delia back in England, how she made him laugh, "Ok, husband, if you want me to I will listen, but you, you will have to follow me to work." "No problem wifey, no problem at all, you lead, and I will follow." Greg thanked GOD under his breath, because he knew how stubborn this woman could be once she set her mind to it, past experiences had taught him that.

Delia was still wondering what her darling ex husband could possibly want from her; perhaps he was seeking her forgiveness, but why now, what was he up to, well she would find out soon enough.

Soon enough they got to the garden Delia got out of her pickup and started unloading her plants and seedlings for planting. Greg came up to her and offered her his assistance, which she accepted. Finally the unloading was done. Delia told Greg she was

Chapter Seven

ready to listen to what he had to say, and offered him a drink, which he accepted, as she prepared to listen. "So speak to me Greg, what is it you want to talk to me about," she said to him, finding to herself that he was taking long to start, after he had taken such a giant step in coming to find her. "Well I don't quite know where to start," he said. "The beginning is always a good place, I mean you must have had an idea of topic before you came to see me, so that's probably the way you should go," she replied. "Okay, first of all, I want to apologise to you for not being there for you when you needed me the most. I was so caught up in my own grief; I didn't recognise you or your pain. I know it was very selfish of me especially as they were our children so I apologise for that. "Ok, said Delia, "What's second?" "Secondly, he continued as if she had not spoken, "I would like to ask you if it is possible for us to try to be civil to each other." "You know something Greg," she said, "it puzzles me that after all this time, we've been doing our own thing and you not giving a damn about whether I was alive or dead, why suddenly would you want to come to me wanting to apologise and be asking that we be civil to each other. What is all this about Greg? And please don't bullshit me, I'm too old for your foolishness." Greg looked at her and wished he'd thought more about this; he was not enjoying the way she was sitting there looking at him. He remembered that look only too well, the look that told him to be very careful what you say mister or else.

  He cleared his throat "Your cousin is pregnant with my child," he said looking her straight in the eyes. Delia frowned,

Delia's Story

"My cousin? Which cousin? Is pregnant with your child?" She hissed at him. "Your cousin Christine" he answered. "I must be in the twilight zone," said Delia, "this is not for real, why my cousin?" There were tears in her eyes and she brushed them away not caring if he noticed or not. "My cousin Christine is pregnant with your baby?" "Yes," said Greg, "and I thought I should tell you about it so that she would not have to lie to you." "So my cousin is having your baby, repeated Delia, "keeping it a bit closer aren't you lover, when did this all happen?" she asked him. "It's like this, we work at the same place and we started having lunch together. At first she was reluctant to begin with because of you, but then things mellowed out and we started seeing each other outside of work. We found we liked each other's company and now she is pregnant," he told her. "Anyway, I could not have you back is it? You wouldn't have me back if I wanted, and I like your cousin; what's wrong with your cousin?" Delia was looking at him with a strange puzzled look on her face, he was starting to feel uncomfortable, why was she looking at him like that? "So tell me Greg she said, are you the reason why my cousin got raped by that filth Kenroy? Are you the man she caught cheating on her? Tell me Greg are you?" Greg's mouth went dry, he hadn't realised that Delia knew about his infidelity, he did not like the way she was blaming him for her cousin getting raped though, not one bit. "I suppose you could say I was the one she caught in bed with another woman yes but, as for the rapist, well, the only place he will be doing any more raping is hell," he said with anger in his voice. "Ooo, Ooo, what do you mean? Tell me more, she asked

Chapter Seven

him, don't stop now." "Don't worry about what I just said, it's of no importance, but as for myself and Christine..." "No Greg," cut in Delia, "you will tell me what you meant about the rapist and hell. I want to know." "There is some things you should not know love," he told her smiling, "so leave it alone ok." "Nope, you will tell me and you will tell me now. If this has anything to do with you and my cousin having a relationship, then I have a right to know and you will tell me." "Wow I didn't know you cared," he answered with a touch of sarcasm in his voice. "Listen Greg, you are beginning to piss me off; before you cause me to sin, quit stalling and start talking" said Delia, who at this time was in no mood for foolishness from him, and he could see that in her eyes. "Kenroy is dead, he and his two brothers all dead but not buried" he told her. "Yes, but how did they die and when?" she asked impatiently. "Come on Greg, talk to me; you wanted to talk and I am listening."

"Okay, you remember when the magician went missing? Well, his brother Michael came to me and told me about it because he needed my help. I agreed to help him because we go back a long way. When Michael told me about the woman getting raped by Kenroy, he'd said her name was Christine, but I did not think anything of it. Then he started talking about Delia and I said to myself it was too much of a coincidence, Delia and Christine had to be you and your cousin. I was already feeling bad about Christine finding me in a compromising situation, but then you were mentioned, I simply lost my senses, so I offered Michael my help in the hope of finding this Kenroy person. I know this might sound a bit warped to you but something inside me snapped when I heard you had been victimised by that filth. I felt it my duty to do something about it and so I did. The brothers died in a house fire, their house that is, and Kenroy had an accident of a cliff hanging kind,"

"What's a cliff hanging kind of accident Greg?" asked Delia, who had been hanging on to every word he had just spoken. "He and his bus went over the side of a cliff with a little help from yours truly." "And Michael was with you all the time when all of it was happening?" she asked. "Yes, he was," answered Greg. "But this is all too much, you just killed three people and you are all right with yourself and Michael too, wow," she said shaking her head. "Oh and Delia, said Greg " nobody know about this, it was for a just cause ok, I mean look at what they did, rape abduction never mind the stress it caused everyone, yeah man they deserved it, so this is just between me and you right, husband and wife secret ok? Christine doesn't have to know any of what I just told you and neither does the magician. She asked him "Does this mean Christine doesn't know you know she was raped?" "What do you think?" he answered, "Yes Greg I get your drift, your secret is safe with me."

By the time they were finished talking, it was way past lunch so Delia decided to stop for the day, storing away her wares she thanked Greg for making her day so very interesting. She told him she had forgiven him for the past and hoped his relationship with her cousin lasted, and then she kissed him on both cheeks to prove to him that she meant everything she had just told him.

Chapter Seven

Then each got into their own vehicle and headed back to town. On parting, Greg told her he would be in touch. She told him to feel free to drop by anytime, he had earned that privilege. Greg smiled and thanked her as he headed west towards Princess Margarette Street, whilst Delia turned east and headed home to Goodwill.

     She still could not quite believe all what she had been told today and yes it was unfortunate Greg and Michael had not found Theo, but the police had and he was now safe in the States. The Masters' brothers however, had not been so fortunate. They had messed with the wrong people, wanting to be wrong and strong, but God doesn't sleep she told herself, and no one would never hear that story from her lips not even Christine or Theo for that matter; it was between her and her ex husband.

Christine came home to find good mood music playing in the house and the smell of baking wafting its way up her nostrils from the kitchen; she could taste it. Her cousin was baking her favourite biscuits, chocolate and coconut chip. She thought her cousin must really be happy. Christine went into the kitchen; Delia was so preoccupied with what she was doing, she only noticed her cousin when she kissed her on her cheek. "Hi Cuz" said Delia "how was your day?" "My day was fine," answered Christine, but not as good as yours obviously, the way things are looking, are we expecting someone?" "No, why?" asked Delia. "Well you're so happy, and it's a long time since I've seen you this happy" her cousin replied. "You're being silly, said Delia, "I'm always happy. But if you must know, I received some interesting news today and it elated me so much I had to do some baking, I might do some writing later, but please Cuz, don't ask me to tell you what it was I heard. I'm not allowed to repeat it, okay." "Okay," said Christine, "well if you will excuse me, I am going to my room to change."

Delia returned to her singing and baking while Christine went to her room to phone Greg. She was a little upset that her cousin could not share her secret with her, she figured Greg must have spoken to her cousin about the pregnancy and made her promise not to tell, so she would phone him to find out.

The phone rang once and went straight to the voice mail; ten minutes later she tried again, this time he answered. "Hi Chris, how are you today and what's up?" "Have you spoken to Delia today?" she asked him. "Why do you ask" he answered, "well! Said Christine, "I've just got in from work and she's in the kitchen singing and baking. When I asked her why she's in such a happy state, she said to me that someone told her something today, but she's not allowed to repeat it and when my cousin says she can't repeat, then she won't repeat." "Well that's a good thing isn't it, but yes I did speak to her today. I told her about the pregnancy and explained the problem, and she' fine with it." Christine was overjoyed, "She's fine with me having your baby?" "Yes Chris," said Greg, "she's fine with it." Christine said bye to Greg and placed the receiver in its cradle. She changed her clothes and went to join her cousin in the kitchen.

Chapter Eight

Time passed, Christine was in the fourth month of her pregnancy and was showing. She was loving every moment of it; her shape was fuller, her breasts were getting bigger the morning sickness had passed and Greg was spoiling her rotten. Delia remembered when she was the one being spoilt by Greg, with his lavish gifts and loving attention, she was happy for her cousin. Delia rubbed her stomach and caught herself just in time, in case she drew any attention to herself. Her mind went on to Theo and she wondered what he would be like as an expecting father. She had spoken to him earlier on that day, asking him if he knew when he would be back on the island. He'd said that Christmas might be possible, but he would have to make sure, since Christmas time always seemed to be the busiest time of the year for Hollins & Hollins, Solicitors Extraordinaire. She was in two minds about seeing him again; one part of her ached for his touch, his warm embrace, to feel his hot breath on her body, just to hold him. Mmm she thought; but the other half of her wasn't in any great rush to see him. He might find out about the secret she had been keeping from everyone, something she was keeping to herself. She knew it would have to come out eventually, but in the meantime it was her secret, her pregnancy, hers alone and she would enjoy it.

Delia's Story

Delia knew it would be a great hullabaloo when they found out about it, so she decided she would go away for a while, visit one of her aunts on one of the other islands and figure out the situation. She would leave Christine in charge of her business with Greg to help her. She knew the two of them could run the business all they had to do was follow the instructions she gave them and it would be extra income for them with a baby to take care of.

Theo was having the time of his life back in the States, partying every weekend starting from Thursday all the way to Sunday; then he would get up and go to work, back to the daily humdrum of being an accountant. He was missing Delia badly and partying was his own personal way of dealing with it. He had spoken to her recently; he spoke to her most nights and sometimes in the mornings. He was missing her so much that he was having nightmares of never seeing her again. Sometimes the dreams were vibrant with their lovemaking, and that would just make matters worse for him. He wondered how she was coping with his absence. Had she gone back to her gardening? Was she seeing someone else? He knew his thought were just idle thoughts, something to torture himself with, he could not help it. He knew what a beautiful woman she was and was sure that other men could see it. He was tired of city life; he needed some more country in his blood. He was feeling the stress that city life brings, he needed an outlet, he needed something, and he needed Delia. She could calm the beast in him, she with her magic spell, that she

Chapter Eight

had woven about him so well, bounded by her charm and that body of hers, they fitted perfectly; a complete one. He needed to stop torturing himself like this. The only way he could do that was as he was doing now, work and party, but he would have to cut down on the partying, it was beginning to take its toll on his stomach, he was bulging a bit. He should start going to the gym again, that would help and definitely cut down on those microwave dinners he has taken a shine to recently. He had gotten lazy, he used to cook for himself, but since he was so busy wallowing in his self pity he could not find the drive for cooking anymore; there was always the Chinese takeaway or pizza hut to feed himself with.

There had been times when he had been tempted to call on Wanda, to help him ease some of his more animal pressures, but that had only been because he knew how easy it would be to call on her. How easily it would have been manipulating her into his way of thinking, just in case she tried to refuse. She was easy bait, and he had had enough of easy bait. He wanted something lasting and hard to get; he had found that something with Delia, even though he had taken advantage of her generous nature back in the hospital on the island. It had occurred to him whilst he was lying on the hospital bed, that after leaving the island and going back to the States, he might never get the opportunity to taste the fruits of Delia's labour, the spell she had woven so well, without realising. He knew she would never let him make love to her under that condition, that was probably why he had that fever. It had been tormenting his mind, and so he used his feverish state to get Delia into his bed. It had not been an easy job; she did it only because she wanted to help him, and help him she did, more than she could have realised. He finally admitted to himself, He brought himself face to face with the man in the mirror, told himself the truth, that it was not the sex after all, there was something about Delia, she was a woman of substance and he could gladly put his life in her hands, she could do all that was expected of a woman, she was gentle as a dove and just as beautiful, she made him feel complete even though more often than not he would make a fool of himself, but she allowed him to be himself and she laughed with him not at him. She was the perfect woman for him he really was not interested in playing around, and there was so much more to discover about her. Wanda was just part of him denying how he felt about Delia, Sex was just an excuse, he's been pierced by Cupid's arrow and it had Delia's name on it. Now he needed a fix, and she was the hit, but she wasn't anywhere close by, she was over there, back on the island.

Wanda sat sipping on a white rum on the rocks and smoking a joint, watching him from the balcony across the street. She had been watching him quite a while now; she wanted to be closer to him and had changed her address while he was on holiday. She wanted to see whom it was about to replace her in his life, since he was no longer interested in her, since he had decided that what they had was no longer sufficient to keep him, but he was wrong. She wanted him then at the party, and she wanted him now, even

Chapter Eight

more than ever. What? Did he think he could just break off the relationship without discussing it with her? After she, had given him so much of her time and body. She thought they had a good thing going on, she could not see why they should not still be together. What was wrong with some men, why are they never satisfied, why do they go around making whores of women? Why do they have to treat us women as if we are listed down somewhere as a case of Use and Discard when what might seem better comes along. However, if and when we women do what they do what they do, we are classed as the lowest of the species. She was not going to make this easy for Theo, she would find a way to make him pay for the hurt, oh but how she wished he would call and ask if it was ok for him to come on over. She knew what time he left the apartment in the morning, what time he got to work on the best of days, what time he had lunch, what he had for lunch; she was in check with most of his local jaunts. She had taken up wearing wigs and different colour hairpieces, altering her appearance so that she could be in the same place as Theo, without him noticing her.

She had noticed that since coming back from his holiday, he has been quite the bachelor, keeping his pants to himself, although on the odd occasion he looked as if he was tempted to touch, but that was short lived. He treated her like a stranger whenever their paths should cross and that really pissed her off, sometimes she thought about having him killed or crippled, then she could be his nurse, be the one to look after him, be there for him in his time of need and then he would have no choice, but to be grateful enough to keep her in his life; that thought lasted only a short time. She picked up her binoculars that were lying next to the rum; she sipped on her drink. She could see him better with the help of her binoculars that she purchased for this said purpose. Lost in her little world she could see him walking around his apartment naked, not a stitch of clothing. The stomach bulge he was getting from all the fast food and beer was not that bad, but if he carried on god alone knows what he would look like. His manhood was slapping his thighs as he walked, looking firm and ready for some action. She could taste him. Wanda touched herself as she felt the hunger for him rise at the pit of her stomach and the throbbing between her thighs, but he was unaware of all this happening, unaware of her spying eyes, as he sat down sprawled on his settee to watch television. She played with herself as she watched him and imagined it was he.

The shrill of the phone made her jump, and brought her out of her quest at hand. She entered the apartment through sliding doors to answer the call. It was her work place, wanting to know when she would be well enough to come back to work. Saying they were short staffed and she has been sick for the past two weeks. Now they were curious to know if she still needed the job. Wanda was looking a little worst for the wear, she had given up taking care of herself as she used to, she would just sit and mope, mourning for Theo as though mourning for a dead loved one, never to see him again even though he lived just across the road,

Chapter Eight

and as time passed she got worse, she had given up caring, her world had ended. Wanda lied and told them that she had to see the doctor again the following day and she would let them know the results as soon as she got it. The voice on the phone said ok, Wanda said goodbye and placed the phone back in its cradle and went back to the balcony to continue her observation of Theodore Samson. She was feeling the need for him badly.

He was not there; he was nowhere to be seen. She searched frantically, readjusting the lens on the binoculars, but still no sign of him. She jumped up from where she sat, ran back into the apartment and headed for the telephone. She called his number... no answer; she called it again and again... still no answer. She called his place of work. The receptionist told her that he was not available and would not be available for the next couple of weeks, perhaps she would like to call back then.

    Wanda cursed her bad luck and slammed down the phone. She hurried to her bedroom and threw on the first thing she laid her hands on, which happened to be a pair of black track-suit, which were laid at the foot of her bed, along with trainers and sunshades. She finger combed her hair and headed for the front door, slamming it shut before realising that her front door keys were still inside on the coffee table. She did not give a damn, she was interested only in finding Theodore she told herself sternly, as she stepped through the swinging door onto the pavement, sniffing the cool air and wondered which direction she should

Delia's Story

take. She looked left and decided to go right. After all, knowing the kind of business minded person he was and since coming back from the island, he had been looking so lost and lonely, not the lively person she used to know, he might have headed for the main part of the city, gone to the bank or even the travel agents. Yes, that was it, he must have gone right, he might be thinking of taking another trip to the island to be with his new love. Why else would he take time from work, after he only just got back to work... yes that had to be it. So right she continued and headed for the city.

Delia was standing in the reception area of the Canfield Airport, passport in hand and one medium sized suitcase at her side, another ten minutes and she would be boarding the Liat Airplane standing out there on the airfield waiting to take her to her destination, she would be spending some time in a non descript little village called Port of Panic, in St Thomas with her aunt Eugene and family for a while. She had explained the situation to her aunt, who then made preparations for Delia to come and spend some time with her. Delia was glad. No work, just the pleasure of relaxation and enjoying my secret, she thought to herself. Plenty of time to find an explanation for everyone concerned when she got back.

Christine had been overjoyed at Delia's proposal for her to take over the business while she was away. She had been a bit dubious and quarrelsome about her cousin wanting to leave the

Chapter Eight

island, but when Delia told her that their aunt wanted her to spend some time with the family in Port of Panic, she relented. Time spent in Port of Panic did a lot of good for Delia. She had not spoken to Christine in a while and she was soon due to have the baby. Delia did not relish the idea of going back home just now. She would have to find a way to tell her cousin the bad news. Christine would be furious with her, she might not even want to speak to her again, but she would deal with it.

The sun was shining brightly, with a gentle breeze blowing amongst the trees. Delia went and sat under a mango tree growing at the side of her aunt's house. Her aunt was outside hanging out the washing on the line that linked from the house to a guava tree standing nearby, laden with fruits yellow, red and green, different colours of ripeness, waiting for someone to come along and ease it of its heavy load.

Delia loved her aunt and family very much, Jasper and Gavin, twins aged 17, and Uncle Jones, her husband. They were a very loving family, you could feel the love as you entered into the house. She remembered one morning she went to the kitchen and found her aunt and uncle in each other's arms kissing, and had broken away when they noticed her standing there. There was nothing they would not do for each other, and she was included in that. Delia remembered when she first got here, the family would not let her raise a finger to help with the housework. They just kept telling her to relax, take it easy. She had begged and begged her aunt to let her help in the kitchen. She needed something to do and she was feeling a little guilty at playing tourist. Her aunt

Delia's Story

finally succumbed to her begging and allowed her to help. No-one mentioned her pregnancy and she liked it just fine. Her stomach was nice and big, her baby was healthy according to the doctor she visited on the island, and she could tell by the kicking she was getting every now and then in her tummy. Rubbing her tummy, Delia got up from where she sat under the mango tree, stretched and made her way to the houses. She was feeling a little tired and she could feel the baby getting restless. Her aunt stopped her as she entered the house. "You feeling alright Sugah?" she asked, "because you looking a bit flushed." "Oh, I'm okay, just a little tired," answered Delia. Her aunt came over to her and placed her hands on her hands on her stomach. "I think the baby want to be free from his prison," her aunt said to her. "No, I still have some time to go before that happens" said Delia, "You mark my words, that baby is going to be here soon, real soon." Saying that, aunty GENE kissed Delia on her forehead patted the stomach again and left Delia standing at the doorway while she went out to finish the washing. Delia stood there staring at her aunt's back as she went out the door. She looked at her stomach and smiled, then continued to her room to lie down for a while.

Aunty Gene, had in her time, delivered a lot of babies as a midwife, but she was now retired. She seemed to have a knack for knowing when babies were ready to escape the encampment of the womb, and she knew without the shadow of a doubt Delia would be having her baby in the next forty eight hours. She had seen the look in Delia's eyes and when she had placed her hands on Delia's stomach, she had felt it for sure. Anyway, she would

Chapter Eight

make sure to keep an eye on her niece and see that there was plenty of wood for boiling water and clean towels because premature or not, there was a baby wanting to be born. She called the twins, telling Jasper to go cut more wood and Gavin to make sure the towels were enough and available. Her husband was at work, he delivered goods for one of the large stores in town, and it would be a little while before he came home. She would tell him about it when he did, heading for the kitchen singing, "The Lord's my shepherd," at the top of her voice, to prepare her family their supper.

Delia lay on her bed writing, she was trying to write a letter to Theo but could not find the words, and instead she wrote.

Dearest Theo:
Be not afraid of the words I write to you,
Misconstrue not the love I speak so true,
I love the Sun, she shines so bright, I love the moon, the stars at night.
I love the light that shines in your eyes, just like the stars they shine with delight.
I love to love, that is so true, since God is love and love is good, I do not wish to be misunderstood.
I do not wish to frighten you away, so come to me my love, come to us freely and stay.

Delia fell asleep. She did not even know when, but as she slept she dreamt that she was back in Goodwill. Christine, Greg

193

Delia's Story

and Theo were in the dream. Wait, Christine was lying down in the middle of the living room on Delia's bed. Greg was standing by her side, wiping her forehead with a cloth and Theo was dressed up as a doctor ready for theatre. Christine was screaming and cursing, she was like a crazy woman. Greg was telling her to push and Theo was pulling something from between her legs; Delia could not see what it was, but he was pouring with sweat and the screaming was getting worse. Finally Theo pulled out a net, a great big fishing net. Wrapped up in the net was two little mermaids and they looked just like her twins. Delia jumped; she jumped out of the dream and woke up. She was sweating and her stomach was hurting, a crampy feeling was taking place at the base of her stomach. She hugged her stomach and curled up in the bed, but the feeling only continued to get worse, the pain was getting extreme. She had no time to worry about her dream; she had to get to her aunt before the pain got worse. She slowly got out of bed and made her way towards her aunt's bedroom, it was dark outside her room, the switch for the light was at the other side of the room. As Delia made her way across the room her stomach tightened up so much she thought she would faint from the pain it was causing. She banged her foot against the sofa and she screamed. Lights came on in her aunt's bedroom and then in the living room as her aunt came rushing to her rescue, and Uncle Jones one step behind. He moved his wife out of the way and picked Delia up from the floor where she was and carried her to her bedroom and laid her on the bed.

Chapter Eight

Aunty Gene had taken one look at her niece and knew she was almost ready to give birth, Delia was contracting. She could see that and the contractions were close, very close by the look of pain on Delia's face. She helped Delia get comfortable, while her husband went to phone the doctor. Gavin and Jasper were now awake and in the kitchen putting wood on the fire for the hot water needed in the bedroom by their mother, who was ready to bring their little cousin into this reality.

Everyone was busy doing their duty. The boy's running back and forth carrying wood, making sure there was enough supply of water and fetching clean towels. Aunty gene constantly checking, making sure her niece and baby was alright, Uncle came back and reported that the doctor would be as soon as possible. Delia laid on the bed thinking about Theo, wishing she had told him about her pregnancy, as the contractions continued to rack her body with pain. Her eyes were red from crying as the tears rolled silently down the side of her face, pass her ears, landing on her pillow. She didn't care who saw her tears, she knew her aunt would understand. The doctor arrived and prepared himself for the delivery, aunty Gene played nurse. After washing his hands and putting on his gown, the doctor went over to examine Delia; while aunty Gene filled him in on her progress, telling him how close her contractions were before giving him the chance to ask. Delia paid no mind to the conversation going on between the two of them, even if she was the one being discussed. She was ready to push. She started to push; the pain was too much, she screamed. Her aunt was wiping the sweat from her brow and talking to her softly, trying to soothe her, but the pain; Delia called for Theo. She knew it was pointless, she hadn't told him about this, she was sorry. She cried, she pushed, the doctor stooping between her legs talking about the baby crowning. He could see the top of its head. Delia could feel the baby wanting to be free. She grabbed her aunt's right hand and squeezed it, as she gave the biggest push she could manage and she felt the baby slip out of her. She heard the doctor shouting it's a boy, and then a slap and the baby started to cry.

Delia was crying, sobbing great big sobs. Her aunt went over to the doctor, helped him to free the baby from the umbilical cord, then took the baby from him and placed him in Delia's outstretched arms. Delia looked at her son. His head was covered in jet black curls, he had Theo's features. She felt a love rise from her as she held him to her breast and kissed him on his forehead, then she thanked God.

After cleansing the room, everyone gathered around Delia's bed, congratulating her on the birth of her son, remarking what a good-looking boy he was and said a prayer thanking God for his miracle. The baby weighed seven pounds. The doctor was telling them that it was quite good considering the baby was premature. He had a strong pair of lungs and it seemed a healthy appetite as he watched Delia breastfeeding the baby for the second time since his delivery. He stayed around for a while making sure that mother and baby were okay and left when he was satisfied with their progress.

Chapter Eight

Theo phoned Delia but got Christine instead. When he asked for Delia, Christine told him she had gone to St. Thomas and had not returned as yet. Theo thanked her and hung up the phone. So Delia was in St. Thomas. All the time she'd been phoning him, she had not mentioned one word about going there or even that she was already there. Why had she not told him about it? What was going on? Was she with someone, had she found somebody else? Is that why she failed to mention it to him? Theo knew he was being silly. He knew Delia was not that kind of person, but he thought they had no secrets between them, so why not that piece of information? He got up from the bed where he was sitting and got ready for work, all the while torturing himself about Delia and her reasons for being in St Thomas. At work, he could not concentrate on the pile of accounts waiting on his desk to be accounted for, barking at anyone who tried to approach him. No matter how he tried to focus, he kept seeing the image of Delia in the arms of another man; the man in his dreams, he had not seen that man for a good while. He could not think of any other person or reason why it should not be him, whoever he was. He was convinced; he had to find out for himself. He would go to St Thomas, but first he needed the address where Delia was staying, and then he would book his flight.

Christine phoned Delia to find out when exactly when she would be returning to the island and to fill her in with all the latest happenings, the kind of information you would not hear of the radio or television. Aunty Gene answered the phone. "Hello aunty, how are you and the family?" Christine asked. "Oh, God is

Delia's Story

good, everyone is fine thank you and yourself?" said her aunt. "I'm doing well," said Christine. "What about the baby, when is it due?" asked her aunt. "Oh in about four weeks time, and he's doing fine," said Christine. Aunty, is Delia around? Can I speak to her please? Christine asked, not really wanting to get into a long conversation with her aunt. "Hold on," said her aunt, if you just hold on a minute I will call her for you, in the meantime you take care and feel free to call anytime." "Thank you aunty," said Christine then she waited as her aunt went to call Delia. "Hi Cuz," said Delia, as she picked up the receiver and placed it her ears. "How you doing?" "I'm not doing fine," answered Christine I'm missing my cousin who is in St Thomas, has been there for ages and has got me thinking she's not in a great hurry to come home." "Sorry Cuz, it's not intentional, but aunty Gene made me promise to stay with her a while at least till the end of this month. She said she hardly ever sees me. So now that I am with her, she wants to make the most of me. You know how she can be? But I promise you, I will be home before you know it and in time to see my little cousin come into the world ok, so don't fret. Anyway I thought you would enjoy having the place to yourself and Greg, playing happy couples," said Delia. "I am, but I miss you, the place is not the same without you," said Christine. "Don't fret Cuz, it's all under control, I love you. I won't let you down okay?" "If you say so," said Christine, "If you say so. Oh by the way, Theo phoned for you. Didn't you tell him you were going to visit St Thomas?" "No, said Delia, "I didn't tell him. I don't know why, before you ask. I just wanted to think without his presence. If he knew where

Chapter Eight

I was it would be different, at least that's what I told myself." "Okay then," said Christine, "I'm sure it made sense to you at the time, but we lesser mortals are a bit baffled." "Anyway what did he say?" asked Delia. "He didn't say anything," said Christine. "He asked for you, I told him you had not returned from St Thomas, and he said thank you, goodbye and hung up." "Oh well, not to worry," said Delia. "I will call him later when he's home from work. So tell me Cuz, are you ready for the great day? Have you got a bag packed just waiting for takeoff?" "I feel excited every time I think about me having a baby. I can't wait; Greg can't wait. He's more impatient than I am and as for being ready, my bags have been packed for the past month. Greg saw to that. I only had to watch," said Christine. Delia could hear the excitement in her cousin's voice and she was happy for her. This would be her first time at motherhood, Delia had been there before, but had been robbed of the opportunity. Now she had been given a second chance. Both she and Greg with different partners of course, but nonetheless, she gave thanks. "Anyway listen Cuz, got to love you and leave you for now, You caught me in the middle of something, and with all our nattering I almost forgot, but take care and say hello to Greg for me. Love you baby and she hung up the phone leaving Christine with the receiver in her hand at the other end, looking at it and wondering if her cousin had a pot burning on the fire. Then she placed the receiver back in its cradle.

Delia's Story

Delia had to rush off the phone because she heard the baby crying. She wasn't sure if Christine had heard him or not. She rushed to the bedroom and found her son already up in aunty Gene's arms being comforted, her aunt who smiled at her as she entered the room.

"I'm going to miss him when you go back home. You know I miss you already. It's been such a long time since I've had a baby in this house. This family is going to miss you both terribly." Delia smiled and kissed her aunt "We're going to miss you too. I have had such a wonderful time here. I never realised how much I missed your influence in my life, you, uncle and the twins. I love you all dearly and I miss you already, but now I will do my best to keep in touch, and you can see your god son as often as is possible okay," said Delia to her aunt as she watched the tears fall from her aunt's eyes and fall on the baby's blanket.

"Thank you Sugah," said her aunt. "And you can tell me to mind my own business, but when are you going to tell the father about his son? Please don't take too long. A boy needs his father in his life, a role model. You understand what I mean don't you Sugah?" "Yes aunty, I understand and I will tell him soon, I promise." "Fine," said her aunt, "fine," as she sat down on the edge of the bed playing and making funny noises at the baby cradled in the crook of her arm.

Delia sat down on the bed next to her aunt, watching, as she made funny faces at her son who had not been named as yet. She was thinking about Theo, how surprised he was going to be when she found the words to tell him. She figured he would be

Chapter Eight

angry; angry that she had not told him about her being pregnant and that it was his; her keeping it a secret. Oh yes, he would be angry, but his anger would abate eventually. The more she thought about it, the more convinced she became that she should write to him, tell him about his son in a letter, he would read the letter and then scream, but at least by that time she would be prepared for the blasting, whether by phone or in person.

When Theo got home that afternoon he called Christine. "Hi Christine, it's me Theo." "Hi Theo," she answered. "Listen," he said. "I want to apologise for this morning. I seemed to have forgotten my manners." "That's ok," she answered. "It happens to the best of us." "Thank you for understanding," he replied. "Anyway I was wondering if is it possible for you to let me have the address in St Thomas where Delia is staying, I want to drop her a note." "No problem," said Christine. "If you just hold on one moment, I will get it for you." She wasn't gone long. She gave him the address. He thanked her and was about to hang up the phone when he heard her asking about his health. "I'm doing fine and yourself? He asked. "Oh yes, I heard you and Greg are about to become parents." "Yes, and were doing fine," she answered. "That's good, I'm glad to hear it," he replied. "Anyway, I'm going to write this note to Delia so take care, ok." , he hung up the phone, leaving Christine standing at the other end with the receiver in her hand, wondering why it was that Delia and Theo always left her hanging on the line. She placed the receiver back

Delia's Story

in its cradle and went back to what she had been doing before the phone rang.

Theo did not know what to say in the note to Delia. His thoughts were in such disarray. He started to write, 'Hi baby, how you doing? I'm cool, missing you like crazy. How is St Thomas? What are you doing their business or pleasure?'

Theo looked at what he had written; he read it twice then screwed it up and tossed it to the carpet. He continued to do that for a while and had to stop when he ran out of paper. He stood up and paced the floor. He went to the phone, picking up the receiver. He called their line company and made reservations for a flight to St Thomas at the end of the week, which was two days away. Then he remembered that he would have to find an excuse to give to his workplace, but that would not be a problem and if it was? Then they would have to terminate his post, because he was going to St Thomas "by hook or by crook" as his Gran used to say.

Wanda stood at the entrance of her building and watched Theo. She watched him as he got into the taxi parked in front of the apartment building where he lived, but for how much longer? she wondered. His simple luggage placed carefully in the boot of the car, he slammed the boot shut, and got in the front passenger side of the car, shutting the door and off he went, out of her life forever and heading to God knows whom. The tears fell slowly at first, running slowly down her cheeks. She felt its warmth and wiped it away with the back of her hands, but still the tears kept on falling.

Chapter Eight

Her heart ached. She wanted to die. She knew this would have happened, but she could not help how she felt about him. She loved him from the bottom of her heart, but truly he had changed. He was not the man she once knew. She wondered if she really knew him at all.

It was tough having to admit it to herself, even if it caused her pain, knowing how pointless and stupid it was being in love with someone who treated you like you don't exist; crying over spilt milk that had truly turned sour, but still she ached for him. She headed for her car, she needed to see this through, so she followed him to the airport.

One hour later, standing in the shadow of a giant of a man, dressed in his well pressed khaki safari suit, heading for wherever, stood Wanda, still dressed in her black tracksuit and shades, plus visor for effect,. She smiled as she watched him step up to the receptionist dressed in her red and blue uniform, with matching cap and shoes, not a hair out of place. The receptionist took his passport from him and checked him in, placing his luggage on the scales to check the weight, nodding and smiling in his direction. She was saying something to him that made him smile. Wanda could not hear what was being said, but noted the receptionist flirting with him, he paid it no mind. He got his passport and papers back and walked away, not looking left nor right, just straight to his destination. Not even the sound of a little girl screaming for her lost toy had any effect on him. He just kept going, straight to whom so ever the lucky lady was. She wished him well as she watched him disappear.

Delia's Story

    Wanda turned and headed back to her car, back to what was left of her life. The tears were pouring; she wanted a drink. She needed a drink very badly, a drink to dull her ache. Perhaps a couple or even a bottle of white rum might do it. Oh well, we will see, she told herself. Wanda was so lost in her thoughts. She stepped off the pavement between parked cars to cross the road, heading to her car. She did not look left or right, the tears still pouring. She did not see the car approaching.

Chapter Nine

The weather was lovely in St Thomas when the plane landed at the airport, a gentle breeze coming in from the sea to calm the raging heat. half dressed natives chatting happily with each other as they went back and forth about their business. Theo liked the vibes; he hired a car and got himself a map of the island. He asked questions and directions of a police officer standing outside the airport, then headed towards "Port of Panic" or whatever it was the place was called. His mood had not changed. His work mates had been overjoyed when he asked for time off. They had given in to him gladly. He had become unbearable. "A bear with a sore head" that's what they called him. He really did not care what they thought of him, he had other business to attend to and that was that.

Port of Panic was not so difficult to find and neither was the address that Delia was staying at. As he approached the house, he noticed Delia, who had just finished writing a poem about the beautiful gift she had been given. Their son. His eyes were so much like his mother's and yet again a lot like his father's. She was sitting under a mango tree and she was breast-feeding a baby. Theo could not believe his eyes. "What in God's name was going on?" he asked himself. He stopped the car and just sat there looking, but not believing what his eyes was showing him. He sat

205

Delia's Story

there for a while, scratching his head, then started up the car and drove back to the hotel where he would be staying while in St Thomas. He called for room service and ordered a bottle of the Island's finest rum with a bucket of ice in case he needed to chase the rum. Theo figured to himself, if the baby belonged to Delia, then it did not takes much maths to add up and make it his, without the shadow of a doubt. But how and why had she not told him about the pregnancy? Why had she kept it a secret? He poured himself a large drink and downed it in two gulps. He felt the drink hit the bottom of his stomach and remembered he had not eaten for the day. He did not care, he poured another drink, and he wondered what the baby looked like, if it was a boy or a girl? He tried to calculate the time between his stay at the hospital and now. It was about seven to eight months. Delia must have had a premature birth. As far as he knew, there had not been anyone else in her life when they got acquainted apart from her one time husband Greg.

    He got up and switched on the television standing in the corner, trying to find something else to focus on, trying to get the image of Delia breast-feeding the baby out of his head. He watched the news being read by a pretty Caribbean lady, still trying to get the picture of Delia out of his head. Theo's cell phone started ringing. He turned down the volume on the television and answered the phone. "Who is this?" he enquired roughly. "My, you sound like you're in a good mood. Been getting a lot of calls lately have you that you don't recognise my number anymore?" asked Delia. "Hi girl, how you doing?" he

Chapter Nine

answered. "Sorry about the rough talk but I've got this blinding headache." "Mm, I see, well I am doing fine, in fact I am feeling "blooming marvellous" as the English would say," answered Delia. "That's good. How's your aunt and her family?" He asked, "Oh they are the best, everybody is doing fine," answered Delia. "So how long did you plan to stay in St Thomas?" he asked her. "Well I've been here long enough already and Christine is cursing me. She wants me back in time for the birth of her baby, so I guess I will be going home in about two weeks time, why do you ask?" she wanted to know. "Did you want to come and spend some time with me?" "Well I was thinking about it," he answered. "That would be nice," she said to him. "I have been missing you too; it's been too long without you." "Don't worry baby, things will work out. I miss you very much, that is why I have to come back home," he told her. "That would really be the thing," she answered, "And we have much to talk about." "Mmmm, I'm sure we do. Anyway I'm going to say goodbye for now. Someone else is trying to contact me, but we will speak soon." With that he hung up the phone and went back to his drinking.

 Delia did not know he was on the island. She did not know he knew her secret and how it was torturing his head, but she was right when she said there was a lot to talk about, because he needed to know what the hell was going on.

 That night he did not sleep very well. He was awake for most of the time, and when he did manage to fall asleep, it was a matter of minutes before he was woken up by the call of a cock crowing in the distance, telling the people it was time to get up.

Delia's Story

He got up, had a shower, brushed his teeth and got dressed. He went downstairs to see what was on offer for breakfast. After breakfast, he went for a walk round the island, buying gifts for Delia, his parents and the baby, which he would have to keep for himself until he was "in the know." On his travel round the island he was fortunate enough not to meet anyone who knew him. He did not want Delia to know he was on the island, not just yet anyway. He came across a shack with a sign advertising boat rides, so he decided to go for a boat ride. He hardly spoke a word to the boatman, apart from when he went to inquire and hire and then when he returned to shore saying thank you and goodbye. The owner of the boat must have thought him rude, but he did not care, he had other things on his mind. He remembered the night at the hospital when he had wished for Delia to have his child, he had been serious at the time, had meant every though, so had this wish come true, was he a dad, Does he know anything about being a dad, would Delia allow him to be a part of his life, what would she want from him, when will she tell him if that is the case? He went back to the hotel and drank some more. He was at a loss, he did not know what to do with himself. He phoned his parents, not telling them where he was, just in case they spoke to Delia and knowing his mother's love for Delia, she would not hesitate in letting her know. They were doing well and keeping fine. After speaking for a while, he promised to be down for Christmas. They said their goodbyes. Then he phoned Michael, but got no response.

Chapter Nine

He decided to go for a swim. If he remembers correctly, he had seen a swimming pool in the hotel grounds. and after his swim he would phone Delia, as he was tired of not knowing. He wondered how old the baby was.

Delia was not surprised by Theo's call, but her heart skipped a beat at the sound of his voice. Baby Timothy was asleep on the sofa next to her and she felt guilty at not having told Theo about him. Every time she spoke to him the feeling got worse. "Hi sugah, how you doing?" he asked. "Oh, I'm doing fine." "That's good to hear," he replied, "but Sugah can I just tell you something that's been bugging me for a long time now?" "Ah come on, you know you can tell me anything. What is it that's bugging you? Do you know that every time we talk on the phone, I get hungry for you? I wonder to myself whether you are lying down on a bed or sitting on a chair, if you are smiling and do you get horny when you think about me?" "Well," said Delia, who was at this time feeling very hot and "horny" as he put it, "To tell you the truth I'm feeling that kind of way now. How I wish you were here," she told him. "You do, do you? Well that can easily be arranged if you really mean it," he responded. "Yes, but what about work?" she asked. "What about it?" he asked. "Well could you take time off now? I mean don't you have to give them notice?" she asked him. "Normally yes, you would have to, but there are occasions when they make an exception," he answered. "And what would that entail?" she wanted to know. "Oh, it's nothing for you to worry your head about, but do you really want me to come and join you or not?" he asked her. Delia knew she had no choice but to say yes, but she took her time in answering. Looking at the baby next to her sleeping quietly she said, "Yes I would love for you to come and join me. How long do you think it would take before you get here?" she asked him. "I will surprise you. I will phone you when I land at the airport. Better still, why don't you just give the address to me and I will link with you instead?" he said to her. "Yes, but won't you need me to pick you up?" she asked, trying to hide the panic in her voice. "No not really. I will just hire a car and make my own way," he answered. "You don't mind do you? I mean, why take you away from whatever you might be doing, I will be alright and if I get stuck I will call you ok?" "Ok, then its arranged, I will see you when I see you," said Delia, "And I you" he replied." "Listen I'd better go and get things moving. Take care of yourself for me. Bye for now." "Ok, see you soon" answered Delia as she listened to him hang up the phone at his end.

She picked up her son, smiled at him as he opened his eyes and said, "Well my little man, you are going to see your daddy soon, real soon if god is willing." Then she hugged him to her breast and made her way to the kitchen, where her aunt was busy preparing the family's supper.

Theo laughed out loud after putting away the phone. Delia had put her foot right in it, caught herself in her own trap and he had played it against her, pinned her up against the wall so to speak, Theo had figured that if he out rightly suggested to Delia that he should visit her she might refuse, so he played it so that she would be the one to do the inviting, that way he gets what he wanted without a problem.. He was hot for her, all that was true,

Chapter Nine

but it was not just about satisfying his libido. It was also the case of needing to know what in God's name was going on. She would not be ready for his appearance at her aunt's house in the morning. He had thought of surprising her tonight, but had thought better of it. He figured she might take it for granted that it would be at least a couple of days before he would arrive in St Thomas, so tomorrow morning would be ideal. He would still catch her off guard.

The next morning, bright and early, Theo paid up and cleared out of the hotel where he was staying. He needed Delia to think that he had just arrived. He would book himself into another hotel on the island and hopefully things would work out as he planned.

Delia was in the living room when she heard a car door shut, but she paid it no mind. It was customary to hear the slamming of car doors coming from the neighbours. Either they were taking the children to school or going to work. The door knocked. She wondered who it might be and got up to answer it, but at the same time the phone started to ring. Being closer to the phone she answered it. The call was for her uncle, so she went to the bedroom to fetch her aunt. Aunty Gene took Timothy from her; he had finished feeding, and she offered to wind him. The door knocked again so Delia went to answer it.

On opening the door, Delia stopped short. Her eyes flew open, and so did her mouth. Theo burst out laughing at her facial expression. "Girl, you better shut your mouth before you catch a

Delia's Story

fly!" he said to her as she stood there holding the door, supporting herself against it. "So aren't you going to invite me in?" he asked.

Aunty Gene had finished with the call on the telephone. She made her way to the door to find out what was happening, she saw a gentleman standing on her doorstep and heard him asking Delia if she wasn't going to invite him in. She figured the gentleman on the doorstep must be Theo. He had the same colouring as the baby and there was a similarity in their looks, there was no denying it. She went forward past Delia, who it seemed was in shock and stuck to the door, introduced herself to him, asking who he was. Theo told her and so she invited him into the house. Then she took Delia from of the door and after shutting it, followed Theo, who was at the time leading Delia to a chair to sit down and then he did the same.

He turned to face Aunty Gene and said "I never realised she would be this shocked at seeing me." He turned back to Delia. "Aren't you going to say something Sugah?" he asked. "I think I'd better go and make her a cup of hot, sweet tea," said Aunty Gene. "Would you like one for yourself?" He declined the offer. After making sure Delia drank the tea, and was feeling better, Aunty Gene excused herself, taking the baby with her.

Chapter Ten

"So you made it," said Delia. "Boy that was quite a shock you gave me just then." "Well I did say I would surprise you," answered Theo. "Yes," agreed Delia, "that you most certainly did." "So don't I get a kiss or a hug or something?" asked Theo, smiling in her direction. "Well ok, you can have a hug now. As for the something, maybe later," answered Delia teasingly. "First I want to know how you got here so quickly." "That," he said, "is for me to know and for you to find out." "Fine," she replied, 'but how long are you planning to stay away from work?" "As long as it takes for me to do what I have to do," he told her. "And what exactly is it you have to do?" asked Delia. "Oh this and that," he answered.

"By the way," he asked her, trying to change the subject, "Is there a hotel close by that I can book myself into?" "Yes," she said. "There's a couple of them not so far from here." "Cool," he replied, Can you do me the honour of booking a room for me at one of them?" "No problem," she told him. "It would be my pleasure." She got up to go and do as he asked. Theo sat there watching her. She looked radiant. There was something about her; he put it down to her having a baby. Yes, she was looking real fine; he felt the familiar stirring in his loins, but this time it was worse. He had been a long time without her, in fact without a woman. Delia felt his eyes on her. She looked back at him and smiled.

Theo was thinking how he would love to undress her, damn never mind undressing her, just having her right there, where she stood with the phone to her ears; right there, right now, but Aunty was close by in one of the rooms behind shut doors. He would wait, he had managed this long. A little while longer won't kill him. "I've booked you a room at the Seaside hotel, so anytime you're ready I will take you there," she told him as she placed the receiver back in its place. "How about now? Is that possible?" he asked her. "If you give me a minute just to let aunty know, then I am all yours," she replied as she skipped across the floor and entered one of the rooms behind the closed door.

Half an hour later they were at the Seaside hotel collecting the keys from the desk clerk. In his room Delia was feeling a little nervous; she had butterflies in her stomach. She watched him as he stripped off the suit he had on and stood before her in his boxers and socks. She looked at his masculinity. How she wanted him. She was sure he could see it in her eyes as she tried to look away. He pulled her to him and held her against his chest. She could smell his odour. Aftershave mixed with his own body smell, and she could feel the fire burning between her thighs and that feeling in her stomach. He put her away from him and looked her in the eye. He said, "I'm going to have a shower, will you join me?" "No thanks," she replied, "I'll just wait here till you've

Chapter Ten

finished." "Spoilsport," he answered. "Where is your sense of adventure?" He left her sitting on the bed as he headed for the bathroom, returning some time later wrapped in a towel that was just big enough to conceal his manhood.

Delia pretended not to notice him standing there in front of the mirror creaming his skin, but could not help catch her breath as the towel he had wrapped around him fell to floor by his feet. He heard her gasp. He started to laugh at her expression, her eyes wide open and full of desire. Theo noticed how her nipples were taut against her top. He stopped his laughing. He went to her where she sat on the bed, standing in front of her in all his nakedness. She looked up at him, seeing the hunger in his eyes. She got up to meet him. He took her in his arms and started to kiss her. He was hungry for the feel of her flesh against his. He wanted to savour the taste of her lips. He could feel her desire, her heart was thumping against his chest, or was it his against hers, he wasn't quite sure. He lifted her up and she wrapped her legs round him. Delia was on fire. She wanted him. She wanted him more than she had ever wanted anyone before. Theo turned and placed her on the bed, stripping her of the clothes she had on. He groaned at the sight of her nakedness. He ran his hand down the length of her body, teasing as he went along, as he had been dying to do for so long. Delia moaned and arched her body up to meet him as he played with her. Her hand were stroking his torso, turning him on. She could feel his heat. She took his manhood in her hands and played with it, rubbing it against her skin. Theo groaned. He took it from her and guided it to where he knew she wanted to feel it the most and she cried. She cried his name; the feeling was too much. She had missed him so much, feeling the muscles as they pumped inside of her. She could hear him calling her name, her nails ripping down his back. She was in heaven and so was he. She wasn't sure how much more she could take, her body shaking with passion. She could not control her body anymore, it was under his command, and she could feel him as he pumped away on top of her, sweat pouring down his body. "Oh Theo!" How much she had missed that feeling. She was crying out and didn't even realise. He could feel her sweetness; he could smell their juices as they mingled together. It was like a drug spurring him on. This woman, how much and how long? But, they wouldn't have to wait any longer, he felt her muscles contract as they squeezed his penis and he felt his muscles contract and the two of them exploded together, feeling each other shaking with passion, sweat pouring off him and falling on her naked body.

They fell asleep wrapped up in each other. Delia jumped out of her sleep. She jumped out of the bed, waking Theo, who looked up at her and smiled. "What's the rush?" "I have things to attend to," she told him. "Ok, I'll just put on some clothes and drop you back to your aunt's place." "No, it's ok. I'll get a ride and see you tomorrow." Boy it's amazing how time passes when a person is enjoying themselves, thought Delia, the scent of their lovemaking still lingering on her. She loved it. She wished she had more time to bask in it. She smiled as she ran into the house to attend to her son. I guess tomorrow will be here soon enough and I will have to confess my sins.

Chapter Ten

The morning was hot and bright, the sun was already on his mission across the island. The sea breeze coming in through the blinds woke Theo. He jumped out of the bed, one thought on his mind, Delia and the passion she woke up in him. He could not keep putting his mission on hold, he had not been able to control himself last night, it was like a bug; he had it so bad that whenever he was in Delia's presence he could not think straight. However, today he would find out what it was he needed to know. He would not let his passion get in the way. He was meeting with Delia today and was certain it would be a day of revelation.

Delia was watching Pastor Benny delivering a Pentecostal sermon on the God channel when Theo arrived at the house. Her aunt had gone out with the twins and the baby, so Delia was free to do what she wanted for a couple of hours and she planned to spend it sightseeing with Theo. They ended up having a picnic. Delia was enjoying herself. Theo was quite the gentleman. He waited on her hand and foot, paying every attention to their conversation. They went for a dip in the sea, and he dried her when they came back to shore. They made love again. Theo could not prevent it, the touch of her skin against his, and she did not fight against it. She wanted him as much as he wanted her, he could feel that. It seems that he could never have enough of her, or was it never enough time to have her, because it seemed he wanted her all the time. It was always soon time to head home.

The drive home was quiet. Delia was enjoying it, It gave her time to think. She was thinking about telling Theo about the baby when he turned and looked at her. "Sugah can I ask you something?" he asked quietly. He said it so seriously she did not know what to think. "Is your aunt baby-sitting for someone?" "No," she replied. "Then whose baby is that I keep seeing in the house? Is it her grandchild?" he asked "No Theo," answered Delia a little sharply, it is not her grandchild, nor does he belong to the twins, but to stop you from making a fool of yourself any longer, the baby is mine, mine and yours if you want him. I fell pregnant after the hospital incident and when I found out, you were already back in the States. I was scared that you would not want to know, scared that you would deny what happened in the hospital, and so I came here to St Thomas to have him. I have not told anyone, not Christine, not my uncle, not anyone. The only people who knows about him is my Aunty Gene, her family, and now you." "You were scared to tell me about my baby? How could you be scared after all we have been through?" he asked her. "Well I don't know, I just was," she answered. Theo was annoyed and Delia could sense that. She could understand his being annoyed, but still, he could try to understand where she was coming from.

Theo tried to see reason but he could not. His knuckles were white from holding the steering wheel so tight. He felt like slapping Delia, but he was not a man who raises his hands to women. She had been terribly selfish. At least she could have told him and found out his reaction, rather than assume how he would react; he really thought she knew him better than that. He wondered if she had any pictures of the pregnancy, but from the way she was speaking he assumed she did not. "So is it a boy?" he asked. "Yes and his name is Timothy" she replied. Theo tried to

Chapter Ten

picture his son, his first born. He had always imagined being at the birth of his children, especially his first-born, but Delia had taken that away from him when she decided to keep him to herself and then lie to him about it. At least he had found out and he was going to make sure she did not make that same mistake twice; he was not going to allow her or his son to be too far away from him. Theo was so engrossed in his thoughts he failed to stop at the house, he drove right past. Delia had to call him back to the present. "You've gone past the house," she shouted at him as he looked at her, wondering why she had disturbed his thought flow. "Oh so sorry," he said, and proceeded to correct his mistake.

Aunty Gene was sitting outside with the baby in her arms. "Oh my!" she said. "Judging by the look on your faces I would say you have spoken and Theo knows the little man here in my arms is his son?" "Right," said Delia and Theo in unison. "Good, then here is your son Theo," said Aunty Gene. "Introduce yourself to him," placing the baby in Theo's outstretched arms, then made her excuses as she turned and left them to it.

"So have you had Timmy blessed as yet?" asked Theo. "No, not yet," replied Delia. "I was waiting to tell you about it first." "Oh, so you were going to tell me about him eventually?" replied Theo with a touch of sarcasm. "And" continued Delia, "I was wondering if you might want to add another name to the one he has already and if he could have your surname." "That's mighty grateful of you," said Theo, as he turned to look at Delia, then back at the baby in his arms. "I think I will call him Doriel, Timothy Doriel Samson. What do you think?" he asked Delia.

Delia's Story

"What do I think? I think if you want to name your son Doriel that's fine by me," said Delia. "Anyway I think it is a nice name, Timothy Doriel Samson. So now that we have his name settled, perhaps we should go and speak to the priest about having him blessed," she said to him. "Okay, but what about my parents, I would like them to be at the blessing," Theo told her. "Well, I thought we could have him blessed here in St Thomas and then when we get back home have him christened. That way everyone can have piece of the action and not feel left out. We just have to decide on the god parents." "Yes I hear you," said Theo, "and I agree." "Okay, we can ask Michael and Greg to be Timothy's godfathers and I'm sure you want your Aunt to be his godmother." "Yes I would," answered Delia, "and I know she would enjoy being his godmother." "So that's settled then," said Theo. "Now it's just a matter of talking to the priest." "Yes," said Delia, "but first let's go talk to aunt and uncle about the arrangements."

Aunty Gene thought it was a good idea, except she thought that Delia ought to have Christine come over and let her know what was happening. Delia did not think it was such a good idea. She figured if Christine came over to St Thomas, the shock would send her into early labour. She thought it best to wait till she got home, but this was the one time her aunt did not listen to what she had to say.

Christine got the telephone call from her aunt. She was a bit baffled at the call. Aunty Gene had the power to make her feel like a child who had been caught with their fingers in the cookie

Chapter Ten

jar. She was the only one, not even her mother could do that to her, and whenever she had mentioned it to Delia, she would laugh and tell her it was all in her head. However, when her aunt told her she intended to keep a surprise party for Delia, Christine relaxed. She knew she would be taking a risk with the baby due soon, but it was for a good cause. She told her aunt she would be there and she also had to promise not to mention any of their conversation with Delia. Aunty Gene had learnt a lot in her life. She knew how people could be, especially village folks back on the island. So, if Christine found out about Delia's baby here in St Thomas, it would be better for all.

Exactly what Delia feared would happen, happened. The same day Christine arrived and found out about the baby, she began ranting and raving, like a crazy person. She could not believe Delia could keep such a thing from her. "Cuz, do you remember the time you came home and found me singing in the kitchen and baking?" asked Delia. "What, the time when you told me you had a secret and you could not share it?" asked Christine. "Yes that time," answered Delia. "Well what about it?" asked Christine. "You thought I was talking about you didn't you? Asked Delia and carried on without waiting for a reply from her cousin. "I know you did, but that was not the case, I was talking about myself. I fell pregnant after sleeping with Theo while he was in the hospital. When I found out I was pregnant, you also found out you were pregnant at that time, so I let you get your lime light, plus I

221

Delia's Story

wasn't sure about Theo's reaction, so I kept it to myself. I could not stay in Goodwill, because then people would have found out sooner than I would have wanted, and you know how slanderous people can be. Well, I got in touch with Aunty Gene, told her my predicament and she said I should come to St Thomas and spend some time with her, so I did." "Well I never did!" exclaimed Christine, as she stood there in front of Delia her stomach bulging, looking ready to burst. "So you my cousin sneaked off, running away with your pregnant self, not telling anyone about it. That is so disgusting Delia. What were you thinking? You did not even tell Theo about it. After all you two have been through. Boy you must have been thinking some madness! I am really surprised at you." "Okay I get your point," Delia said, "but everything has worked out fine. Theo knows he has a son, so you can stop now Chris." Delia was losing her cool with her cousin. Today of all days; today she had been happy to see her cousin arrive; today she thought now that Theo knew everything she would not have to go through it again, but she had been wrong, she had to go through it again with her cousin. "You know Cuz; I thought if anyone would have understood my predicament it would have been you. It seems to me how easy you forget when it was you doing the running away not so long ago." "Yes, but my situation was different," argued Christine. "There was no baby involved. I had been abused. You were in love and I know he loves you too. Anyway, it is done and I have a playmate for your son, my little cousin. They can grow up like brothers." Listening to her cousin, Delia felt a little sad. She had been thinking whether she should go back

Chapter Ten

to the States with Theo for a while, or if she should get him to stay here in Dominica with her and Timothy. She loved her cousin, but she hoped she would not keep going on about the "betrayal" as she now called it, she hadn't betrayed anyone, she was just thinking about what was her best options were at the time. Theo was happy, she was happy and that was the important thing. "So you see, there's a bright light in this situation already." "My son and your son growing up like brothers," repeated Delia. Christine was holding her stomach and looking at Delia, her face changing colour. "Cuz, I think mister is ready to make his acquaintance you know. I am wet; oh yes my water has broken for real, I think you should call the doctor." said Christine softly, wincing as she felt the second spasm in the pit of her stomach. "Oh and Cuz, you really should hurry." Just as Delia was about to run for help, Christine grabbed her arms. "I think perhaps you should stay and just scream for help, I need you here, with me." "Ok," said Delia. "But just let me get to the door and call someone from the living room to call the doctor or Aunty Gene. Just lie down on my bed and make yourself as comfortable as you can. Soon come."

It's a good thing I changed my bedding this morning thought Delia, or Christine's baby would be landing on a not so clean sheet. Christine refused to let go of her arm. She started doing her breathing techniques. She had been attending the baby birth clinic with Greg and now it was coming in useful, but the pain, the contractions really did hurt. She tried to lie down on the bed and only managed with Delia's assistance.

Delia's Story

While assisting her, Delia was shouting for someone, anyone who could hear her to call for the doctor please. Christine was sweating. Delia had helped her to get comfortable and still no one had answered her call, the family had decided to give them some space to discuss matters and it looked like they had forgotten about them. The baby was coming. Delia ran to the bowl of water she had covered on her dresser. She washed her hands and attended to her cousin. The baby was coming, and there was the blood; she did not like the sight of blood but she would cope. She quickly grabbed some clean towels belonging to Timothy, and placed it beneath her cousin, still wondering, why no one had not been to check on the two of them. She waited for the baby to make his way into her waiting hands. Someone was knocking the bedroom door, Delia shouted for the person to come in.

It was Theo. He had wondered why they had been taking so long in the bedroom, so he had come to investigate. He saw the situation, assessed it and ran back into the living room to call the doctor and also telling everyone in the room at the same time.

Greg rushed into the bedroom and made his way to Christine's side to comfort her, Aunty Gene was shouting for hot water, placed herself next to Delia and waited for the baby to come. They didn't have to wait very long. He came into the world screaming at the top of his lungs, everything in place and looking as a baby should, messy.

Chapter Ten

Delia was happy for her cousin, everything had turned out fine, she had delivered her cousin's baby, The doctor had arrived and checked out both mother and son. Greg was crying uncontrollably, Delia had to take him out of the room, making up some excuse about having him help her in the kitchen, and comforted him. She knew why he was crying and she, only she understood because she, had been in the same position. She still understood him better than anyone he knew and they both knew that, but they also knew that they could not let it become a problem for their partners.

Christine was in seventh heaven, she loved her baby on sight. He looked to her like a little bundle of joy, her joy, and nothing was going to take that feeling away from her, not even Greg, she loved Greg but this was a different kind of love. She could not believe that Delia had helped her deliver the baby. She loved her cousin, but this would make their bond even stronger. They had grown up together and Delia had always been there for her. She has been like her mother and bigger sister all rolled into one. Now they would be bringing up their sons together. How good GOD is thought Christine, as she silently prayed and thanked him. They had all prayed together after the baby was born, as was the tradition, but this one was from her personally, thanking him for everything, she had been through with her cousin and for him placing her in her life.

Aunty Gene was very proud of her niece, she was so proud of her she decided to throw her a party, a surprise party, she got the help of her husband, she did not even tell the twins, they loved Delia so much they might let it slip, The best hotel in town

Delia's Story

was booked for the occasion, the best caterers but with Auntie's menu and assistant, The biggest cake the oven could bake, everyone in the neighbourhood who could keep a secret was invited and all this to be held the same day as the blessing for baby Timothy and for his new born cousin, that way no one would know what was going on, they would just think everything was a part of the blessing arrangements. Christine and Greg decided to name him Michael, after his best friend and Theodore, as a thank you to Theo for all he had done to assist her in her time of need and also made them godfathers Christine made it to be known that her son could not have anyone but Delia as godmother, especially as it was she who brought him into the world.

Three weeks later, Delia, now Mrs Theodore Samson, and Christine, Mrs Beau Pierre flew back to Dominica with Theo's parents in tow. They had flown over to St Thomas for the big occasion and to be introduced to their grandson.

The wedding and blessing had all been rolled into one affair; everyone who was anyone was there. Uncle Joseph gave Delia away and Uncle Jones gave Christine away. Michael had been best man for both couples and the twins attended Delia and Christine as their pageboys. Family who had not been seen for decades turned up. Theo's Calypsonian friends and acquaintances were there, even the media turned up for the occasion. The Prime minister for the Island was a friend of Theo's dad. He was there with his security and all this had taken place at the Sea Side Hotel,

Chapter Ten

who had been most honoured to house the event for The Magician as they preferred to call him.

Aunty Gene was happy for them, she was also happy her house had been blessed by the birth of two baby boys and she had gotten to spent some quality time with both her nieces, her family reacquainted.

But happiest of all was Theo, not only had they married and had a son, but Delia had another secret to tell, she was pregnant again and this time it was their secret.

Lightning Source UK Ltd.
Milton Keynes UK
15 May 2010
154199UK00001B/10/P